Masters of the Universe

Masters of the Universe

✳

HAYEK, FRIEDMAN, AND THE BIRTH OF

NEOLIBERAL POLITICS

Daniel Stedman Jones

PRINCETON UNIVERSITY PRESS

Princeton & Oxford

Copyright © 2012 by Daniel Stedman Jones
Published by Princeton University Press, 41 William Street,
Princeton, New Jersey 08540
In the United Kingdom: Princeton University Press, 6 Oxford Street,
Woodstock, Oxfordshire OX20 1TW

Requests for permission to reproduce material from this work should be sent to
Permissions, Princeton University Press

press.princeton.edu

All Rights Reserved

ISBN 978-0-691-15157-1

LIBRARY OF CONGRESS CATALOGING-IN-PUBLICATION DATA
Jones, Daniel Stedman.
Masters of the universe : Hayek, Friedman, and the birth of neoliberal politics / Daniel
Stedman Jones.
p. cm.
Includes bibliographical references and index.
ISBN 978-0-691-15157-1 (hbk. : alk. paper)
1. Neoliberalism—History. 2. Economic policy. 3. Economics—Political aspects. I. Title.
HB95.J66 2012
320.51—dc23   2012002523

British Library Cataloging-in-Publication Data is available

This book has been composed in Arno Pro

Printed on acid-free paper.∞

Printed in the United States of America

1 3 5 7 9 10 8 6 4 2

To my parents,

Sally Alexander and Gareth Stedman Jones

Contents

Acknowledgments

This project germinated over the many years I spent at Oxford University and working in public policy at the London-based think tank, Demos. There are always more people to thank than can fit into a space such as this, but clearly, some people deserve special mention. I had always wanted to conduct a study of transatlantic policy and thought of starting a project on U.S.-UK policy transfer with my great friend and colleague at Demos, Rachel Jupp. The chance to pursue the idea did not come until I returned to graduate study, initially to complete my master's degree in political theory and American politics in the Political Science Department at the University of Pennsylvania.

The opportunity really opened up when I began to work with Professor Michael Katz in the History Department at Penn. I owe my greatest thanks to Michael, who encouraged me to switch departments from Political Science and inspired me to stay for the doctoral program in history. His quiet authority and demanding inquisitiveness were the most important spurs to my graduate education in general and this book in particular. I must also thank the other members of my committee, Professor Warren Breckman and Professor Thomas Sugrue, both of whom provided invaluable comments, help, and encouragement throughout the years I spent on the book. Conversations with both of them (and with Michael) kept me focused and allowed the project to develop manageably. I should also thank my two closest friends and colleagues at Penn, Daniel Amsterdam and Tim Weaver. We kept each other sane amid the inevitable highs and lows of graduate work. I would also like to reserve a special thanks for Professor Peter Hennessy at Queen Mary College, London, who very kindly advised me on the British research for this book. Without his help, the project would have been more limited in intellectual scope and imagination. I am also very grateful to Professor Daniel Rodgers of Princeton University, whose book, *Atlantic Crossings,* was one of the major beacons behind this project and who acted as a tough but fair examiner for my PhD. Finally, Chris Alsopp and Robert Skidelsky gave generously of their time to read drafts of the chapters on economic policy. Responsibility for the overall approach and any remaining errors in the text, however, is solely my own.

I thank all of the interviewees who generously gave their time and helped bring this project to life through their insights and remembrances: Anneliese Anderson, Martin Anderson, John Blundell, Eamonn and Stuart Butler, Leon Brittan, Jim Boughton, Ed Crane, Andrew Duguid, Ed Feulner, John Hoskyns, Michael Howard, Geoffrey Howe, Douglas Hurd, Peter Jay, William Keegan, Norman Lamont, Tim Lankester, Nigel Lawson, Madsen Pirie, John Redwood, George Shultz, and Robert Skidelsky. I also thank the archivists at the Ronald Reagan Presidential Library, the Hoover Institution at Stanford University, the Conservative Party Archive in the Bodleian Library, and the Thatcher Archive at Churchill College, Cambridge, who were efficient and helpful whenever I needed attention. In particular, Diane Barrie and Andrew Riley were unfailingly patient and provided essential assistance and advice. Professor Mary Chamberlain kindly lent me the recording equipment I used to conduct my interviews for the project.

I want to thank my editors at Princeton University Press, Ian Malcolm and Al Bertrand, without whom the book might never have seen the light of day. I am also grateful to all the staff at the press, especially Hannah Paul and Debbie Tegarden, for making the book's publication a smooth and thoughtful process.

Many friends and family members provided encouragement and a temporary home during the course of my research in London, Oxford, Cambridge, Philadelphia, California, Washington, D.C., and New York, among them Christopher Glass, Adam Solow, Laura Scarano, Jenny Suen, Alexis Sampietro, Larissa and Conrad Persons, Jake Stevens, Clara Heyworth, Tanya Naps, Verity, Elizabeth, and Mark Allen, Cate and Mike Styer, and William Poole. My family, Abigail, Nigel, Miri, Joseph, Molly, and Talia, gave unstintingly the love and support that make me happy and capable. Beatrice Riley helped me in more ways than I can say while I revised and finished the manuscript. Finally, I thank my parents, Sally Alexander and Gareth Stedman Jones, to whom this book is dedicated.

DANIEL STEDMAN JONES
March 2011

Timeline

Decade	United States	Britain
1900s	1900–1930 High tide of American Progressivism	1906–14 New Liberal government of Herbert Henry Asquith enacts welfare reforms
1910s	1917–18 United States joins the war	1914–18 World War I
1920s	1929 Wall Street crash	1926 The General Strike
1930s	1932 FDR elected and New Deal begins 1933–1945 Democrat Roosevelt administration	September 1939 Outbreak of World War II
1940s	April 1945 FDR dies, replaced by Harry Truman 1945–53 Democratic Truman administration 1945 World War II ends	May 1945 Clement Attlee prime minister 1945–51 Labour government 1948 National Health Service founded by Nye Bevan
1950s	1950–53 Korean War 1953–61 Republican Eisenhower administration 1955–75 Vietnam War	1951–64 Conservative government 1951–55 Winston Churchill prime minister 1955–57 Anthony Eden prime minister 1956–57 Suez Crisis 1957–63 Harold Macmillan prime minister
1960s	1960 JFK elected 1961–63 Democratic Kennedy administration 1963 JFK assassinated 1963–69 Democratic Johnson administration 1968 Richard Nixon elected 1969–74 Republican Nixon administration	1963–64 Alec Douglas-Home prime minister 1964–70 Labour government Harold Wilson prime minister

Decade	United States	Britain
1970s	1974 Watergate scandal; Nixon resigns 1974–77 Republican Ford administration 1976 Jimmy Carter elected 1977–81 Democratic Carter administration	1970–74 Conservative government Edward Heath prime minister 1974–79 Labour government 1974–76 Harold Wilson prime minister 1976–79 James Callaghan prime minister 1979 Margaret Thatcher elected 1979–1997 Conservative government
1980s	1980 Ronald Reagan elected November 1988 Republican Reagan administration 1981–89 George H. W. Bush elected 1989–93 Republican Bush administration Fall of the Berlin Wall October 1989	1982 Falklands War

Abbreviations

AEA—American Economic Association
AEF—American Economic Foundation
AEI—American Enterprise Institute
ASI—Adam Smith Institute
CPS—Centre for Policy Studies
FEE—Foundation for Economic Education
FHA—U.S. Federal Housing Administration
HIPs—UK Housing Investment Programmes
HUD—U.S. Department of Housing and Urban Development
IEA—Institute of Economic Affairs
IHS—Institute for Humane Studies
USPHA—U.S. Public Housing Administration
WVF—William Volker Fund

※

Introduction

The ideas of economists and political philosophers, both when they are right and when they are wrong, are more powerful than is commonly understood. Indeed the world is ruled by little else. Practical men, who believe themselves to be quite exempt from any intellectual influences, are usually the slaves of some defunct economist. Madmen in authority, who hear voices in the air, are distilling their frenzy from some academic scribbler of a few years back. I am sure that the power of vested interests is vastly exaggerated compared with the gradual encroachment of ideas. Not, indeed, immediately, but after a certain interval; for in the field of economic and political philosophy there are not many who are influenced by new theories after they are twenty-five or thirty years of age, so that the ideas which civil servants and politicians and even agitators apply to current events are not likely to be the newest. But, soon or late, it is ideas, not vested interests, which are dangerous for good or evil.

JOHN MAYNARD KEYNES, *The General Theory of Unemployment*, 1936

Neoliberal ideas—monetarism, deregulation, and market-based reforms—were not new in the 1970s. But as Keynes suggested, they were the ideas to which politicians and civil servants turned to address the biggest economic crisis since the Great Depression. This book is about why this happened, and how the neoliberal faith in markets came to dominate politics in Britain and the United States in the last quarter of the twentieth century up to the financial crisis of 2008.

The demise of the postwar economic settlement had been hastened by a series of catastrophic events: the Vietnam War, the first oil shock of 1973, and the near collapse of industrial relations in Britain. The Keynes-inspired policies that governments had relied on to deliver a golden age of prosperity and rising incomes for the generation after 1945 seemed exhausted. The collapse of the Bretton Woods international monetary system in 1971 indicated the end of the experiment with fixed exchange rates. The assumption that there was a relatively simple and manipulable trade-off between inflation and employment, the famous Phillips Curve (named after the New Zealand Keynesian economist William Phillips), proved to be a dangerous illusion. Repeated balance-of-payments crises were the most prominent symptom of the so-called "British disease" of industrial decline. In both Britain and the United States, the appearance of stagflation—simultaneous stagnant growth and inflation—meant that governments felt forced to change course.

An alternative policy agenda was ready to replace New Deal and Great Society liberalism, British social democracy and Keynesian economic policy. New approaches to macroeconomic management, the deregulation of industry and financial markets, the "problem" of trade union power, urban deprivation, and the lack of affordable rents or housing appeared to Keynes's "practical men" in power as both appealing and available responses to the economic and political crises of the 1970s. Politicians on the right and, just as important, on the left turned to the proposals of figures like Friedrich Hayek, Ludwig von Mises, Milton Friedman, George Stigler, and James Buchanan (all of whom, except Mises, were Nobel Prize winners) when the chimera of stability based on the Bretton Woods Agreement was dispelled. These thinkers were representative of what has become known as neoliberalism. It is hard to gain historical perspective on neoliberalism. The term has become divorced from its complicated and varied origins. It is too often used as a catch-all shorthand for the horrors associated with globalization and recurring financial crises. But transatlantic neoliberalism, as used in this book, is the free market ideology based on individual liberty and limited government that connected human freedom to the actions of the rational, self-interested actor in the competitive marketplace.

Neoliberal ideas had been generated slowly over fifty years or so by "academic scribblers" in Europe and the United States. In the interwar years, neoliberalism emerged from debates among liberals responding to the rise of trade unions, universal suffrage, and wartime administrations that had consolidated late nineteenth-century and early twentieth-century trends toward growth in government and bureaucracy. New political movements, such as the New Liberalism of H. H. Asquith and David Lloyd George in Britain, saw the state not as an obstacle to freedom but as a way to expand it for more citizens through the introduction of new forms of social insurance and pensions. In the United States, progressive reformers drew on new scientific approaches to social problems in Europe. The specter of communist revolution was ever present after the overthrow of tsarist Russia by the Bolsheviks in 1917. A worrying political phenomenon appeared in the form of Mussolini's Black-shirts. In all these trends, many liberals saw threats to existing freedoms.

The appeal of socialism and the prospect of revolution gave added urgency to the debate among economists over the viability of economic planning. In Cambridge during the 1920s, John Maynard Keynes attempted to solve the problem of economic downturns by developing proposals for countercyclical public spending. In Vienna in 1920, meanwhile, leading Austrian school economist Ludwig von Mises elaborated the socialist calculation problem: whether economic resources can be allocated efficiently in a planned economy. This question was later refined by Hayek, Mises' student and Keynes's friend and adversary, who argued that the price mechanism operated as an information processor that sent unique, comprehensible signals to producers and consumers that were impossible for planners to replicate. After the Wall Street crash of 1929, capitalism seemed in apocalyptic crisis. Hayek debated with Keynes his proposal to use fiscal policy to tackle the fluctuations of the business cycle. The argument culminated in the publication of Keynes's *General Theory of Employment, Interest and Money* (1936), which transformed economic policymaking by seeming to offer a solution to recessions.[1]

The Great Depression made many early neoliberals of the Austrian school, the Freiburg school, and the London School of Economics (LSE) accept the need for forms of intervention and social provision to complement the state's primary role as sustainer of the market order. This was true of Hayek, his friend and later colleague at the LSE Karl Popper, and also Henry Simons, a leader of the first Chicago school of economics. In Germany the Freiburg school, who became known as the ordoliberals (after the journal *Ordo*, the movement's leading organ after 1948), sought to harness state power to maintain a market order. In this they departed from laissez-faire doctrines of the nineteenth century and the modern activist liberalism of Lloyd George and Franklin Delano Roosevelt and aimed to reconstruct a *neo*-liberalism that remained true to the classical liberal commitment to individual liberty. Neoliberalism therefore emerged in the interwar period as a nuanced response to a very different set of conditions—the experience of war and depression, and the onset of fascist, Nazi, and communist totalitarianism—from those obtaining in the late twentieth century, when the word became a byword for market liberalization and globalization.

After 1945, Hayek and Friedman first helped to create, and then to synthesize, a neoliberal policy program and political strategy. In 1947, Hayek brought a disparate group of intellectuals together in Switzerland to discuss how liberalism could be defended in the face of the challenge of "collectivism"—an all-encompassing term that included Nazi and Soviet totalitarianism, New Deal liberalism, and British social democracy. The group adopted the name the Mont Pelerin Society. Then, in his 1949 article, "The Intellectuals and Socialism," Hayek drew on the successes of the British Fabian Left to argue that individual liberty within the framework of free markets could only be protected by an elite-driven and elite-directed strategy of opinion formation. Like Keynes, Hayek believed that ideas seeped into policy only very slowly. Therefore, the way to ensure that free markets triumphed was to focus on changing the minds of the "second-hand dealers in ideas," the intellectuals. The strategy was clear: neoliberal thinkers needed to target the wider intelligentsia, journalists, experts, politicians, and policymakers. This was done through a transatlantic network of sympathetic business funders and ideological entrepreneurs who ran think tanks, and through the popularization of neoliberal ideas by journalists and politicians.

In the following decades, the neoliberal center of gravity shifted from Europe to the United States, especially the University of Chicago. Hayek's status as a founding thinker was unchallenged, but it was Milton Friedman, a tireless public intellectual and campaigner for free markets, who showed the most talent as a proselytizer of neoliberalism. Other Chicago economists, among them George Stigler, Aaron Director, Ronald Coase, and Gary Becker, opened up new areas to free market analysis. Hayek was also based in Chicago during the 1950s in the Committee on Social Thought (his Austrian economics not being entirely welcome in the Economics Department). He, too, was relentless in his policy activism. Allied to Chicago economics was Buchanan's and Tullock's Virginia school of public choice. Rational choice theory, inspired by William Riker at the University of Rochester, like the Chicago and Virginia approaches, also used utility-maximizing and rationally based economic models to explain politics, government, and other areas of social and political life. These U.S.-based neoliberals formed the intellectual nodes at the heart of a transatlantic network of think tanks, businessmen, journalists, and politicians, who spread an increasingly honed political message of the superiority of free markets.

The sharpened neoliberal philosophy that resulted from these developments should be separated from the academic contributions made by Austrian, Chicago, and Virginia school economists. Friedman himself insisted that his technical and empirical work as an economist was distinct from his political philosophy and activism. His research was supposed to be open to rigorous empirical testing and was therefore theoretically open to change; his advocacy of the virtues of markets, by contrast, was a product of his strongly held political beliefs. But undoubtedly, Hayek's, Friedman's, Stigler's, Buchanan's, and Tullock's free market views were lent credence by their academic achievements. Their scholarly success meant that politicians, public officials, and civil servants were much more likely to take neoliberal ideas seriously when they resonated with a new set of problems, just as Keynes's ideas had during the Great Depression.

In the mid-1970s, neoliberal insights into macroeconomic management and regulation first took hold in the administrations of Democratic president Jimmy Carter and Labour prime ministers Harold Wilson and James Callaghan. Carter began to deregulate the transportation and banking sectors, and appointed Paul Volcker chairman of the Federal Reserve. After 1975, Wilson, his successor Callaghan, and Chancellor Denis Healey oversaw deep spending cuts and the abandonment of the long-cherished postwar goal of full employment in favor of targeting inflation. These neoliberal-influenced policies broke through on the left because liberalism, social democracy, and Keynesianism seemed toothless in the face of stagflation. But even in the 1960s there was evidence of a change in approach among British and American policymakers across a range of fields, especially with regard to trade unions, welfare, housing, and urban development. There was a greater willingness to look at market-based solutions in areas of perceived policy failure, such as affordable housing and urban renewal.

Despite this evidence of incremental policy change, the neoliberal legacy would not simply be the instigation of a gradual shift away from reliance on state provision to experimentation with markets. Instead, the initial appeal of neoliberal proposals led ultimately to a widespread acceptance, by the 1980s, of an overarching philosophy of free markets. This was unnecessary. That certain neoliberal proposals spoke to the problems of the 1970s—stagflation, worsening industrial relations, the breakdown of antipoverty and welfare strategies, and the collapse of economic competitiveness—did not make the larger faith in markets an essential accompaniment. Indeed, it was the boundless belief in markets and deregulation that, a generation later, led to the collapse of the international financial system in 2007–8. Moreover, the philosophy of markets contrasted with the more compromising positions of the early neoliberals themselves. This leap was made by an energized political Right after the elections of Margaret Thatcher in 1979 and Ronald Reagan in 1980. The way in which neoliberal ideas—about individual liberty, free markets, and deregulation—translated into electorally successful programs in Britain and the United States between the 1940s and the 1980s is the story of this book.

The Three Phases of Neoliberalism

The history of neoliberalism has at least three distinct phases. The first lasted from the 1920s until about 1950. The term began to acquire meaning in inter-war Europe as the Austrian school economists and the German ordoliberals sought to define the contours of a market-based society, which they believed was the best way to organize an economy and guarantee individual liberty. "Neoliberal" was embraced by participants at the famous Colloque Walter Lippmann, organized in Paris in 1938 by the French philosopher Louis Rougier to consider the implications of Walter Lippmann's book, *The Good Society* (1937). The term was chosen because it suggested more than a simple return to laissez-faire economics. Instead, neoliberalism would reformulate liberalism to address the concerns of the 1930s. Present, among others, were Hayek, Alexander Rüstow, Wilhelm Röpke, and Mises, as well as the French economist Jacques Rueff and the Hungarian British polymath Michael Polanyi. These men, along with others from Europe and America, would later form the Mont Pelerin Society with Hayek, Röpke, and Albert Hunold in 1947.

The influence of Mont Pelerin liberalism was apparent in Milton Friedman's essay, "Neo-liberalism and Its Prospects," published in 1951.[2] Though little noticed and in many ways oddly unrepresentative of his thought, Friedman's article can be seen in retrospect as an important bridge between the first and second phases of neoliberalism, between the concerns of the predominantly European founding figures, located in Austria, London, Manchester, France, Switzerland, and parts of Germany, and a subsequent generation of thinkers, mainly though by no means all American, located especially in Chicago and Virginia. Of course, the "first Chicago school" of economics, comprising Frank Knight, Jacob Viner, and Henry Simons, played its part in neoliberalism's formation, but most early neoliberals were preoccupied with European concerns.

The second phase of neoliberalism lasted from 1950 until the free market ascendency of Thatcher and Reagan in the 1980s. At the zenith of New Deal liberalism and British social democracy, when neo-Keynesian approaches to economic policy were at their height, much of this period was a superficially lean time for neoliberals. Outside Germany, they lacked concrete political success in the 1950s and 1960s. Instead, neoliberalism generated intellectual coherence and matured politically. It grew into a recognizable group of ideas, and also into a movement. An increasingly confident group of thinkers, scholars, businessmen, and policy entrepreneurs developed and refined a radical set of free market prescriptions and promoted their agenda. Ironically, it was also in this period that the use of "neoliberal" by its proponents became less common. This was odd at a time when American neoliberal thinkers in particular were defining it ever more precisely in the spheres of industrial organization, monetary policy, and regulation. But this was probably because the term meant little in an American context.

Characteristic of the Chicago approach was the "methodology of positive economics," out of which emerged Friedman's revival of monetarism and Stigler's theory of regulatory capture. This empirical bent was allied to new theories and research endeavors, subsidized by sympathetic business finance and developed in the 1950s and 1960s, about the relatively harmless nature of monopoly and the positive role of large corporations. From the Chicago perspective, the more worrying manifestation of monopoly was trade union power. The Chicago approach marked a sharp contrast, however, with European neoliberalism and even with the adherents' own departmental forebears, such as Frank Knight, Jacob Viner, and, most important, Henry Simons. German ordoliberals, for example, always took the need for robust antimonopoly policies seriously. In parallel with the technical work of the Chicago economists, Friedman's polemical arguments, put forward in *Capitalism and Freedom* (1962)—the "American *Road to Serfdom*," as Philip Mirowski and Rob

Van Horn have called it—presented the market as the means both to deliver social goods and to deliver the ends, the good life itself.[3]

A third phase of neoliberalism, after 1980, was driven by the advance of an agenda of market liberalization and fiscal discipline into development and trade policy. Neoliberalism broke out of the predominantly North Atlantic and Western European confines of elite academia and domestic national politics and spread into many global institutions, especially in the former communist countries and the developing world. Its principles were adopted by economists and policymakers of the International Monetary Fund (IMF), the World Bank, the World Trade Organization (WTO), the EU, and as part of the North American Free Trade Agreement (NAFTA). The 1980s and 1990s were notable for the notorious "structural adjustment" policies pursued through these institutions and agreements. These were summarized in 1989 by the British economist John Williamson as the now renowned "Washington Consensus" and included tax reform, trade liberalization, privatization, deregulation, and strong property rights.[4] The certainty with which such policies were introduced has been much criticized by economists such as Joseph Stiglitz and Paul Krugman, as well as by uncompromising opponents of capitalism in the antiglobalization movement, which famously erupted at the WTO meetings in Seattle in 1999.

This book focuses on the second phase of neoliberalism. During these years the early debates about the proper relationship of the market to the nascent welfare state, or about the "compatible" economic interventions envisaged by Karl Popper's theory of "piecemeal social engineering," coalesced into a complete rejection of economic planning, social democracy, and New Deal liberalism. A moderate tone had characterized books like Hayek's *The Road to Serfdom* (1944) or Popper's *The Open Society and Its Enemies* (1945), and the programs envisaged in Lippmann's *The Good Society* (1938) or Henry Simons's "Economic Policy for a Free Society" (1946). Such works were fairly positive about the need for social and welfare safety nets. But after the formation of Hayek's Mont Pelerin Society in 1947, neoliberal scholars began to depart from such accommodations, which were a legacy of the 1930s and the 1940s, and a position less troubled by doubts about the virtues of markets emerged.[5] More strident advocacy of free markets, deregulation, and the power of incentives for rational expectations came from Chicago, Virginia, and Rochester. Such ideas were pushed by think tanks such as the Institute of Economic Affairs (IEA) or the American Enterprise Institute (AEI) in the 1950s and 1960s.

Although the theory from Chicago and Virginia became cruder and the pens of Friedman, Stigler, and Buchanan grew stronger in their valorization of the market after 1950, the concomitant effect in the political sphere was that neoliberal ideas became clearer and more stark. For example, bodies like the IEA and the AEI argued that social and economic inequality was necessary as a motor for social and economic progress. (Hayek, too, in his later work developed a more "evolutionist" approach to social and political philosophy.)[6] A simplification of the message helped neoliberal ideas gain significant purchase in the public debates that accompanied the varying crises of liberalism and social democracy of the 1960s and 1970s, something their champions, such as Friedman, were acutely aware of. Simplicity added force to neoliberal messages and meant policymakers noticed, particularly when the economy on both sides of the Atlantic changed for the worse.

Neoliberalism had the added appeal of appearing at one with traditions and myths of American individualism. Support for neoliberal policies from politicians such as Barry Goldwater and Ronald Reagan did not mean they thought of themselves as neoliberal. In the American context, neoliberal ideas usually crept in under the radar, subsumed under the banner of rugged individualism or libertarianism, a movement distinct from, though overlapping with, conservatism. These two traditions were expertly fused with other forms of social and religious conservatism by Reagan. An important dimension of this phase of the history of neoliberalism was, therefore, how politically palatable, mainly economic neoliberal policy prescriptions combined with forms of social and cultural conservatism reacting strongly to 1960s liberal permissiveness. It was a combination that ultimately attracted policymakers and the public in the United States after 1968.

Some observers, especially politicians involved in the Conservative (British) and Republican (U.S.) administrations of the 1980s, have been skeptical of Keynes's argument that "academic scribblers" influence politics, arguing instead that the economic reality of Britain and the United States led to the election victories of Thatcher and Reagan. In essence, the policies were successful because they were the right ones. Yet the historical process described here, whereby ideas broke through to be adopted by political parties, provides a perfect example of how ideas move, change, become distorted, and sometimes even mix with their polar opposites in the messy world of electoral politics, policy, and government.[7] Unlike the histories, memoirs, and commentaries that have sought to paint a cosy picture of inevitability or triumph in the rise and success of New Right politics, much of the research presented here shows just how unpredictable, patchy, and surprising were the ways in which the neoliberal influence was felt. But before beginning this story, it is essential first to consider the distinctive development of neoliberalism as a conceptual category in history and in wider public debate in order to situate the arguments presented in this book.

Neoliberalism and History

As political scientist Rachel Turner has pointed out, the term neoliberalism is used with lazy imprecision in both popular debate and academic scholarship.[8] The outlines of the term's history are widely assumed, although usually without a clear understanding of what is meant by the label. This is perhaps unsurprising as historians have only just begun to examine its genesis and assess its real significance. The problem of definition is further complicated because liberalism, neoliberalism, "New Niberalism," New Democrats, New Labour, and neoconservative all mean different things on either side of the Atlantic.

Efforts at definition, such as Philip Mirowski and Dieter Plehwe's edited volume, *The Road from Mont Pelerin* (2009), have emphasized the dynamic nature of neoliberalism. The essays focus on a "neoliberal thought collective," which is deliberately confined to the scholars and theorists of the Mont Pelerin Society. There is a welcome rigor in limiting discussion of neoliberalism to the society, its members, and their output, given the flabby use to which the term is often put. Yet such a narrow definition risks missing some of its larger political significance, especially in the second phase of the history of neoliberalism. The term neoliberalism is used more broadly in this book. Rather than being attached to a specific group of scholars and politicians of any single organization, the book deals with neoliberalism both in terms of the thinkers and ideological entrepreneurs who put Hayek's strategy into action and in terms of the application of neoliberal ideas after 1970. It therefore complements the debates involving the Mont Pelerin Society and moves beyond them, into wider politics.

Neoliberalism was a conflicted political movement. The kind of purposeful action evident in the statecraft of Margaret Thatcher and Ronald Reagan sometimes conflicted with the ideal of a market-based organicism, particularly apparent in Hayek's evocations of Edmund Burke.[9] Politicians like Margaret Thatcher, Ronald Reagan, Jack Kemp, and Nigel Lawson (none of whom were members of the Mont Pelerin Society) argued that their policies formed part of a lineage that stretched back to the classical liberal political economy of David Hume, Adam Smith, David Ricardo, and the liberals of the Manchester school, Richard Cobden and John Bright. This trajectory they also saw as building on the ideas of Hayek, Friedman, and Buchanan in more recent times.[10] Such claims reflected a distinctive view of the history of liberalism; they signified the appropriation of certain neoliberal tropes. These politicians, for example, liked the liberalism of John Stuart Mill's *On Liberty* but not his *Utilitarianism*.

Neoliberals, whether authoritarian or libertarian, distrusted the "New Niberalism" of L. T. Hobhouse, or that of William Beveridge and John Maynard Keynes, for its faith in government intervention. They also disliked Lyndon Johnson's Great Society and the British social democracy of Clement Attlee, Nye Bevan, and even Conservative Rab Butler (the "But" in "Butskellism," the famous description given to postwar British politics by the *Economist's* Norman Macrae). Above all, they hated Franklin Roosevelt's New Deal. The political heterogeneity of neoliberalism, just like the variety of scholars and disciplines associated with the Mont Pelerin Society itself, calls for serious historical explanation. How *did* neoliberalism come to have a much wider meaning than that which Hayek and his followers and supporters might have wished for during their debates and meetings of the society?

While neoliberal ideas certainly did bear many superficial similarities to classical liberalism and the laissez-faire liberalism of the Manchester school, they also contained important elements not present in earlier forms of liberal thought. As recent scholarship has begun to show, the early neoliberals—in Austria, Paris, Switzerland, and Germany, at the LSE, and in Manchester and Chicago—were clear in their criticisms of both classical liberalism and what they perceived as the excesses of laissez-faire.[11] Subsequently, in the postwar decades, neoliberal scholars, politicians, and policymakers began to build on this initial critique in even more expansive ways, in part through a linkage of free markets to freedom per se. Some of the important divergences from, and differences between, earlier forms of liberalism and neoliberal thought are explained in detail in chapter 3.

Until recently, the debate about neoliberalism was dominated by memoir and journalism, which treated it as a political and economic fact rather than as a historical phenomenon in want of explanation. Discussion of neoliberalism has focused on its current reality as a category of existing policy rather than on its origins, development, and (past) effects. A historical perspective has been sorely lacking. Research by historians such as Angus Burgin and Ben Jackson has begun to remedy this state, particularly in relation to the 1930s and 1940s, by thickening our understanding of the animating impulses of the early neoliberals and, by implication, of the contrast between these early years and what came later. But despite these efforts, the history of neoliberalism remains dominated by two diametrically opposed interpretations, both of which are severely limited.

The first of these is the myth of the historical inevitability of neoliberal success. This myth is fostered not just by the intellectual and political participants, it is reinforced by some historians and social and political scientists. The best and most scholarly example of this approach, applied particularly to Britain, is Richard Cockett's *Thinking the Unthinkable*, which illustrates the central role played by British think tanks in the collapse of the postwar consensus in macroeconomic policy in Britain.[12] On the United States, George Nash paints a nuanced picture of the conservative intellectual ascendancy and in particular the story of "fusionism," the fusion of the different strands of American conservatism advocated and espoused by William F. Buckley and put into practice by Reagan. The book lays bare the bewildering complexity and contradictory nature of the American New Right.[13] Also in this vein have been biographies of the leading political figures, such as Barry Goldwater, Enoch Powell, Ronald Reagan, and Margaret Thatcher, and their memoirs and those of their colleagues, especially Geoffrey Howe, Nigel Lawson, and Alan Greenspan.[14]

Neoliberalism offers a lens through which to view a transformation across the political spectrum, not just of the Conservative or Republican Party. The rightward shift of politics in Britain and the United States is not simply a story of the rise or success of a particular new brand of conservatism. The success of neoliberal ideas was not a straightforward by-product of the rise of the New Right or the triumph of Thatcherism. The change in economic policy during the 1970s was more profoundly about the success of proposals that transcended narrow party affiliation. The terrible prevailing economic conditions ensured that monetarism, deregulation, and trade union reform acted as Trojan horses for a more polemical neoliberal faith in free markets by breaking through into the policy programs of Carter and Callaghan. The significance of this fact—that accepting the need for changed policies in certain distinct economic policy areas need not have implied the wholesale acceptance of free markets—has largely been overlooked. Much of the historiography fails to connect Reagan's and Thatcher's policies with their respective Democratic and Labour Party antecedents except to say that they were reluctant or forced converts to an alien ideology. Too often the adoption of certain key policies by Labour or Democratic administrations during the 1960s and 1970s is assumed by conservative commentators to have been a sham, or by left or liberal observers to be a source of shame. These views miss important elements in the successes and failures of the neoliberal political project.

A second major interpretation of neoliberalism, popular with its critics, sees it as the monolithic and pernicious manifestation of U.S. power over global policy. In this view, neoliberalism arrived, fully formed in the policy toolkits of Chicago economists, sometime after General Augusto Pinochet's violent usurpation of Salvador Allende's democratically elected government in Chile in 1973, to torment the poor populations of the developed and, especially, the developing world. In this version, the "Chicago boys" in Chile are held to be the first group to push a destructive program of market liberalization, which was subsequently imposed through the "structural adjustment" policies of the IMF, the World Bank, and the U.S. Treasury Department.[15] Friedman and Hayek are identified as the original thinkers and Thatcher and Reagan as the archetypal politicians of Western neoliberalism. Neoliberalism here has a pejorative connotation. The British Marxist geographer David Harvey, for example, argues that "neoliberalization" was really a highly effective form of class warfare on behalf of finance capital, in China as well as in the West.[16] Andrew Glyn has pointed to the crisis of profitability for business during the 1970s as the impetus behind market-based reforms in the developed world.[17] More popularly, Naomi Klein has referred to neoliberalism as "the Shock Doctrine" of "disaster capitalism," which feeds on catastrophes such as 9/11, the war in Iraq, and Hurricane Katrina.[18]

Such analyses contain valuable insights, especially in regard to the corrosive relationships among business, finance capital, and political power. Yet they are incomplete. As Mirowski has pointed out, it is a mistake to reduce neoliberal ideas to neoclassical economics as these writers tend to.[19] Neoliberal ideas came to be dominated by Chicago economics in the public mind but were actually a cocktail, united not just by a belief in the superiority of markets—or, more reductively, corporations—but also by a distrust of state authority, intervention, and bureaucracy. Similarly, the intellectual and political strategies pursued by neoliberals in the postwar period opened up new bridges between the academy and politics. A new type of political organization was cemented through the success of the free market think tanks set up in the United States and Britain, such as the AEI, the Foundation for Economic Education, the Institute of Economic Affairs, the Heritage Foundation, the Centre for Policy Studies, the Cato Institute, and the Adam Smith Institute. The men who ran these organizations—and they were all men—F. A. Harper, Leonard Read, Ralph Harris, Arthur Seldon, Anthony Fisher, Ed Feulner, Ed Crane, Eamonn and Stuart Butler, and Madsen Pirie, were ideological entrepreneurs who spread neoliberalism. Their success left a lasting legacy in terms of policy activism that had characteristically different effects in each country.

But neither the "inevitablist" school, on the one side, nor the Marxist or neo-Marxist camp on the other will do. Notable efforts at comparative assessment of British and American policies under Reagan and Thatcher by the political and social scientists Paul Pierson and Monica Prasad aside, the literature fails to view the rise of neoliberalism in its proper transatlantic context.[20] The historiography is patchy and either too insular or too global in scope. Such shortcomings led to misunderstandings about the nexus of Europe, Britain, and the United States, so crucial in the formation of neoliberal ideas, and the crystallization of these ideas in the postwar period. The specifically European problems and traditions central to the intellectual formation of Hayek, Popper, and Mises should not be understated despite their subsequent "Anglicization" or "Americanization." These influences— for example, the fear of Nazi totalitarianism and the bundling together of diverse opponents, progressive, liberal, socialist, and social democratic politics, under the label "collectivism"—had a bearing, sometimes indirectly, on how neoliberalism was developed later by American theorists such as Friedman or Buchanan.

The nuances of postwar neoliberalism, the relationship of its political and organizational character to the thought of its main academic representatives, and the way such ideas were mediated through an ideological infrastructure and international network have yet to be fully explored by historians. The transatlantic character of neoliberalism has often been taken for granted without its origins and development being properly excavated. The extent to which neoliberal policy insights differed from neoliberal political philosophy and the ways in which neoliberal ideas took hold in left mainstream politics have not been taken seriously. The degree to which neoliberalism is seen as the ideology of a malevolent globalization by critics has prevented an understanding of the sources of its broad popularity, as it was dressed up in the rhetoric of the Republican and Conservative Parties, among electorates in the United States and Britain.

Transatlantic Neoliberal Politics

At the core of transatlantic neoliberal politics was an economic argument. This was the monetarist critique of neo-Keynesianism and the promotion of free markets. Allied to this, and crucial to its political success, was a reaction to the so-called permissive society that was epitomized by the upheavals of 1968 (in the United States, this coincided with a powerful opposition on the right to the civil rights movement) that was ever-present in the programs of political neoliberals in power. Another dimension of neoliberal politics was the determined prosecution of the Cold War against Soviet communism. But the economic critique was the special motivating force in neoliberal politics. In the midst of the calamities of the 1970s, the economic case against the perceived follies of Keynesian demand management and large-scale social spending in favor of targeting inflation and trade unions carried with it a powerfully compelling logic. Economic ideas were central to Thatcher and Reagan winning power.

Though some of the outlines of the story of neoliberal politics are familiar, this book makes three distinctive historiographic contributions. First, it complements the existing scholarly literature on conservatism, liberalism, the rise of the Right, and neoliberalism itself, through an emphasis on the underappreciated real significance of the transatlantic nature of neoliberalism—it didn't just happen in different places at the same time, it happened across and between them. Daniel Rodgers in *Atlantic Crossings* (1998) traces a transnational network of fin-de-siècle and early twentieth-century progressives who sought collective solutions to perceived unbridled capitalism in Europe and the United States and shows that the roots of the New Deal lay in shared analyses and answers developed by American and European reformers. Partly inspired by this approach, this book situates neoliberalism in its proper transatlantic context.

The origins of the New Right in the United States and Britain in general, and of the politics of Margaret Thatcher and Ronald Reagan in particular, are sometimes assumed to have been coincidental. Their closeness has been presented as an accident of time, place, and personality. A view encountered among interviewees for this book, such as Martin Anderson and Peter Jay, for example, holds that the importance of this coincidence became manifest only after Thatcher and Reagan took office, not least through their shared approach to the Soviet Union and the Cold War. Alternatively, the existence of a transatlantic connection, often observed simply through the intimacy of Reagan and Thatcher themselves, has been vaguely asserted without proper investigation of its nature. This narrow perspective covers up the deeper associations, parallels, and, most important, the differences between neoliberal politics in Britain and in the United States.

The actual amount of daily policy exchange between the Thatcher and Reagan governments and their members appears to have been limited, though significant.[21] The history of enterprise zones, treated in chapter 7, is an important example of explicit transatlantic policy transfer. The idea traveled across the Atlantic from Britain in the person of Stuart Butler, who moved from the Adam Smith Institute, which he founded in 1977 with his brother Eamonn and Madsen Pirie, to become one of the most senior figures at Ed Feulner's Heritage Foundation in Washington, D.C., after 1979. It is perhaps surprising that there were not more examples like this. But despite the relative paucity of direct exchange, the relationship between the ideas of the two administrations, and their shared histories, are crucial to understanding the political influence and impact of neoliberalism. The divergent priorities of the Thatcher and Reagan administrations often gave neoliberal policies starkly separate and specific local effects.

Second, the book focuses on the intellectual history of the political development of neoliberal thought. It is based on extensive primary research in archives in California, Washington, D.C., New York, London, Oxford, and Cambridge, including the papers of Friedrich Hayek, Karl Popper, Milton Friedman, the IEA, and the Conservative Party. It also draws on a series of research interviews with politicians, advisers, members of the Reagan White House and Thatcher government, and representatives of the leading British and American neoliberal think tanks. The interviews add color to the narrative and reveal some of the motives and justifications of the participants, but more important, reading between the lines, they illustrate many of the contradictions inherent in the application of neoliberal theory to politics and government. Neoliberal policies were supported by such disparate figures as Chicago economist Henry Simons, Austrian philosopher Karl Popper, Virginia "public choice" theorist James Buchanan, and even Labour Party minister Edmund Dell. Neoliberal political symbols have included Chilean dictator Augusto Pinochet, Conservative politician Keith Joseph, former chairman of the Federal Reserve Alan Greenspan, and arguably even former Democratic president Bill Clinton and British Labour Party prime ministers Tony Blair and Gordon Brown. The frictions implied by these associations illustrate some of the problems already alluded to in reaching any single definition of neoliberalism.

There were, and still are, several neoliberalisms to be discussed, both separately and in combination. This complexity is revealed in the relationships between neoliberal thought and the classical Enlightenment, the French Revolution and conservative reactions to it, the American Revolution and its product, the U.S. Constitution, the liberalisms of Manchester and Mill, and the new political movements of the twentieth century. Addressing these connections provides a clearer view of what it opposed: Marxist and British Fabian socialism, social democracy, the One Nation group and paternalist Conservatism, the New Deal, the Great Society, and totalitarianism of the Left or Right. Such analysis reveals the specific character of varieties of neoliberalism, their roots as well as their orientations in power. A focus on ideas allows a greater appreciation of the limits of neoliberal influence and challenges the loose use of the term neoliberal as a general conceptual category.

The third historical innovation offered is a study of neoliberalism as a political movement as well as an intellectual one. It reveals the manner in which a body of thought was imperfectly translated into policy and, ultimately, into politics. The process by which ideas were mixed with power involved compromise, but it also involved the creation of a vast network that achieved a large measure of political influence. In this sense, it is a history of how neoliberal organizations and ideas meshed with the reality of power. What emerges, especially in chapters 6 and 7, is a detailed picture of economic and social policy. How Austrian, Chicago, or Virginia theory was applied to concrete social and economic problems and clashed with or complemented competing traditional, conservative, liberal, or populist electoral imperatives presents a vivid image of the fudges and opportunities of politics. Politicians of different stripes and priorities could pick and choose from a menu of neoliberal offerings. Peter Jay, James Callaghan's British ambassador to the United States between 1977 and 1979 and economic commentator for the *Times* newspaper, became a monetarist from the late 1960s without believing that economic freedom was limited to the pursuit of profit. Jay reminds us that it is possible to believe in the efficacy of competitive markets without wishing for the destruction of the welfare state. The spectacularly symbolic collapse of Soviet communism after 1989 obscured this truth and led some Democratic and Labour Party politicians to support policies that continued the agenda of the radical Right.[22]

The side effects of the unqualified advocacy of markets by Thatcher and Reagan during a period of rapid globalization were visible in the communities that had sustained damage from the decline in manufacturing, especially in Britain, in the 1980s. Thatcherite economic policy was often hostile toward the affected groups, many of which had traditionally supported their political opponents in the Labour Party. In the United States, Reagan was able to fashion a new Republican coalition that knit together a seemingly explosive combination of working-class Reagan Democrats with big business interests. The examination of ideas, policy, and politics in a single transatlantic frame brings this messy reality into focus and affords a clearer view of the history of neoliberal politics. Together, these three elements provide a new appreciation of the relevance of neoliberalism in its various guises and results in Britain and the United States.

In 1979, Margaret Thatcher became British prime minister, and in 1980 Ronald Reagan became president of the United States. Despite different cultural inflections and national contexts—the legacy of slavery and segregation in the United States, immigration and empire in Britain, and a federal system in contrast to a centralized government—each entered office with a manifesto based on free markets and a critique of the social democracy and New Deal liberalism that had dominated political culture in both countries since the war. In Stuart Hall's famous phrase, each constructed an electorally potent politics of "authoritarian populism" that roundly defeated dazed opponents in the Labour and Democratic Parties.[23] Neoliberalism was the coherent, if loose, body of ideas best placed to capitalize on the opportunities created by the social and economic storms of the 1970s. Deep-seated social and economic trends had erupted into crises, dislocation, and urban breakdown. But later on, the electoral successes of Thatcher and Reagan during the 1980s enabled a wholesale political and philosophical shift to a new neoliberal ideology based on markets. The move was away from a belief in the efficacy and moral power of government and toward an unguarded faith in the individual, and in free markets as the deliverer of freedom.

Thirty years after this breakthrough moment in the 1970s, it was clear that faith in markets had outstripped the enthusiasm even of many of the leading neoliberal advocates of the postwar decades. During the frenzy of the financial crisis of 2007–8, neoliberal ideas—defined by a guileless faith in the efficiency of markets and their virtues—were blamed for the greed apparent on Wall Street and in the City of London. Widely held beliefs about the unquestioned superiority and self-correcting nature of the market, espoused by those such as former head of the Federal Reserve Alan Greenspan, had created a deregulated financial sector that brought the international economic system to the point of collapse. Despite a brief resurrection of neo-Keynesian stimulus packages to aid recovery from the credit crunch, in early 2009, the dominant impulse among British and American policymakers was to return to the pre-2007 status quo rather than to attempt a root-and-branch reform. This was obvious in the refusal of either the British or the U.S. government to challenge seriously the financial sector in the aftermath of a glaring example of unregulated market failure. Instead, the same economic technocrats who had presided over the policies that had contributed to the crisis in the first place were tasked with cleaning up the mess. Former members of Clinton's core economic policy team such as Larry Summers and Timothy Geithner, for example, became respectively director of the National Economic Council and treasury secretary under President Barack Obama after Obama's election in 2008.[24]

As Paul Krugman, another Nobel Prize–winning economist, put it in his retrospective assessment of the life and achievements of Milton Friedman, the "laissez-faire absolutism [promoted by neoliberals like Friedman] contributed to an intellectual climate in which faith in markets and disdain for government often trumps the evidence."[25] Such evidence, as we will see, reveals a decidedly mixed record in the two areas this book deals with in detail—macroeconomic strategy, and affordable housing and urban policy. As the economic sociologist Jamie Peck has argued, the ideal of the pure free market has always been unattainable, as utopian an idea in its own way as the Marxist illusion of a classless society.[26] The political, theoretical, and cultural transformation wrought by neoliberal politics after the 1970s brought with it a series of social and economic consequences, not least in the failure of successive governments to consider the broken communities their policies left behind. Such a radical change in political culture and public debate from social democracy to a market-driven society was not planned or mapped out in advance. Luck, opportunism, and a set of contingent circumstances played the most crucial roles. Above all, it was far from inevitable.

1

✳

The Postwar Settlement

In our day these economic truths have become accepted as self-evident. We have accepted, so to speak, a second Bill of Rights under which a new basis of security and prosperity can be established for all regardless of station, race, or creed.

Among these are:

> The right to a useful and remunerative job in the industries or shops or farms or mines of the Nation;
> The right to earn enough to provide adequate food and clothing and recreation;
> The right of every farmer to raise and sell his products at a return which will give him and his family a decent living;
> The right of every businessman, large and small, to trade in an atmosphere of freedom from unfair competition and domination by monopolies at home or abroad;
> The right of every family to a decent home;
> The right to adequate medical care and the opportunity to achieve and enjoy good health;
> The right to adequate protection from the economic fears of old age, sickness, accident, and unemployment;
> The right to a good education.

All of these rights spell security. And after this war is won we must be prepared to move forward, in the implementation of these rights, to new goals of human happiness and well-being.

—Franklin Delano Roosevelt,
State of the Union speech, January 11, 1944

In January 1944, President Roosevelt outlined to Congree his vision of a postwar society defined by social and economic citizenship rights. At the same time, Friedrich Hayek's classic polemic, *The Road to Serfdom*, was at the publishers in London. Where Roosevelt saw an opportunity to embed and expand the liberal gains of the New Deal, which had been cemented by the war effort, Hayek and his friends saw only the threat of encroaching socialism, collectivism, and totalitarianism. As the war raged to a close, it was possible to see the clash of two diametrically opposed worldviews: American New Deal liberalism and British social democracy, on one side, and a distinctive critique that formed the basis of transatlantic neoliberalism on the other. There was no doubt, however, that Rooseveltian New Deal liberalism was in the ascendance in the United States, while Prime Minister Clement Attlee's government began to build in Britain the postwar settlement symbolized by the foundation of the National Health Service by Minister of Health Aneurin (Nye) Bevan in 1948.

To many on the progressive left, the slow unraveling of Roosevelt's expansive vision in the postwar period is one of the great laments of recent U.S. history. But despite the failure of the Democrats to achieve everything Roosevelt had promised (most obviously, universal health care, something partially redeemed by President Barack Obama in 2010), Harry S. Truman's Fair Deal, the GI Bill, and the 1949 and 1950 expansions of Social Security set the tone for American liberalism's advance.[1] At the same time in Britain, Beveridge's 1942 *Report on Social Insurance and Allied Services* inspired a demand that postwar reconstruction be built on the welfare state creation of the early twentieth-century New Liberal governments of Asquith and Lloyd George. Indeed, in May 1945 an ungrateful electorate dumped Winston Churchill and the Conservative Party from office and replaced them with Attlee's Labour Party. One of the great reforming governments, Labour implemented Beveridge's proposals for a cradle-to-grave welfare state and, again through Nye Bevan's leadership as secretary of state for health, initiated a high-specification public housing building initiative to replace Britain's bombed-out housing stock.

Here were two countries with very different systems and circumstances that nevertheless felt similar social and liberal-democratic impulses at mid-century. A legacy of the Great Depression of the 1930s was to make unemployment, poverty, and freedom from want the chief concerns of voters, who demanded of their leaders that their societies would "never again" suffer from such indignities and degradations at the hands of market failure.[2] Reformist liberals and moderate conservatives in Britain, and liberal Republicans and conservative Southern Democrats (for whites, at least) in the United States, were as fully committed to these aims as supporters of the Labour and Democratic Parties were.[3] Political culture, conversation, and elections in both the United States and Britain were dominated by the thinkers and parties of the center and left in 1945. Fifty-five years later, at the dawn of a new millennium, a new creed reigned, one the speculator and philanthropist George Soros has called "market fundamentalism."[4] Part of this change was driven by a movement whose origins were visible in the final years of World War II. Transatlantic neoliberalism, and the movement that spread its agenda, emerged from a critique of what Hayek and others referred to as the "collectivist" character of the politics of President Roosevelt and Prime Minister Attlee. This critique was motivated by a profound fear of totalitarianism, the threat of which they saw in the blind acceptance of government and administrative expansion in the first half of the twentieth century. But it would take a transformation in primarily economic structures, mixed with events and circumstances, not just policies, to create the conditions under which these new ideas could take hold in the political programs of the Conservative and Republican Parties, and thus influence government action. That would not happen until the late 1960s and, especially, the 1970s.

But in this chapter it is first necessary to describe the contours and limits of the political settlement in Britain and the United States in the middle of the twentieth century. How far was there consensus among the political elites and publics in both countries? What was the political and intellectual paradigm that the neoliberals viewed with such foreboding? The shape of politics and society in Britain and the United States had fundamentally changed as it had developed through the experiences of two world wars, Progressivism, Fabian socialism, the Great Depression, and the New Deal.

Both Britain and the United States underwent economic and political transformations in the first half of the twentieth century. The size of government expanded exponentially in both countries. For example, in 1900, total central government expenditure in the United States amounted to $521 million. This compared to £193 million in Britain. By 1949, government expenditure had reached $39 billion in the United States and almost £3.5 billion in Britain. By 1990 the federal government was spending $1.3 trillion in the United States and £158 billion in Britain.[5] The income tax was introduced in the United States after the Sixteenth Amendment to the Constitution was ratified in 1913. This was quickly reflected in increased government revenue from taxation. In 1900, federal government revenue amounted to $567 million. By 1949, total revenue was $41.5 billion, of which $26.7 billion was from the income tax and $3.8 billion was from payments into the Social Security fund.[6] In Britain in 1900, the government received £140 million, of which £29 million came from income and property taxes. In 1949 the government received £4.1 billion, of which £1.85 billion came from income and property taxes.[7] These figures illustrate the growth in the presence, scope, and power of government in both countries as policymakers, driven by increasingly insecure populations, built large-scale welfare states in response to the economic collapse of the 1930s and world war in the 1940s.

By the end of the war, in 1945, however, the economic positions of the two countries were in stark contrast. The United States had emerged from the war with unprecedented global power and affluence, while Britain had been brought to its knees by a war whose graphic cost had taken its toll in terms of dead bodies and towns and cities destroyed during the Blitz. The cost of the defeat of the Nazis propelled Britain toward the loss of its imperial possessions. Compounding the difficulty of Britain's position was the fact that the devastation wrought by the war came on top of the far-reaching economic collapse of the 1930s. A new approach to economics to deal with these crises was demanded and duly arrived in the ideas of the Liberal economist, John Maynard Keynes. Keynes constructed a theory that developed the concept of macroeconomic management of fiscal and monetary policy as a response to the Great Depression. Keynesian prescriptions would now be adopted by the politicians of Britain and the United States, and would dominate the mainstream of the economics profession. Macroeconomics focuses on economy-wide phenomena such as employment levels, interest rates, and fiscal and monetary policy, as opposed to sector-specific, microeconomic policy. Keynes's *General Theory of Employment, Interest and Money*, published in 1936, and Keynes's leading role in the postwar negotiations that led to the creation of the Bretton Woods international monetary system, had set the terms by which Western governments were to manage stable economies in peacetime. In the wake of the disasters of the 1930s, full employment was to be the primary goal of economic policy. The desire to avoid the dole queues pervaded the establishments of both Britain and the United States as much as it did the working classes.

Keynes argued that governments could beat the business cycle through fiscal policy or large-scale public investment when demand in the economy was either sluggish or in recession. By pumping money into the economy, practicing government intervention through deficit spending, or boosting consumption through tax cuts, policymakers believed they had a set of tools with which to ensure high employment and continued economic growth. This recipe seemed to offer politicians and publics alike what they most wanted: the prospect of full employment and increased prosperity. Keynes's followers pushed these ideas beyond what the man himself would have envisaged. As Robert Skidelsky, Keynes's biographer, has suggested,

> [Keynes] thought governments could manage total spending power only in a rough and ready way which would still be an improvement on laissez-faire. But the next generation carried this project much further. They thought the problem of limited knowledge facing the central manager was a contingent one, and that as statistics improved, so would the possibility of control. This reached its apogee in the "fine tuning" approach of the 1960s.[8]

This neo-Keynesian approach, alongside the welfare state (though of course provision was less comprehensive in the United States than in Britain), formed the bedrock of U.S. and British economic policy of the 1950s and 1960s. It was the era of "Butskellism," as described by Norman Macrae in the *Economist*, so called after senior British Conservative Rab Butler and Attlee's successor as Labour leader Hugh Gaitskell.[9]

In the United States the New Deal marked a revolution in government during the 1930s. Roosevelt's administration, after his election in 1932, reformed the banking sector, supported the farmers, and created large-scale public employment programs through the Public Works Administration, the Civil Works Administration, and the Works Progress Administration in order to defeat the Depression. A welfare state, if one limited in several important ways, was enacted through the Social Security Act of 1935. Labor unions were recognized and their rights assured through the National Recovery

Administration and, especially, the National Labor Relations Act, known as the Wagner Act, also of 1935. A system of regulation of the stock exchange and the financial sector, since repealed, was created through the Glass-Steagall Act (1933), which separated the commercial and speculative operations of banks and established the Securities and Exchange Commission and the Federal Deposit Insurance Corporation. A rudimentary structure of support for home buyers and the homeless was put in place with the creation of the Federal Housing Administration and the U.S. Housing Authority. Mortgages were to be provided at subsidized rates, and public housing was created in the United States for the first time.

Taken as a whole, the New Deal enshrined the federal government's role in American life and legitimized government activism. But the gains of the New Deal were limited in important ways.[10] First, the American welfare state, unlike Britain's, did not proceed along universalist lines. At the insistence of the congressional Southern Democrats, blacks, casual and agricultural laborers, and women were initially excluded from Social Security and unemployment insurance, and welfare was left to the states to administer.[11] This ensured that blacks in the South, for example, received few or no benefits. Universal health care, implicit in Roosevelt's Committee on Economic Security's plans, was not attempted, let alone enacted, until the Obama administration made it a priority. A large vociferous opposition, meanwhile, was never reconciled to a program it saw as counter to all American traditions of individual initiative and liberty. Out of this opposition would emerge some of the most significant business funders of the neoliberals after World War II, including such figures as William Volker and Laurence Fertig. The finance provided by the anti–New Deal businessmen was crucial to the successful promotion of free market ideas in the postwar United States.

What Peter Hennessy has called the "British New Deal" was a mixture of the reforms of Herbert Henry Asquith's and David Lloyd George's Liberal governments of 1906–22 and Attlee's Labour government of 1945–51.[12] It was confirmed and accepted by the long Conservative Party administrations of 1951–64, which did not attempt to reverse its key components or chart a radically different course. The postwar consensus, as it was known in Britain, involved a universal welfare state combined with nationalization of "the Commanding heights" of the economy and public utilities, which, by 1951,

Labour had achieved—the Bank of England, railways, road haulage, civil aviation, coal, steel, electricity, and gas.

The British welfare state was created in stages. The Liberal governments of Henry Campbell-Bannerman and Herbert Henry Asquith between 1906 and 1916 introduced means-tested pensions for the elderly and means-tested unemployment insurance, labor exchanges for the unemployed, limited means-tested health insurance, and sickness benefits for workers.[13] The system, however, was patchy, and many citizens were left out of its provisions. If the New Deal marked the emergence of a new form of liberalism in the United States, the enactment of these early reforms marked the split between the nineteenth-century Victorian liberalism of Gladstone and a new progressive and activist liberalism in Britain. Gladstonian liberalism had been built on laissez-faire and free trade. The New Liberals, by contrast, saw impediments to freedom in poverty, sickness, and squalor.

The postwar Labour government, inspired by the Fabian socialists and William Beveridge, among others, built on these early reforms by introducing universal pensions, unemployment insurance, and Nye Bevan's National Health Service.[14] Beveridge, like Keynes a member of the Liberal Party, was a main architect of both the Liberal and Labour reforms. He was a contradictory figure. According to his biographer, Jose Harris, "Far from being a consistent 'liberal collectivist', he veered between an almost total commitment to the free market and an equally strong commitment to a semi-authoritarian administrative state."[15] His personality epitomized the conflict in twentieth-century liberalism, torn between its classical and laissez-faire heritage and a radically new kind of interventionism. However, both Beveridge's and Keynes's ideas were central to the developments that the neoliberals feared and opposed.

At the heart of both New Deal liberalism and the British Liberal and Labour reforms was a happy conception of the state so long as its power was in the hands of an enlightened and expert policy elite. The famous Brain Trust around Roosevelt and the progressive liberal civil service personified by Beveridge and Keynes fit exactly this notion of top-down reform for the benefit of society as a whole. The progressive liberal project was not revolutionary. It was born of a desire to preserve and defend liberal democracy and the capitalist system. However, it was also based on a belief that a "middle way," as Keynes put it, was possible. Once the economic disorder of the 1930s had been replaced by war, liberals saw a ray of light. In both Britain and the United States there was a belief that the wholesale mobilization of the economy and society for the war effort had pointed the way to how social objectives might be achieved in peacetime. This, of course, was a judgment that the neoliberals vehemently challenged.

Among political elites on both sides of the Atlantic—civil servants, politicians, senior public officials, and academics—there was a shared set of assumptions about many of the most important elements of economic and social policy. The need for a welfare state and for the government to take an active role in the economy were accepted. This is a partial picture, however. In the United States especially the picture is too complicated to describe simply as a consensus. The onset of the Cold War in the late 1940s had ensured a continual ideological struggle between not just communists and capitalists but also American conservatives and liberals.[16] Equally, there were deep fissures and often violent conflicts in the cities and urban centers between blacks and whites.[17] This struggle was conducted in both subtle and confrontational ways, as was to be seen in the struggles over desegregation and in the constantly shifting boundaries between the inner city and the suburbs.[18] In the South, racial politics dominated, and indeed, the power of white southern politicians would be one of the most significant bellwethers of U.S. politics throughout the postwar period as they transferred their support from the Democratic Party to the Republicans after the passage of the Civil Rights Act (1964) and the Voting Rights Act (1965) by Lyndon Johnson.[19] In the 1930s and 1940s, the conservative Southern Democrats had been responsible for many of the most important limits on New Deal legislation through their insistence on the exclusion of blacks. The growing and unsustainable split in the Democratic Party was foreshadowed by the segregationist, "Dixiecrat" presidential candidacy of Strom Thurmond in 1948, which carried five Deep South states against President Truman.

In Britain, society underwent social and economic changes that would become more important as the 1950s turned into the 1960s. The end of empire brought mass immigration from the former colonies to the British mainland for the first time.[20] West Indians and South Asians began to move to Britain in large numbers. Britain's economy, meanwhile, had been ravaged by the war. The late 1940s were a period of what David Kynaston has called "austerity" and sacrifice.[21] British policymakers and citizens alike were forced to come to terms with the loss of Britain's global role. This was catastrophically revealed by the Suez crisis of 1957. Prime Minister Anthony Eden's failed attempt to face down General Gamal Abdel Nasser without American support showed that Britain could no longer act alone in international affairs, a bitter pill for the political establishment to swallow.

This was how the United States and the UK looked in the middle of the twentieth century. It was a world that offered hope for many progressives that the worst social and political problems might be overcome once peace arrived. But this hopeful outlook was also seen by some critics as laced with utopianism and a misplaced faith in the virtuous nature of government action. In particular, a group of thinkers emerged to puncture the optimism. It is to these writers, Karl Popper, Ludwig von Mises, and Friedrich Hayek, that we now turn, for they were the standard-bearers of a new set of ideas that would, later in the twentieth century, transform the intellectual landscape and fundamentally reshape the practice of public policy in both Britain and the United States.

2

✳

The 1940s

The Emergence of the Neoliberal Critique

There is more than a superficial similarity, between the trend of thought in Germany during and after the last war and the present current of ideas in the democracies. There exists now in these countries certainly the same determination that the organisation of the nation which has been achieved for purposes of defence shall be retained for the purposes of creation.

FRIEDRICH A. HAYEK, *The Road to Serfdom*, 1944

As World War II drew to an end and an uneasy peace dawned, Friedrich Hayek began to develop an intellectual and organizational strategy to protect and maintain "the free society." His strategy, which he laid out in his article "The Intellectuals and Socialism," looked to the influence of the early twentieth-century American progressives and British Fabian socialists and argued that defenders of liberty would have to develop a similar organizational and intellectual strategy. During the war, Hayek worked at the London School of Economics (LSE, founded by the Fabian socialists Beatrice and Sydney Webb in 1895), which had been exiled to Cambridge because of the bombing. He stayed with his longtime friend and intellectual adversary John Maynard Keynes and sought to build on the rhetorical force of his coruscating polemic, *The Road to Serfdom*, by establishing a society of scholars who could defend the core tenets of what he saw as the freedom of the individual.

The result of Hayek's efforts was that a sympathetic group of intellectuals from Paris, Austria, Switzerland, Germany, Manchester, the LSE, and Chicago came together under his leadership to form a kind of neoliberal international.

("Neoliberalism" was the term these scholars had chosen to describe their approach at the Colloque Walter Lippmann in 1938.) The group called itself the Mont Pelerin Society after the venue of its first meeting, which was held in Vevey, Switzerland, April 1–10, 1947. But what would this movement created in the Swiss mountains be based around? What would unite its participants and hold it together? What would enable neoliberalism to expand beyond the Mont Pelerin Society and break through into the political mainstream, first in Britain and the United States, and then around the world? What was the neoliberals' distinctive view of liberty? The answer was to be found in a comprehensive critique of political, economic, and social life that was elaborated in the work of many scholars in the 1930s and 1940s. Its central themes were synthesized in three important books: *The Open Society and Its Enemies* (1945), by Karl Popper, *Bureaucracy* (1944), by Ludwig von Mises, and *The Road to Serfdom* (1944), by Friedrich A. Hayek.

Attempts had been made in the years preceding the establishment of the society, most famously at the Colloque Walter Lippmann, in Paris in 1938, which had been convened by the French philosopher Louis Rougier to debate the future of the free society, inspired by Walter Lippmann's book, *The Good Society* (1937). These scholars had aimed to reconstruct a theory of liberalism because they felt that classical liberalism was under assault. Indeed, at this meeting the term neoliberal was suggested by Alexander Rüstow and was chosen as the name for a movement to revive market liberalism. It was always a problematic term, and alternatives such as "individualism," "positive liberalism," and even "left-wing liberalism" were suggested. But, according to François Denord, the label was chosen for strategic reasons: to "be "neoliberal" implied one recognized that laissez-faire economics was not enough and that, in the name of liberalism, a modern economic policy was needed."[1] Many of those who would go on to join the Mont Pelerin Society had been present at the Colloque Walter Lippmann in Paris—Hayek, Ludwig von Mises, Wilhelm Röpke, Alexander Rüstow, Michael Polanyi, Raymond Aron, Bertrand de Jouvenel, and Jacques Rueff—but its purpose was soon overwhelmed by the outbreak of war.

This time, however, the society established at Mont Pelerin succeeded in laying firm ground for a transatlantic neoliberal movement. In many ways, Hayek's creation marked a transition point from one phase of the history of neoliberalism to another. The origins of neoliberalism in its first phase as an intellectual development that sought to theorize liberalism anew had been clear for some time in the work of scholars in Austria, London, Germany, and Chicago in the interwar years who sought to move beyond laissez-faire and to fight totalitarianism of the right and the left. The next, second phase of neoliberalism as a mature and organized intellectual and eventually political movement began with the society's formation. The society helped create a transatlantic neoliberal network that would, as its members saw it, combat the New Deal and social democratic political establishments in Britain and the United States. It also provided a haven for like-minded scholars from all over the world to combat the forces of collectivism (occupying for Hayek a spectrum all the way from Nazism and Soviet communism to New Deal liberalism and Attlee's social democracy), which Hayek had identified in *The Road to Serfdom* as posing a threat to individual liberty. Hayek became the leader of this movement through the prominence and clarity of his message in the book and also because of his tenacity at organizing and fundraising.

The scholars who came together around Hayek in 1947 (as well as the odd businessman, journalist, and think tank member) were bound together by a deeply held conviction that freedom was under threat in the developed world. They were especially worried about trends they perceived in Britain and the United States in the preceding fifty years, countries that Hayek and Mises had identified as the homes of liberty. The society's statement of aims, drafted mainly by the LSE economist Lionel Robbins (like Hayek, an old antagonist of Keynes), struck an apocalyptic tone:

> The central values of civilisation are in danger. Over large stretches of the Earth's surface the essential conditions of human dignity and freedom have already disappeared. In others they are under constant menace from the development of current tendencies of policy. The position of the individual and the voluntary group are progressively undermined by extensions of arbitrary power.[2]

The encouragement, maintenance, and protection of free market capitalism were at the core of the members' understanding of freedom. This defining feature of the Western democracies had to be upheld if the tide of ideas was to be turned.

The three books by Austrian emigrants, Karl Popper, Friedrich Hayek, and Ludwig von Mises, were conceived in reaction to a political and economic landscape in the 1940s that was hostile to their views. The ideas they promoted were to have a profound influence on the intellectual development of neoliberalism in Britain and the United States in the postwar period. Each began to articulate a neoliberal alternative to discredited nineteenth-century laissez-faire economics, on the one hand, and New Deal liberalism and British social democracy on the other. Hayek's *The Road to Serfdom* and Mises' *Bureaucracy* responded directly to the events and catastrophes that had befallen Europe in the 1930s and 1940s. Popper's *The Open Society and Its Enemies* was a little less direct as it was addressing the history of political thought. Together, they developed a critique of contemporary politics that provided the foundation for what we might think of as neoliberalism today. They articulated a distinctive view of historical development, of the history of ideas, and of the practice of politics that, taken together, systematically undermined each pillar of the New Deal, in the United States, and the social democratic state in Britain.

Hayek's, Mises', and Popper's ideas did not yet form a positive alternative political agenda, however. The detailed policy challenge to Keynesianism, the regulation of capitalism and the welfare state, would come later when a less compromising and more forthright set of neoliberal ideas was developed by others, a transatlantic community of scholars, think tanks, journalists, politicians, and policymakers, funded by sympathetic businessmen. But such a self-confident and expansive free market program as did emerge later, especially in Chicago and Virginia in the 1950s, 1960s, and 1970s, would not have succeeded without the robust philosophical ballast that was provided by Hayek's, Popper's, and Mises' analyses of the West's predicament. In *The Road to Serfdom*, *The Open Society*, and *Bureaucracy*, then, it is possible to see the beginnings of a recognizably neoliberal worldview.

The arguments put forward in these books caught fire at this moment in the 1940s because they chimed with the fears and insecurities of a world haunted by the phantom of Hitler's National Socialism and cast down by the drawing across Europe of the Iron Curtain and the beginning of the Cold War. Their hold on the political imagination, especially in the United States, however, cannot be explained simply on the basis of the searing critiques of European forms of totalitarianism they provided. Hayek and Mises in particular also spoke to popular tropes of rugged individualism and the fear and distrust of government authority that ran deep in American society. Karl Popper's *The Open Society* is important for different reasons. His concept of "piecemeal engineering" illustrates the willingness of early neoliberal thinkers in the 1940s to reach an accommodation with the seemingly adverse environment in which they found themselves. Popper envisaged a basic level of government intervention, especially in education, that would help ensure the progress of mankind through innovation and trial and error. He believed he was united with the motives of most socialists, if not with their means—he described liberals, progressives, and socialists as the "humanitarian camp."

Such pacts with collectivism were never envisaged by Mises, whose abhorrence of the New Deal was unmitigated. They were frowned on by Hayek, too. But there is no doubt that Popper's idea was an extreme example of a willingness to make certain compromises with the emerging welfare state in order to safeguard the larger goal of the market society (though his conciliatory approach was almost entirely absent in later manifestations of neoliberal thought).[3] Thus, the three major works, all published within a year of each other at the end of the war, represent the flowering of an early neoliberalism, which had cross-pollinated in interwar Austria, Germany, France, Britain, and the United States. This early neoliberalism, though superficially recognizable, was very different from what would come to be thought of as neoliberalism by the century's end. The early neoliberals were marked by their desire to move beyond both laissez-faire economics and the New Deal. Later neoliberals, defined by the Chicago emphasis on unregulated markets, were much less ambiguous in their opposition to the welfare state and to the need for government intervention in the economy.

The contribution of Hayek, Mises, and Popper built on the academic debates among scholars in Europe and the United States in the 1930s and 1940s—arguments in which Hayek and Mises had themselves participated—about the merits of central planning versus free markets as the organizing principle of economic activity in society.[4] Their analyses undermined the central supports of what would later be thought of as the postwar settlement—the progressive and social democratic belief in collective solutions to social needs, their accounts of history and political thought, and the organizational structure, bureaucracy, that had developed to manage problems such as poverty and want—and the theoretical assumptions that underpinned them.

Popper provided an account of the history of political ideas that showed how the "collectivist" thought of Plato, Hegel, and Marx had become rooted in Western philosophy. The true basis of Western civilization, individual liberty, and reason had consequently been lost. Mises attacked the bureaucratic mentality that he claimed had corroded the fonts of human initiative, to be found in individualism and the profit motive, while Hayek presented an analysis of political and economic life, drawing on themes that were present in both Mises' and Popper's work, that aimed to expose the slippery path on which Western societies had, in his view, embarked by accepting the encroachments and interventions of government bureaucracies. According to Hayek, individual freedom was threatened.

Other influential works of the time were important to the development of neoliberalism: Walter Lippmann's *The Good Society* (1937), which had inspired the Colloque Walter Lippmann; Ayn Rand's libertarian novels *The Fountainhead* (1943) and *Atlas Shrugged* (1957), which would influence the future head of the Federal Reserve, Alan Greenspan, among many others; Mises' own magnum opus, *Human Action* (1949); the articles of the Chicago economist Henry Simons (which are treated in the next chapter); and Henry Hazlitt's *Economics in One Lesson* (1946) are just a few of the possible examples. But the work of these three Austrian émigrés was particularly important for the development of a coherent attack on progressive liberalism and social democracy.

Like many other intellectuals, scientists, and academics, Mises and Popper had fled Germany and Austria during the 1930s because of the Nazi seizure of power and persecution of the Jews. Mises left Vienna for Switzerland in 1934 because of his Jewish heritage. Popper did the same in 1937, emigrating first to New Zealand and then, through Hayek's influence, moving to Britain to work at the LSE in 1946. Hayek himself had arrived at the LSE in 1931 as a visiting lecturer before gaining a permanent position as a result of the popularity of his lectures and the patronage of Professor Lionel Robbins, an opponent of Maynard Keynes. (Robbins was later a member of the Mont Pelerin Society.) All three Austrian thinkers were imbued with preoccupations and concerns instilled by the cataclysm that had unfolded in Europe between the wars. In this sense, they were largely responding to European, and even particularly German, trends that had led mankind, as they saw it, to the terrors of National Socialist totalitarianism and world war.

To all three writers, communism, especially because of its influence on Western democratic policymakers, was a renewed threat as great as that posed by Nazism and fascism. They believed that the terrible outcome of total war was the result of profound Europe-wide cultural traits and ideas from which the United States and Britain were, relatively speaking, free. Mises and Hayek in particular looked to both these countries for hope. The New Deal, therefore, was a problematic development. Hayek, for example, worried that Jewish exiles from Hitler's Germany brought dangerous totalitarian philosophies with them as they escaped abroad, ideas that, though free of Nazi racial policy, would nevertheless cause harm. Hayek's point was that many had left because of racial persecution rather than because they disagreed with the totalitarian direction of Germany per se: "We should never forget that the anti-Semitism of Hitler has driven from his country, or turned into his enemies, many people who in every respect are confirmed totalitarians of the German type."[5] Many of Germany's leading academics, Hayek suggested, had actually supported the Nazi program:

> The way in which, in the end, with few exceptions, [Germany's] scholars and scientists put themselves readily at the service of the new rulers is one of the depressing and shameful spectacles in the whole history of the rise of National Socialism.[6]

The European origins of neoliberalism, then, arose out of this devastating experience.

Hayek, alongside Lionel Robbins, had fought intellectual battles with Maynard Keynes in the 1930s over their different approaches to monetary policy and the nascent area of macroeconomics. Mises had supervised the elaboration of Austrian economic theory through his *Privatseminar* in the 1920s. Popper had spent twenty years writing and rewriting the attack on historicism that would finally see the light of day in *The Open Society*.[7] But not until the closing months of the war was battle truly joined between two competing visions of society. The first assault in a new Cold War of ideas came in these Anglo-Austrian critiques. Their target was not simply collectivism or even, more simply, communism, socialism, or Nazism. Instead, they saw in the encroachment of state intervention on every aspect of social and economic life a creeping totalitarianism. They argued that this was imperceptibly implicit in the blind adoption of collectivism as the first principle for the solution of social problems. But the development of this approach to policy, for these Austrian thinkers, eroded basic individual liberty, which was the foundation of a free society.

Karl Popper and *The Open Society*

Karl Popper was born in Vienna in 1902 to middle-class parents who had converted from Judaism to Christianity.[8] He studied to become an auditor at the University of Vienna, taking a range of subjects, including physics, math, and psychology. Like many students of the time, Popper was initially attracted to socialism. He volunteered for the Austrian Communist Party and later joined the Association of Socialist School Students and became a member of the Austrian Social Democratic Party. Popper witnessed a death during a demonstration in June 1919, an experience that shattered his nascent worldview.[9] As a result, he became disillusioned with left-wing ideas and subsequently became a staunch advocate of liberal democracy. Popper received his doctorate in psychology in 1928 and worked as a secondary schoolteacher in Vienna in the early 1930s. In 1937 he left Austria and emigrated to New Zealand, where he lectured in philosophy at the University of Canterbury. He moved to the LSE in 1946, just after the publication, with Hayek's help, of *The Open Society and Its Enemies*.

Primarily a philosopher, Popper also wrote extensively on social and political theory throughout his life. Crucial to a neoliberal perspective was his distinctive emphasis on the importance of rationality in scientific research. His first major book, *The Logic of Scientific Discovery* (1934), developed Popper's key idea of falsifiability, according to which scientific theories, while they may never be proved true absolutely, may be disproved with a single counterexample. Thus, according to Popper, critical rational debate and trial and error were the best foundations of scientific progress. This insight underpinned, for example, Milton Friedman's and the Chicago school of economics' empirical approach, which was outlined in Friedman's famous 1953 article, "The Methodology of Positive Economics."[10] As Friedman wrote to Hayek much later, in 1975, about his methodology:

> Consider the proposition that a theory can be true yet untestable. I have no doubt that is correct. But now let us go on to the next stage that an

individual asserts that he knows a particular theory to be true though untestable. Suppose another individual disagrees with him. How is the difference to be resolved? In the praxeological [Mises' Austrian theory of economics, articulated in *Human Action*[11]] context, only by either conversion or force. The belief in the theory becomes of the nature of a religious belief. Contrast this with the procedure implicit in the kind of methodological approach I would support. You believe a particular theory to be true; I believe that theory to be false or a different theory true. We do not argue for the moment the issues. Rather we agreed between us on what set of facts if observed would lead you to accept my theory and what set of facts if observed would lead me to accept your theory. We thus have a peaceful method of reconciling disagreements between us.[12]

Friedman contested Hayek's belief that someone could know something to be true while being unable to put that knowledge properly to the test. Instead, he argued that Popper was right, that any theory must be capable of repudiation by disproof or by being tested so as to show the "inconsistency of observations with implications."[13] Popper, though himself educated in the laboratory of Austrian economics, challenged the Austrian school of economics' emphasis on theory over practice in the study of economics.

The Open Society and Its Enemies was published in two volumes in 1945. Popper had difficulty finding a publisher for the book until Hayek came to his aid. Cambridge, Longmans, and Macmillan all rejected the book. Finally, Hayek's and Popper's other good friend, the art historian Ernst Gombrich, managed to persuade Routledge in London to accept it. For this help, Popper was eternally grateful to Hayek. The correspondence between the two of them during their battle to get the book published was constant and touching. Their letters discussed its themes and also those of Hayek's own *Road to Serfdom*, which shared many of the same preoccupations. The letters are fascinating for what they reveal about both men's motives in writing these influential books.

Popper saw his book as a contribution to the "war effort," but he despaired of finding a "good title."[14] Popper presented Hayek with three options: "(1) the Open Society and its Enemies[,] (2) A Social Philosophy for Everyman (or, if it is not too pretentious, For Our Time), (3) the Flight From Freedom (or From the Open Society)."[15] Hayek was skeptical of Popper's suggestion of *The Open Society* as a title:

> Part of the reason for the delay of my reply was that I wanted to think further on the vexed title question but I am afraid I have not really had time to do so. I do not think the "Open Society" should appear in the title: it does not immediately convey the meaning it assumes in the book. The Flight From Freedom would be good if a book with an almost identical title had not recently appeared. "A Social Philosophy for Everyman" (or "For Our Time") is a little too neutral but may be relatively the best. Personally I still think the Conflict of Political (or Social) Ideals better but it is far from ideal.[16]

In the end, Popper stuck to his guns and went with *The Open Society and Its Enemies*. Hayek was less keen on this title because he felt "the open society" was too vague a term. He was much more preoccupied than Popper was with a vision of individual liberty grounded in the free market.

Hayek was particularly keen, however, to read Popper's draft because, as he put it, "it seems to be extraordinarily close to what I am doing myself at present" [in *The Road to Serfdom*].[17] Popper wanted Hayek's views to ensure he had not made any basic errors of economic reasoning. As he put it in a letter to Hayek,

> I had been looking forward to your judgment with a mixture of hope and fear; after all, in the economic field I am a typical dilettante, and although my book does not contain, or pretend to contain, anything new in this respect, I was wondering whether a real economist would agree with what I say.[18]

Their exchange of letters displayed the spirit of two comrades-in-arms in a struggle against collectivism. But Popper was not as willing as Hayek and Mises were to prioritize the free market above all else. This is evident in *The Open Society*, which illuminates his fear that the Western democracies had fallen under the influence of the wrong-headed collectivist ideas of Plato, Heraclitus, Hegel, and Marx. But Popper, more so than Hayek, also saw his task as one of reunification of liberals, progressives, and socialists.

He wanted to get "over the fatal split in the humanitarian camp"—Popper's emphasis—and work at "uniting the vast majority of liberals and socialists (as it were, under the flags of Mill and Lippmann)." Mill represented the fusion of two traditions, those of classical liberalism and utilitarianism, and Lippmann was the critic of totalitarian tendencies in American society during the 1930s.[19]

Popper's hope for renewed unity in the "humanitarian camp" was clear in his approach to the Mont Pelerin Society when Hayek began to canvass opinions in 1946 about what form the society should take. Popper argued that some socialists ought to be invited to participate.[20] This attitude was in stark contrast to that of both Hayek and especially Mises, who wanted like-minded liberals to participate. But Popper throughout his life believed the market was only one of several aims for the open society. Speaking in an interview just before he died in 1994, Popper reflected,

> Well I do believe that in a way one has to have a free market, but I also believe that to make a godhead out of the principle of the free market is nonsense. If we do not have a free market, then quite obviously the things that are being produced are not being produced for the consumer, really. The consumer can take it or leave it. His needs are not taken into account in the process of production. But all that is not of a fundamental importance. *Humanitarianism*, that is of fundamental importance.
>
> Traditionally, one of the main tasks of economics was to think of the problem of full employment. Since approximately 1965 economists have given up on that; I find it very wrong. It cannot be an insoluble problem. It may be difficult, but surely it is not insoluble!
>
> Our first task is peace; our second task is to see that nobody be hungry; and the third task is fairly full employment. The fourth task is, of course, education.[21]

As this passage makes clear, Popper's complex humanitarianism cannot be characterized as typical even of early neoliberalism.

In this earlier period, neoliberal thinkers such as Henry Simons, Hayek, and even Friedman himself were much more open to some of the innovations of the welfare state (arguably they had to be, given the intellectual and political climate).[22] Despite Popper's more positive attitude toward progressive politics, placing individualism at the center of his thought made him an early neoliberal, while his scathing assault on historicism provided intellectual ammunition to neoliberal critics of Plato, Hegel, and Marx. As he remained a member of the Mont Pelerin Society until his death, his philosophical differences with Hayek and Mises were relatively minor. Looking back, Hayek wrote of Popper in 1983, "We became close friends in the few years we were together at the London School of Economics, but I would not wish to say which of the two of us had the greater influence on the other (Not for quotation!)"[23] Popper and Hayek continued to correspond for the rest of their lives, and remained firm friends.

Volume 1 of *The Open Society and Its Enemies* dealt with the ancient ideas of Plato, Aristotle, and other Greek philosophers such as Heraclitus. Volume 2 treated, as Popper saw it, their modern equivalents, Hegel and Marx. Popper believed that the tradition created and sustained by these thinkers, which he called historicism, posed a threat to the ideals of a free society because they undermined individual liberty. The work provided an intellectual defense of critical rationalism as the basis for social development and progress through an account of the conflict between open and closed, or tribal, societies. The open society had developed, according to Popper, through the growth of commerce and free trade. He identified currents of thought that he considered to have been the parents of totalitarianism. Popper argued that the ideas of these historicist thinkers still posed a threat because of the intellectual confusion they fostered about what exactly the free, or open, society was based on.

The Open Society described the betrayal of Western civilization by a group of thinkers who had misunderstood the roots of liberal democracy and individual freedom:

> [The book] attempts to show that this civilisation has not yet fully recovered from the shock of its birth—the transition from the tribal or "closed society", with its submission to magical forces, to the "open society" which sets free the critical powers of man. It attempts to show that the shock of this transition is one of the factors that have made possible the rise of those reactionary movements which have tried, and still try, to overthrow civilisation and to return to tribalism. And it sug-

gests that what we call nowadays totalitarianism belongs to a tradition which is just as old or just as young as our civilisation itself.[24]

Popper's central target was historicism. According to Popper, historicism assumed a set of immutable laws of historical development that governed human affairs. Historicism was the doctrine that history is controlled by specific evolutionary laws whose discovery would enable the prophecy of the destiny of man.[25] Popper held that such an approach began with Plato.

Plato, Popper argued, was the first to set up the collective as greater than the individual. The collective was embodied in the state, which was the vehicle of human development or disintegration. For Plato, all change marked the dilution of the original and perfect state. Through Plato's belief in the corruptibility of institutions and constitutions, he had set up a fantastical ideal, a utopian (or, for Popper, a dystopian) vision of the perfect state that was impossible to sustain. For Plato, the perfect state was something that would only deteriorate and decay through change and reform and was, in this sense, a deeply conservative concept. The aristocracy and "philosopher kings," who were to be the rulers, were set up, for Popper, just like any other type of class rule. Slavery, of course, was an integral part of Plato's ideal. Plato revealed himself, according to Popper, not as a progressive but as a totalitarian whose ruling class was based, like others, on racial, tribal, and economic interests.

Popper highlighted Plato's definition of the differences between rulers and ruled, between the members of the elite and the slaves. He thought that this illustrated that Plato had constructed a concept of the master race *avant la lettre*: "The aim of breeding the master race is thus established, and shown to be attainable. It has been derived from an analysis of the conditions which are necessary for keeping the state stable."[26] Plato thus introduced a biological character to the perfect state that clearly presaged the claims of fascism and Nazism. All individual goals or needs were to be subordinated to the furtherance of a racially and economically exclusive group of rulers. Their wisdom trumped all. For Popper, this represented an essentially closed and tribal society and was an obstacle to the development of the kind of critical rationalism among the citizens that allowed individuals to take responsibility for their own ethical choices. This was because truth was detached from reason in such a scheme:

"For the benefit of the city", says Plato. Again we find that the appeal to the principle of collective utility [based in the homogeneous ruling caste] is the ultimate ethical consideration. Totalitarian morality over-rules everything, even the definition, the Idea, of the philosopher. It need hardly be mentioned that, by the same principle of political expediency, the ruled are forced to tell the truth. "If the ruler catches *anyone else* in a lie . . . then he will punish him for introducing a practice which injures and endangers the city. . . ." Only in this slightly unexpected sense are the Platonic rulers—philosopher kings—lovers of truth.[27]

Truth becomes an elastic concept in the service of the state and the imperatives decided by the wise rulers on behalf of the larger community. The link in Popper's mind with the police states of Mussolini's Italy, Hitler's Germany, and Stalin's Russia is obvious.

According to Popper, Plato had attempted to destroy individualism as a creed because he saw it as the greatest impediment to his perfect system:

Why did Plato try to attack individualism? I think he knew very well what he was doing when he trained his guns upon this position, for individualism, perhaps even more than equalitarianism [which Popper distinguished from egalitarianism, the difference between opportunity and outcome] was a stronghold in the defences of the new humanitarian creed. The emancipation of the individual was indeed the great spiritual revolution which had led to the breakdown of tribalism and to the rise of democracy. Plato's uncanny sociological intuition shows itself in the way in which he invariably discerned the enemy wherever he met him.[28]

For Popper, individualism, combined with altruism, was the foundation of Western civilization.[29] Plato had constructed a totalitarian morality that subjected each individual to the force of the collective will. Plato sought to restore the tribalism that Popper argued was characteristic of the closed society. This eagerness to defend and promote individualism was at the heart of the alternative philosophy that Popper, Hayek, and Mises were writing in New Zealand, London, and New York but directing at continental Europe and the United States. They were attempting to oppose New Deal liberalism and social democracy, which they saw as taking from the individual his ability to make free choices. Individualism was something they believed to be central to the Anglo-Scottish-American Enlightenment tradition of economic and political thought and something that might best be protected in Britain and the United States. These twentieth-century considerations provided the background for Popper's arguments about ancient political philosophy.

Popper's other quarry were Hegel and Marx, who in his view built on the tradition begun by Plato and Aristotle. As he put it, "Hegel is the renaissance of tribalism."[30] Hegel was the father of modern historicism and developed the ancient totalitarianism of Plato:

> Hegel's success was the beginning of the "age of dishonesty" (as Schopenhauer described the period of German Idealism) and of the "age of irresponsibility" (as K. Heiden characterises the age of modern totalitarianism); first of intellectual, and later, as one of its consequences, of moral irresponsibility; of a new age controlled by the magic of high-sounding words, and by the power of jargon.

Historical prophecy, like that of Plato, Hegel, and Marx, he maintained, had become confused with reasoned hypothesis through the scientific claims of dialectics and historical materialism:

> A careful examination of this question has led me to the conviction that such sweeping historical prophecies are entirely beyond the scope of scientific method. The future depends on ourselves, and we do not depend on any historical necessity.
>
> The various social philosophies which raise claims of this kind, I have grouped together under the name *historicism*. Elsewhere, in *The Poverty of Historicism*, I have tried to argue against these claims, and to show that in spite of their plausibility they are based on a gross misunderstanding of the method of science, and especially on the neglect of the distinction between *scientific prediction* and *historical prophecy*.[31]

For Popper, belief in historical inevitability was not simply wrong, it also raised a practical problem: it eradicated the incentive to behave responsibly. It was easier for people to do nothing. Such a view was anathema to a defender of individual choice and freedom. Popper further argued that such ideas took hold in times of crisis:

> It seems as if historicist ideas easily become prominent in times of great social change. There can be little doubt, I believe, that Heraclitus's philosophy is an expression of a feeling of drift; a feeling which seems to be a typical reaction to the dissolution of the ancient tribal forms of social life. In modern Europe, historicist ideas were revived during the industrial revolution and especially through the impact of the political revolutions in America and France. It appears to be more than a mere coincidence that Hegel, who adopted so much of Heraclitus' thought and passed it on to all modern historicist movements, was a mouth-piece of the reaction against the French Revolution.[32]

For Popper, the 1940s were clearly such a moment of great social change. The era was therefore also a moment of danger because the depression of the 1930s had been followed by the devastation and dislocation of world war. Historicist ideas thrived in such moments. Indeed, they had influenced National Socialism, fascism, and the New Deal through the emphasis of all these movements on state intervention and government management of economic and social life.

If Hegel's dialectics provided the intellectual cover for a virulent new form of totalitarianism through its effacement of contradiction through synthesis, Marx had mounted an attack on the modern and open mode of economic organization: capitalism. Marx's historicism, according to Popper, was "economism," "the claim that the economic organisation of society, the organisation of our exchange of matter with nature is fundamental for all social institutions and especially for their historical development."[33] Though crucial to his argument, the part of the book devoted to Marx posed unexpected problems for Popper's attempts to get the book published. Hayek had written to Popper that the section on Marx was the weakest. He had told Popper that the weakness of this section meant that Lionel Robbins felt he could not support the book for publication. Hayek wrote,

> I cannot deny that, so far as I was myself concerned, I also felt a certain slackening of interest in that part, although this, in the case of an econo-

mist, who for the past twenty years had had [sic] to read one exposition and criticism of Marx after another, would not prove that the part is excessively long.[34]

Popper himself felt that the section on Marx was one he had struggled over in the course of many years of drafting and rewriting. He agreed with Hayek that interest dimmed in this part of the text; however, he replied, "I wrote the Marx part with the undoubtedly naive but ardent belief that it is possible and worthwhile to try to convert Marxists, and that one must do one's best to meet them as far as possible (the fact is that I have succeeded in converting even some prominent ones)." But most of all, Popper added, "I simply cannot rewrite the thing for the hundredth time. . . . This time it must be the end."[35]

What was the alternative for Popper, the antidote, to the body of dangerous ideas he labeled historicist? His answer was that a considered attempt at reform to blunt capitalism's excesses should be made. Popper agreed with Marx that economic organization was fundamental to the new types of political identity. But inequality should be addressed not by class war but through pragmatic reform. This might be done by government, although Popper worried that state intervention would concentrate too much power in its hands.[36] Concentrations of power were especially dangerous for Popper. According to Popper, there were two types of intervention:

> The first is that of designing a "legal framework" of protective institutions (laws restricting the powers of the owner of an animal, or of a landowner, are an example). The second is that of empowering organs of the state to act—within certain limits—as they consider necessary for achieving the ends laid down by the rulers for the time being. We may describe the first procedure as "institutional" or "indirect" intervention, and the second as "personal" or "direct" intervention. (Of course, intermediate cases exist.)[37]

The first type of intervention was best because it was less open to abuse. According to Popper, only the first method allowed for "adjustments in the light of discussion and experience."[38] The problems arose with the second form of intervention, when discretionary powers were granted to the state that would be difficult to control:

The use of discretionary powers is liable to grow quickly, once it has become an accepted method, since adjustments to discretionary short-term decisions can hardly be carried out by institutional means. This tendency must greatly increase the irrationality of the system, creating in many the impression that there are hidden powers behind the scenes, and making them susceptible to the conspiracy theory of society with all its consequences—heresy hunts, national, social, and class hostility.[39]

According to Popper, people did not understand the significance of the distinction between clearly delineated powers under the rule of law and discretionary powers. Hitler's seizure of power was an extreme example of the possible results of discretion.

People—individuals—must take responsibility for making decisions in their own lives. These decisions must not be left to leaders, politicians, or bureaucrats. This, Popper admitted, meant taking an irrational leap of faith like any other—putting faith in critical reason. However, to choose irrationalism was disempowering and allowed for the tyrannies Popper saw as being justified through the various strands of historicism:

> By thus abandoning reason, they split mankind into friends and foes; into the few who share reason with the gods, and the many who don't (as Plato says); into the few who stand near and the many who stand far; into those who speak the untranslatable language of our own emotions and passions and those whose tongue is not our tongue. Once we have done this political equalitarianism becomes practically impossible.[40]

Irrationalism allowed "might is right" arguments because of the inevitability of the historical prophecy, its stages, and the relative unimportance of the individual and her rights. The individual's role was reduced to that of a cog in the historicist machine. Instead, Popper said, "A social technology is needed whose results can be tested by piecemeal social engineering." The rational individual must be empowered pragmatically through "piecemeal engineering"—through trial, error, and criticism.[41]

The opposite of piecemeal engineering was "utopian engineering" of the sort implied by communist, socialist, or indeed National Socialist revolution:

What I criticise under the name Utopian engineering recommends the
reconstruction of society as a whole, i.e. very sweeping changes whose
practical consequences are hard to calculate, owing to our limited experiences. It claims to plan rationally for the whole of society, although
we do not possess anything like the factual knowledge to make good
such an ambitious claim. We cannot possess such knowledge since
we have insufficient practical experience in this kind of planning, and
knowledge of facts must be based upon experience. At present, the sociological knowledge necessary for large-scale engineering is simply
non-existent.[42]

This criticism of utopian plans, as we will see, was similar to both Hayek's and
Mises' critique of planning. It was impossible for the planner to have enough
information and knowledge to make a plan effective, though Popper left open
the theoretical possibility that it might at some point in the future.

According to Popper, there were only two types of government, tyranny
or that which can be freely changed without violence. The real classical inspiration for Popper's notion of rational freedom was Socrates. The "new faith
of the open society, the faith in man, in equalitarian justice, and in human
reason, was perhaps beginning to take shape" in his person.[43] This alternative
tradition, according to Popper, needed to be recovered. The individual had to
be empowered:

What I have tried to show is that the choice with which we are confronted is between a faith in reason and in human individuals and a
faith in the mystical faculties of man by which he is united to a collective; and that his choice is at the same time a choice between an attitude that recognises the unity of mankind and an attitude that divides
men into friends and foes, masters and slaves.[44]

Popper's challenge was that the West recover its philosophical moorings
through the application of critical reason to social problems within the framework of liberal democracy, free market capitalism, and a renewed emphasis
on individual liberty. As he put it in a letter to Hayek in 1944 after he had
read *The Road to Serfdom*, we "have a duty progressively to rationalise the
irrational."[45] If Popper railed against the erosion of critical faculties implied

by historicist ideas, and Hayek's chief fear, in *The Road to Serfdom,* was the incremental effects of well-meaning state action, Mises' target was a particular practical and philosophical orientation that was bound up with a rigid bureaucratic mode of organization, one that was both inefficient and corrosive of individual freedom. It was an outlook that Mises thought would undermine the free market society.

Ludwig von Mises and *Bureaucracy*

Ludwig von Mises was born twenty-one years before Popper, in 1881 in Lemberg, Galicia (then in the Austro-Hungarian Empire, later a part of Poland, and now in the Ukraine).[46] Like his younger friend and protégé Hayek, Mises was born into an old Austrian aristocratic family. His father was an engineer and his uncle had been a prominent member of the Austrian Liberal Party. Like Popper, Mises began his intellectual development as a left-wing interventionist. However, while studying law at the University of Vienna, Mises was influenced by the work of the founder of the Austrian school of economics, Carl Menger. The Austrian school believed in the power of the free market and in a set of unalterable economic laws centered on the individual. Government action could prevent the successful operation of these laws but it could not avoid their logic if economic success was desired. This was why Austrian economics was relatively outcast, according to Mises:

> To maintain the theory that there are such things as economic laws was deemed a kind of rebellion. For if there are economic laws, then governments cannot be regarded as omnipotent, as their policies could only succeed when adjusted to the operation of these laws. Thus the main concern of the German professors of the social sciences [of the German Historical School] was to denounce the scandalous heresy that there is a regularity in economic phenomena.[47]

The special focus of Austrian economics, and that of Mises and Hayek in particular, was the power of the price mechanism to allow the spontaneous organization of the economic life of autonomous individuals. Menger's work thus exposed Mises to the typically Austrian emphasis on the individual and the free market.

Mises received his doctorate from the school of law in 1906. Around this time he attended the lectures of another Austrian school economist, Eugene Bohm-Bawerk. Bohm-Bawerk was a tenacious backer of the gold standard as a guarantor of currency stability. The belief in the gold standard became a staple of the Austrian approach and an important difference with the second Chicago school (whose acknowledged leader, Milton Friedman, always supported floating exchange rates). During the 1920s in Vienna, Mises conducted a private seminar series that included a number of important economists in regular attendance. Hayek (as well as occasionally his LSE colleague, Lionel Robbins) and Fritz Machlup, for example, were regular attendees.[48] Mises taught at the University of Vienna until 1934, when he left for Switzerland, eventually emigrating to the United States in 1940. He remained in the United States until his death at age ninety-two, in 1973, teaching at New York University from 1945 to 1969. His classic treatise on economics, *Human Action*, was published in 1949. During his time in America, Mises' salary at NYU was paid by anti–New Deal businessmen such as Lawrence Fertig rather than by the university itself, a mark of how unfashionable his free market beliefs were.[49]

Bureaucracy was a short polemic published in the United States by Yale in 1944. It was written as a direct response to the advance in the West of what Mises referred to as "bureaucratism." Mises was animated by a characteristic concern to defend the potential of the United States, the country he had made his home, to resist a trend that he argued was a particular motif of the European political tradition. *Obrigkeit*, Mises suggested—the notion of a government "the authority of which is not derived from the people"—was alien to Americans, whose government was famously declared by Abraham Lincoln, in his Gettysburg Address, to be "of the people, by the people, for the people."[50] In the nineteenth century, the French aristocratic historian and observer Alexis de Tocqueville, a hero of Hayek and Mises, wrote of the vibrancy of local and community civic life in the United States.[51] By contrast, according to Mises, Europe had a long tradition of authoritarian and autocratic rule, which had been made frighteningly clear in the crises of the liberal democracies of Northern and Western Europe in the interwar period.

In *Bureaucracy,* Mises drew a contrast between the bureaucratic mode of management and the strictures imposed through a system governed by profit. Under a profit system, businesses and their operations were necessarily accountable to consumers. Bureaucratic management was instead unaccountable and generative of its own internal impulses, which were removed from people's real needs and wants. Such impulses, Mises suggested, change the nature of governmental power and distorted outcomes. Bureaucratic organizations accrue more and more responsibilities, but because the king, despot, or government that initially delegated the authority does not want its powers to be used independently by local, provincial, or sector-specific governors or managers, it introduces codes, regulations, and decrees that limit and change the nature of their power. Thus, initiative and innovation are stifled:

> The whole character of their management changes. They are no longer eager to deal with each case to the best of their abilities; they are no longer anxious to find the most appropriate solution for every problem. Their main concern is to comply with the rules and regulations, no matter whether they are reasonable or contrary to what was intended. The first virtue of an administrator is to abide by the codes and decrees. He becomes a bureaucrat.

Thus the incentive structures of bureaucratic administration and organization tend to produce twisted results.

Bureaucracy was taking over the government of the United States, Mises suggested, especially through the policies of the Roosevelt administration and the New Deal. But, he argued, the transformation in the U.S. administration had deeper roots in the late nineteenth century and continued with the Progressive era of social reform. Mises worried that the shift was becoming all-encompassing and irreversible:

> The characteristic feature of present-day policies is the trend toward a substitution of government control of all economic activities, for thorough government planning, and for the nationalisation of business. They aim at full government control of education and at the socialisation of the medical profession. There is no sphere of human activity

that they would not be prepared to subordinate to regimentation by the authorities. In their eyes, state control is the panacea for all ills.[52]

The New Deal had been democratic, in the strictly electoral sense, according to Mises, but "it is obvious that delegation of power can be used as a quasi-constitutional disguise for dictatorship."[53] Mises saw in Roosevelt and the policies of the 1930s and 1940s the threat of a similar usurpation of power that had occurred in Nazi Germany, though it would happen incrementally rather than suddenly and might well appear benevolent at first. But, he suggested, the United States, with its love of individual liberty and democracy, the traits Tocqueville had first noticed in the 1830s, was in a much more robust position to resist such a development than Germany, with its military and authoritarian traditions, had been.

The spread of bureaucratism, however, was not just harming the public sector. The increased regulation of business it instituted also threatened the private sector and carried the danger of the bureaucratization of business with it:

> It is an open question whether Secretary Ickes was right in saying: "Every big business is a bureaucracy." (*NY Times Magazine*, January 16th, 1944, p. 9) But if the Secretary of the Interior is right, or as far as he is right, this is not an outcome of the evolution of private business but of the growing government interference with business.[54]

Mises argued that a strict separation between business, governed by the profit motive, and public service, governed by democratic accountability, was crucial. But government ought to be small, with as much left in private hands as possible. Unlike Ronald Reagan, one of neoliberalism's political practitioners, Mises did not believe in business leadership in the public sector.[55] According to Mises, this would not work because the role of the businessman changed as soon as he assumed a public function:

> It is vain to advocate a bureaucratic reform through the appointment of businessmen as heads of various departments. The quality of being an entrepreneur is not inherent in the personality of the entrepreneur; it is inherent in the position which he occupies in the framework of market

society. A former entrepreneur who is given charge of a government bureau is in this capacity no longer a businessman but a bureaucrat. His objective can no longer be profit, but compliance with the rules and regulations.[56]

In a direct contradiction of the way that later neoliberals would conduct public policy in the 1980s and 1990s, such as through the internal market introduced by Margaret Thatcher into Britain's Health Service, Mises *did not* believe it was possible to mix market mechanisms and public tasks. He stated, "no reform could transform a public office into a sort of private enterprise."[57] Instead, the state's role had to shrink, and it was reasonable to expect that markets would "accomplish those services that the consumers deem most urgent."[58]

Mises was thus a free market libertarian, espousing a pure ideological position that was probably untenable for any successful politician of the late twentieth century. No politician could abolish the income tax or the public education system. Business was both simple and harsh. The enterprise is judged simply by whether it makes or loses money—by the bottom line. However, to allow bureaucratic managers to function with the backing of the state allowed them to evade crucial problems. As Margaret Thatcher pointed out in an interview in 1993, this would allow the managers of public offices to draw on the public purse, which was a recipe for slackness and inefficiency.[59] According to Mises, the problem was not that managers might be corrupt or criminally negligent but rather that "every service can be improved by increasing expenditures."[60] A good public sector manager would therefore fight for more funds and resources. The only way to limit the discretion of such a manager was through rules and regulations:

> The management is under the necessity of abiding by a code of instructions; this alone matters. The manager is not answerable if his actions are correct from the point of view of this code. His main task cannot be efficiency as such, but efficiency within the limits of subservience to the regulations. His position is not that of an executive in a profit-seeking enterprise but that of a civil servant, for instance, the head of a police department.[61]

It was therefore impossible to manage a public enterprise except through bureaucracy. This point was also made forcefully in interviews later by Milton Friedman and by Margaret Thatcher's chancellor of the exchequer in the 1980s, Nigel Lawson, and became a watchword of the neoliberal approach to politics—the incentives that bear on public sector managers and bureaucrats are such as to increase pressure on public expenditure, which was nearly always (and certainly in Friedman's case) a bad thing.[62] This perceived insight was also a starting point for the Virginia school of public choice theory, led by James Buchanan and Gordon Tullock in the 1960s and 1970s.[63]

Mises built up his critique of bureaucracy through a comparison with what he saw as the virtues of the private enterprise alternative. He defined bureaucracy not so much as a particular institutional form but as a mode of thinking and organization necessary to the relationships implied by public sector management, as the "way in which the offices of the government and municipalities are operated."[64] The profit motive unhindered, according to Mises, precluded the bureaucratic management of private enterprise. Mises suggested that public opinion, and the political parties in its thrall, seek to impede the profit motive and replace it with "service." There was a difference between the innovation and experimentation at the heart of entrepreneurial activity and the priorities of bureaucratic service:

> To say to the entrepreneur of an enterprise with limited profit chances, "behave as the conscientious bureaucrats do," is tantamount to telling him to shun any reform. Nobody can be at the same time a correct bureaucrat and an innovator. Progress is precisely that which the rules and regulations did not foresee; it is necessarily outside the field of bureaucratic activities.[65]

The difference between the incentives built into the bureaucratic system based in government regulation and intervention compared to those that operated under private enterprise was that the profit motive placed a high premium on improvement. Without this there could be no progress.[66]

This was not how things had appeared to the architects of the British welfare state in the interwar period, William Beveridge, Sidney and Beatrice Webb, and John Maynard Keynes, or to the policy experts that surrounded Roosevelt in the 1930s, Harry Hopkins, Frances Perkins, or Rexford Tugwell, for example. For them, public service was a duty and a privilege, a noble vo-cation for educated experts and their talents. The ethos of service did not require profit. Instead, the knowledge and reason of what Keynes referred to as the right-thinking elite would solve intractable problems of government and public affairs. According to Mises,

> The answer to be given to these bureaucratic radicals is obvious. The citizen may reply: You may be excellent and lofty men, much better than we other citizens are. We do not question your competence and intelligence. But you are not the vicars of a god called "the State." You are servants of the law, the duly passed laws of our nation. It is not your business to criticise the law, still less to violate it. In violating the law you are perhaps worse than a good many of the racketeers, no matter how good your intentions may be. For you are appointed, sworn, and paid to enforce the law, not to break it. The worst law is better than bureaucratic tyranny.[67]

The rule of law must govern the free market and a small constitutionally defined arena of public service, but this framework must not include loose powers for agencies, public authorities, and their leaders that are not carefully proscribed through legislation. These points echoed the forceful complaints of the critics of the New Deal.

Mises' criticisms led him to suggest that the problem was the entire politi-cal system—governed by a bureaucracy that alienated and detached power from its proper democratic source:

> It is quite correct, as the opponents of the trend toward totalitarianism say, that the bureaucrats are free to decide according to their own dis-cretion questions of vital importance for the individual citizen's life. It is true that the officeholders are no longer the servants of the citizenry but irresponsible and arbitrary masters and tyrants. But this is not the fault of bureaucracy. It is the outcome of the new system of government which restricts the individual's freedom to manage his own affairs and assigns more and more tasks to the government. The culprit is not the bureaucrat but the political system. And the sovereign people is still free to discard this system.[68]

He argued there was a conflict of interest in the bureaucrat as a voter because as such, he was both an employer and an employee. A large public sector would always be a threat to democracy because of this basic conflict. Political parties try to outdo each other in offering incentives and sweeteners to gain the support of the public sector employees—as in, for example, pork barrel spending by Congress.[69] But, Mises argued, there was still time for the systemic trend toward a growing public sector to be resisted through free elections in the United States and Britain.

Another effect of the growth of bureaucracy was, for Mises, the patronage of intellectuals and professors who had "trustworthy" views rather than those who countered or challenged the prevalent orthodoxy about the state and its omnipotent role. Like Popper, Mises saw a similarity between the bureaucratic mentality and Plato's utopia, in which the large majority of the ruled served the rulers. He thought that "all later utopians who shaped the blueprints of their earthly paradises according to Plato's example in the same way believed in the immutability of human affairs."[70] He went on,

> Bureaucratization is necessarily rigid because it involves the observation of established rules and practices. But in social life rigidity amounts to petrification and death. It is a very significant fact that stability and security are the most cherished slogans of present-day "reformers." If primitive men had adopted the principle of stability, they would long since have been wiped out by beasts of prey and microbes.[71]

The point, for Mises, about the market and its spontaneous forces of economic organization was that neoliberalism was a theory that, unlike Marxism, did not entrench the interests of particular classes or ideas. Instead, the market liberated the individual to experiment and thus to improve:

> The anonymous forces operating on the market are continuously determining anew who should be entrepreneur and who should be capitalist. The consumers vote, as it were, for those who are to occupy the exalted positions in the setting of the nation's economic structure.[72]

This created a fundamental equality of access and potential success, if not of results.

The market was thus a fundamentally democratic arena for Mises. It re-warded those things that people wanted and voted for with their feet and wal-lets. Unsuccessful businesses, products, managers, and entrepreneurs were subject to its ruthless discipline, and greater efficiency and the unhindered operation of the free market resulted in more effective delivery of social and economic goods and services. This was one reason why, according to Mises, wherever possible it was better to allow private market mechanisms to de-liver public goods: the results would be cheaper and more useful. That was the theory, anyway, and Mises was perhaps the most uncritical of markets of all the neoliberals. His ideas about the almost democratic nature of markets were radical. He asserted a new basis of popular legitimacy that was not de-pendent on elections, political processes, or other accountability structures. Instead, the market mechanism itself operated as a responsive hub around which consumers reigned supreme. For Mises' former student and colleague Friedrich Hayek, too, neoliberalism was not "a stationary creed."[73] This was one of the most important reasons, according to Hayek, for the superiority of the free market as a way of organizing economic life.

Friedrich Hayek and *The Road to Serfdom*

Karl Popper had assaulted the historicist philosophies that had done so much harm to a humanitarian individualism, and Mises had critiqued the bureau-cratic mentality at the heart of state institutions and political organizations. Hayek drove home a polemical attack on the drift of Western policy toward collectivism.

Friedrich August von Hayek was born into a moderately wealthy aris-tocratic and intellectual family in Vienna in 1899. His father was a biolo-gist, botanist, and policymaker who worked on social welfare issues for the Austro-Hungarian government before World War I. Friedrich Hayek grew up in imperial Vienna before volunteering to join the army at the outbreak of the war in 1914. Hayek survived without serious injury and was decorated for his bravery. After the war, Hayek decided to pursue studies in law and political science at the University of Vienna and received doctorates in both disciplines, in 1921 and 1923, respectively (he also permanently dropped the "von" from his name in 1919). After completing his studies, Hayek spent a year working as a research assistant to Professor Jeremiah Jenks at NYU between 1923 and 1924.[74] Hayek returned to Vienna before an invitation from Lionel Robbins brought him to the LSE as a visiting lecturer in 1929.

At the LSE, Hayek soon entered into debates with Keynes about the role of monetary policy and the viability of planning in the economy. He became Tooke Professor of Economic Science and Statistics in 1931, at age thirty-two, and joined an established group of free market advocates led first by Edwin Cannan, the editor of a distinguished edition of Adam Smith's *The Wealth of Nations*, and afterward by Cannan's protégé, Robbins.[75] This group was later joined by Popper and Ronald Coase, another future member of the Mont Pelerin Society who, like Hayek, also won the Nobel Prize in Economics (in 1991), and who moved to the United States in 1951 before settling at the University of Chicago in 1964, where he joined Friedman and George Stigler in the Economics Department. Hayek fell in love with Britain and developed a lasting admiration for its history, traditions, and institutions, believing it to be in many ways the home of liberty. He developed strong bonds with Robbins at the LSE and Keynes at Cambridge and became a British citizen, remaining close to the country for the rest of his life through his only son, Lawrence, who settled there after his father left for Chicago in 1951.[76]

Of the three works, Hayek's *Road to Serfdom* had the most lasting political impact. Written in haste while the LSE was exiled to Cambridge during the Blitz, according to Popper, to whom Hayek sent a copy of the draft, *The Road to Serfdom* was "frankly a political book." But Popper thought it "without question one of the most important political books I have ever seen."[77] *The Road to Serfdom* was published in Britain in March 1944, at the end of a fevered period of eighteen months during which the Beveridge *Report on Social Insurance and Allied Services* (1942), the government's white paper on employment (1944), and Beveridge's own report on full employment (1944) all appeared and were debated widely. In *The Road to Serfdom*, Hayek took aim at this drift among Western policymakers toward central planning.

Hayek's view of the dangers of "collectivist" central planning, which he equated with socialism, arose from an analysis of the development of human thought and freedom close to Popper's in *The Open Society*:

> We have progressively abandoned that freedom in economic affairs
> without which personal and political freedom has never existed in the

past.... We are rapidly abandoning not the views merely of Cobden and Bright, of Adam Smith and Hume, or even of Locke and Milton, but one of the salient characteristics of Western Civilisation as it has grown from the foundations laid by Christianity and the Greeks and Romans. Not merely nineteenth and eighteenth-century, but the basic individualism inherited by us from Erasmus and Montaigne, from Cicero and Tacitus, Pericles and Thucydides, is progressively relinquished.[78]

Hayek explicitly linked this idea of Western civilization with the Judeo-Christian tradition. This linkage brings him close to traditional conservatives like Edmund Burke, with whom Hayek identified:[79]

But the essential features of that individualism which, elements provided by Christianity and the philosophy of classical antiquity, was at first fully developed during the renaissance and has since grown and spread into what we know as Western Civilisation—are the respect for the individual man *qua* man, that is, the recognition of his own views and tastes as supreme in his own sphere, however narrowly that may be circumscribed, and the belief that it is desirable that men should develop their own individual gifts and bents.[80]

Hayek's view of human nature mixed the traditional conservative acceptance of man's fall from grace coupled with a Burkean belief in his cumulatively held wisdom and the modern political philosophical belief in rational self-interest as man's strongest motivating force.

Hayek's view of human nature made him suspicious of what he worried was Popper's susceptibility to certain forms of interventionism. For example, Popper thought that "we do use means (law courts, police) in order to keep crime under control, and child labour; and we may be able to end wars by similar means. All this is no doubt legitimate; and so is the attempt to control poverty and one-sided exploitation, and to try to eliminate it."[81] This partiality, Hayek felt, went against the grain of a society based on the freedom of the individual to pursue her economic self-interest. But even with the best intentions guaranteed, according to Hayek, the realization of a political philosophy based on government planning and state intervention in the economy would be impossible because of the natural limits to human knowledge.

Hayek wrote to Popper when he was trying to help him publish *The Open Society* about the concept of "piecemeal engineering." He questioned why his friend supported such an approach to social and economic problems and explained his own aversion to such an idea:

> I can now also better explain my strong dislike for your term "partial engineering". If the aspect of the "engineering type of mind" which I there discuss as the reason for the strong inclination of most engineers for a centrally planned society is correct, your term is almost "a contradiction in terms". It is briefly that it is of the nature of an engineering job that all the knowledge if concentrated in a single head, while it is the specific character of all truly social problems that the task is to utilise knowledge which can not be so concentrated.[82]

Hayek therefore compared Popper's concept to his own arguments about the impossibility of central planning. Hayek's view of the impossibility of planning stemmed directly from a limited view of human capacities—it was impossible for people to hold all the information necessary to make rational decisions on behalf of everyone. Such interventionism would also confound a society characterized by liberty and spontaneous order. In response, Popper clarified what he meant by the term and attempted to narrow any disagreement with Hayek about what he saw as their common approach to social and economic progress:

> I am very greatly impressed by your criticism of my term "piecemeal engineering". I happen to dislike the "engineering type of mind" too, and I see now intuitively more clearly your objections. If I could, I would change my terminology. Your remark that in the engineering case "all knowledge is concentrated in a single head" (or, at any rate, in a very few heads) "while it is the specific character of all truly social problems that the task is to utilise knowledge which cannot be so concentrated" is one of the most illuminating and striking formulations I have ever heard on these problems. This really is a fundamental difference. In a way, it fits in with one idea which I mention in the critical part of my article, viz., that the concentration of power and the possessions of social knowledge exclude each other to a certain extent. Your point

is immensely interesting, but I never meant this "engineering attitude of mind" when I spoke of piecemeal engineering; what I meant was the careful and conscious trial- and -error attitude of mind; the attitude of looking, on the one side, for institutional reforms, on the other hand, for the unavoidable blunders which are, in the social case, precisely due to the fact that we shall only find out from those on whose toes we have stepped that we have done so. (And if we have concentrated power, we shall not find out.)[83]

This approach, for Popper, was crucial to his project of uniting the "humanitarian camp" around the methodology of critical rationalism.

In their letters, Hayek and Popper constantly debated the theme of language and terminology. Much of the discussion is obscured, however, by the concept of freedom. The word is used by Popper, for example, to establish what he thinks Hayek and he are in agreement about:

> I too feel that our tendencies are fundamentally the same: for individualism (I am using the term in my sense), for freedom as the necessary condition of everything else, and against pseudo-science, dogmatism, dilettant [sic] radicalism. I think I fully appreciate your remark that we are fighting the same battle on different fronts, and I was glad about your hint that my approach (and terminology) might possibly gain "a certain audience" with whom reasoning is notoriously difficult.[84]

The reader of these letters today is struck, however, by the weight that such elastic terms as "individualism" and "freedom" are meant to carry. It is not at all clear that Hayek and Popper mean the same thing when they use these terms. As if to acknowledge this very point, Hayek wrote back to Popper when discussing the prospective title of *The Open Society*, that "it is now unfortunately almost imperative to avoid the word freedom in the title, so much nonsense has it had to cover in recent years."[85] If Hayek was concerned with the drift of Western policymakers toward collectivism in general, it may be that Popper was more worried about any reproduction of the conditions for totalitarianism. In a discussion of the French social theorist Auguste Comte, he described to Hayek what he saw as the real problem:

Where the scientistic enthusiasts fail, I believe, is not the idea that mankind may, to some extent, control its fate, or lift itself out (as many individual men have done, especially if we take the metaphor spiritually) by its bootstraps. It is, rather, the holistic exaggeration of this idea which is so mistaken, and so repulsive in its hysterical wish for power. I feel certain that we agree on this point.[86]

Thus, for Popper, it is the potential for totalitarian tendencies in the utopian projects of many of those on the left that make them unacceptable and dangerous. The belief that man can better himself was an admirable and important aim, but it had to be tempered with modesty about the tools at our disposal to achieve such a goal.

Despite these nuances in Hayek's and Popper's views, it is clear they were extremely close to each other during this period in the 1940s, especially when their views are contrasted with the view of Hayek's great friend and academic adversary John Maynard Keynes, who was working to plan the peace with the Americans, including developing the Bretton Woods monetary system with Harry Dexter White. Keynes famously wrote to Hayek after reading *The Road to Serfdom* that he believed intellectually talented and morally unimpeachable experts could create the "good society."[87] Keynes argued that Hayek's view of humanity was likely to prove wrong, especially in the United States, which he took to be the highest testing ground for ideas as well as being, after World War II, the leader of the developed world. Instead of ditching ideas of efficacious government, Keynes said, in a famous line,

> what we need is the restoration of right moral thinking—a return to proper moral values in our social philosophy. If only you could turn your crusade in that direction you would not look or feel so much like Don Quixote. I accuse you of perhaps confusing a little bit the moral and material issues. Dangerous acts can be done safely in a community which thinks and feels rightly which would be the way to hell if they were executed by those who think and feel wrongly.[88]

Keynes's views were typical of liberalism's twentieth-century metamorphosis into a creed that espoused intervention and technical expertise by enlightened officials imbued with public service. Similar ideas animated the New

Dealers. But they also represented everything that Hayek and his friends were fighting against. Quite to the contrary, Hayek thought that people of good intentions, in trying to create a society that functioned according to high ideals, might "in fact unwittingly produce the very opposite of what we have been striving for."[89] Such a pessimistic view placed Hayek close to the heart of all those American businessmen, politicians, and others who had never been reconciled to Roosevelt's policies. The neoliberal movement grew out of such tensions in the postwar period in the United States.

In place of activist government and central planning, Hayek sought a carefully circumscribed role for the state. Hayek's vision was intimately bound up with the rule of law within which markets would operate effectively and individual liberty would be preserved. The rule of law would guarantee a basic negative freedom, which was the state's legitimate function outside of defence and the protection of its citizens. It also implied a fundamental acceptance of substantive inequality—an essential feature of neoliberal ideas throughout all three phases of its history. An understanding of inequality as unavoidable, even desirable, gets at the crux of the conflict between neoliberal ideals and those of New Deal liberals or social democrats—there was an acceptance of the rectitude of different outcomes for different individuals for neoliberal theorists. Any notion of greater equality of outcome that could be produced by redistributing income or resources was a utopian idea that, lacking a precise rational meaning, was open to manipulation by a despot or a government.

By contrast, in a free market system, the individual was paramount. Different individuals had different capacities, which would be valued differently in the marketplace. Such inequality of outcome was fine because, according to Hayek, at least everyone had equal access to the market. Inequality did not matter because social mobility was possible, and for anyone who lost out, their own initiative would give them the opportunity to succeed through repeated attempts. If they were unable or unwilling to make such attempts, then it was not the role of government to treat individuals unequally by compensating for someone's lack of success:

> A necessary, and only apparently paradoxical, result of this is that formal equality before the law is in conflict, and in fact incompatible, with any activity of the government deliberately aiming at a substantive ide-

al of distributive justice; it must lead to the destruction of the Rule of Law. To produce the same result for different people, it is necessary to treat them differently.[90]

Here the idea that redistribution and greater equality were not simply disincentives to initiative but actually morally debilitating emerges as a crucial dimension of neoliberal thought. (Later on, academics such as political scientist Charles Murray in his book on American social policy, *Losing Ground* [1984], and even liberal Democratic politicians such as Daniel Patrick Moynihan in his controversial report on the African American family [1965], would tap into such beliefs through their emphasis on the age-old distinction between the deserving and the undeserving poor.[91] A belief in inequality was at the root of arguments among neoliberal welfare reformers from the 1960s on about egalitarian welfare policies and the culture of dependency they supposedly produced. Some deserved their chance to advance and others did not—the division usually fell between those who worked and those who did not, such as the notorious "welfare moms." This type of debate occurred on both sides of the Atlantic and culminated in welfare reform under Bill Clinton in 1996 and in various attempts at reform under Margaret Thatcher, John Major, and Tony Blair in the 1990s.)

According to Hayek, then, collective endeavors had to be kept to a minimum so that there would be no danger of subjugating the individual and her various desires and values. For in a planned system, there would inevitably be the problem of a scale of values and of who was to decide among them. Instead of government or the ruling group making such decisions on our behalf, under a free market capitalist system "common action is thus limited to the fields where people agree on common ends. Very frequently these common ends will not be the ultimate ends to the individuals but means which different persons can use for different purposes."[92]

For Hayek, it was "not the source of power but the limitation of power which prevents it from being arbitrary."[93] Thus mere overall democratic control, as with Mises, would not prevent the abuse of coercive power. For Hayek, the danger was the appeal of socialism. Socialism was the antithesis of freedom, according to Hayek, but it had mistakenly become equated with liberty as well as equality because of its appeal to an optimistic vision of social, technological, and economic progress. Hayek argued that such a utopian view of the aims of socialism was a disastrous misreading:

Where freedom was concerned, the founders of socialism made no bones about their intentions. Freedom of thought they regarded as the root-evil of nineteenth century society, and the first of modern planners, Saint-Simon, even predicted that those who did not obey his proposed planning boards would be "treated as cattle."[94]

Hayek suggested that socialists had appropriated the term freedom for themselves when what they really meant was wealth (and its expropriation):

> But [it] would only heighten the tragedy if it should prove that what was promised to us as the Road to freedom was in fact the High Road to Servitude. Unquestionably, the promise of more freedom was responsible for luring more and more liberals along the socialist road, for blinding them to the conflict which exists between the basic principles of socialism and liberalism, and for often enabling socialists to usurp the very name of the old party of freedom. Socialism was embraced by the greater part of the intelligentsia as the apparent heir of the liberal tradition: therefore it is not surprising that to them the idea of socialism's leading to the opposite of liberty should appear inconceivable.[95]

For Hayek, then, a reunification of socialism and liberalism of the sort Popper sought was fundamentally impossible because for socialists, the individual was not important. The larger ends of a socialist society were to be realized at the expense of the individual's needs or wants, whereas for liberals, the individual was sacrosanct. The two philosophies were in irreducible conflict. According to Hayek, socialism was a breed of collectivism.

The problem of collectivism, like Mises' bureaucratism and Popper's Platonic or Hegelian historicism, also brought with it a moral problem: the problem of the "end of truth." All individual desires and acts must be subsumed under the overarching social purpose as defined by the collectivist state:

> It is entirely in keeping with the whole spirit of totalitarianism that it condemns any human activity done for its own sake and without ulterior purpose. Science for science's sake, art for art's sake, are equally abhorrent to the Nazis, our socialist intellectuals, and the communists. *Every* activity must derive its justification from a conscious social purpose.[96]

Reality ceases to be empirically based and becomes something to be handed down and shaped by the powerful according to their plans for society—their monopoly on truth. Intellectual freedom should not be undermined and eroded simply because, Hayek scathingly suggested, most people do not have the capacity for "independent thought."[97]

However, Hayek, at this stage of his career, was also attempting to construct an alternative to crude nineteenth-century laissez-faire economics. This preoccupation with moving beyond both laissez-faire arguments and the new forms of interventionism espoused by the British Edwardian New Liberalism or the liberalism of Roosevelt and the New Deal was central to the research of the early neoliberals—the German neoliberals Walter Eucken and Franz Bohm (as well as Wilhelm Röpke and Alexander Rüstow, who was one of the first to coin the term neoliberal, this group was also known as the ordoliberals and is discussed in the next chapter), Henry Simons and Frank Knight at Chicago (also discussed in the next chapter), and Hayek, Popper, and Robbins in London at the LSE during the 1930s and 1940s.[98] According to Hayek, opposition to socialist and collectivist planning should not be confused with a "dogmatic laissez-faire attitude."[99] The state was essential to guarantee the conditions of free competition. But, like Mises, Hayek was a strong advocate of the spontaneity of markets. The price mechanism organized free individuals into a functional system governed by supply and demand. It got rid of the need for coercion implied by planning:

> This [spontaneous and complex diversity] is precisely what the price system does under competition, and which no other system even promises to accomplish. It enables entrepreneurs, by watching the movement of comparatively few prices, as an engineer watches the hands of a few dials, to adjust their activities to those of their fellows. The important point here is that the price system will fulfil this function only if competition prevails, that is, if the individual producer has to adapt himself to price changes and cannot control them.[100]

Nevertheless, Hayek, like Popper, believed that the benefits of competition could be complemented by certain regulations and restrictions, such as health and safety, or perhaps even those directed at certain social outcomes.

But where should the line be drawn? Which social outcomes were reasonable to justify state intervention and which were not? This was Keynes's main criticism of Hayek when he read *The Road to Serfdom*:

> You admit here and there that it is a question of where to draw the line. You agree that the line has to be drawn somewhere, and that the logical extreme is not possible. But you give no guidance whatever as to where to draw it. In a sense this is shirking the practical issue. It is true that you and I would probably draw it in different places. I should guess that according to my ideas you greatly underestimate the practicability of the middle course. But as soon as you admit that the extreme is not possible, and that a line has to be drawn, you are, on your own argument, done for, since you are trying to persuade us that so soon as one moves in the planned direction you are necessarily launched on the slippery path which will lead you in due course over the precipice.[101]

This devastating critique is not entirely fair to Hayek, who did give guidance as to the limits of laissez-faire economics.[102] For example, he saw a legitimate role for government in the regulation of the monetary system, the prevention of private monopolies, and the supervision of natural monopolies—something that would distinguish him from members of the second Chicago school such as Aaron Director or Milton Friedman, who, after 1950, reversed the emphasis of early neoliberals on antimonopoly.[103] For Hayek, writing in *The Road to Serfdom*,

> The only question here is whether in the particular instance the advantages gained are greater than the social costs which they impose. Nor is the preservation of competition incompatible with an extensive system of social services—so long as the organisation of these services is not designed in such a way as to make competition ineffective over wide fields.[104]

However, the standard of where to draw the line between when to intervene and when not to was a subjective one on the part of the government seeking to intervene, and necessarily so, because each government, or indeed each individual, would draw it in a different place. This unpredictability was the

fundamental problem Keynes had noticed. In Hayek's statement it is possible to imagine the justification of the New Deal or Nye Bevan's National
Health Service. So, while Hayek wanted to critique the idea of the middle
way associated with Roosevelt, Keynes, and the mixed economy, he ended
up sounding as though he might support it. Again, this is indicative of the
fact that the primary target in the work of early neoliberalism, and especially that of the Austrians, such as Hayek, was totalitarianism. Totalitarianism of the sort witnessed in Soviet Russia was similar to that of Nazi Germany. The key point about totalitarian systems was that it aimed toward a
total negation of the individual, his wants, desires, and needs. "The various
kinds of collectivism, communism, fascism, etc. differ between themselves
in the nature of the goal," according to Hayek, but they all want to "organise
the whole of society and all its resources for this unitary end, and in refus-
ing to recognise autonomous spheres in which the ends of the individuals
are supreme."[105] There was no compromise with totalitarianism. Accommodations with certain aspects of the welfare state, on the other hand, especially with people's memories of the Great Depression still so fresh,
were possible.

Keynes's criticisms ran deep. Many years later, Hayek gave an insight into
his anger at the public misrepresentation, as he saw it, of the arguments of
The Road to Serfdom in his correspondence with the American Keynesian
economist Paul Samuelson. He blamed Samuelson for the propagation of the
idea that he, Hayek, thought the road to serfdom was inevitable in his famous
economic textbook: "I seem to have discovered the source of the false allega-
tion about my book *The Road to Serfdom* which I constantly encounter, most
resent and can only regard as a malicious distortion which has largely succeeded in discrediting my argument."[106] He went on,

> I believe you will have to admit, if you look at the book again, that your
> assertion is wholly unfounded and has probably become the main
> cause of the prejudice which has prevented people from taking my ar-
> gument seriously. I am afraid that I cannot take this matter lightly. By
> creating this myth you have done so much harm to the development of
> opinion that I must insist on a public retraction and apology in a form
> commensurate with the extent of circulation of your book.[107]

Hayek was outraged at what he saw as the distortion of his message, an important part of which was the ability of free individuals in society to alter their course. The existence of elections meant that a society could choose to claw back government power as well as to give it away.[108]

Another crucial element of Hayek's analysis centered on the potential for complacency among democratic publics. An example is the idea that the planning and regulation of the economy didn't matter because only the economic sphere would be affected. For Hayek, this was a myth. It was precisely the increased control over economic affairs through government interference that revealed the thin end of a wedge. In his belief that no liberty was possible without the economic freedom of the individual in the marketplace, Hayek again came close to Mises. The increased involvement of an interventionist government in the economy eroded, as Hayek saw it, the fundamental foundations of freedom as understood within the paradigm of Western civilization. This is a point that left the neoliberals vulnerable. Winston Churchill's ill-judged speech during the 1945 election campaign, in the run-up to a vote that Churchill lost in a landslide, suggested that the Labour Party might need "some kind of a Gestapo" to enact socialism in Britain, a view that fell flat with an electorate that just did not believe the most exaggerated claims about democratic parties of the left.[109] (Attlee's mildness did not help Churchill, either).

For Hayek and Mises, the economy could not be separated from other arenas of social and political life. Economic freedom created the conditions for all other freedoms. As Hayek put it,

> The authority directing all economic activity would not merely control the part of our lives which is concerned with inferior things; it would control the allocation of the limited means for all our ends. And whoever controls all economic activity controls the means for all our ends and must therefore decide which are to be satisfied and which not. This really is the crux of the matter. Economic control is not merely control of a sector of human life which can be separated from the rest. It is the control of the means for all our ends.[110]

This was a fundamental point. Economic freedom could not be separated from political or civic freedom. There could be no freedom without economic liberty. This idea, alongside Mises' description of a laissez-faire society constructed on the "democratic" power of the consumer, would form the basis for Milton Friedman's claims in *Capitalism and Freedom* (1962) that human freedom rested in the market, a development discussed in the next chapter.

There is also an interesting convergence here worthy of note. Both the New Deal liberals and the British social democrats pitched their egalitarian ideas on the grounds that political freedom was inadequate without some economic security—a basic assumption that has a long history on the left. Economic freedom, as constructed by neoliberals, was a hollow concept because it was beyond so many people's reach. As Keith Tribe has argued, in Hayek's discussion of the pernicious influence of the German statist tradition (which stemmed back to Bismarck and the Prussian *Rechtsstaat*), he refused to credit political reformers' attempts to address the stark realities of life during the Industrial Revolution.[111] The center of gravity for liberals, in the latter part of the nineteenth century, moved from a concern about the potential for harm in government regulation and intervention to a conviction that necessary social reform entailed improving the lot of the mass of people affected by industrial capitalism's savage inequalities. Without economic freedom, political or civil rights meant substantively little. The neoliberals also believed that political and civil freedom were not enough. But for them the linkage was defined by the freedom of the individual in the marketplace to buy and sell as she pleased. Here we have another fundamental difference between the value placed on the market as the deliverer of freedom and the idea that the market presents an obstacle to freedom whose harshest effects must be blunted so that freedom might flourish—between negative and positive liberty, as Isaiah Berlin famously presented the division.[112]

Hayek saw the conflict between the free market and the state as a choice, upon which rested the future of the freedoms that Western democracies cherish:

> The choice open to us is not between a system in which everybody will get what he deserves according to some absolute and universal standard of right, and one where the individual shares are determined partly by accident or good or ill chance, but between a system where it is the will of a few persons that decides who is to get what, and one where

it depends at least partly on the ability and enterprise of the people concerned and partly on unforeseeable circumstances.[113]

Thus, Hayek believed that negative liberty was all that could be guaranteed by government through the rule of law and the supervision of the competitive order. But it was a negative liberty supported by meritocracy. An attempt to engineer positive liberty, on the other hand, brought with it the danger of enslavement. The desire of policymakers and publics alike for a measure of economic security in the wake of war and depression was understandable. But Hayek thought that the dangers of unintended consequences in the expansion of government power necessary to guarantee positive liberty outweighed the protections that the universalist welfare state might provide for those in need. According to him, there were two types of security:

> These two types of security are, first, security against severe physical privation, the certainty of a given minimum of sustenance for all; and, second, the security of a given standard of life, or of the relative position which one person or group enjoys compared with others; or, as we may put it briefly, the security of a minimum income and the security of the particular income a person is thought to deserve.[114]

Keynesian approaches to economic management as laid out in *The General Theory of Employment, Interest and Money* (1936) privileged certain groups over others, according to Hayek.[115] For example, inflation and its effects benefited consumers at the expense of saving and investment. Economic security could only be purchased at the price of equalitarian, in the Popperian sense, freedom, the liberty of all before the law and the freedom of access of everyone to the market. If we want to conserve freedom, according to Hayek, "we must regain the conviction on which the rule of liberty in the Anglo-Saxon countries has been based and which Benjamin Franklin expressed in a phrase applicable to us in our lives as individuals no less than as nations: 'those who would give up essential liberty to purchase a little temporary safety deserve neither liberty nor safety.'"[116]

The moral results of "collectivism" were thus more important than its "moral basis" or the motivations behind it:[117]

We must now return briefly to the crucial point—that individual freedom cannot be reconciled with the supremacy of one single purpose
to which the whole society must be entirely and permanently subordinated. The only exception to the rule that a free society must not
be subjected to a single purpose is war and other temporary disasters
when subordination of almost everything to the immediate and pressing need is the price at which we preserve our freedom in the long run.
This explains also why so many of the fashionable phrases about doing
for the purposes of peace what we have learned to do for the purposes
of war are so misleading: it is sensible temporarily to sacrifice freedom
in order to make it more secure in the future; but the same cannot be
said for a system proposed as a permanent arrangement.[118]

Hope lay with the United States and the UK, where traditions of human liberty had, according to Hayek, been best preserved.[119] At same the time, Hayek
was very worried about the damage that was being done to the traditions of
individualism and freedom, even in those two countries:

> The virtues these people possessed—in a higher degree than most other
> people, excepting only a few of the smaller nations, like the Swiss and the
> Dutch—were independence and self-reliance, individual initiative and
> local responsibility, the successful reliance on voluntary activity, non-
> interference with one's neighbour and tolerance of the different and queer,
> respect for custom and tradition, and a healthy suspicion of power and
> authority. Almost all the traditions and institutions in which democratic
> moral genius has found its most characteristic expression, and which in
> turn have moulded the national character and the whole moral climate of
> England and America, are those which the progress of collectivism and its
> inherently centralistic tendencies are progressively destroying.[120]

Hayek believed these things needed to be first fought for in the realm of ideas.
It is perhaps important to remember here Hayek's status as an exile from Aus-
tria (a culture dominated by German statism) and his happy relationship with
Britain, where he became a citizen. His assertion of Britain and the United
States as the homes of liberty was surely reinforced by this experience. Hayek
was acutely aware of the socialist success, through the Fabian Society espe-

cially, in influencing the development of social democratic policies, which were taken up by the Conservative and Liberal Parties as well as the Labour Party. Hayek's admiration for the political successes of socialists is almost as keenly felt as his admiration of British and American political culture. He believed that a similar movement had to be created for the defense of free markets and individual liberty. This led him to think about creating an organization that would bring together like-minded scholars from across Europe and the United States.

The Mont Pelerin Society
and *The Intellectuals and Socialism*

The Road to Serfdom was a huge success and a bestseller in both Britain and the United States as soon as it came out. No other book of Hayek's would receive such popular acclaim. Its popularity with a mass audience was ensured by the publication of a condensed version of the book in the *Reader's Digest* that appeared in the United States in April 1945. A promotional book tour across the United States followed publication. Hayek was hailed as a celebrity when he arrived in New York.[121] The book attracted American admirers, such as Leonard Read, the founder of the Irvington, New York–based free market think tank, the Foundation for Economic Education (FEE, discussed in chapter 4), who were drawn to Hayek's criticisms of liberals and collectivist conservatives. This helped Hayek pursue his plans to establish a transatlantic group to defend "the free society."[122]

The historian Max Hartwell, himself a member of the Mont Pelerin Society, has suggested that Hayek's plans for the society grew out of a belief that Western civilization was under threat from the historical trends in favor of collectivism outlined in *The Road to Serfdom*. His and others' similar ideas needed to be backed up with action in the form of a group that would share their thoughts and observations in the face of the domination of the academy by supporters of planning, socialism, and government intervention. They were further motivated by a fear of the renewed onset of totalitarianism evident in Stalinist Russia's advance into Eastern and Central Europe. Soviet Communism had not been attacked directly in *The Road to Serfdom* because Russia was still allied to Britain and the United States in the effort to defeat

Hitler. Now the communist threat behind the iron curtain, as Churchill described it in 1946, was at the forefront of the concerns of the scholars and activists surrounding Hayek. With communism on the advance militarily, the fears of communist influence on the Western democracies was real. Such a neoliberal network would facilitate opportunities and contacts that might help to change the intellectual and political climate in the West to one that would be more congenial to free markets and individual liberty. It would also provide a forum to counter the intellectual appeal of socialism.

According to Hartwell, five major groups, four in Europe and one in America, formed the basis of the Mont Pelerin Society's early membership. The first group comprised those based in England, at the LSE and in Manchester. In addition to Hayek, this group included Lionel Robbins, Edwin Cannan, Arnold Plant, William H. Hutt, Ronald Coase, Karl Popper, John Jewkes, T. S. Ashton, Cecily Wedgwood, and Michael Polanyi. These intellectuals were predominantly economists, but also historians, philosophers, and journalists. The second group consisted of Austrian exiles from Nazi rule in the United States, including Gottfried Haberler (who had been at Harvard since the mid-1930s), Fritz Machlup (who went first to the University of Buffalo, then to Johns Hopkins in Baltimore, and then to Princeton, where he remained until his death in 1983), and Ludwig von Mises (who had by this time moved to New York and was based at NYU). A third group, centered on Paris, had emerged out of the Colloque Walter Lippmann of 1938. This group included French liberal sociologists, economists, and philosophers, among them Louis Rougier, Raymond Aron, Jacques Rueff, M. Bourgeois, and E. Mantoux. The Colloque Walter Lippmann had anticipated the aims of the Mont Pelerin Society, primarily the urgent need to defend the classical liberal principles of individual freedom. The membership of the fourth group came mainly from those who had remained in Hitler's Germany, from the Freiburg school and Munich, a group of scholars that become known as ordoliberals, who had pushed the idea of the social market in the 1920s and 1930s (see chapter 3). These included the future German chancellor Ludwig Erhard, A. Weber, Walter Eucken, Wilhelm Röpke, and Franz Böhm. The last group consisted of Americans mainly from the University of Chicago, such as Frank Knight, Milton Friedman, George Stigler, Aaron Director, and Henry Simons (also discussed in chapter 3).[123]

Hayek wanted to keep the membership of the organization broad to ensure wide engagement and debate in its meetings, though as we have seen, not as broad as Popper would have liked. Certain nuances of view emerged during the discussions that surrounded the first meeting, which took place in Mont Pelerin, Switzerland, in 1947. Uniting the membership was a vaguely defined belief in the need to fight to protect freedom—a formulation that allowed for much disagreement. As we have seen, Popper thought that "what we need is peace and mutual confidence within the camp of humanitarianism, and the great majority of socialists is in this camp." Others disagreed. Mises, for example, wrote to Hayek in late 1946 from New York about his plans for the society's first meeting, worried that too many socialist sympathizers might be invited:

> The cause of this lamentable failure [to safeguard freedom from totalitarianism] was that the founders of these movements [of liberal and social democratic reform] could not emancipate themselves from the sway of the very ideas of the foes of liberty. They did not realise that freedom is inextricably linked with the market economy. They endorsed by and large the critical part of the socialist programs. They were committed to a middle-of-the-road solution, to interventionism.[124]

For Mises, these views were dangerous. As such, they were ideas the society should be fighting not courting. The potential watering down of free market advocacy, continued Mises, was the most important point:

> The weak point in Professor Hayek's plan is that it relies upon the cooperation of many men who are known for their endorsement of interventionism. It is necessary to clarify this point before the meeting starts. As I understand the plan, it is not the task of this meeting to discuss anew whether or not a government decree or a union dictate has the power to raise the standard of living of the masses. If somebody wants to discuss these problems, there is no need for him to make a pilgrimage to Mont Pelerin. He can find in his neighborhood ample opportunity to do so.

The point of the meeting and the society, for Mises, should be to pursue an agenda that took the inimical nature of government action for granted and decided what should be done about it.

Hayek was often less dogmatic than his friend. As we have seen in *The Road to Serfdom*, he was ready to allow some forms of government intervention to ensure social services or a minimum level of sustenance, for example. Equally, it is apparent from his correspondence with Leonard Read of the FEE in Irvington that he did not believe market forces ought to trump the imperatives of postwar reconstruction. As Hayek commented to Read about the American journalist Henry Hazlitt (author of the bestselling introduction to free market economics, *Economics in One Lesson*, published in 1946), whose study of the postwar economic situation had queried the lack of conditions attached to American loans to Europe and suggested that they be halted until conditions had been met,

> It is possible to agree with practically every word in his conclusions and yet doubt the advisability of giving the impressions [*sic*] that at this moment the complete cessation of American lending would be anything less than a major calamity. I agree particularly that it is of the first importance that the effects of these loans should not produce serious inflation in America, and that it is of the greatest importance that the Americans should give the example of sound policy. And the most important point is of course that the loans will help only if they induce the government to use the time gained to put their own economies in order. But while that is probably true it seems to me extremely dangerous to state this publicly by saying that "as a contribution to revival the conditions are much more important than the loan itself."[125]

Hayek's objection to the public discussion of the conditions for American lending (what became Marshall Plan aid) because debtor nations would find such intrusions into their affairs politically intolerable. Hayek was thus a robust defender of the independence of the historically great European powers—when he saw fit. In this kind of debate, Hayek was much more pragmatic than some of his supporters and colleagues. He was also often a staunch advocate of European and British interests in arguments and discussions with his American colleagues and supporters.

The American contingent was vital when it came to finance.[126] In the beginning the assistance was fairly modest and consisted in paying for the American-based members' attendance at meetings. For example, Leonard Read suggested that Mises could attend the Mont Pelerin meeting as a representative of his Foundation for Economic Education. Read also helped to organize a dinner in New York at the Canadian Club in the Waldorf Astoria in May 1946 for "intimate discussion" between Mises, Hayek, Read, and Hazlitt.[127] The FEE had offered to help Hayek, to which he replied with a letter requesting a long "list" of American books, to be sent "individually" so as to avoid problems with import licenses.[128] H. C. Cornuelle, the executive vice president of the FEE, replied to Hayek:

> The books you requested have been ordered and we shall send them to you, separately, as soon as possible. We are pleased to do this and hope they will be useful to you. Do not hesitate to ask us for any assistance of this kind.
>
> With best wishes,
Sincerely yours,
H. C. Cornuelle[129]

Such help became more bountiful during subsequent years as major funds such as the William Volker Fund (WVF) and the Earhart Foundation provided substantial support for scholars and resources for free market activism (see chapter 4). Quite often, such as with the Free Market Study funded by the WVF at the University of Chicago and supervised by Hayek, the influence of funders was much more significant. The WVF's efforts to control the substantive work of the project were only partially successfully resisted by Hayek. Van Horn and Mirowski write that Harold Luhnow and the officers of the WVF were not "mere pecuniary accessories to the rise of the Chicago School: they were hands-on players, determined and persistent in making every dollar count, supervising doctrine as well as organisation."[130]

Central to Hayek's thought, then, was intellectual organization. As we have seen, he was convinced of the importance of the battle of ideas. In 1949, after the success of *The Road to Serfdom* and the establishment of the Mont Pelerin Society, Hayek published an important article that laid out a rationale for a transatlantic network of defenders of individual liberty and the free market to combat the influence of the left. In all democratic countries, Hayek believed, and

> in the United States even more than elsewhere, a strong belief prevails that the influence of the intellectuals on politics is negligible. This is no doubt true of the power of intellectuals to make their peculiar opinions of the moment influence decisions, of the extent to which they can sway the popular vote on questions on which they differ from the current views of the masses. Yet over somewhat longer periods they have probably never exercised so great an influence as they do today in those countries. This power they wield by shaping public opinion.[131]

Hayek was deeply impressed by the influence of the British Fabian Society in developing social policy in the UK through its books, the LSE, and the infiltration of government and social institutions with an educated elite of public servants. A movement that took seriously the successes of the Fabians would be somewhat different from the plans of some for a "Liberal International," as he wrote to Popper:

> Our effort therefore differs from any political task in that it must be essentially a long-run effort, concerned not so much with what would be immediately practicable, but with the beliefs which must regain ascendance if the dangers are to be averted which at the moment threaten individual freedom.[132]

This was his primary motivation for founding the Mont Pelerin Society. He thought that winning the intellectual struggle would lead, in the long term but not before, to political success as well.

Hayek argued that the way in which ideas filtered into the political and public mainstream was through the influence of intellectuals, whom he called "second-hand dealers in ideas."[133] By intellectuals, he meant a diverse group of individuals whose *actual* expertise in any specific area was usually limited at best but whose authority to comment and pontificate on all sorts of matters was rarely questioned by wider society:

The class does not consist of only journalists, teachers, ministers, lecturers, publicists, radio commentators, writers of fiction, cartoonists, and artists all of whom may be masters of the technique of conveying ideas but are usually amateurs so far as the substance of what they convey is concerned. The class also includes many professional men and technicians, such as scientists and doctors, who through their habitual intercourse with the printed word become carriers of new ideas outside their own fields and who, because of their expert knowledge of their own subjects, are listened to with respect on most others. There is little that the ordinary man of today learns about events or ideas except through the medium of this class.[134]

Hayek thought that this intellectual class held views with a blatantly liberal (in the progressive American sense of the term), socialist, or progressive bias.

The predisposition toward interventionist ideas among intellectuals reinforced their public status as long as such ideas were more broadly popular, and vice versa. The effect of this culture of conformity was a kind of mutually reinforcing circle that was deeply damaging to intellectual diversity and the public scrutiny necessary for effective debate:

It is specially significant for our problem that every scholar can probably name several instances from his field of men who have undeservedly achieved a popular reputation as great scientists solely because they hold what the intellectuals regard as "progressive" political views; but I have yet to come across a single instance where such a scientific pseudo-reputation has been bestowed for political reasons on a scholar of more conservative leanings.[135]

According to Hayek, experts were too often judged by their political sympathies instead of by the excellence or otherwise of their academic work. Their results, and the consequent reputation they enjoyed within their specialist field, mattered less than whether they were adherents of "fashionable general ideas."[136] The intellectuals helped propagate these general ideas through their public and political actions. The results of technical knowledge became divorced from public debate because they were interpreted for the public and

filtered by intellectuals with a socialist or collectivist bias. Public debate became characterized by the vague repetition of notions given weight through
being repeated by intellectuals:

> It is no exaggeration to say that, once the more active part of the in-
> tellectuals has been converted to a set of beliefs, the process by which
> these become generally accepted is almost automatic and irresistible.
> These intellectuals are the organs which modern society has developed
> for spreading knowledge and ideas, and it is their convictions and opin-
> ions which operate as the sieve through which all new conceptions
> must pass before they can reach the masses.[137]

Defenders of individual liberty and the market, according to Hayek, had a
duty to counter this trend by generating their own long-term influence in the
climate of ideas. In this way, the legislation, policy, and politics of the future
would change for the better to reflect the principles of their view of the free
society.

Hayek's essay had a profound influence on those around him at the time.
But it was a strange manifesto in that it emphasized utopian dreams, exactly
the sort of folly for which Hayek supposedly attacked the socialists. It was
also affected by Hayek's limitations as a writer in English, his second language. Some, like Leonard Read, who secured its publication in the *University
of Chicago Law Review* in 1949, thought its meaning hampered by Hayek's
awkward prose style:

> [*The Intellectuals and Socialism's*] limitation, as I see it, is in the writing.
> In too many places your meaning is obscured, by reason of the language
> arrangement in setting forth the ideas.
>
> This piece is far too important to be limited to those who, having
> done considerable thinking in this area, can deduce your brilliant
> meanings.[138]

In the drift toward socialism among the intellectuals, Hayek sensed a laziness
that imperiled the bases of freedom. A message such as this carried enough
force that the prose style really didn't matter. Instead, the fervor it carried, and
which was felt at the time by other neoliberal readers and supporters, made it

such an important strategic statement. It is worth quoting Hayek's conclusion in full as it served as the call to arms for the transatlantic neoliberal movement that grew up after 1945:

Does this mean that freedom is valued only when it is lost, that the world must everywhere go through a dark phase of socialist totalitarianism before the forces of freedom can gather strength anew? It may be so, but I hope it need not be. Yet, so long as the people who over longer periods determine public opinion continue to be attracted by the ideals of socialism, the trend will continue. If we are to avoid such a development, we must be able to offer a new liberal program which appeals to the imagination. We must make the building of a free society once more an intellectual adventure, a deed of courage. What we lack is a liberal Utopia, a program which seems neither a mere defense of things as they are nor a diluted kind of socialism, but a truly liberal radicalism which does not spare the susceptibilities of the mighty (including the trade unions), which is not too severely practical, and which does not confine itself to what appears today as politically possible. We need intellectual leaders who are willing to work for an ideal, however small may be the prospects of its early realisation. They must be men who are willing to stick to principles and to fight for their full realisation, however remote. The practical compromises they must leave to the politicians. Free trade and freedom of opportunity are ideals which still may arouse the imaginations of large numbers, but a mere "reasonable freedom of trade" or a mere "relaxation of controls" is neither intellectually respectable nor likely to inspire any enthusiasm.

The main lesson which the true liberal must learn from the success of the socialists is that it was their courage to be Utopian which gained them the support of the intellectuals and therefore an influence on public opinion which is daily making possible what only recently seemed utterly remote. Those who have concerned themselves exclusively with what seemed practicable in the existing state of opinion have constantly found that even this had rapidly become politically impossible as the result of changes in a public opinion which they have done nothing to guide. Unless we can make the philosophic foundations of a free society once more a living intellectual issue, and its implementation a task which challenges the ingenuity and imagination of our liveliest minds [sic]. But if we can regain that belief in the power of ideas which was the mark of liberalism at its best, the battle is not lost. The intellectual revival of liberalism is already underway in many parts of the world. Will it be in time?[139]

It was not too late, as events in subsequent decades proved. But it took a generation for Hayek's strategy of ideological purity to bear fruit.

Hayek's emphasis on utopia was not pursued in the political strategies of the neoliberal intellectuals and think tanks that spread the revival of free market ideology in the postwar period. If anything, the market as neoliberalism matured was presented as clear common sense, whose basic logic was inescapable. Of course, this presentation was fantasy. Some markets succeeded and others failed. The ideological case for the superiority of the market in all areas of economic and social life all of the time amounted to a political faith as utopian as any other. The difficult questions, then as now, were when markets work best and when they fail to succeed at all. The most striking thing about Hayek's statement is how much of his pure ideological vision did come to pass in Britain and the United States after 1980. The free market became the organizing principle for microeconomic reform, especially through the privatization of state assets, nationalized industries, public utilities, and public services. Trade unions were vanquished and the power of labor was diluted. Exchange controls were abolished. The financial markets were progressively deregulated. Market mechanisms became the models for the operation of health care. Of course, the institutions of the welfare state, the progressive income tax, and universal public education remained, although even in these areas, public funding and support had been downgraded by the end of the twentieth century. It is hard to think of another "utopia" to have been as fully realized. The purity that Hayek advocated was meant as an optimistic and ideological and intellectual tactic rather than a blueprint. The results have been extraordinary.

Hayek's cogent presentation of the case for an alternative ideological infrastructure to transform the "climate of opinion," as opposed to the emphasis on utopianism, was followed by neoliberal supporters and activists. Hayek's article had a powerful galvanizing effect on many of the creators and leaders of the transatlantic network of neoliberals—liberals "in the old sense of the word"—that Hayek and his ideas helped bring to generate in the post-war period.[140] It remained for flesh to be put onto the bones of the skeleton conceived by the early activists of the Mont Pelerin Society. The members of the society were intellectuals and academics, and tended to revert to their universities between meetings and return to their work. What the movement needed was a group of individuals who would popularize and promote neo-liberal ideas beyond their scattered and isolated academic homes. The ideas contained in *The Road to Serfdom* had already gained the attention of many members of the business elite, such as Jasper Crane of DuPont Chemicals, who were central to the anti–New Deal coalition. This network is the subject of chapter 4. But by the end of the 1940s, the foundations of a program and an intellectual and political strategy were in place.

Popper, Mises, and Hayek had assailed the characteristic features of New Deal liberalism and British social democracy as they saw them. Popper was the least comfortable with a crude free market program, and this was reflected in his less prominent role in the growth and maturation of neoliberal politics after 1945. But he had provided a cogent attack on Plato, Hegel, and Marx that gave intellectual armory to neoliberalism. Hayek had emerged as the in-tellectual and organizational leader of a new movement. His unwillingness to compromise philosophically about the superiority of markets in "The Intel-lectuals and Socialism" was followed by Milton Friedman and other Chicago economists. It was also followed by many of the fervent ideological entrepre-neurs who ran the neoliberal think tanks and promoted free market ideas. Mises was least noticed at the time, but it was perhaps his unalloyed vision of markets that emerged victorious in the long run. His view of bureaucracies influenced the Chicago economists, the Virginia public choice theorists, and, most important of all, the businessmen who funded transatlantic neoliberal politics. Businessmen liked Mises because he argued that corporations were the drivers of social and economic progress. Without the support of such rich individuals and foundations the movement could never have got off the ground. His conception of consumption as a fundamentally democratic act and the marketplace as a forum for expression was far-sighted. It became a core component of the arguments made on behalf of markets by supporters of the Thatcher and Reagan governments in the 1980s.

Popper and Hayek had articulated the beginnings of an alternative that they based on individual liberty and limited but strong government to maintain the competitive order and free market capitalism. Mises was less keen on government of any sort. But at this stage and in these works, these writers had not yet constructed a detailed and coherent alternative political or economic agenda. They were still too affected by what had happened in continental Europe from which they had all escaped. They were not able to foresee the wealth and general prosperity of the postwar period. The second Chicago school, and Milton Friedman and George Stigler in particular, were primarily responsible for the generation of a set of workable alternative policies. Instead, Popper, Mises, and Hayek had sounded a siren call, a warning about the tragic possibilities of the direction in which Western politics, economy, and society seemed to be moving. But the critique they had generated gave substance to the movement that Hayek in particular would lead. The detailed character of transatlantic neoliberalism and the network that was responsible for its successful diffusion are the subject of the next two chapters. But its beginnings, in the ideas of Popper, Mises, and Hayek, marked the first steps that would launch transatlantic neoliberalism from the academy into policy and politics.

3

✳

The Rising Tide

Neoliberal Ideas in the Postwar Period

The stage is set for the growth of a new current of opinion to replace the old,
to provide the philosophy that will guide the legislators of the next generation
even though it can hardly affect those of this one.

MILTON FRIEDMAN, "Neo-liberalism and Its Prospects," 1951

After 1945, a distinct neoliberal worldview was built on the foundations of
the critique of New Deal liberalism and social democracy synthesized in
the writings of Ludwig von Mises, Friedrich Hayek, and Karl Popper. During the thirty years after the publication of Hayek's essay, "The Intellectuals
and Socialism," in 1949, a transatlantic movement was launched and moved
into a preeminent position. Its main tenets—philosophical, political, and
economic—were worked out in detail by scholars such as Milton Friedman,
George Stigler, Gary Becker, James Buchanan, and Gordon Tullock, as well
as Hayek and Mises, and the locus of research activity, though by no means
all of it, moved from Britain and Europe to the United States, to Chicago and
Virginia in particular. In the same period, a network of people, organizations,
and money spread the new gospel on either side of the Atlantic Ocean. By
the 1970s a body of diagnoses and policy prescriptions was aided by an institutional infrastructure that injected neoliberalism into the political bloodstream of both the United States and Britain. The adrenaline generated by the
movement and its ideas in the Conservative and Republican Parties radically
changed the political and economic life of both countries. This chapter and
the next are about the ideas and organizations that made up transatlantic neoliberal politics.

In vital respects, the 1940s marked the beginnings of neoliberalism. In this decade, a powerful attack on the interventionist bent of British and American society was allied to an assertion of the supremacy of the free market and a strategy for its revival. Early neoliberals in Europe and the United States, during the 1930s and 1940s, felt they were rethinking liberalism afresh, so as to move beyond both older nineteenth-century laissez-faire economics and the interventionist liberalism of FDR, Keynes, and Beveridge. The legacy of the unemployment of the 1930s and World War II was to cement progressive and social democratic ideas in British and U.S. politics after 1945. The resultant dominance of such politics placed neoliberal thinkers on the defensive.

But for nascent neoliberalism and opponents of the New Deal and social democracy, the postwar political settlement was not as much of a drought as it seemed. The critiques of Hayek, Mises, and Popper, the formation and funding of the Mont Pelerin Society in 1947, the stirring of anticollectivist noise that accompanied the onset of the Cold War, the emergence of the Dixiecrats in the South (southern conservative Democrats whose politics were defined by race and segregation), and the successful constraints imposed by Congress on President Harry Truman's Fair Deal in the late forties all indicated a new conservative readiness to attack the dominance of the Democrats in the United States. At the same time, Britain's Labour Party, exhausted and having achieved most of its aims, lost power, to be replaced by the Conservative Party in 1951. Neoliberalism was one tributary to this sea of opposition to the postwar dispensation, particularly in the United States, much of which occurred at the grassroots level rather than among political elites and policymakers. In the late 1940s and 1950s, neoliberalism flowed alongside anticommunist, anti-immigration, and traditional conservative streams. By the late 1970s, however, transatlantic neoliberalism had become the preeminent reservoir for alternative Republican and Conservative social and economic policy ideas (and often for the Labour Party and Democratic Party, too).

This chapter examines how neoliberal ideas developed a sharper focus and an icy coherence. By the 1970s, neither Milton Friedman's intelligent loquaciousness nor Ronald Reagan's warm sentiments could disguise a philosophy that was built on a cold and abstract individualism and a theory as much based in the harsh principles of free market discipline as it might have been in any more positive notion of progress. And yet the vision was still very much a utopian one, centered on a fantasy of the perfect free market. Moreover, the basis for this alternative political philosophy had been laid by the 1950s. Mature neoliberalism, when it emerged, was much more aggressive in its advocacy of free market models as the solution to all manner of policy problems and compromised much less with mainstream New Deal or Great Society liberalism and social democracy. When the political philosophies of some of the main thinkers—Milton Friedman, Henry Simons, James Buchanan, and George Stigler, as well as Mises and Hayek—are examined, it is possible to situate and define more clearly transatlantic neoliberalism in relation to other political and economic philosophies. Neoliberalism differed from the classical liberalism of Adam Smith. It was defined by an emphasis on what these thinkers saw as the crucial relationship between economic and political liberty, a relationship that also placed neoliberal ideas at the center of both civil rights and Cold War debates about the nature of freedom.

That transatlantic neoliberal politics stemmed from the powerful critique developed in the 1930s and 1940s originating in ideas and debates about the future of liberalism that were circulating in Vienna, Freiburg, Switzerland, Paris, and at the London School of Economics (LSE), presents only a partial picture. For a fuller explanation, it is necessary to examine at least three further crucial currents without which the development of postwar neoliberalism cannot be understood. First, there were important progenitors in the United States in the first Chicago school, before 1950 (resembling like-minded scholars at the LSE, led by Edwin Cannan, Lionel Robbins, and Hayek himself). Although Frank Knight is usually cited as a leader, economist Henry Simons was actually the central Chicago figure in terms of the history of neoliberalism. He proposed arguments similar to those of his European neoliberal friends, including Hayek, about the future of liberalism in the 1930s and 1940s. Simons's influence on Friedman was also vital to the latter's development of monetary theory.

Second, there was a self-consciously neoliberal political movement in West Germany during the 1950s, the "social market" economy. This grouping, the first to flower into an actual governmental project, was linked to the Mont Pelerin Society through its finance minister, Ludwig Erhard, and main theorists, Walter Eucken and Wilhelm Röpke. The intellectuals who formulated this distinctive German neoliberalism in the 1920s, 1930s, and 1940s, and to whom Hayek was close, were known as ordoliberals, for their association with the journal *Ordo*. German neoliberalism was characterized, like

Simons's thought, by the strong state supervision of the competitive order. In recognition of the unsettling and troublesome effects of the market, ordoliberalism theorized a powerful state role in addressing the social impact of markets, as well as their successful operation. This meant an acceptance of both a welfare state and a strong role for antimonopoly legislation in the *Soziale Marktwirtschaft*. These elements were markedly absent from Chicago economics. The movement found favor in the policies of the Christian Democratic governments of Konrad Adenauer and Erhard himself.

Last, the encroachment of Chicago theory on many different policy spheres in the United States was followed by the development of public choice theory and rational choice approaches in the 1960s. Both built on the assumptions of neoclassical economics, and especially the concept of the individual as a rational utility-maximizer. Too often in the accounts of its critics, such as Naomi Klein, David Harvey, or Andrew Glyn, neoliberalism has been assumed to be little more than a reflection of the dominance of neoclassical economics.[1] In fact, many of the distinctive contributions of neoliberal economists took rational utility-maximizing individuals operating within a general equilibrium model for granted, whether they were closer to Léon Walras, Alfred Marshall, or Kenneth Arrow. Neoliberals were not usually exercised by the questions of how such neoclassical models could be proved or whether they worked. Instead, the ideas of rational and public choice theory assumed the utility of the rational actor model that lay at the core of neoclassical assumptions, then extended those assumptions' application to the hitherto untouched arenas of politics, regulation, and government. This new research was done both within the Chicago school, through George Stigler's idea of regulatory capture, for example, and also from without, by William Riker at the University of Rochester and his followers in the rational choice school of political science. It also came from the work of James Buchanan, who earned his PhD in economics under Friedman's tutelage at the University of Chicago, and Gordon Tulluck, also Chicago-educated, who went on to become the leaders of the Virginia school of public choice theory. This important convergence expanded neoliberal thought's perceived explanatory power into new and important areas that had previously been ignored by economists. The work of these other key economists is therefore also central to any proper understanding of the development of transatlantic neoliberal politics.

At the heart of many of these developments in the postwar period was the figure of Milton Friedman, who, along with Hayek, became the most important neoliberal activist and theorist, as well as the leader of the Chicago school of economics (in fact, there were at least two Chicago schools, as we shall see). The ideas, published and unpublished, of Milton Friedman warrant detailed exposition to understand how academic debates around the various neoliberal ideas crystallized into a coherent and powerful message of political and economic reform. Such an analysis of Friedman's work and of the roles played by other important figures at Chicago in the 1950s, such as Friedman's brother-in-law Aaron Director, Stigler, Edward Levi, Coase, Becker, and also Hayek himself, helps to explain how neoliberalism coalesced within the academy in the United States.

But despite the importance of various individual thinkers, the fundamentally collaborative approach that the various neoliberal groups brought to their transatlantic academic conversations across disciplines and between countries and continents was important. It was not simply the project of one or two writers. No one or two thinkers should be thought of as canonical, either.[2] Nevertheless, the crisper and more effective promotion of free markets and deregulation that emerged out of the Chicago school and the Virginia school did begin to supersede the more ambivalent and accommodating European and early Chicago considerations of the role of the market that had dominated in the years before 1950. This emboldening perhaps also reflected the very different sort of public debate in the United States from that undertaken in European countries immediately after the war. Such discussions, in the United States, were shot through with considerations of race, anticommunism, and the unique responsibilities of being a superpower, rather than economic survival and recovery, which were the dominant themes in Europe. Friedman and his colleagues felt themselves to be full participants in these public discussions about the role of the United States in the world, and of economic freedom within its borders, even to the extent of feeling themselves to be actual ideological protagonists in the Cold War itself.

The Two Chicago Schools: Henry Simons, Milton Friedman, and Neoliberalism

Together with Austrian economics and the group of scholars at the LSE in the 1940s, the Chicago school of economic theory was perhaps the most influential group in terms of the development of transatlantic neoliberal politics in the 1950s and 1960s.[3] There were actually two Chicago schools, based at the University of Chicago, comprising both sitting faculty and Chicago-trained economists: the first existed during the interwar years and the second developed after 1946, during the 1950s and 1960s. The difference between the two was more generational than doctrinal, although substantial divergence did exist between the methodologies of the first and second Chicago schools. Frank Knight, Jacob Viner, Lloyd Mints, and Henry Simons led the first during the 1920s and 1930s.[4] Unlike their intellectual progeny, these thinkers' primary focus was on pure economic theory, with an emphasis on Marshallian neoclassical marginalism. The "marginalist revolution," codified by Keynes's teacher at Cambridge, Alfred Marshall, and begun almost simultaneously by the French mathematical economist Léon Walras, the Italian engineer and economist Vilfredo Pareto, and the British logician and economist William Stanley Jevons, was the idea that consumers would maximize their utility by matching their consumption to the prices of the various goods they wanted according to a rational order of preference. This insight was profoundly influential on the economics profession as a whole and became a core tenet of early Chicago economics as well.

But the Chicago school has been notoriously difficult to pin down, even by those who studied and taught there. According to one of the second Chicago school's leading lights, George Stigler (who, although he earned a PhD from the University of Chicago, only joined the economics faculty from Columbia University in 1958):

> The Chicago School has always been a phrase whose accuracy varied inversely to its content. The leading figures of the School in the 1930s were highly diverse: Knight was the great philosopher and theoretician, almost in a Marxian sense; Viner was studiously non-dogmatic on policy views; Mints was a close historical student of money, and restricted himself to that field; Simons was the utopian. None of the school had any interest in quantitative work, and indeed—like the rest of the economics profession—none (except Viner) had serious reservation that his understanding of economic life was incomplete or mistaken.[5]

Stigler's caustic last comment is perhaps apt for economists in general, as he points out, and it certainly helps to convey some of the intellectual confidence that emanated from the Great Lakes.[6] The influence of these early Chicago economists of the 1930s and 1940s in relation to the development of neoliberal thought was due to their role as teachers of the leading figures of the second Chicago school, which included Friedman, Aaron Director, Stigler, Gary Becker, Ronald Coase (who had initially been at the LSE with Hayek and Robbins), and Edward Levi.[7] These later figures developed an aggressively pro–free market research program that was coupled with the marketing talent possessed by some of the most famous of all postwar American public intellectuals. This talent for promotion was also reflected in the fact that many of them won the Nobel Prize in Economics, including Friedman, Stigler, Coase, and Becker.

Hayek was also based in Chicago during the 1950s, having moved there from the LSE in 1950 to take up a post as a professor in the Committee on Social Thought. This position was not in the Economics Department itself, a situation that partly reflected the discomfort other members of the department felt toward someone so clearly identified with the Austrian tradition.[8] The Austrian and Chicago traditions differed in their methodological emphases. The Austrian tradition believed that economics was a science based in axiomatic truths. The Chicago school, especially the second, favored an empirically based approach to research in order to prove its hypotheses. But the appointment also reflected a desire on Hayek's part to retreat from the economic arguments about the Great Depression and the merits of planning, which he had debated with Keynes in the 1930s. He began to direct his efforts at questions of political and moral philosophy. Hayek's position in Chicago was very important because he acted as a bridge between various colleagues and significant sources of business finance such as the William Volker Foundation (WVF). Seen in this way, Hayek's years in Chicago enabled him to supervise and develop the intellectual and political strategy he had elaborated earlier in "The Intellectuals and Socialism."

Rob Van Horn and Phillip Mirowski have argued that Hayek's coordination of the establishment of the Free Market Study at Chicago in the late 1940s and early 1950s and, at the suggestion of Henry Simons, his insistence that Friedman's brother-in-law, the economist Aaron Director, run the program, show that Hayek's role in the development of the second Chicago School was much more pivotal than previously thought.[9] They have illustrated that a decisive spur to the growth of the second Chicago school came from this attempt by Harold Luhnow, the president of the WVF, and Hayek to instigate a free market project (which became the Free Market Study) that would produce an American version of *The Road to Serfdom*. This eventually materialized in Milton Friedman's *Capitalism and Freedom,* published in 1962.

The project revealed the insidious influence of the funders over the academic content of the Free Market Study. Initially it was meant to be located at Princeton University and headed by monetary economist Friedrich Lutz. However, Hayek settled on Chicago because of the presence of Henry Simons and other congenial and like-minded pro–free market economists. The result was that the WVF helped fund Aaron Director's position at the university as well as an ongoing research program that looked into questions of monopoly, labor, and the role of the corporation:

> Corporations, in particular, were inevitably characterised as passive responders to outside forces. In economics, the only market actor accused of misusing power was the trade union, which was uniformly treated as illegitimate, whereas any other instance of market power, as in the case of monopoly or oligopoly, was either treated as harmless and temporary or attributed to some nefarious state policy.[10]

According to Van Horn and Mirowski, "It is important to realise that, for Hayek, these negotiations [with Luhnow, Director, and, before his untimely suicide in 1946, Simons] over Chicago and the parallel construction of what became Mont Pelerin were all part of the same common endeavour."[11] Such a view simplifies the differences between Hayek and the Chicago school over issues such as the business cycle (see chapter 4). These debates constantly risked dividing the Mont Pelerin Society into rival Friedmanite and Hayekian camps. But it is undoubtedly true that Hayek, as well as Friedman, played a central role throughout the 1950s in the establishment of Chicago as a central hub for neoliberal thought.[12]

The second Chicago school issued a flood of work in the 1950s, 1960s, and 1970s that argued for free market policies. The school successfully engaged in a kind of economic imperialism through the colonization of new policy pastures with ideas of market liberalization, an imperialism that was married to a deep commitment to methodological individualism and empirically based research. Chicago economists argued that free market analyses should occupy new fiefdoms, such as law, regulation, the family, welfare, and sex, that had previously been considered outside the realm of markets. Chicago economists presented a benign picture of monopolies and a hostile picture of labor and trade unions, which they argued were a much more serious threat to the successful operation of the free market economy than vertically integrated corporations. In these commitments, the second generation was more cohesive and very different from the first, whose ideological pluralism contained a more theoretical bent. Of those who made up the first Chicago school, Henry Simons especially was fundamental to the history of American neoliberal thought. Simons was Friedman's mentor and Hayek's friend, and, as Stigler put it, can be thought of as "the Crown Prince of that hypothetical kingdom, the Chicago School of Economics."[13]

Henry Calvert Simons was born in Illinois in 1899 into an upper-middle-class family, the son of an attorney and an "imperious" "southern belle."[14] He left home at age seventeen to study economics at the University of Michigan. A brilliant student, Simons pursued graduate study first at the University of Iowa, where he met Frank Knight, who became his doctoral supervisor and brought him to Chicago. He settled at the University of Chicago during the 1930s and 1940s and eventually became a professor of economics there in 1945, a year before his early death from suicide.[15] Simons's main work focused on the Great Depression, monetary theory, and the business cycle. A vociferous critic of the New Deal, which he thought had exacerbated the Depression and introduced an unwarranted expansion of government activity, Simons was a crucial influence on Friedman's monetary theory (examined in chapter 5). Like most economists of the 1930s, Simons advocated a program that would prevent a future economic collapse such as that which followed the stock market crash of 1929. Simons held many policy views Friedman disagreed with, such as a belief in greater equality through progressive taxation, the public ownership of "natural" monopolies, the curtailment of advertising, and a commitment to "many welfare functions."[16] But he also argued for rules that would preclude the exercise of discretionary authority in monetary policy and economic policy more generally, something that would later preoccupy Friedman.[17]

Simons's student Milton Friedman was the central figure and the leader, along with George Stigler, of the second Chicago school. Friedman was born in Brooklyn in 1912, the son of Hungarian Jewish immigrants.[18] His parents ran a dry goods store. He grew up in New Jersey and studied for a bachelor's degree at Rutgers University, where he majored in mathematics. While at Rutgers, Friedman was taught by the future chairman of the Federal Reserve during the economic dramas of the 1970s, Arthur Burns. He took a master's degree at the University of Chicago in 1933, where he fell under the influence of Knight, Viner, and Simons. Friedman married Rose Director, the sister of Aaron, his future colleague at Chicago. He won a fellowship and spent a year studying statistics at Columbia University in New York. Unable to find an academic job, something he later felt was due to anti-Semitism, he was at this time a supporter of the New Deal and went to work for the National Resources Committee in Washington in 1935. An avowed Keynesian during this period, Friedman continued in government service, except for a brief interlude as assistant professor in economics at the University of Wisconsin–Madison, until 1943. He had further stints at Columbia and the University of Minnesota, and eventually earned his PhD from Columbia in 1946, after which he was appointed to teach economics at the University of Chicago.

For the remainder of his professional academic career, Friedman taught and researched in Chicago, though he also worked for the National Bureau of Economic Research. In 1954–55 he spent a year as a visiting fellow at Gonville and Caius College of Cambridge University in England, where, among others, he taught the British economist Samuel Brittan. He also befriended Stanley Dennison, one of the few anti-Keynesians left at Cambridge University during the 1950s and a fellow member of the Mont Pelerin Society. Throughout his life, Friedman also worked with policy think tanks and research institutes in many countries, especially Great Britain, where he wrote several pamphlets and reports for the Institute of Economic Affairs (IEA) during the 1960s and 1970s, mainly on monetary policy and inflation. He also wrote for the Centre for Policy Studies (CPS) and the Adam Smith Institute (ASI). On retirement in 1977, Friedman moved to the Stanford-based think tank, the Hoover Institution, where he remained until his death in 2006.

Henry Simons exerted a powerful and always acknowledged influence on the young Friedman.[19] Simons's most important essay, published in 1934, proposed an unapologetic program of laissez-faire, for "freedom of enterprise," in response to the Great Depression and in place of Roosevelt's New Deal.[20] Laissez-faire, he thought, was the policy that would guarantee all the freedoms, economic and political, that people held dear:

The existence (and preservation) of a competitive system in private industry makes possible a minimizing of the responsibilities of the sovereign state. It frees the state from the obligations of adjudicating endless, bitter disputes among persons as participants in different industries and among owners of different kinds of productive services. In a word, it makes possible a political policy of laissez-faire.[21]

He argued that for capitalism to work properly, government should refrain from economic life except for certain carefully demarcated functions. For Simons, the state, not the market, had failed during the Great Depression. This was because of the expansion of state activity through increased regulation and by intervention to provide greater employment through the creation of a plethora of new agencies epitomized by the Works Progress Administration. Additionally, the New Deal administration, through its meddling with relative prices, had failed to protect the competitive environment. According to Simons, "the so-called failure of capitalism (of the free-enterprise system, of competition) may reasonably be interpreted as primarily a failure of the political state in the discharge of its minimum responsibilities under capitalism."[22]

By presenting the Great Depression as a problem compounded by government action, Simons anticipated Friedman's own claims about the Federal Reserve in his and Anna Jacobsen Schwartz's *Monetary History of the United States* (published in 1963, this book argued that the Fed had turned a small recession into a depression through incompetent management of monetary policy). However, Simons was also very clear that government should protect the rules needed for competition by fighting monopoly in all its guises:

The policy [laissez-faire], therefore, should be defined positively, as one under which the state seeks to establish and maintain such conditions that it may avoid the necessity of regulating "the heart of the contract"— that is to say, the necessity of regulating relative prices. Thus, the state is charged, under this "division of labor," with heavy responsibilities and large "control" functions: the maintenance of competitive conditions in industry; the control of the currency (of the quantity and value of the effective money); the definition of the institution of property (especially with reference to fiscal practices)—not to mention the many social welfare activities.[23]

These sentiments were echoed closely in a paper by Friedman from 1951 that drew explicitly on Simons's work, although this early emphasis on antitrust would subsequently be largely abandoned by the second Chicago school after the work of the Free Market Study.[24]

Friedman, in this 1951 paper, titled "Neo-liberalism and Its Prospects," is one of the first American writers to claim the neoliberal moniker explicitly (though the term, as we have seen, was in fairly common usage among European neoliberals in the 1930s and 1940s). The paper is therefore a useful marker of the moment when neoliberalism became a self-conscious political and economic concept in the United States.[25] The paper articulates the key components of a viable state whose purpose, like Simons's concept of the state in his "Positive Program for Laissez-Faire," is the creation and sustenance of a "competitive order."[26] Friedman argued that the state should be limited if essential, instead of the expansive state revealed in the regulatory and legislative encroachments of New Deal liberalism. But laissez-faire, according to Friedman, lacked the necessary ingredients for the success of free markets (at least as he conceived it in the immediate postwar years). In his criticisms of laissez-faire, Friedman was clearly drawing on the ideas of the early neoliberals of the first phase of the movement's intellectual development in the 1930s and 1940s, many of which were synthesized and articulated in the work of Hayek, Popper, and Mises, to present a picture that went beyond the famously limited night watchman state. Instead, he presented a vision of a state that played a central role in the establishment and maintenance of the free market.[27]

In this short essay Friedman argued that the rise of collectivist ideas in the first half of the twentieth century had highlighted a basic weakness in the laissez-faire policies of nineteenth-century Manchester liberals such as Richard Cobden and John Bright. This philosophy, he wrote,

> assigned almost no role to the state other than the maintenance of order and the enforcement of contracts. It was a negative philosophy. The state could do only harm. Laissez-faire must be the rule. In taking this position, it underestimated the danger that private individuals could through agreement and combination usurp power and effectively limit the freedom of other individuals; it failed to see that there were some functions the price system could not perform and that unless these oth-

er functions were somehow provided for, the price system could not discharge effectively the tasks for which it is admirably fitted.[28]

Collectivist ideas—which Friedman, like Hayek and Mises before him, conflated with socialism and New Deal liberalism—had also failed because socialism had been found wanting in crucial respects:

> It has become abundantly clear that nationalisation solves no fundamental economic problems; that centralised economic planning is consistent with its own brand of chaos and disorganisation; and that centralised planning may raise far greater barriers to free international intercourse than unregulated capitalism ever did. Equally important, the growing power of the State has brought widespread recognition of the extent to which centralised economic control is likely to endanger individual freedom and liberty.[29]

Friedman advocated "the New Faith" of neoliberalism as one that would avoid the failures of both collectivism and laissez-faire approaches. In a perhaps conscious echo of Keynes, he proposed a "middle road" (Friedman understood the power of Keynesian ideas, as well as how to promote them—something he would prove by becoming an arch policy propagandist himself). The central point of the paper, made forcefully, was that both laissez-faire policies and collectivism had failed, a development that called for a new theory of liberalism—of *neoliberalism*—that would

> accept the nineteenth century liberal emphasis in the fundamental importance of the individual, but it would substitute for the nineteenth century goal of laissez-faire as a means to this end, the goal of a competitive order. It would use competition among producers to protect the consumer from exploitation, competition among employers to protect workers and owners of property and competition among consumers to protect the enterprises themselves. The state would police the system, establish conditions favorable to competition and prevent monopoly, provide a stable monetary framework, and relieve acute misery and distress. The citizens would be protected against the state by the

existence of a private market; and against one another by the preservation of competition.[30]

The inspiration of Henry Simons is clear in the elaboration of the outlines
of a comprehensive neoliberal worldview in this essay. First, in this passage,
Friedman describes the main elements of a neoliberal theory of the state in a
conscious rendering of Simons's ideas. But he goes beyond Simons and the
other early neoliberals when he hints at a faith in self-regulation, in the self-
correcting nature of free markets.[31] Second, Friedman emphasizes the relationship between economic and other types of freedom, especially individual
democratic and political rights, which were placed at the heart of his vision
of society.

Friedman's essay can be seen as radical in some ways, for example in its belief in the need for a "new" theory of neoliberalism, as opposed to those who
claimed that what they were engaged in was a revival of classical liberalism.
But in fact, Friedman displays an affinity with a more moderate form of neoliberal thought. This sympathy is evident in his advocacy of a strong role for
the state in the supervision of competition. This was something from which
he—with many of his Chicago colleagues—would later depart. But his artic-
ulation of such a compromise position, akin to that of Hayek and Popper, as
well as Simons, also bears the hallmark of the influence of the group of thinkers who formed the Mont Pelerin Society on Friedman, who himself was a
founding member. By 1950 Friedman had attended three meetings of the society—in Mont Pelerin and Seelisberg in Switzerland and in Bloemendaal in
Holland. The papers discussed at the meetings ranged from "Free Enterprise
or Competitive Order," by Hayek, to "The Future of Germany," by Wilhelm
Röpke, to "Trade Unions and the Price System," by William Hutt, and "Labour and Management," by Stanley Dennison.[32]

After "Neo-liberalism and Its Prospects," Friedman rarely used the label
neoliberal. Consequently, the paper marks a fascinating moment in his own
intellectual growth and can also be seen as a symbolic cutoff point dividing
early neoliberalism from its more strident successors, the point at which the
more moderate accommodations characteristic of the early neoliberalism of
Henry Simons, with its muted acceptance of "many welfare functions" and
the like, had apparently reached their apogee of influence within the Mont
Pelerin Society and in the burgeoning neoliberal movement as a whole. In

this essay, Friedman argued for a position he would never publicly support again.

Another salient dimension in Simons's thought, to which, as I have suggested, Friedman alluded in "Neo-liberalism and Its Prospects," was the connection between economic and political liberty. In "For a Free Market Liberalism," Simons argued that

> Smith, and Bentham especially, stand out, I think, as the great political philosophers of modern democracy. Their special insight was that political and economic power must be widely dispersed and decentralised in a world that would be free; that economic control must, to that end, be largely divorced from the state and effected through a competitive process in which participants are relatively small and anonymous; and that the state must jealously guard its prerogatives of controlling prices (and wages), not for the purpose of exercising them directly itself but to prevent organised minorities from usurping and using them against the common interest.[33]

The description of Adam Smith (and arguably Bentham too, who moved between autocratic and democratic means in his utilitarian theory) as a philosopher of modern democracy is both anachronistic and wrong. But the elaboration of the similarities between the dispersal of political power implied by democracy and that of economic power through the market does help to illuminate where neoliberals felt themselves close to the Enlightenment liberalism of Smith.

As with Hayek, Popper, and Mises, Simons was concerned to differentiate the Anglo-Scottish-American Enlightenment tradition from the nineteenth-century German one:

> Germany never accepted English liberalism; and even her best scholars rarely understood Adam Smith and Jeremy Bentham and the tradition of thought identified with them. On the other hand, the German creed was always congenial to our own powerful minorities, seeking special favours from the state, and to politicians who lived by such dispensations. Its emphasis upon social legislation appealed to the finest sentiments and led us, sensitive about our so-called "backwardness,"

into imitative measures subtly but deeply incompatible with our democratic tradition.[34]

NO NEW PARA Simons, then, also blamed German statism, bureaucratism, and welfarism for corrupting Anglo-American liberalism. His primary
complaint was that the German tradition, which encompassed, in different
ways, both Hegel and Bismarck, focused too heavily on the collective (embodied in the Prussian *Rechtsstaat*) and subjugated individual interests to the
larger nation.[35] Simons, like Hayek and Mises, saw a similar trend occurring
in the United States in the 1930s and 1940s, primarily brought about through
the policies of the New Deal.

The Enlightenment, Adam Smith, and Neoliberalism

Both intellectual and political neoliberals have always wanted to claim classical liberalism as their own. In place of the tradition of German statism, which
Hayek, Simons, and Popper had all criticized harshly, Hayek, Robbins, Simons, Mises, Popper, Friedman, Stigler, Coase, Buchanan, Hartwell, and their
colleagues, followers, and supporters claimed the heritage of Anglo-Scottish
Enlightenment liberalism. Yet neoliberalism departed from the classical political economy of the Scottish Enlightenment in its unambiguous view of the
free market and its effects. This difference makes any affirmed alliance between classical Enlightenment liberalism and neoliberalism deceptive.

The relationship of neoliberal ideas and Adam Smith especially, given
his status as conservative hero and father of modern economics, is significant because it helps reveal the distinctive character of neoliberalism and
its claims. If the nuanced economic theories of the various figures that have
been described so far in this book were sometimes at odds, a coherent intellectual and political strategy nevertheless emerged with force and clarity
in the postwar years. Neoliberal politics became unified around some basic
themes that were themselves transformed by the historical exigencies of the
mid-twentieth century. For example, a cold war of ideas began alongside the
military maneuvers and espionage of the United States and the Soviet Union
almost as soon as World War II ended, a contest that recast the relationship
between economic and political freedom in the minds of many leading think-

ers on the right and left. For neoliberals like Friedman, the Cold War necessitated the unambiguous advocacy of the superiority of the market. A robust historical tradition of economic liberty, which was suddenly identified with U.S.-style industrial capitalism, was felt to be essential. This need for a recognizable history led neoliberals to appeal to the authority of Smith and other Enlightenment figures, such as David Hume.

Such a linkage was appealing because it lent intellectual heft to theories that contradicted the political assumptions of the postwar period.[36] The supposed seamless line from Smith to Hayek and Friedman thus became a rhetorical strategy as much as a belief in the heritage itself. The placement of neoliberal ideas in a lineage that stretched back to the Enlightenment helped disguise where those ideas diverged, for example, in the crude Chicago emphasis on the near universal failures of government intervention. For Smith and Hume the market was a central dimension of eighteenth-century commercial society, a source of dynamism and social and economic change. But these Scottish writers were also ambivalent about these developments. Manners and morals, for Smith and Hume, were the necessary glue to hold a civilized society together amid economic transformation. The invisible hand of the market was not a straightforward concept, despite subsequent conservative portrayals otherwise. For Adam Smith, humans were motivated by a desire for security and good government, a desire that could not be reduced to pure self-interest or selfishness. Instead, as Nicholas Phillipson has argued, Smith perceived in humans "an aesthetic sensibility," which led people to pursue order and convenience for their own sake, "behaviour which Smith in one of his more poetical moments would attribute to the workings of the Invisible Hand."[37]

Time and again, though, neoliberal writers such as Hayek, Mises, Friedman, Coase, or Stigler emphasized the need to recover lost or forgotten truths—the value of individual liberty, the invisible hand of the free market, and the virtues of limited government—that had been lost in the headlong rush to collectivism. Hayek wrote in the first sentence of his magnum opus, *The Constitution of Liberty* (1960), "if old truths are to retain their hold on men's minds, they must be restated in the language and concepts of successive generations."[38] Neoliberal thinkers therefore often insistently repeated what (they thought) Adam Smith had always maintained: that freedom consisted in the individual liberty to engage in the marketplace voluntarily and

unhindered. In Smith, according to Friedman, the origins of the crucial connection of economic and political freedom were to be found. *The Wealth of
Nations* (1776) had, after all, introduced the new discipline of political economy. The state and the market had yet to become polar opposites.

A good example of the neoliberal discussion of Smith's classical liberalism
came in a series of retrospective papers prepared for the bicentennial of the
publication of *The Wealth of Nations* in 1976. Some were given at a conference held by the Mont Pelerin Society at St. Andrews in Scotland (Milton
Friedman, George Stigler, Ronald Coase, and Max Hartwell, among others,
gave papers). Friedman's approach to Smith, in these papers, provides an illuminating counterpoint to his essay on neoliberalism written twenty-five years
earlier. The later essays reveal a starker neoliberal philosophy than the one he
had professed in the early 1950s:

> Adam Smith was a revolutionary. He was attacking an entrenched sys-
> tem of governmental planning, control and intervention. His attack
> reinforced by social and economic changes ultimately succeeded, but
> not for some seventy years. By today we have come full circle back to
> the kind of arrangements that Adam Smith was attacking in 1776. His
> book is just about as pertinent an attack on our present structure of
> governmental control and intervention as it was on the structure of his
> time. We once again need a move away from that structure and toward
> that system of natural liberty Adam Smith favored.[39]

Smith, Friedman claimed, was "a radical and revolutionary in his time—just
as those of us who today preach laissez-faire are in our time." It is notable that
in 1976, Friedman is willing to describe himself as a defender of laissez-faire,
a philosophy that he had argued in 1951 was seriously flawed.[40] This new willingness to use laissez-faire reflected a change in the political and economic atmosphere in the 1970s. The goal of the eradication of unemployment had by
this time given way to the battle with inflation as the central policy aim in the
fight against stagflation. It was no longer so important for Friedman to claim
that his project was a reformulation of liberalism. By the 1970s, liberalism had
been discredited in the United States in many people's eyes, a reflection of
the perceived "excesses" of the 1960s and dissatisfaction with the economic
situation. Thus, although the use of the term laissez-faire shrouded new ele-

ments in Friedman's economic and political philosophy—a clearer sense of
the need to use the state to enforce the conditions for free markets and to
transfer economic power from government to corporations—he once again
felt comfortable using it as a shorthand for deregulation, tax cuts, and the introduction of market mechanisms into new spheres such as education as well
as industry.

Friedman's describes Smith as "a radical and revolutionary," a characterization that illustrates Friedman's own distinctive philosophy as one of impatient and active social and economic reform. It conflicts with conservative
interpreters of Smith who appropriated his thought and falsely conflated his
ideas with those of Edmund Burke by 1800. By the end of the nineteenth
century, the view of Smith as what Beatrice Webb in 1886 called the "Em-
ployers Gospel" had come to define Smith, along with Burke, as an economic
conservative.[41] This conservative view still colors his reputation today when
conservative politicians refer to Smith as a staunch proponent of the self-
interested man in the marketplace. The myth of Smith's popular reputation as
a conservative, or indeed as a proto-neoliberal, prompted scholars like Istvan
Hont, Michael Ignatieff, Andrew Skinner, and Emma Rothschild to place him
back in his proper eighteenth-century context.[42] Unlike with Edmund Burke,
it is not obvious where Smith stood on the French Revolution, the litmus test
of politics at the end of the eighteenth century (and beyond). There is also
evidence that he agreed with major elements of the Girondin program, but
this was buried by reactionary followers in the wake of the perceived excesses
of the revolution.[43]

Smith's view of the state and market is alien to most modern readers. According to Rothschild, Smith thought that markets "were established by
states, or imposed by them upon recalcitrant traders. States were great ram-
bling societies, which include the governments of parishes, guilds, incorpora-
tions, and established churches."[44] Smith's mental universe make it impossible
to interpret him as conceiving of markets as separate from government actions, and any view of Smith must be complemented by an appreciation of his
complex view of human morality. Rothschild writes of Smith's final revisions
to his *Theory of Moral Sentiments*:

> They are written in a tone of sometimes powerful indignation, as when
> Smith speaks, for example, of the "mean principle of national preju-

dice," or of the "corruption of our moral sentiments" which follows from the disposition almost to worship, the rich and powerful."[45]

Smith's resurrection as the quintessential conservative economist in the nineteenth century laid the ground, then, for the twentieth-century neoliberal assumption that he was also unproblematically theirs.[46]

There were three major and interconnected elements of Smith's thought that were important for neoliberalism. First, his argument in favor of the power of the free market was based, it was suggested, in human nature. Smith was crucial for his emphasis on concrete reality, humans as they really were. His description of economic life in *The Wealth of Nations* was not utopian; it was presented as a description of economic history. James Buchanan, a leader of public choice theory (see below), for example, understood Smith as the creator of the science of *is* as opposed to the philosophy of *ought*. He wrote to Hayek in 1966 about Smith:

> My tendency is always to think in terms of specific examples, and I was led by your argument to think of the implied normative ethics of Smith, an aspect that has never, to my knowledge, been properly discussed. To Adam Smith, man behaved in a certain way, and from this base, he constructed his theory. Turning your point around in one sense, we could say that this, in Smith, was really little different from saying that man "ought" to behave in this way, if certain social objectives were to be attained.[47]

The science of political economy, for Buchanan, amounted to the same thing as political and moral philosophy. The *is* was the *ought* in Smith, according to Buchanan. Smith's descriptive focus gave credence to the oft-repeated claim by supporters that capitalist society was a closer reflection of actual human behavior, as opposed to fantastical socialist or communist dreams of human benevolence, altruism, and generosity.

Ronald Coase picked up the point about human nature in his paper delivered at the 1976 Mont Pelerin Society conference on Adam Smith's view of man. Coase believed that Smith's conception of human nature did not lead to any conflict—what the Germans have famously referred to as "Das Adam Smith Problem" of reconciling *The Wealth of Nations* and *The Theory of Moral*

Sentiments. Recent scholarship has shown that the two are consistent. *Theory* was, alongside *Wealth of Nations*, another plank of what Phillipson has shown to be Smith's projected "Science of Man," a universal Enlightenment project of unprecedented ambition, which was meant to include history, aesthetics, and law, as well as ethics and economics.[48] With a slightly different twist, Coase also argued that Smith's multilayered view of man's nature laid out in *The Theory of Moral Sentiments* was perfectly compatible with the market economy of *Wealth of Nations*. But the depiction of Smith's view of man, as presented by Coase, is mostly grimly narcissistic. Coase wanted to show that, far from there being an Adam Smith problem, Smith's view of human nature was based in sympathy and benevolence *and* self-interest. Together, these traits bolster the case for the market:

> It is sometimes said that Adam Smith assumes that human beings are motivated solely by self-interest. Self-interest is certainly, in Adam Smith's view, a powerful motive in human behaviour but it is by no means the only motive. I think it is important to recognise this since the inclusion of other motives in his analysis does not weaken but rather strengthens Adam Smith's argument for the use of the market and the limitation of government action in economic affairs.[49]

According to Coase, benevolence was limited: it stemmed from Smith's understanding of sympathy as based in self-love. Thus, although Smith's notion of benevolence, for Coase, could be a motivating force behind human actions, "it is strongest within the family and that as we go beyond the family, friends neighbours and colleagues, and then to others who are none of these, the force of benevolence becomes weaker the more remote and casual the connection."[50]

On the other hand, the market required the interaction and cooperation "of multitudes" of perfect strangers who could not be expected to feel benevolent toward each other. Therefore, benevolence was useless. Instead, self-interest took over to ensure that this kind of cooperation occurred to the benefit of all:

> Looked at in this way, Adam Smith's argument for the use of the market for the organisation of economic activity is much stronger than it is

usually thought to be. The market is not simply an ingenious mechanism, fuelled by self-interest, for securing the cooperation of individuals in the production of goods and services. In most circumstances it is
the only way in which this could be done.[51]

Thus, for Coase, man's almost Swiftian nature—his self-obsession manifested
in his love for those who mirror most closely himself, his family, and his
selfishness, in terms of his pursuit of economic self-interest—was actually a
boon. Each element of human nature fitted together to produce the successful operation of the free market economy.

Coase's article is a sophisticated attempt to reconcile a more complex view
of Smith with a neoliberal view. He acknowledges that Smith's view of man
cannot be reduced to that of a rational utility-maximizer. But, in Coase's view,
incorporating as it did a rather bleak view of human benevolence, there was
still no space left for government or collective action to solve social or political problems:

> Nor does government regulation or operation represent a possible way
> out. A politician when motivated by benevolence, will tend to favour
> his family, his friends, members of his party, inhabitants of his region
> or country (and this whether or not he is democratically elected). Such
> benevolence will not necessarily redound to the general good. And
> when politicians are motivated by self-interest unalloyed by benevo-
> lence, it is easy to see that the results may be less satisfactory.

Instead, he sees the logic of the free market as in perfect tune with human
nature as it actually is, limited in its benevolence. For George Stigler, too,
Friedman's colleague at Chicago and economist of regulation, as he pointed
out in his paper on the successes and failures of Smith's economics, Smith
"put into the centre of economics the systematic analysis of the behavior of
individuals pursuing their self-interest under conditions of competition."[52]
This economic behavior reflected human nature, but our imperfections, far
from being devastating to us, were instead ordered, strained through the free
market sieve, toward constructive economic ends. Both Stigler and Coase appeared to ignore the fact that Smith did advocate government intervention

to deliver education and to address basic social needs, which reflected their partial reading of him.

The second element in Smith's thought of significance to the neoliberal rediscovery was his argument for progress arising from the free actions of self-interested individuals engaged in the marketplace as if by some Invisible Hand. Smith's famous statement of the idea of the invisible hand comes in book 4, chapter 2, of *The Wealth of Nations*. Here, Smith argued, the individual was

> led by an invisible hand to promote an end which was no part of his intention. Nor is it always the worse for the society that it was no part of it. By pursuing his own interest, he frequently promotes that of the society more effectually than when he really intends to promote it. I have never known much good done by those who affected to trade for the public good.[53]

The unintended effects of self-interested individuals and their actions in the market lay at the heart of the neoliberals' interpretation of Smith and their critique of government intervention, for it enabled them to argue that the grand utopian aims of socialists, social democrats and New Deal liberals were achievable, more efficiently, through private means. The market alone would ensure the most efficient allocation of resources.

Hayek's theory of the spontaneous power of markets drew heavily on Smith's idea of the invisible hand, as did Milton Friedman's various outpourings on the benefits of capitalist exchange. Coase also emphasized the unseen logic behind the various elements of human nature operating in harmony with the free market economy, as we have seen. Stigler took the implications of the idea even further by suggesting that Smith's argument for the invisible hand underlay the discipline of economics as a whole: "The proposition that resources seek their most profitable uses, so that in equilibrium the rates of return to a resource in various uses will be equal, is still the most important substantive proposition in all of economics."[54] (Stigler's view also goes some way to explain the ease with which neoliberalism has been reduced by some to mere neoclassical economics.)

The implication of Smith's invisible hand, in the neoliberal view, was that the state was unnecessary to the delivery of the "good life" because the market left alone would deliver it better. This also had become a central ideological claim on behalf of free market capitalism in the Cold War against totalitarian communism and its Western collectivist cousins. As Friedman put it in 1976,

> [The invisible hand] is a highly sophisticated and subtle insight. The market, with each individual going his own way, with no central authority setting social priorities, avoiding duplication, and coordinating activities, looks like chaos to the naked eye. Yet through Smith's eyes we see that it is a finely ordered and delicately tuned system, one which arises out of man's actions, yet is not deliberately created by man. It is a system which enables the dispersed knowledge and skill of millions of people to be coordinated for a common purpose.[55]

The influence of Hayek and Mises is readily apparent in this passage. Friedman suggests that the only efficient and practicable means of organizing information in a noncoercive way was through the price mechanism. Like Hayek, Friedman thought it impossible for government planning to substitute for the market, the job of organizing a free society. For example, in his Mont Pelerin paper on Smith, Friedman quotes *The Wealth of Nations* mockingly against Hubert Humphrey, Lyndon Johnson's vice president and the Democratic presidential candidate in 1968:

> "The statesman, who would attempt to direct private people in what manner they ought to employ their capital, would not only load himself with a most unnecessary attention, but assume an authority which could safely be trusted, not only to no single person, but to no council or senate whatever, and which would be nowhere so dangerous as in the hands of a man who had folly and presumption enough to fancy himself fit to exercise it." Has any contemporary political writer described Hubert Humphrey more accurately, or devastatingly?[56]

The specific reference was to the Humphrey-Hawkins Act of 1978, signed into law by President Carter, which marked a halting return to the tools of Keynesian economic management as a response to the crises of the 1970s (see chapter 6). Friedman's criticism is unsurprising, coming from someone who was an economic adviser, from the 1960s to the 1980s, to Barry

Goldwater and Presidents Nixon, Ford, and Reagan. With Hayek and Mises, Friedman believed that the claims of socialists, liberals, and progressives alike to know best how to achieve social progress and attend to economic needs were fatally hubristic. The socialist calculation debate, in which both Hayek and Mises had participated, had demonstrated a logic that Friedman agreed with. For the Austrians, planning, whether dirigiste or socialist, depended on impossible levels of knowledge on the part of the planner about social and economic preferences. At the same time, in order for planning decisions to be made successfully, conditions had to be static enough to avoid unintended consequences. For Hayek, Mises, and Friedman, this mix was a confused swirl of wrong-headed notions.

Belief in limited government is the third dimension of Smith's thought that was important for neoliberals. Again invoking the invisible hand, Friedman argued that where markets operated to generate the greater good despite the individual intentions of market actors, the situation in politics was reversed. The invisible hand at work in political life had a malevolent influence as the noble intentions of interventionists produced terrible outcomes. Smith had identified the culprit, Friedman argued, in the man of system who played with human beings as if arranging the different pieces on the chess board:

[Quoting the *Wealth of Nations*] "which have no other principle of motion besides that which the hand impresses upon them; but that, in the great chess-board of human society, every single piece has a principle of motion of its own, altogether different from that which the legislature might choose to impress upon it. If those two principles coincide and act in the same direction, the game of human society will go easily and harmoniously, and is very likely to be happy and successful. If they are opposite or different, the game will go on miserably, and the society must be at all times in the highest degree of disorder."

The failure to understand this profound observation has produced an invisible hand in politics that is the precise reverse of the invisible hand in the market. In politics, men who intend only to promote the public interest, as they conceive it, are "led by an invisible hand to promote an end which was no part of their intention." They become the front-men for special interests they would never knowingly serve. They end up sacrificing the public interest to the special interest, the interest of the consumers to that of producers, of the masses who never go to college to that of those who attend college, of the poor working-class saddled with employment taxes to the middle class who get disproportionate benefits from social security, and so down the line.[57]

Friedman is consciously thinking of his friend George Stigler's theory of regulation here, the idea that the regulators are captured by the regulated (see discussion below).

The irrational outcome of capture identified by Stigler, which is produced by the rational interactions of administrators with special interests, was central too in Friedman's thought. It is reflected in the idea that government, the collective, should not decide any more than is absolutely necessary on behalf of individuals, though the problem of when and where the precise limits were was exactly the difficulty that Keynes had identified in Hayek's *The Road to Serfdom* (1944). But such a system led only to market distortion at best, and more likely to corruption, according to Friedman. Thus, he always argued for tax cuts of any type—including, for example, the tax limitation amendment implied by Proposition 13 in California during the 1970s—because they reduced the amount government could spend of other people's money. According to Friedman, "enemies of freedom attribute all defects in the world to the market and all advances to beneficent governmental intervention. As Smith stresses, improvements have come in spite of, not because of, government intrusion into the marketplace."[58] But Friedman's and Hayek's interpretation of the invisible hand, as Rothschild suggests, missed the troubled cocktail implied in Smith's own thought—his ironic sense of detachment—and consequently misunderstood the resonance Smith himself intended. Self-interest did not imply selfishness for Smith, though he knew that is what selfish people imagined their self-interest to be. Enlightened self-interest, for Smith, on the other hand, came with moral cultivation and sympathy. The problem with these three components of the neoliberal interpretation of Smith is that they missed fundamental features of his corpus, and thus subsequent neoliberal ideas were erected on confused foundations. The neoliberals took Smith outside his time, place, and politics and reduced the grand scope of his thought to three principles.

Economic and Political Freedom: Milton Friedman and Cold War Neoliberalism

Friedman acknowledged the difficulties with Smith for his own brand of thought. He admitted that Smith had advocated for more government action than Friedman himself thought advisable. For example, Smith had proposed three appropriate functions for government. The first two—protection from invasion and the fair administration of justice, defense, and security—were unobjectionable. But the third, for Friedman, was problematic:

> The mischief is done by the third, "the duty of erecting and maintaining certain public works and certain public institutions, which it can never be for the interest of any individual, or small number of individuals, to erect and maintain; because the profit could never repay the expense to any individual or small number of individuals, though it may frequently do much more than repay it to a great society."
>
> This third duty is mischievous because on the one hand, properly interpreted, it does specify a valid function of government; on the other hand, it can be used to justify a completely unlimited extension of government. The valid element is the argument for government intervention from third party effects—or "external economies and diseconomies" in the technical lingo that has developed. If a person's actions impose costs or confer benefits on others for which it is not feasible; the third party effects are involuntary exchanges imposed on other persons.[59]

Friedman argued that Smith had misunderstood the nature and potential harm that "third party effects" could do to market processes. Here, like his mentor Simons, and Hayek in *The Constitution of Liberty* (1960), Friedman promotes a role for government and state action in the supervision of fair competition. But he argues that markets and governments have been judged by double standards:

> The major consideration that gives rise to significant third party effects of private actions is the difficulty of identifying the external costs and

benefits—if that were relatively easy, it would be possible to subject them to voluntary exchange. But this same consideration hinders government actions, making it hard to evaluate the net effects of external costs and benefits in taking supposedly corrective government action. In addition, governmental actions have further external effects, via its method of finance and via the danger to freedom from the expansion of government.

Perhaps the major intellectual fallacy in this area in the past century has been the double standard applied to the market and to political action. A market "defect"—whether through an absence of competition or external effects (equivalent as recent literature has made clear to transaction costs) has been regarded as immediate justification for government intervention. But the political mechanism has its "defects" too. It is fallacious to compare the actual market with the ideal political structure. One should either compare the real with the real or the ideal with the ideal. Unfortunately, Smith's working lends itself readily to this fallacy.[60]

But Smith was not thinking in terms of the twentieth-century New Deal state and its successes and failures, although he did go further than Friedman in his advocacy of public administrative action. He argued, for example, that government should take responsibility for education and infrastructure, something Friedman thought the market could operate through vouchers and competition between alternative providers.[61] Smith's conception of the moral individual, essential to his thought, Friedman avoided altogether. Smith was concerned that people's "disposition to admire the rich and the great, and to despise or neglect persons of poor and mean condition," led to "the corruption of our moral sentiments."[62] Friedman was concerned instead with the best environment in which individual liberty could operate securely. In other words, for Friedman, people could do what they wanted best in a free market society so long as it did not harm anyone else.

Morality was almost always absent in the writings of Hayek, Friedman, and Buchanan. In this sense, as a political philosophy neoliberal thought was fundamentally based in dry economic processes rather than values. Hayek defines freedom negatively in *The Constitution of Liberty*, as "that condition of men in which coercion of some by others is reduced as much as possible."[63]

Hayek certainly admired and paid homage to Anglo-American traditions of constitutionalism and the rule of law, but he was not, on the whole, concerned with individual behavior. Friedman constructed a radical individualism that saw the marketplace as the breeding ground of democratic and human rights. This dimension of his thought marks a radical break with the classical tradition of Smith and Hume, who were fundamentally republican, not democratic, in their orientation.

Neoliberal thought began, as we have seen, with a reductive reading of Adam Smith's premise of man as a rational, self-interested actor. Human liberty depended on the economic individual, whose freedom in the marketplace, in the neoliberal view, was commensurate with human freedom more generally.[64] From this basic idea, all other propositions followed. At root, Friedman, Hayek, Mises, Buchanan, and other neoliberal thinkers from the 1940s through to the 1970s and beyond have held a limited view of human nature—though the neoliberal view contained hints of the conservatism of Burke, especially in Hayek's thought. They believed that the only certain, observable part of that nature was that people operated according to their own interests to maximize their utility. As Friedman argued,

> The liberal conceives of men as imperfect beings. He regards the problem of social organisation to be as much a negative problem of preventing "bad" people from doing harm as enabling "good" people to do good; and, of course, "bad" and "good" people may be the same people, depending on who is judging them.[65]

The neoliberal conception of man as purely selfish is a caricature, though this was often the second-hand interpretation of their ideas which came later, as, for example, in the "greed is good" culture famously depicted in Oliver Stone's 1987 film, *Wall Street*. For Hayek and Friedman, men might be good and bad.

It is more accurate to say that for the neoliberal, the market is where prosperity is delivered most efficiently. As Mises put it in a letter to Hayek in which he commented on his plans to set up the Mont Pelerin Society in 1946,

> Laissez-faire does not mean: let the evils last. It means: let the consumers, i.e. the people, decide—by their buying and by their abstention from buying what should be produced and by whom. The alternative

to laissez-faire is to entrust these decisions to a paternal government. There is no middle way. Either the consumers are supreme or the government.[66]

(This passage is typical of Mises—he flatly rejects any idea that neoliberalism could be a "middle way," as Friedman had suggested in his 1951 essay.) A crucial dimension of the neoliberal idea is revealed in this passage: the marketplace is the primary arena in which freedom is experienced and expressed. It is also where consumers manifest their wishes—the things for which there is a demand get made and delivered and things that are not good enough or desirable enough wither away and die. Government, aside from its primary duty to protect the physical safety of the citizenry, should be limited to the supervision of competitive and thriving markets. For it is here that people make their most *real* choices, unencumbered by good intentions. The explicit linkage of political with economic freedom here was forceful and of a different order than the relationship implied by Smith, who always had a sense of the possibility that *sometimes at least* people may not know what they want and that at other times, the fact that a market delivered what people wanted underpinned an unfortunate and undesirable herd mentality.

Ludwig von Mises had the more accurate perspective on Smith in terms of his relationship to neoliberal ideas, however. He agreed that Smith was an important figure whose legacy was carried forward by neoliberals. But he had no illusions about the limits of Smith's relevance to the middle of the twentieth century (this passage also reveals some of Mises' fiery sense of injustice at not being recognized by the mainstream economics profession). Mises in his 1952 introduction to *The Wealth of Nations* issued a warning:

Nobody should believe that he will find in Smith's inquiry information about present-day economics or about present-day problems of economic policy. Reading Smith is no more a substitute for studying economics than reading Euclid is a substitute for the study of mathematics. It is at best a historical introduction into the study of modern ideas and policies. Neither will the reader find in the *Wealth of Nations* a refutation of the teachings of Marx, Veblen, Keynes, and their followers. It is one of the tricks of the socialists to make people believe that there are no other writings recommending economic freedom than those of eighteenth-century authors and that in their, of course, unsuccessful attempts to refute Smith they have done all that is needed to prove the correctness of their own point of view. Socialist professors withheld from their students—not only in the countries behind the Iron Curtain—any knowledge about the existence of contemporary economists who deal with the problems concerned in an unbiased scientific way and have devastatingly exploded the spurious schemes of all brands of socialism and interventionism. If they are blamed for their partiality, they protest their innocence. "Did we not read in class some chapters of Adam Smith?" they retort. In their pedagogy the reading of Smith serves as a blind for ignoring all sound contemporary economics.

Read the great book of Smith. But don't think that this may save you the trouble of seriously studying modern economic books. Smith sapped the prestige of eighteenth-century government controls. He does not say anything about the controls of 1952 and about the Communist challenge.[67]

The Cold War context roundly evoked here by Mises—an important theme that will be explored in more detail presently—was also central to the development of transatlantic neoliberalism.

Smith's legacy was also used and abused by politicians such as Margaret Thatcher. A myth of eternal verities first articulated by Smith, restated by the classical liberal and English politician John Stuart Mill (though only in *On Liberty*), rediscovered and understood by Hayek, and adapted by Friedman, was propagated. The myth was mutually reinforcing. It helped convey an impression of philosophical depth on the part of the politicians, and it flattered the intellectual egos of neoliberal academics, who claimed Smith, making them feel politically important and part of a rich canon. But in the actual relationship between the ideas of Friedman, Buchanan, Hayek, Mises and those of Adam Smith, as opposed to this mythical one, it has been possible to see some of what was new about neoliberalism. It was a virulent faith in the individual and his economic behavior under market conditions rather than any conception of cultivated behavior, manners, or Smithian moral sympathy that was important to neoliberal thinkers. Moral behavior was not usually considered relevant (though later Reaganite and Thatcherite policies and rhetoric revived certain age-old moral tropes, these had nothing to do with neoliberal free market economics). For the neoliberal theorists, market processes generated a flourishing freedom and prosperity, which individuals could do with as they willed. Transatlantic neoliberalism, unlike Smith's liberalism, was generated out of a different set of historical forces, by the Cold War, the New and Fair Deals, the postwar Labour governments of Clement Attlee, and a belief in the rising collectivist tide. These worries led neoliberal writers, from a belief in the link between free markets and democracy and human freedom, to articulate their faith in individual liberty in apocalyptic terms as a struggle between free societies and communist totalitarianism.

Friedman's significant contribution to neoliberal thought was his connection of economic freedom with political freedom, published in *Capitalism and Freedom* (1962). This went beyond Mises' belief in the market as the arena in which humans express themselves. Friedman suggested that the common division of the economic and political spheres was false:

> It is widely believed that politics and economics are separate and largely unconnected; that individual freedom is a political problem and material welfare an economic problem; and that any kind of political arrangements can be combined with any kind of economic arrangements. The chief contemporary manifestation of this idea is the advocacy of "democratic socialism" by many who condemn out of hand the restrictions on individual freedom imposed by "totalitarian socialism" in Russia and who are persuaded that it is possible for a country to adopt the essential features of Russian economic arrangements and yet to ensure individual freedom through political arrangements.[68]

Friedman's book had eventually realized the wish of Harold Luhnow of the WVF for an American *Road to Serfdom*.

Friedman's belief was that an economy free from government intervention meant that political power was divorced from economic power. The market, for example, protected the ability to dissent:

> In a capitalist society, it is only necessary to convince a few wealthy people to get funds to launch any idea, however strange, and there are many such persons, many independent foci of support. And, indeed, it is not even necessary to persuade people or financial institutions with

available funds of the soundness of the ideas to be propagated. It is only necessary to persuade them that the propagation can be financially successful; that the newspaper or magazine or book or other venture will be profitable. The competitive publisher, for example, cannot afford to publish only writing with which he personally agrees; his touchstone must be the likelihood that the market will be large enough to yield a satisfactory return on his investment.[69]

Commerce and the profit motive allowed anyone to push a political agenda, regardless of the proprietors' agreement with its content. The only consideration for the owner was whether or not the writer could pay. The market guaranteed basic political freedoms by ensuring that alternatives were always available. For example, the existence of a private market economy, according to Friedman, was a protection during McCarthyism because accused government employees had an alternative to public employment where they could not be persecuted in the same way.[70]

The free market also provided a barrier to the worst kinds of discrimination and prejudice. The market is an impersonal force that guarantees equality to all because it "separates economic activities from political views and protects men from being discriminated against in their economic activities for reasons that are irrelevant to their productivity—whether these reasons are associated with their views or their color."[71]

As already noted, Friedman argued that the imperfections of free market capitalism were unfairly compared with the utopian ideal of a socialist or communist alternative. This was due, according to Friedman, to the prevailing attitudes of the 1920s and 1930s, when liberal and progressive intellectuals in the United States were caught up in the wave of optimism surrounding the establishment of Soviet communism in Russia at the same time as the stock market crash seemed to indicate the demise of capitalism. According to Friedman,

> The attitudes of that time are still with us. There is still a tendency to regard any existing government intervention as desirable, to attribute all evils to the market, and to evaluate new proposals for government control in their ideal form, as they might work as if run by able, disinterested men, free from the pressure of special interest groups. The

proponents of limited government and free enterprise are still on the defensive.[72]

Friedman spent little time reflecting on any alleged market failures (devoting instead a large slice of his academic efforts and reputation to exonerating the market for the devastation caused by the Great Depression in *A Monetary History of the United States*, written with Anna Jacobsen Schwartz and published in 1963, a year after *Capitalism and Freedom*—discussed in chapter 5).

The experience of government failure in the United States and the West was the key point for Friedman in *Capitalism and Freedom*. It was indicative of the Chicago emphasis on the need for theory to be backed by empirical proof. The failures of state intervention as witnessed, according to Friedman, in the decades after the New Deal enabled people to compare "the actual with the actual." For Friedman, the evidence of government failure served as a call to arms in the Cold War:

> Wrote Marx and Engels in *The Communist Manifesto*: "The proletarians have nothing to lose but their chains. They have a world to win." Who today can regard the chains of the proletarians in the Soviet Union as weaker than the chains of the proletarians in the United States, or Britain or France or Germany or any Western state?[73]

So he didn't confine his argument to the Soviet Union. Friedman expanded his list of examples to include what he saw as the follies of the Progressives, the New Deal, and the postwar policies of both Democratic and Republican administrations—railroad regulation, income tax, monetary reform, agricultural subsidies, public housing, labor law, and social security legislation.

Friedman also pointed to foreign aid, public power projects, and urban redevelopment programs as areas of government expansion in which the state had at best missed its targets and at worst done great harm:

> The greater part of the new ventures undertaken by government have failed to achieve their objectives. The United States has continued to progress; its citizens have become better fed, better clothed, better housed, and better transported; class and social distinctions have narrowed; minority groups have become less disadvantaged; popular cul-

ture has advanced by leaps and bounds. All this has been the product of the initiative and drive of individuals co-operating through the free market. Government measures have hampered not helped this development. We have been able to afford and surmount these measures only because of the extraordinary fecundity of the market. The invisible hand has been more potent for progress than the visible hand for retrogression.[74]

But a restoration of the presumption against intervention and government action was required if future progress was to be guaranteed. Economic freedom must be assured if political and other freedoms were to remain intact:

The preservation and expansion of freedom are today threatened from two directions. The one threat is obvious and clear. It is the external threat coming from the evil men in the Kremlin who promise to bury us. The other threat is far more subtle. It is the internal threat coming from men of good intentions and good will who wish to reform us.[75]

Throughout *Capitalism and Freedom*, like Hayek in *The Road to Serfdom*, Friedman is at pains to make the link between the good intentions of Western policymakers and Soviet communist totalitarianism to the east insistent and explicit. His two-front strategy consistently identifies New Deal liberalism with socialism and even communism, and suggests that his own ideas belong to the lineage of classical liberalism. The Cold War of ideas is waged through association—just as the McCarthyism of which he was tepidly critical.

Instead of government intervention, both Friedman and Hayek advocated free market solutions to the most intractable policy problems in *Capitalism and Freedom* and *The Constitution of Liberty*. In *The Constitution of Liberty*, published in 1960, Hayek examines most of the major social and economic issues: the welfare state, labor unions, social security, taxation, monetary policy, housing and town planning, agriculture and natural resources, education, and research.[76] Hayek advocates, for example, the abolition of agricultural subsidy and right-to-work laws. Similarly, in *Capitalism and Freedom*, Friedman treats money, international finance, taxation, monopoly, business and labor, education, welfare, and poverty. Here, for example, Friedman argues for the privatization of Social Security and the abolition of trade tariffs. Most famously, and tenaciously, Friedman was a lifelong campaigner for a school vouchers program and the establishment of a market in elementary and secondary education because he thought it would drive down costs, increase efficiency, and ensure the delivery of better education to those who were poorly served by public education.

This belligerent element in Friedman's thought, the sense that the war of ideas between socialism and free market capitalism was a life-or-death struggle, is most obviously explained by the fervid atmosphere of Cold War politics. Academics were active combatants in the perceived apocalyptic global fight between two alternative visions of society. For example, when James Buchanan, one of Friedman's students at the University of Chicago in the late 1940s, applied for a job as an economist at the Federal Reserve, Friedman was asked to provide a reference. In a passage typical of the period, the Federal Reserve posed the question:

> Do you have any information indicating that the applicant is now or has ever been a member of any organization which advocates the overthrow of our constitutional form of Government in the United States or that there is any reason to question his loyalty to the United States.

Friedman replied:

> I do not know anything about the organizations he belongs to; but I do know that he is completely and unquestionably loyal to the United States and the American way of life. He is a strong believer in the virtues of a free market, free enterprise, free price economy, and a strong opponent of any extension of government interference with the activities of individuals. These sentiments are, of course, fundamentally opposed to those of socialism or communism.
>
> Buchanan is one of the ablest students we have had at Chicago since I have been here. He will unquestionably be a distinct asset to you if you can persuade him to join your staff.[77]

Neoliberal intellectuals, in particular economic and political theorists, felt themselves foot-soldiers in the fight against communism. *Capitalism and Freedom* marked a deliberate attempt by Friedman to enter the fray.

It should be added here that this dimension of neoliberal thought—the dependence of democratic and political freedom on economic freedom—also provided a foundation for neoconservative U.S. foreign policy in relation to the Eastern bloc, especially Poland, and the Soviet Union under Ronald Reagan, for example, during the last years of the Cold War in the 1980s. It also underpinned the arguments of figures such as Deputy Defense Secretary Paul Wolfowitz and UN Ambassador John Bolton during the second Iraq war (2003) when they argued that a democratic Iraq would help provide a beacon of freedom in the Middle East. In another troubled example, Friedman condemned the bloody violence in 1989 in Tiananmen Square but was not perturbed by the problem that political repression and undeveloped democracy in China might pose for his arguments about the political power of free markets. He suggested that Communist China, since Deng Xiaoping's market reforms, had become significantly freer. He also pointed to the successes of the East Asian "tiger economies" and the former Soviet bloc countries in Eastern Europe as evidence for the intimate connection between capitalism and freedom: "In all those cases, in accordance with the theme of this book, increases in economic freedom have gone hand in hand with increases in political and civil freedom and have led to increased prosperity; competitive capitalism and freedom have been inseparable."[78]

These arguments have been extremely influential both in terms of academic debates and in terms of economic and foreign policies in the West after 1970. They are also indicative of the radical nature of neoliberalism in its third and internationally influential phase. Free markets and liberal democracy went together and could not be separated, according to Friedman. This case was most triumphantly made by Francis Fukuyama after the collapse of the Berlin Wall.[79] Such theses help to explain the shift in attitudes toward state and market that have transformed the world in the last third of the twentieth century.

The German Economic Miracle: Neoliberalism and the Soziale Marktwirtschaft

The political philosophy put into practice in Germany after World War II was a second source of neoliberal inspiration. The economic policies of Christian Democratic German chancellors Konrad Adenauer and Ludwig Erhard (who was first Adenauer's finance minister) were founded on the ideas of a group of thinkers known collectively as the Freiburg school. This group, some of whose members escaped Germany during the Third Reich while others stayed, referred to their ideas, which were developed in the interwar period, as neoliberal.[80] The relative success of this project in restoring the health of the German economy, in combination with American Marshall Plan aid, became a propaganda success for the West—the United States and Western Europe—in the Cold War.

Under Adenauer and Erhard, war-ravaged Germany experimented with free markets as an alternative to the totalitarianism of the right and left that had destroyed Germany and then divided Europe. This approach, the "social market economy" of the German "economic miracle" of the 1950s, mirrored many of the themes that had been outlined by Friedman in his 1951 essay. This was no accident, in light of the interaction of the Chicagoans and the Germans in the Mont Pelerin Society after 1947. But the German neoliberals saw themselves as defenders of the utility and efficiency of free markets, complemented by an awareness of, and desire to achieve, social justice. In this concern for social justice, their ideas were also clearly similar to those propounded by Henry Simons at the University of Chicago in the 1930s. But this emphasis on the need for a social safety net was something that the second Chicago School left behind after 1950 (unless it could be delivered more efficiently and at a profit through the private market).

The origins of the *Soziale Marktwirtschaft* lay in the thought of German economists and legal theorists of the interwar period, such as Wilhelm Röpke, Walter Eucken, Franz Bohm, and Alfred Müller-Armack (who coined the term "social market economy").[81] As Carl Friedrich, the Harvard political scientist and Nazi exile, commented at the time,

> The key slogan is the "social market economy" (*Soziale Mark-twirtschaft*), an economy which is definitely "free," as compared with a directed and planned economy, but which is subjected to controls, preferably in legal form, designed to prevent the concentration of economic power, whether through cartels, trusts, or giant enterprise.[82]

Also known in Germany as ordoliberalism (because of its association with the German journal *Ordo*, founded by Walter Eucken and Franz Bohm in 1948), neoliberalism was distinguished from both classical liberalism and nineteenth-century laissez-faire approaches.[83] Instead, as with Simons, the state was expected to play a central role in ensuring the conditions for fair competition in the economy. The German ordoliberals saw the state as intimately involved with economic life. Friedrich again:

> The neo-liberals see economics as "embedded" in politics, and are convinced that economic and political systems are interrelated. In a very striking study concerning this relationship, Franz Böhm, one of the leading thinkers of the neo-liberal movement, comes to the conclusion that a market is an economic form of a political democracy.[84]

This is fascinating when placed alongside Mises' claims about the role of the consumer in the market. The German neoliberals referred to Mises as a paleoliberal because they thought of him as an unreconstructed defender of laissez-faire.[85] The key difference was that the economic benefits of competition as guaranteed by the state were to be balanced by the need to address social problems. The way was left open for a robust welfare state (which allowed the German Social Democrats to sign up to the neoliberal approach through the Godesberg program of 1959).[86]

Hayek's relationship with German neoliberalism was more complicated— surprisingly, perhaps, given his close connection to Mises. For example, he wrote for *Ordo*, the movement's main journal, served on its editorial board, and was sometimes associated with the Freiburg school. But Hayek was much more critical of the state's role in the economy than most of the other German neoliberals. His association with them, however, also stemmed from the close involvement of some of the German neoliberals with the Mont Pelerin Society. Of the social market economists, Röpke, Eucken, Erhard, Müller-Armack, Bohm, H. Ilau, K. Friedrich Maier, and A. Rustow were all members by 1951.[87] According to Max Hartwell, historian and fellow society member, "Hayek believed that it was Röpke's influence that, in the German-speaking part of Europe, had been the most important for the existence of a neo-liberal movement beyond the circle of specialists in the universities."[88]

German neoliberalism attracted the attention of American observers aside from Friedrich. For example, there was a feature on the "social market economy" in a special bulletin of the American Institute for Economic Research, based at the Massachusetts Institute of Technology, in 1959. The report was read in the Nixon White House and is found among the papers of the White House Central Staff.[89] In the bulletin, subtitled "Research Report on Ludwig Erhard's Achievements," the authors describe German neoliberalism as the philosophy of "Eucken, Röpke and Erhard." The report identifies the strong role reserved for the state in policing the market as the novelty of Erhard's approach as finance minister:

> Thus, the "newness" of Neoliberalism consists to a large extent in a new appreciation of the positive role of the State in creating the legislative, juridical, and monetary framework necessary to a viable market economy.[90]

The policies it identifies with Erhard—the abolition of price controls, currency stability and battling inflation, antitrust laws, and a "war on special interests"—could equally well be attributed to Hayek or Friedman (with the exception of the currency issue, on which Friedman was always an advocate of floating exchange rates, and antitrust, on which he came to believe that legislation was unnecessary).[91]

The MIT report also misleadingly suggests that the German neoliberals rejected the welfare state, something that does not tally with the German emphasis on social welfare. (It is also unlikely that Friedman and Hayek would have agreed that the "State must be in ultimate control of economic policy rather than businesses or industries.")[92] The more favorable view of the state was highlighted in the *Bulletin:*

> The Neoliberal has enormous respect for the market as the only mechanism by which an advanced industrial society can solve its economic problem and yet preserve its liberty. But he also knows that the borders of the "civitas humana" extend far beyond the market, that the market is really only a means to an end. If he has an axe to grind it is in behalf of human freedom.[93]

The ordoliberal approach to the "social question," in similar fashion to Bismarck's introduction of pensions in the 1870s, was primarily conservative. As Ralf Ptak has shown, the basic approach "had a greater affinity with conservative than with classical liberal positions." The motivation was classically conservative: "stability and security for the working class was prerequisite to securing the market economy," a program that "fundamentally differed from left-wing calls for egalitarian redistribution."[94]

The closeness between the German approach and that of Henry Simons, economist of the first Chicago school of the 1930s and 1940s, illustrates the origins of neoliberalism in different and earlier contexts and debates than those of the postwar United States. The similarity between Simons and the German originators of the social market economy during the 1930s reveals other ways in which the neoliberalism of Friedman, with his emphasis on market solutions to social problems in place of a government-run welfare state, moved in a more immoderate direction than many of his European friends and colleagues in the Mont Pelerin Society between the 1950s and the 1970s. First, through their pioneering emphasis on the social question and the relationship between the legal and competitive orders, according to Ptak, the German neoliberals deserve enormous credit in "acknowledging the destructive potential of the market economy."[95] This dynamic and devastating power of capitalism was rarely acknowledged, for its negative effects at least, by Friedman and Hayek. Second, Simons shared with the Germans a strong belief in the importance of antimonopoly, or antitrust, something that Friedman, Aaron Director, and Edward Levi, the law school dean who participated in the WVF-funded Chicago Free Market Study project on monopoly during the late 1940s and 1950s, all rejected.[96] In contrast to Germany and other parts of Europe, the different historical, cultural, and geographic traits of the United States, especially its deep-rooted cultural obsession with the rugged individualism of the frontier, also played their part in generating these different emphases and made the country fertile ground for a more radicalized version of neoliberal political theory.

The German example had a powerful formative effect on British observers, too, in part because it represented the first successful political experimentation with neoliberal ideas. John Hoskyns, the future head of Margaret Thatcher's Policy Unit between 1979 and 1982, recounted that "the great [Ludwig] Erhard" had abolished the imposed Allies' currency and created the Deutschmark in the face of the opposition of the occupying authorities in June 1948. Adenauer's Christian Socialist government lasted from 1949 to 1963, and then Erhard replaced Adenauer as chancellor until 1966. He suggested that Erhard was an inspiration because he had "opened the whole economy with no [economic or trade] protection[s]."[97] Geoffrey Howe and Nigel Lawson, future chancellors of the exchequer under Thatcher, were also both influenced by the German model. Howe "became aware" of the "social market economy" and intrigued by the combination of free markets and the social market, a concern he identified with the "One Nation" Toryism that was being rediscovered and redefined in 1950s Britain by radical young Conservatives (see next chapter).[98] Lawson said that the features of the two economies that he admired most during the 1950s and 1960s were the "dynamism" of the United States and the "Erhard settlement" in West Germany.[99] Norman Lamont, another future Conservative chancellor, echoed these sentiments.[100]

Regulatory Capture, Public Choice, and Rational Choice Theory

These disparate developments—the growth of neoliberal ideas and the practical application of neoliberal policies in the United States and Germany in the postwar years, which built on the work that had been done in the 1930s and 1940s in Austria, Germany, Switzerland, France, and Britain—had by the end of the 1950s created a recognizable body of thought. The connection of liberty with the market, rationality, and self-interest provided fertile terrain for other scholars to expand neoliberal ideas in new directions. The third current of ideas in the development of political neoliberalism in the 1950s and 1960s in the United States was also dominated by Chicago-influenced scholars.

George Stigler, first at Columbia University and then at the University of Chicago after 1958, and James Buchanan and Gordon Tullock, both Chicago-trained economists whose academic base was at the Virginia Polytechnic Institute (and later at George Mason University in Fairfax, the so-called Virginia school of political economy), extended the analysis of man as a utility-maximizing individual into the realms of politics, government bureaucracy, and regulation through their elaboration of public choice theory and "constitutional economics" in the 1960s. Another group of scholars led by William Riker at the University of Rochester developed rational choice as a new methodology in political science at the same time. Together, these two groups posited that politics, government, and the public sector should not be considered apart from the rest of the economy. Instead, according to these writers, politics and government formed an arena in which the same principles and incentives applied as those that were relevant to the market and the wider economy. Other economists, such as Peter Bauer at the LSE and the University of Chicago's Gary Becker, the 1992 Nobel Laureate in Economics, extended the logic to, for example, international aid and development policies, and sociological human behavior such as the family.[101] These new forays forged an extension of neoliberal economic principles into spaces that had hitherto been analyzed from very different perspectives. They also helped the neoliberal view of free markets seep into mainstream public and political consciousness.

George Stigler, according to a later director of the IEA, John Blundell, was the most influential neoliberal thinker in Britain, together with Friedman and Hayek. He was considered the joint leader of the second Chicago school of economics.[102] Born in Seattle in 1911, Stigler was Friedman's contemporary and great friend. His PhD work was supervised by Frank Knight, and he, too, was influenced by Henry Simons. He earned his doctorate in 1938 from the University of Chicago but began teaching there only in the late 1950s, after serving during the war on the Manhattan Project to develop the atom bomb and later as a faculty member at Columbia University. Stigler, like Friedman, worked regularly throughout his career with think tanks in Britain, with the London-based IEA, as well as in the United States, and advised presidents and politicians. Another Nobel Prize winner, in 1982, Stigler is most famous for his contribution of an economic theory of regulation, which became an important dimension of public choice theory in the 1960s.

Stigler pointed out that the state was a source of resources for which control, industries, and firms competed for. In a paper sent to President Nixon in 1971 summarizing his thesis, he argued that two basic assumptions underlying analyses of government regulation were wrong.[103] The first was the belief that regulation operated in the wider public interest. The second was

> essentially that the political process defies rational explanation: "politics" is an imponderable, a constantly and unpredictably shifting mixture of forces of the most diverse nature, comprehending great acts of moral virtue (the emancipation of the slaves) and of the most vulgar venality (the congressman feathering his own nest).[104]

These two common ideas about regulation, according to Stigler, lacked the explanatory power of a "profit-maximizing" methodology. For Stigler, the problem of regulation was one of "discovering when and why an industry (or other group of like-minded people) is able to use the state for its purposes, or is singled out by the state to be used for alien purposes."[105]

Stigler argued that firms in particular industries sought four things from state regulation, all of which would enhance profitability. The first of these was direct public subsidy to a particular sector through cash grants or bailouts. The second was the control of the market entry of new competitors through, for example, protective tariffs. The third was the encouragement of complementary products or the suppression of substitute products: as Stigler put it, "the butter producers wish to suppress margarine and encourage the production of bread."[106] "The fourth class of public policies" desired by industry had to do with price fixing.[107] These four types of regulation, in the state's gift because of its monopoly of coercive force, were most often pursued through legislation, or sometimes through occupational licensing that helped write oligopolistic, monopolistic, or exclusionary rules. At the core of Stigler's theory was the notion of "regulatory capture," the proposition that regulation would be dominated by the interests of the regulated. As such, ideas of neutral public administration and government acting in the public interest should be treated with skepticism:

> The idealistic view of public regulation is deeply imbedded in professional economic thought. So many economists, for example, have denounced the ICC [Interstate Commerce Commission] for its pro-railroad policies that this has become a cliché of the literature. This criticism seems to me exactly as appropriate as a criticism of the Great Atlantic and Pacific Tea Company for selling groceries, or as a criticism of a politician for currying popular support. The fundamental vice of such criticism is it misdirects attention. It suggests that the way to get an ICC which is not subservient to the carriers is to preach to the commissioners or to the people who appoint the commissioners. The only way to get a different commission would be to change the political support for the Commission, and reward commissioners on a basis unrelated to their services to the carriers.

> Until the basic logic of political life is developed, [regulatory] re-
> formers will be ill-equipped to use the state for their reforms, and
> victims of the pervasive use of the state's support for special groups
> will be helpless to protect themselves. Economists should quickly
> establish the license to practice on the rational theory of political
> behaviour.[108]

He ends this passage with a joke, but his thesis was serious and managed to
change understanding of the regulatory process. Stigler's thesis was one of the
most important contributions to the field of public choice theory and challenged the efficacy and benefits that the social democratic reformist approach
to capitalism was supposed to achieve.

Public choice theory was first developed in the 1940s and 1950s. Duncan
Black's theory of the median voter (1948), Kenneth Arrow's impossibility
theorem (1951), Anthony Downs's *Economic Theory of Democracy* (1958),
and Mancur Olsen's free-rider problem (1965) are all important founda-
tional ideas in the field of public choice.[109] Rational choice was a related field
that shared many of the same assumptions of the public choice theorists, including especially the work of William Riker and his followers.[110] Rational
choice theory grew out of economics through its acceptance of basic micro-
economic method, which assumes that individuals try to maximize their utility in a given, stable environment. The unifying current in all these ideas was
the relevance of rational self-interest to politics, elections, and state or local
government activity—a much more simple and reductive notion of human
motivation than is seen in Enlightenment economics, or even the early writings of Hayek or Popper.

James Buchanan and Gordon Tullock are considered the "fathers of public
choice" through the publication of their jointly authored book, *The Calculus of
Consent*, in 1962 and the establishment of a research program at the Virginia
Polytechnic Institute.[111] The book was a "formalization of the structure that
James Madison had in mind when he constructed the U.S. Constitution."[112]
Buchanan, yet another winner of the Nobel Prize in Economics (1986), described the "hardcore" in public choice as "(1) methodological individualism, (2) rational choice, and (3) politics-as-exchange."[113] The rationale for its
emergence is described by Buchanan:

As they emerged from World War II, governments, even in Western democracies, were allocating between one third and one-half of their total product through collective-political institutions rather than through markets. Economists, however, were devoting their efforts almost exclusively to explanations-understandings of the market sector. No attention was being paid to political-collective decision making. Practitioners in political science were no better. They had developed no explanatory basis, no theory as it were, from which operationally falsifiable hypotheses might be derived.[114]

Rational choice theory and public choice theory stepped into this breach.

Buchanan and Tullock emphasized the imperfections of the political institutions and agents, the constitutional mechanisms and the voters who, they argued, would compete for their interests just like an individual in the marketplace. Also members of the Mont Pelerin Society, they were deeply involved in the transatlantic neoliberal network and wrote regularly on British policy issues. Buchanan served as a contributing editor to IEA publications. He was involved with the institute's journal and sat on the board, and wrote a number of reports and pamphlets for the institute, including *The Economics of Politics* (1978), in which he laid out the basic principles of the Virginia school's approach to constitutional economics for a British audience. The potential of this field, as Buchanan saw it, lay in "constructing, or re-constructing, a political order that will channel the self-serving behaviour of participants towards the common good in a manner that comes as close as possible to that described by Adam Smith with respect to the economic order."[115]

It was essential for policymakers to work with the grain of human nature—with human self-interest—to avoid the distorted outcomes that Friedman had suggested were likely when the invisible hand worked in reverse. Buchanan was especially interested in the link between economic issues such as taxation and the U.S. Constitution, which had enshrined the separation of powers as its core principle, and a pet project of his was decrying the lack of any "genuinely constitutional analysis in Britain."[116] By this, Buchanan meant that the British parliamentary system lacked proper checks and balances on its authority; it was an elected dictatorship. Perhaps surprisingly, Buchanan and Tullock felt close to the work of John Rawls, the liberal theorist of social justice. But their main political preoccupation was working out how to use constitutional mechanisms to limit state intervention, taxation, and spending. As Buchanan put it in a letter to Hayek in 1965, "public choice" was "politics without the romance":[117]

> It has always been of interest to me how the two parts of the older political economy diverged in this respect. Economics was developed strictly as a science of the "is," as a predictive theory. Politics, by sharp contrast, developed strictly as a science of the "ought," of political obligation, of the obligation of the individual, the norms that he should follow if the social order is to survive. Recently, some of us have tried to extend the economic methodology to politics, but, perhaps of equally neglected importance, is the reverse. That is, the extension of some theory of obligation into economics, or at least some clarification of these murky regions. By this I do not mean to say that we can get very far from accepting the way men do, in fact, behave, when confronted with different alternatives. But we must, I think, also recognise that behavior is conditioned, to a degree, by prevailing rules of conduct, and that these can vary, within limits, from one social group to another. Self-interest within limits: this is the implied ethics of the market place. Does not this suggest some of the troubles with, say, England, today, where, really, the ethics of "fair shares" have become a part of the whole culture? Here it seems to me, we could say that the rules of conduct upon which individuals behave have become precisely those which do not insure group survival, if we measure survival in the standard terms of economics. At least this is one aspect of the problem. Those rules that would insure the attainment of group objectives become those of the deviants.[118]

Buchanan wrote, "Constitutional rules have as their central purpose the imposition of limits on the potential exercise of political authority."[119] This public choice notion applied to politics was very similar to the idea of the state's role as the guarantor of a competitive framework to govern the market in the work of Simons, Friedman, and the German neoliberals. The aim was to set the rules for limited government.

In the 1950s and 1960s, neoliberal thought established a distinct and coherent identity. Its basic concerns—individual liberty, free markets, spontaneous order, the price mechanism, competition, consumerism, deregulation, and rational self-interest—had come together in the ideas of a group of European and American economists and philosophers who developed a radical individualism that broke with the liberalisms of the past, be they classical, nineteenth-century German, or early twentieth-century British or American. They saw themselves fighting the Cold War and defending their vision of the free society. Their ideas were in direct opposition to the dominant political projects of the 1950s and 1960s as well: JFK's New Frontier, LBJ's Great Society, and Harold Wilson's attempted renewal of British social democracy. Friedman, Stigler, Buchanan, and Tullock would become the intellectual standard-bearers of a new political and economic movement in the 1970s, transatlantic neoliberal politics.

Inherent in this set of ideas, however, was a set of uneasy tensions that would create problems in their interpretation, application, and justification in politics and policy in the government policies of the 1970s and 1980s. First, competition and equality of opportunity sat more comfortably together in neoliberal theory than they did in the knotty problems of the distribution of government resources. Second, the evisceration of the idea of a robust public interest or sphere, implied by Chicago economics and public choice theory, may have provided an insight into the workings of some types of public administration, but it simultaneously undermined the bases of democratic authority by exposing the problems of bureaucracy. Public officials would not necessarily service the public good. Instead, public and government institutions could develop their own identities and interests. Third, the individual's role in the market as a consumer conflicted with her role as a citizen in Friedman's, Hayek's, and Mises' ideas about the link between the market and democracy. The result of the neoliberal influence was that politics and the provision of public services were increasingly seen in terms of market processes rather than in terms of citizenship rights. Finally, the rhetoric of freedom and opportunity popular with publics, especially as pushed by Conservative and Republican politicians influenced by Hayek and Friedman, sat uneasily with the inequality, globalization, and deindustrialization wrought by competitive free market capitalism. It has been possible to see these unresolved gaps between the rhetoric of successful electoral politics and the policy reality of social outcomes play out messily in the governmental practice of neoliberalism on both sides of the Atlantic since 1979.

Chapters 5, 6, and 7 examine how neoliberal ideas took hold in two specific policy fields, economic strategy and low- and moderate-income housing and urban policy. Before that, it is necessary to see how neoliberal ideas were able to break through into of the main political parties in Britain and the United States. This was done through a highly effective transatlantic network of people, organizations, and money that spent many years thrashing against the dams before bursting through in a flood during the 1970s. The writers considered in this chapter worked with academic and policy think tanks, foundations, and wealthy individuals in the United States and Britain, as well as in their university and institutional settings, to advance their ideas. This network became the conduit through which neoliberalism flowed into conservative and eventually mainstream politics. It is to this network that we now turn. The next chapter describes the growth of the transatlantic network, whose interactions sparked a process by which the ideas diffused and spread between and beyond the true believers in the 1960s and 1970s.

4

✳

A Transatlantic Network

Think Tanks and the Ideological Entrepreneurs

Historians who seek the meaning of events in the latter part of the twentieth century must look back on gatherings such as this [at the Heritage Foundation in 1983]. They will find among your numbers the leaders of an intellectual revolution that recaptured and renewed the great lessons of Western culture, a revolution that is rallying the great democracies to the defense of that culture and to the cause of human freedom, a revolution that I believe is also writing the last sad pages of a bizarre chapter in human history known as communism.

—RONALD REAGAN, speech to the Heritage Foundation, October 3, 1983

A transatlantic network of sympathetic businessmen and fundraisers, journalists and politicians, policy experts and academics grew and spread neoliberal ideas between the 1940s and the 1970s. These individuals were successful at promoting ideas through a new type of political organization, the think tank. The first wave of neoliberal think tanks were set up in the 1940s and 1950s and included the American Enterprise Institute (AEI) and the Foundation for Economic Education (FEE) in the United States, and the Institute of Economic Affairs (IEA) in Britain. A second wave of neoliberal think tanks were established in the 1970s, including the Centre for Policy Studies (CPS) and the Adam Smith Institute (ASI) in Britain and the Heritage Foundation and the Cato Institute in the United States. These organizations would later directly influence the policies of the Thatcher and Reagan administrations in the 1980s. But in the immediate postwar decades, neoliberal thought might have been confined to academic circles were it not for the growth of a network to spread its message of individual liberty, free markets, low taxes, deregulation, and limited government on both sides of the Atlantic.

The individuals who ran these policy institutes were the ideological entrepreneurs who made neoliberal thought accessible.[1] They helped turn neoliberal thought into a neoliberal political program. They hustled to establish a media presence by raising their profile among sympathetic journalists, and to secure financial robustness for their organizations, and they fought for influence in the political process through the powerful promotion of free markets. With Friedrich Hayek, Milton Friedman emerged as the neoliberal network's beating heart. But it was the ideological entrepreneurs, figures like Leonard Read of the FEE, Ralph Harris of the IEA, and Ed Feulner of the Heritage Foundation, whose organizations connected the network and popularized transatlantic neoliberalism. To a large extent this network was held together by the Mont Pelerin Society.

The think tanks acted as nodes that drew in developing neoliberal ideas from Hayek, Friedman, Buchanan, and their colleagues in Chicago, Virginia, London, and elsewhere and encouraged these writers to discuss their implications for specific policy contexts in Britain, the United States, or internationally. Think tank staff researchers, the editors of their in-house journals and magazines, and local experts, writers, and activists helped apply the abstract contributions of Austrian, Chicago, or Virginia theory. In the process they provided a hard-edged potency for policymakers. The wider political context—defined by Keynesian economics, a commitment to full employment, and the welfare state—into which these think tanks crept was inhospitable and skeptical. But when the economic crises of the 1970s forced politicians and public servants to look around for new ideas, the transatlantic neoliberal network was well established to provide them.

The correspondence between the leading figures of this network reveals the shared sense of waging an ideological war against overwhelming odds. For example, Anthony Fisher, the founder of the IEA (he brought Ralph Harris and Arthur Seldon together to run the think tank in 1955), wrote to Hayek after hearing of his winning the Nobel Prize in Economics in 1974:

> It is one award that you will have least expected to achieve and that will surely make it all the more exciting. The world is in a sorry deteriorating

state. And yet my morale is raised, can I say, ever more often, by some things which are happening.

I enclose a copy of an article of mine which appeared in the Financial Times of all places! ...

I am being introduced to new top executives of multi-national corporations who are becoming aware of the danger. As a consequence of one such introduction I am endeavouring to meet the treasurer of Esso of Indiana or Amoco, hopefully on December 2nd.

I am doing everything I can to free myself from every other activity so that I have as much time as there is in any day to spend on being a catalyst between businessmen and the academic world.[2]

The neoliberal activists such as Fisher believed that collectivism, social democracy, the New Deal, and Great Society liberalism posed a grave threat to the continued existence of Western civilization. They should be thought of as entrepreneurial, not least because some were successful businessmen. More profoundly, despite being cast out and ridiculed by the political mainstream, they worked tirelessly to ensure that free market policies had a voice.

Antony Fisher, Ralph Harris, Leonard Read, William Baroody, F. A. "Baldy" Harper, Ed Feulner, Ed Crane, Eamonn Butler, and Madsen Pirie were all engaged in what they saw as a fight for the survival of individual freedom against the prevalent intellectual and political atmosphere in favor of socialist collectivism in Britain and the United States. They were exceptionally talented at bridging the gap between the technical and academic work of neoliberal scholars and the wider political and public debate. But it took time for their efforts to bear fruit. They required a moment that would force people to pay attention. They were perceived as outsiders by most politicians and journalists in the 1950s and 1960s, and their efforts must have felt like banging their heads against a brick wall. The breakthrough did not happen until some of Friedman's ideas about inflation began to seize those worried about the seemingly endless inflationary spirals of the late 1960s and 1970s. Friedman's own talent for political communication was evident after his famous American Economic Association address of 1967, as we will see in the next chapter.

In both Britain and the United States, during the 1950s and 1960s, neoliberalism had to find a place within conservative politics. For large periods this was either not possible, nor was it obvious that the Conservative and Republican Parties were the most welcoming home for neoliberals. In both parties there was a veneer of apparent agreement over big questions such as the existence of the welfare state, the end of empire, civil rights, desegregation, and the Cold War in the accommodations of the Republican president Dwight Eisenhower and the Conservative prime ministers Winston Churchill, Anthony Eden, and Harold Macmillan.[3] But bubbling beneath the surface was widespread grassroots and intellectual discontent among conservatives on both sides of the Atlantic. The growth of neoliberal politics reflected its capacity in the end to complement dissatisfaction on the right about race, foreign policy, immigration, and social policy. Each of these issues inspired vociferous opposition in the larger conservative movement of the United States and the resurgent Conservative Party in Britain. The opposition generated an atmosphere that enabled nascent neoliberal politics to travel together with anticommunists, anti-immigration populists, antidesegregationists, defenders of the traditional family, and traditional conservatives in a remarkable fusion. This fusion was personified in the American context by Hollywood B-movie-actor-turned-politician, Ronald Reagan.[4] In Britain, the proto-Thatcherite unifier of anti-immigration, neo-imperialist, and free market tendencies was Enoch Powell.[5]

The political atmosphere of the 1960s in the United States seemed to be governed by President John F. Kennedy's New Frontier and Lyndon Johnson's Great Society. In Britain, too, the politics of the left appeared ascendant. Policymakers of both political parties were enamored of experiments with French-style indicative planning, first under Conservative chancellor of the exchequer Reginald Maudling and then under Harold Wilson's Labour governments of 1964–70. The politics of the liberal left in both countries appeared totally dominant after Johnson's reelection in 1964 and Wilson's landslide of 1966. However, the Cold War, the end of empire, civil rights, and desegregation, and later the Vietnam War and the cultural reaction to the perceived permissiveness of the 1960s, all bred disillusionment with the politics of Keynesianism, the welfare state, and corporatist social democracy. The credibility of the liberal Democratic Party and social democratic Labour Party approaches to the social and economic problems of the 1950s and 1960s was stretched. Support for these elements of the postwar political settlement in both countries was undermined by a grassroots revolt over the incendiary issues of race, immigration, and anticommunism.

Against this background, neoliberal thinkers—Friedrich Hayek, Ludwig von Mises, Milton Friedman, George Stigler, James Buchanan, Gordon Tullock, and their students and colleagues—were convinced of the practical and political relevance of their ideas to the problems of the postwar period. Both Hayek and Friedman sought to influence the intellectual climate so that policy changes would follow a changed political context, just as the New Deal of the 1930s in the United States and the Attlee governments' reforms of the 1940s in Britain had been inspired by the writers of the liberal progressive, social democratic, and socialist left of the first half of the twentieth century. These liberal progressive and left-wing intellectuals had capitalized on the atmosphere generated by the Great Depression and World War II. The neoliberal thinkers, and the think tank ideological entrepreneurs who propagated their ideas and turned them into policy, followed Hayek's call in "The Intellectuals and Socialism." They worked to transform the intellectual and ideological landscape so that concrete political successes and policy reforms would follow. Transatlantic neoliberalism thus became a conscious political movement and moved beyond being simply an academic critique.

The first part of this chapter surveys some of the wider trends of conservative politics first in the United States and then in Britain during the 1950s and 1960s. The chapter then examines the individuals and organizations that were key to the construction of the transatlantic neoliberal network. But it is to the historical context of the 1950s and 1960s that we first turn. It was within this setting and in reaction to it that the transatlantic neoliberal network was created, and it was in response to many of its features that neoliberal think tanks, and the ideological entrepreneurs who ran them, first made their mark.

The United States in the 1950s: Fusionism and the Cold War

Transatlantic neoliberal politics must be separated from the other strands of the American conservative movement and British Conservatism in the 1950s and 1960s.[6] In both the United States and Britain, in different ways, free market economics (and politics, as the public choice theorists James Buchanan and Gordon Tullock would have it) was but one branch of a right that was in ideological, if not always electoral, retreat for much of the postwar period.

In 1952, Dwight D. Eisenhower finally reclaimed the White House from the Democratic Party, which had held it for twenty years, first under Franklin Delano Roosevelt in 1932–45, and then through Harry Truman's presidency in 1945–52, when he defeated Adlai Stevenson. A year before, Conservative Winston Churchill returned to power by defeating Labour prime minister Clement Attlee, whose government had by 1951 achieved its aims, and run out of steam. The sedate governments of Churchill, followed by Eden and Macmillan, in the 1950s and early 1960s were interrupted only by the shattering realization wrought by the Suez Crisis (1956–57) of Britain's reduced role in the world.[7]

These administrations in both countries, led by veterans, often of both wars, were centrist in character. They were colored by the searing scars of war and depression. In neither country were the achievements of their Democratic and Labour Party predecessors seriously doubted, let alone challenged by Republican or Conservative leaders. However, as recent scholarship has shown, this consensual image of national politics in the 1950s and early 1960s disguised the rumblings on the right in both countries. There was a hive of activity, both at the grassroots level and among intellectuals, that pointed toward widespread dissatisfaction with the mainstream politics of the Republican and Conservative Parties. In the United States this agitation, violent unrest, and protest, fueled by anticommunism and resistance to the civil rights movement, led to the growth of a conservative movement. In Britain, nothing as coherent or imposing was evident, but there was violent, often racist, anger among poorer white working-class people. These destructive sentiments erupted in the Notting Hill race riots of 1958 and in the violent protests that followed Enoch Powell's notorious anti-immigration "Rivers of Blood" speech in 1968.

It is essential to illustrate briefly this wider historical context in which neoliberals and their transatlantic network operated. At the center of the American Right were the different and sometimes competing priorities of economics, religion, and culture, all of which required reconciliation if the focus of conservatives was not to dissipate ineffectively. The mix of economics, religion, and culture, always present in political debates, was especially explosive in the United States because of the pervasive presence of race-related issues. Economic conservatives were concerned to revive free market policies to replace the government interventions of the Progressive and New Deal eras.

Social conservatives were deeply upset by the upheavals in the social and racial structures of society implied by the twin developments of the civil rights
movement and the welfare state. Cultural conservatives were motivated by
their religious convictions about the superiority of Christian morality and
the Judeo-Christian tradition. In fact, the Religious Right emerged later in
the 1970s to spread the influence of evangelicals, but in the 1950s, too, there
was a powerful brand of traditional conservative thought that, while less fun-
damentalist than what succeeded it, was nevertheless influential. The distinctive feature of the conservative revival in the 1950s and 1960s was the ability
of its disparate elements to unite under the banners of anticommunism and
states' rights. The latter allowed mainstream, nonracist Republican politicians
to capitalize on the South's anger at desegregation, for example.

One of the main reasons why conservatives were able to sustain the
fraught alliance through economic, social, and cultural appeals was the rise of
an alternative establishment to rival the influence of liberalism. George Nash
in his classic study, *The Conservative Intellectual Movement in America*, highlights the fact that conservatism in the United States has been characterized
by many divergent impulses. Indeed, as Nash points out, "the very quest for
self-definition has been one of the most notable motifs of [the many brands
of conservative] thought since World War II."[8] In the 1950s and 1960s, the
conservative movement was not sufficiently united to be capable of political
power. But the germs of its subsequent success were obvious in the theoretical groundwork laid by conservative intellectuals and in the grassroots activism that sprang up in the newly rich and predominantly white suburban
South and West.[9]

Three distinct groups of American conservatism emerged in the 1950s.
The first group was the "new conservatives" and traditionalists, represented
by figures like Richard Weaver, Russell Kirk, Peter Viereck, and Robert Nis-
bet. "Shocked by totalitarianism, total war, and the development of secular,
rootless, mass society during the 1930s and 1940s, the 'new conservatives'
urged a return to traditional religious and ethical absolutes and a rejection of
the 'relativism' which had allegedly corroded Western values and produced
an intolerable vacuum that was filled by demonic ideologies," Nash writes.
In a second group were the committed anticommunists, men such as Whit-
taker Chambers, James Burnham, and Frank Meyer, "former men of the
Left" themselves, who, according to Nash, "brought to the postwar Right a

profound conviction that the West was engaged in a titanic struggle with an implacable adversary—Communism—which sought nothing less than conquest of the world."[10] Finally, the neoliberals themselves (who tended to call themselves libertarians in the American context) were those most influenced by Hayek, Friedman, and the rest. Hayek's *The Road to Serfdom* (1944), and the book tour that accompanied it, for example, enshrined it as a bible for American conservatives in the postwar period.

Together, these three streams flowed into the river of intellectual life on the right in the 1950s and early 1960s and formed the basis of the growth of a conservative establishment that would flourish and rival their liberal opponents. At the same time, a host of organizations, periodicals, and journals sprang up to propagate conservative ideas more widely. For example, Frank Chodorov founded the Intercollegiate Society of Individualists (ISI) in 1953. The ISI was set up to supplement existing academic courses for students with an education in free markets and the Judeo-Christian tradition on campuses across the United States. William F. Buckley, Jr., the ISI's first president and a great friend of Milton Friedman, founded the *National Review* in 1955. Buckley's book, *God and Man at Yale* (1951), one of the seminal conservative books of the period, indicted the liberal academic establishment, especially the emblematic Economics Department at Yale University, for abandoning the creed of individualism. He wrote it "to expose what I regard as an extraordinarily irresponsible educational attitude that, under the protective label 'academic freedom,' has produced one of the most extraordinary incongruities of our time: the institution [Yale University] that derives its moral and financial support from Christian individualists and then addresses itself to the task of persuading the sons of these supporters to be atheistic socialists."[11]

A string of other important books were published by the "new conservatives" and European émigrés such as the "father of neoconservatism," Leo Strauss, the philosopher Eric Voegelin, and the libertarian critic and educational theorist Albert Jay Nock.[12] The American critic and writer Russell Kirk launched the most comprehensive rearticulation of conservative principles in a book that emerged from his doctoral dissertation called *The Conservative Mind,* which was published in 1953. This book surveyed literature, philosophy, and history to present a portrayal of the religious foundations of Western civilization and restated arguments put forward by Edmund Burke about the value of custom and tradition. Underlying all these developments in conservative thought was an important rediscovered emphasis on the eternal and time-honored bases of the Judaeo-Christian tradition, a conviction that Hayek in particular shared. From such beginnings, it was argued, had come the virtues and truths needed to fight the Cold War and that were simultaneously being destroyed by liberal America. They felt that the liberal political and educational establishments were not taking seriously the need to teach and preserve the Judeo-Christian heritage, from which had come the distinctive political and economic freedoms enjoyed by the West. What was lacking from these critiques, however, was a way of fusing all this activity together into something like a coherent "movement"—fusing together traditional, economic, and cultural conservatives. This fusion would be performed by William F. Buckley, Jr.

Although some have argued that the origins of the fusion of cultural and economic politics on the right can be seen in the prewar period, it was the 1950s that witnessed the emergence of distinctively new forms of conservatism.[13] At the same time, a new political climate defined by anticommunism was fostered by the onset of the Cold War and the intense paranoia manipulated and stirred by Joseph McCarthy in the early 1950s. McCarthyism was the extreme manifestation of a cause that could unite conservatives of many different stripes. McCarthyite anticommunism also represented a staging post in the Right's successful manipulation of language and rhetoric in politics. The term "communist" and "communist influence" became a cover for all manner of complaints. Such usages arguably began during the New Deal, with many policies becoming tarred with a communist or socialist brush by right-wing critics of Roosevelt (who often called themselves true liberals). The use of guilt by association phraseology became a favorite tactic of the New Deal's conservative opponents in the 1930s—tarring policies with the "communistic" or "socialistic" brush—a trend that accelerated alarmingly during the second Red Scare of the immediate postwar years.[14]

Language was also used very cleverly in the backlash against desegregation and the reaction to the civil rights movement led by Martin Luther King and the Southern Christian Leadership Conference in the late 1950s and early 1960s. Initially the victories were all on the side of the activists and their white liberal supporters, who successfully employed the language of the U.S. Constitution to appeal to universalist notions of liberty and equality before the law. But as the civil rights movement itself began to fracture after it had achieved the legislative victories of the Civil Rights Act (1964) and the Voting Rights Act (1965), the way was open for a new strategy on the part of Republicans to exploit the racial tensions boiling over in the inner cities of the North. By 1968, the overt racism of the white supremacists had given way to Nixon's more sophisticated "southern strategy," which pushed the buttons of the supposed God-fearing "silent majority" who abhorred violence and instability.

Matthew Lassiter has argued that this exploitation of race was a deeper reflection of the emergence of a powerful suburban class in the South and the West that came to dominate the political landscape.[15] The Republican leadership discovered a language that tapped into the sentiments and concerns of disaffected whites, partly a legacy of George Wallace's insurgency campaigns for president during the 1960s.[16] But, just as important, the predominantly white, affluent suburbs of Richmond, Charlotte, and Atlanta began to turn the civil rights rhetoric back on itself in the violent resistance to busing, the practice of transporting school pupils between school districts to redress social and residential segregation. As Lassiter has suggested, the silent majority rallied round a "color-blind discourse of suburban innocence that depicted residential segregation as the class-based outcome of meritocratic individualism rather than the unconstitutional product of structural racism."[17] The anti-busing campaigners appropriated the language of equal rights and the Constitution to resist any integration of their schools by arguing that government should leave them alone and not interfere in their local communities. Consequently, the lines of racial politics were redrawn so that the language of civil rights became a tool that affluent white communities used to remake existing social and racial inequalities.

The manipulation of language was also a common practice of the various neoliberal think tanks such as the AEI and the FEE in their attacks on New Deal and Great Society policies. A mild British equivalent of such terminology was Conservative Party politicians routinely deriding members of the Labour Party as "socialists"—the Labour Party, however, still considered itself socialist in this period, though not Marxist. Many of the individuals who funded these organizations were originally anti–New Deal businessmen, such as advertising executive Lawrence Fertig and picture frame entrepreneur William Volker. These people and organizations deemed Roosevelt's project socialist. Businessmen of the anti–New Deal coalition fought back in aggressive pro-market campaigns after the war, as both Elizabeth Fones-Wolf and Kim Phillips-Fein have shown.[18] Corporate leaders such as Jasper Crane of Du Pont Chemicals and Lemuel Ricketts Boulwere of General Electric marshaled new strategies to defeat labor and attack the welfare state. For example, Crane was critical to the early funding of the Mont Pelerin Society. But this breed of business conservatives of the anti–New Deal coalition was another stream on the right in the 1950s. The business conservatives were also particular allies of the neoliberals as they were the group most exercised by the importance of free markets and corporate freedom.

McCarthyism was the most visible example of the extreme atmosphere of the 1950s, but anticommunism was not clearly a partisan issue. Many Democrats were also Cold Warriors committed to the destruction of the "evil" of communism, just like their Republican counterparts.[19] This is not to suggest there were not very important differences between the anticommunism implied by Truman's policy of containment, for example, and the anticommunism of those who wished to bomb China or hound New Deal liberals out of the United States as communist fellow travelers. But what is especially important for the rise of conservatism in the United States is the impact of the anticommunist fervor on the development of a movement. Here the blanket concept, "communist," took on a new significance even from the roots of its usage in the New Deal era.

Lisa McGirr's study of Orange County, California, explains the connection between the McCarthy era and the troubled decade of the 1960s. According to McGirr, a particularly nasty and uncompromising anticommunism enabled conservative activists to attack liberalism more generally: "[In Orange County] this variant was a broad rubric that encompassed not simply a rejection of a Soviet-style organization of society but also a rejection of 'collectivism' in all its forms, including federal regulations, the welfare state and liberal political culture."[20] McGirr explores the quotidian existence of a Western community during the 1950s and 1960s and shows how the movement was marshaled through the activities of groups like the John Birch Society, the School of anti-Communism, and Young Americans for Freedom throughout Orange County. Zealous local activists organized campaigns against Deweyan "progressive education," the American Civil Liberties Union, and the encroachment of the federal government. Anticommunism was the respectable cover for fears and resentments among conservatives of a drift in

American society during the 1950s and 1960s toward a more liberal and permissive society.

McGirr sheds light on some of the contradictions that go to the heart of conservatism's resuscitation after World War II. For example, the tension between tradition and modernity was glaring among the conservative activists of Orange County:

> While many of these activists hailed from rural and small-town backgrounds in the Midwest and border South, it is misleading to characterize their mobilization, as contemporary observers often did, as a rearguard action against "modernity." . . .
>
> These men and women embraced modernity but did so selectively. They rejected some elements usually associated with modernity—namely, secularism, relativism, and egalitarianism, believing that a thoroughly modern life could, and should, exclude them—while embracing thoroughly modern lifestyles.[21]

This tension is also laid bare in Gregory Schneider's examination of the history of the Young Americans for Freedom (YAF). Founded in 1960 in Sharon, Connecticut, by M. Stanton Evans on William F. Buckley's estate, the organization became an important conduit for striving young right-wingers and played a crucial role in the conservative takeover of the Republican Party.[22] Schneider argues that the YAF is a prime example of an indigenous grassroots conservatism that has gone largely unnoticed until recently. According to Schneider, "what historians have long ignored, but are beginning to recover, is the tradition of conservative politics in America—the development and shaping of a key set of principles and affectations that eventually led to political activism and the capture of a major political party."[23] What this scholarship shows, along with the growth of the Religious Right, is the vibrancy of local activism that sustains the conservative movement. Even after the excesses of McCarthy in the early 1950s, anticommunism and opposition to civil rights remained the most important conservative rallying calls in the United States.

The journalist E. J. Dionne has argued, in *Why Americans Hate Politics*, that the roots of conservatism's later success lay in the ideological debates that fashioned fusionism in the 1950s. According to Dionne, "conservatism's first political breakthrough was actually an intellectual breakthrough," brokered by the success of William F. Buckley and his colleagues through "a theoretical compromise between conservatives who revered tradition and religion, and those who valued free market economics above all else."[24] This theoretical compromise was possible because of the Cold War and the potential of anticommunism to unite right-wingers and conservatives of all stripes during the 1950s and early 1960s.

The fusion of cultural and economic conservatism through anticommunism paved the way for the later electoral successes of Ronald Reagan and the defeat of a more internationalist liberal Republicanism, most recently represented by George H. W. Bush. The successful fusion of cultural and economic conservatives was allied to the alienation of the South from the Democratic Party in the years after the *Brown v. Board of Education* decision of 1954 to desegregate the public schools. The protest politics of Alabama governor and segregationist presidential candidate George Wallace and Nixon's election ensured a political realignment that benefited the conservative movement and the Republican Party. The *Brown* decision, the civil rights movement, and the reactions to them, as we have seen, contributed to a progressive "southernization" of U.S. politics that was based on the politics of the affluent and suburban South and West. Crucially, conservatives could form a viable electoral majority only in the late 1960s when enough groups were united in opposition to the perceived failings of liberal America led by Presidents John F. Kennedy and Lyndon B. Johnson. That such a majority did form required a complex coalescence of economic, political, and cultural, especially religious, forces. However, it also needed a positive vision and a set of concrete policies that could be communicated to Americans.

Neoliberals contributed to this alternative program, and the transatlantic network that promoted their ideas overlapped and fizzed among these other waves of opposition. Neoliberal politics fit alongside the anticommunists, traditionalists, religious, and fusionist conservatives in a broad church of right-wing activism that was flying under the radar of mainstream politics for much of the period. The radical individualism that inhered in the ideas of Hayek, Friedman, and the others undoubtedly tapped a vast well of American conservative belief. The implications of their attacks on the public sector, public interest, and public administration chimed with the beliefs of the most vehement opponents of Progressivism, the New Deal, and the Great Society. This also made the financing of neoliberal and free market think tanks and policy research in the United States relatively easy.

British Conservatism in the 1950s

The social and political context in the Conservative Party in Britain during the 1950s, though it exhibited some similar activity, was different. There was nothing quite like the internecine struggles over desegregation or McCarthyism. The leaders of the Conservative governments of 1951–64 for the most part, in policy terms, reached an accommodation with the Labour Party settlement of 1945. Their attitude was summed up by Rab Butler, successively chancellor, home secretary, and deputy prime minister in the 1950s and 1960s, in a look back at policy statements since the war: "We have expressed our deep belief in democratic freedom and our anxiety to hold fairly the balance between the independence of the individual and the authority of the state. We showed our determination to maintain and care for the social services." Butler went on to identify the central challenge for the Conservative Party and the country in the postwar years: "The immediate issue today is how to repel the supreme threat of Communist imperialism and how best to preserve what has already been achieved in wealth and welfare."[25] Rab Butler's kind of Conservative was proud to have increased living standards across the board and to have ensured a safety net of well-funded public provision. Butler's statements sum up the political atmosphere of "Butskellism"—the broadly social democratic politics of the Labour leader Hugh Gaitskell and Butler, who had championed universal state education in the 1944 Education Act, which became known as the Butler Act.

Beneath the agreements of the political elites, however, Britain, like the United States, underwent changes in terms of its social and racial composition in the postwar decades as a result of immigration from the former colonies. Asians and West Indians emigrated to Britain and began to settle into new jobs in the social services; a new and rebellious younger generation began to challenge the establishment and transform popular and political culture. These developments, the end of empire, and the social and cultural revolutions of the 1950s and 1960s led many grassroots Conservatives to feel deep dissatisfaction with their party leaders, who appeared to acquiesce in and sometimes even promote such developments. At the same time, a new group of young Tory MPs and intellectuals such as Enoch Powell, Iain Macleod, and Geoffrey Howe began to redefine Conservatism and to challenge the wholesale acceptance of the welfare state and the nationalizations of the Labour governments of 1945–51.

In the early 1950s, several Conservative Party groups came into being at the same time to articulate a fresh policy agenda. The formation of the One Nation group in 1950 and the Bow Group in 1951 marked attempts to pressure the leadership into a more imaginative direction than the general agreement with Labour Party policy favored by the leadership of Churchill, Macmillan, and Butler. As historian Ewen Green has shown, these groups touched a wider middle-class revolt based in concerns about inflation, the trade unions, taxes, and the Conservative compromise with Labour over the welfare state and social policy. This wider revolt, according to Green, was marked by the founding, in 1956, of the protest organizations the Middle Class Alliance (MCA) and the People's League in Defence of Freedom (PLDF), "both of which were highly critical of postwar economic and social reform."[26] The Conservative vote dropped in by-elections in Tunbridge Wells in 1956 and in Torquay, Edinburgh, and Ipswich in 1957. The party actually lost elections in Lewisham North in 1957 and in Torrington in 1958. These were all areas with large middle-class constituencies. Both the MCA and the PLDF had memberships comprised of "natural" Conservative voters, who fought for more free market policies and restrictions of trade union power.[27]

The One Nation group, led by Enoch Powell, Angus Maude, and Iain Macleod, and founded in 1950, wanted to place free market thinking at the center of Tory government policy. Their publications, pamphlets with such titles as *One Nation* (1950), *The Social Services: Needs and Means* (1952), *Change Is Our Ally* (1954), and *The Responsible Society* (1959), resounded with the demands of the MCA and the PLDF. The proposed programs were tangential to the neoliberalism being developed by Hayek and Friedman. For example, the One Nation Tories were skeptical of the relevance of Hayek in the atmosphere of 1950s Britain. As Green writes,

> The One Nation group's *The Responsible Society* noted, rightly, that Hayek had been the 'inspiration' for Churchill's 'Gestapo' speech of 1945 [where he suggested the possibility that Labour in power would

make Britain a police state], but argued that he had inspired 'very little else at the time' or since, because arguments for self-help were not in vogue. But they felt that, as the 1950s drew to a close, opinion was moving in a more Hayekian direction. By 1968 Hayekian assumptions had come once again to provide inspiration for libertarian arguments in the Conservative ranks, and in many ways Hayek's renewed kudos in Conservative circles was symptomatic of this.[28]

Unlike Hayek's sparse social philosophy, primarily concerned with the significance of the economic processes of the market, the One Nation group nevertheless celebrated the contribution of the Conservative Party to Britain's welfare state. But it aimed to supplement this social democratic element with a more radical economic program based on markets.

The Bow Group was set up in 1951 as a think tank within the Conservative Party that was intended to be nonpartisan in that it was open to Conservatives of all different types. Although its membership was broad and inclusive, its chairmen from the 1950s, 1960s, and 1970s included many who went on to become core members of Margaret Thatcher's governments in the 1980s. They included David Howell, Leon Brittan, Michael Howard, John MacGregor, Norman Lamont, and Peter Lilley, all future cabinet ministers. Its leading light during the 1950s was Geoffrey Howe, who became consecutively Margaret Thatcher's chancellor, foreign secretary, and deputy prime minister between 1979 and 1990, until resigning over her increasingly uncompromising leadership style. According to Howe, in a similar vein to Hayek's motivation in founding the Mont Pelerin Society, the Bow Group was established partly to combat the influence of the Fabian Society on Labour Party politics.[29] It had five preoccupations: the state of the union, free market economics, the One Nation tradition, the multiracial Commonwealth, and a realistic appraisal of Britain's position in the world.[30] There was also much crossover, suggests Howe, between the One Nation group, Powell, Macleod, and the Bow Group.

The Bow Group also initiated contacts with like-minded American groups. The Ripon Society of the Republican Party was set up by Emil Frankel in 1961 as a conscious imitation of the Bow Group.[31] The Ripon Society, however, was swimming against the tide of increasing radicalism in the conservative movement in the United States in terms of its vocal support for the civil rights movement. The Bow Group, too, was liberal on racial issues. Its first pamphlet, *Coloured People in Britain* (1951), marked an attempt to grapple with the impact of immigration into Britain from the former imperial colonies. There were also transatlantic contacts through the Bow Group's quarterly magazine, *Crossbow*.[32] The links between these two groups indicate the differences between the two political cultures. A moderate conservative politics defined by social liberalism and free markets was becoming difficult to sustain within the Republican Party in the United States, while in Britain, social liberalism and the welfare state went together in the politics of Macmillan and Butler, leaving little space for free market policies. The political challenges for young Conservative intellectuals in Britain seeking a more radical free market policy agenda were similar to those faced by Republicans in that such an approach remained outside the party mainstream during the 1950s and 1960s. But the emergence of the young leaders of One Nation and the Bow Group showed there were opportunities for neoliberal ideas to find a place within the Conservative Party during the 1950s and 1960s, at least in terms of economic policy. It was just that these opportunities did not, in general, lead to changes in the policy direction of the party leadership.

The political situation in Britain was not characterized by the sustained violent conflicts of the battles for racial equality in the United States, although the waves of immigration from the former colonies were an explosive issue. While there were no Montgomery bus boycotts or Little Rocks in Britain, there were significant upheavals spurred by the end of the British Empire and the immigration that accompanied its replacement by the Commonwealth.[33] Conflicts over housing, social services, and welfare payments simmered as resources were perceived to have drained away to the new residents. The immigration did spark racial violence, resentment, and struggles against the infamous "Rachmanite landlords" in communities like Notting Hill, where the new arrivals settled.[34] Overcrowding was a typical problem associated with immigration in postwar Britain.[35] These tensions exploded spectacularly in race riots initiated by gangs of white youths who attacked West Indian immigrants in Notting Hill and Nottingham in the late summer of 1958. The riots shocked those who imagined that nothing could happen in Britain like the shocking racial violence witnessed in the American Deep South or apartheid South Africa. As historian Peter Hennessy has suggested, "things were never the same again. . . . The tone of British domestic politics shifted and, after a short lag, the politics and the statute law concerning immigration did too."[36]

The shock of Notting Hill had revealed the racial ferment produced by immigration. Racial prejudice was accompanied by real fears about the resources of the British welfare state in the inner cities. The immediate solution for the Conservative government appeared to be to limit the numbers coming into Britain, legislation that was duly passed as the Commonwealth Immigrants Act of 1962. In the process, promises that had been made to prospective immigrants, that they would be able to man the buses and clean the hospital floors, were broken. Tens of thousands entered from the Caribbean and South Asia between 1958 and 1962 as a result of the expected law. Immigration became a staple issue around which the racist and insecure working-class support rallied throughout the 1950s and 1960s. Enoch Powell, of One Nation and health minister in Macmillan's government, led those concerned with immigration through his "Rivers of Blood" speech in which he claimed to speak for the old lady in the street.[37] Despite the volatility of race and immigration as an issue among certain groups of the population, historian Dominic Sandbrook has wryly noted that Britain in this period was a "net exporter of people"—far greater numbers emigrated away than entered.[38] More people left Britain, especially for the former dominions of Canada, Australia, and New Zealand, than arrived to settle from the Commonwealth countries.

The mix of anger and discontent over race, immigration, and housing and the clashes over social resources did not translate into a fervor for free market ideas in Britain either, however. Differences in the attitudes of British and American conservatives were be summed up by Alec Douglas-Home (who was Conservative successor as prime minister to Macmillan in 1963–64). A briefing paper suggested that the consequences of Goldwater winning would be "too awful to contemplate," to which Home added a handwritten marginal note, "it is really terrible that having seen his writings and speeches that he got the nomination—his organisation was doubtless excellent. I suppose it all shows how gullible people are."[39] Home's British ambassador to the United States, Lord Harlech, reported to the prime inister on a Goldwater rally in similar terms: "[One is] reminded of a revivalist meeting with the candidate claiming that the United States had been created by God to carry out some divine purpose." He went on to suggest that he expected a Goldwater victory to be accompanied by "an early recession and heavy unemployment which would in turn lead to increased protection for American Industry."[40]

The disdainful attitudes toward Goldwater Republicanism expressed by the patrician elite were illustrative of the beliefs of Conservative Party leaders in the 1950s and 1960s. But the grassroots right-wing discontent revealed the limits of support for the cosy assumptions of the political leaders at the top. Attitudes among both the young intellectual politicians of the Conservative Party and average party members showed that space existed for a new set of political ideas. This potential was confirmed by the failures of the Labour Party under Harold Wilson, whose experiment with a National Plan through his establishment of the Department of Economic Affairs in 1964 to rival the power of the Treasury, under the volatile and drunken leadership of his deputy George Brown, ended up a damp squib. The Wilson governments' economic policies were, in the end, overtaken amid the recurrent balance-of-payments economic crises of the 1960s and 1970s. It was into this heady mix of issues and activism that the neoliberal network of academics, think tanks, funds, and journalists poured its not inconsequential efforts.

Neoliberal Organization in the 1950s and 1960s

The neoliberals were just one of the many groups and loose affiliations that contributed to the conservative chorus in Britain and the United States. In Britain, the voices of neoliberal spokesmen such as those of the IEA were at best ignored. At worst, individuals such as IEA director Ralph Harris (despite being formerly an economics lecturer at the University of St. Andrews) and Editorial Director Arthur Seldon (also previously a journalist and academic) were considered to be unhinged in their determined advocacy of free market solutions to policy problems, a position thought by most to go against all received economic policy wisdom. In the United States, the belief in the superiority of the market economy was much closer to the political mainstream. But even though America's individualist political culture made it a more receptive environment for the ideas of Milton Friedman and Friedrich Hayek, the American policy establishment of the 1950s and 1960s was similarly sold on the logic of various forms of Keynesian demand management. Consequently, in the United States as well, the neoliberals were sailing against the wind.

Milton Friedman, echoing the ideas in Hayek's 1949 essay, "The Intellectuals and Socialism," from his base at the University of Chicago, also called
for a movement of ideas that would slowly change the postwar ideological
landscape. Since there was a time lag between a shift in the "underlying current of opinion" and a legislative response to such change, efforts should be
made to transform ideas:

> The stage is set for the growth of a new current of opinion to replace the
> old, to provide the philosophy that will guide the legislators of the next
> generation even though it can hardly affect those of this one.[41]

Both Hayek and Friedman facilitated a network that would do exactly
that. Between 1943 and 1980, a web of institutions and people grew up
to spread and popularize neoliberal ideas so that eventually they seemed
the natural alternative to liberal or social democratic policies. In both the
United States and Britain, what journalist Sidney Blumenthal has termed a
"counter-establishment" developed to provide intellectual succour to neoliberal politics in the wake of the increasingly manifest failures of the Keynesian
economic policy consensus during the 1970s.[42] In the 1950s and 1960s the
transatlantic network expanded through the growth of think tanks—Hayek's
"second-hand dealers in ideas."[43] The American think tanks in particular were
also supported by business sources, often American household corporate
names such as Du Pont Chemicals, General Electric, and Coors Brewing
Company.

Kim Phillips-Fein has shown that the major strategy of American business was to fund think tanks and organize campaigns on behalf of free enterprise and against trade unions or strenuous regulation of employment
practices. The economic policy successes of business have been striking when
compared to the relatively unsuccessful Christian conservative attempts to
roll back the sexual and cultural revolutions of the 1960s, for example. As
Phillips-Fein suggests, "by the early twenty-first century, the conservative
movement in power had transformed the tax code, government regulation of
business, and the relationship between the federal government and the states;
in the private sector, the proportion of the working population represented
by labor unions had fallen to levels not seen since before the New Deal."[44] The
anti–New Deal coalition, formed in the 1930s and 1940s, became the nucleus

of a postwar corporate-driven free market resurgence. As Phillips-Fein has shown, the success in World War II was a propaganda victory that enabled business to fight back against the Wagner Act of 1935 (which had guaranteed broad trade union rights to workers) and the more optimistic dreams of liberal Democrats for a more universalist welfare state. But the agenda of a new generation of business leaders was not antigovernment per se:

> They did not claim to stand for social order against the chaos of change; instead, they embraced the forces of transformation. They wanted to empower business, not to reinvigorate lost traditions, and some even wanted to use the state to enforce policies friendly to business or to the market, the hallmark of the neoliberal.[45]

The new focus among the business elite helped spark the growth of a conservative ideological infrastructure needed to influence political reforms in Washington, D.C.

The first major think tanks in the United States were the American Enterprise Institute, founded in 1943, and the Foundation for Economic Education, which was set up in 1946. The AEI came out of the American Enterprise Association, a key anti-New Deal business group that had been established in New York City by Lewis Brown in 1938. The American Enterprise Association was disturbed by the prospect of a continuation of price controls in peacetime once the war was won, and its leadership decided to open an office in Washington, D.C., to agitate on behalf of competitive free enterprise. As the AEI annual report put it on the sixtieth anniversary of its creation,

> The new AEA office, which eventually became headquarters and graduated from "association" to "institute," was the avant-garde [sic] of two momentous developments of the decades to come, both responding to the growing size and power of the federal government: the migration of business and trade associations from commercial centers to the nation's capital and the emergence of the policy "think-tank."[46]

After initial success with the end to price controls after the war ended, the AEI began legislative analyses and policy advocacy on new proposals and started to produce its own tracts on elements of conservative and free market philosophy. In 1954 William Baroody, Sr., joined the AEI as an executive vice president and transformed it. Baroody became the president of the AEI in 1962. He managed to raise the AEI's public profile and brought in leading scholars to work with the institute. Milton Friedman, Gottfried Haberler, and Nixon's future chairman of economic advisers, Paul McCracken, joined its advisory board in the early 1960s. Haberler, like Friedman, was a member of the Mont Pelerin Society. Baroody was also the principal adviser to Barry Goldwater's 1964 presidential campaign. The AEI underwent a tough time after Baroody Sr. handed over to his son in 1978. Despite this decline, many AEI scholars joined the Reagan administration, and it has a claim to being one of the first American think tanks, after the liberal Brookings Institution.

The FEE was established by Leonard Read, the general manager of the Los Angeles Chamber of Commerce, in 1946 in Irvington, New York. Like the AEI, the FEE was supported by many leading businessmen—David Goodrich, of Goodrich and Co.; H. W. Luhnow, president of William Volker & Co. and subsequently also the head of the William Volker Fund; Charles White, of Republic Oil Corporation; Jasper Crane, of Du Pont; and Donaldson Brown, of General Motors.[47] Its primary aim was the economic education of policymakers and the wider public on the importance of the free market through courses, publications, leaflets, pamphlets and books, radio, lectures, and scholarships.

Leonard Read was close to Hayek from the beginning. He brought in other neoliberal writers as well to contribute to FEE. One of its first publications, in 1946, titled *Roofs or Ceilings*, was about the follies of rent control and was written by George Stigler and Milton Friedman.[48] Ludwig von Mises also joined the foundation at its start and wrote a pamphlet, *Planned Chaos*, that was published by the FEE in 1947.[49] The organization acquired its own journal in 1956 when the FEE took over *The Freeman,* a New York–based free market magazine that had existed since 1950. According to Ed Crane, later president of the Cato Institute, "people of my generation [Crane was born in 1944] will often say they came to these [free market] ideas through *The Freeman*."[50] Henry Hazlitt, one of the FEE's founding vice presidents, a member of the Mont Pelerin Society and an editor of *The Freeman,* argued in a retrospective piece from 1984 that the FEE was very influential as one of the earliest think tanks propounding neoliberal ideas:

It is astonishing how soon Leonard's action began to produce important results. Friedrich Hayek, in London, impressed by Read's initiative, raised the money the next year, 1947, to call a conference at Vevey, Switzerland, of 43 libertarian writers, mainly economists, from half a dozen nations. The group of ten of us from the United States included such figures as Ludwig von Mises, Milton Friedman, George Stigler—and Leonard Read. That was the beginning of the still flourishing and immensely influential Mont Pelerin Society, now with several hundred members from dozens of countries.

Another effect of Leonard's initiative soon followed. Other libertarian foundations were set up in emulation. Baldy Harper, who had been working as economist for FEE from its first year, left in 1958 and started his Institute for Humane Studies in 1963 in California. Soon Antony Fisher set up like organizations in England [the Institute of Economic Affairs], Canada, and eventually here.[51]

As a result of Read's successful fundraising, the FEE was able to mass-produce its publications and distribute them widely, often for free (36,000 copies of Friedman and Stigler's paper were distributed by the foundation in 1946). Despite being influenced by Read and the FEE, the leading British free market think tank of the 1950s and 1960s was the IEA, which came to see itself as a different kind of organization altogether.

The IEA was the most important of all the think tanks for the development of transatlantic neoliberal politics to be set up after World War II, certainly in Britain. It was established in 1955 by Antony Fisher. Fisher had been deeply impressed by Hayek's belief in the long-term importance of ideas to political change. He first met Hayek in 1945 while he was planning a more conventional political career as a Tory MP and visited Hayek at his LSE office, where Hayek invited Fisher to join him in the task of changing the intellectual landscape instead.[52] Once Ralph Harris and Arthur Seldon were recruited to run the organization after its launch in 1957, and once Fisher had found the money for the organization (Fisher was an entrepreneur who made millions developing battery chicken farms during the 1950s), the institute metamorphosed into a much more serious academic enterprise than the FEE.

Fisher's approach stemmed directly from Hayek's belief in the influence of ideas, which he had impressed on Fisher at that first meeting. The IEA's aim has since been summarized by John Blundell, president of the Atlas Foundation between 1987 and 1991 and a director of the IEA between 1993 and 2009:

> The IEA has from the beginning concentrated on publishing papers and pamphlets for an intellectual audience, works whose sole concern— in the words of the IEA's first brochure—would be "economic truth" unswayed by current "political considerations". The goal of these efforts, the IEA said, was a society in which people would understand free-market economics "together with an understanding of the moral foundations which govern the acquisition and holding of property, the right of the individual to have access to free competitive markets and the necessity of a secure and honest monetary system."[53]

Men like Fisher, Read, and Baroody were the indefatigable foot soldiers in Friedman and Hayek's ideological war. Fisher wrote to Hayek, after an anniversary dinner, of the serendipitous path to the establishment of the IEA:

> You mentioned "luck" [at an IEA dinner]! No doubt luck is important— but how much is luck if someone finds what he is deliberately seeking?
>
> In 1949 Ralph [Harris] took the trouble to disseminate his ideas at a meeting. I was present in my capacity as chairman of my village Conservative Association—on a Saturday afternoon. I took the trouble to seek Ralph after his talk. I mentioned your advice. He expressed an interest.
>
> I took his name and address. I only wrote 7 years later when I was acquiring limited funds [it was actually six years later]. Was there not an intention on both our parts and consequent action? How much is luck? It is an interesting subject and too long for one letter.
>
> Anyway, your own inspired idea imparted to me in 1945 is still growing and having much more important consequences.[54]

The IEA linked British and American academics, politicians, journalists, and think-tankers.[55] The institute brought together these individuals at conferences and events to discuss free market ideas. They also published and promoted their policy proposals in the media and to policymakers and politicians.

Antony Fisher, described by the president of the Heritage Foundation, Ed Feulner, as "a great adviser and a source of inspiration," worked hard, after the foundation of the IEA, to grow a patchwork of similar organizations around the world.[56] Through what he called the Atlas Foundation, think tanks such as the Fisher Institute in Dallas, the Fraser Institute in Vancouver, the Manhattan Institute in New York City, and the Cato Institute, first in San Francisco and then removed to Washington, D.C., all modeled on the IEA, were established across North America. Many more sprang up all over the world after 1980, especially in Eastern Europe and the countries of the former Communist bloc. John Redwood, once a member of Margaret Thatcher's Policy Unit and a cabinet minister in John Major's Conservative government, has described the neoliberal breakthrough into Eastern Europe in the 1990s after the fall of the Berlin Wall as a "revolution."[57] By the 1990s, it was clear that Fisher's legacy had contributed to the reforms that followed the collapse of the Berlin Wall in 1989. Fisher was a visionary who saw his project as international in scope and aimed at spreading free market, neoliberal ideas all over the world.

Fisher regularly wrote to tell Hayek of his progress in building this global network of institutes. For example, in the year of Ronald Reagan's election to the presidency in 1980, Fisher wrote:

To my knowledge there are now 11 institutes either trying to get started or beginning to run reasonably effectively. I am in touch with other people on every continent, and if I had the time and the money, many other institutes would get going quickly.

Personally, I am just beginning the difficult stage of developing what Ralph Harris and I are calling the Atlas Foundation, with tax-exempt status in England and the United States. First, this I hope will give me a base from which to work outside existing institutes. I have additionally, continued of course, to find the income to run an office and cover all my travels. This has never been easy, but I always somehow seem to manage. It is sad that it is necessary but since the tremendous losses in the Turtle business [a failed business venture that Fisher had invested in], I no longer have the personal resources.[58]

From the correspondence among members of the transatlantic neoliberal network, a picture emerges of individuals like Fisher as resolute campaigners, fundraisers, and organizers. They used their institutions as engines of a renaissance of free market ideas in Britain, the United States, and beyond. Although it is hard to map the direct influence of think tanks on particular government policies, they brought politicians and businessmen into contact with ideas and thinkers through conferences, journals, and newspapers. They reinforced the relationships that were fostered by the Mont Pelerin Society, such as that between Hayek and Fisher. Many think tanks also raised the public profile of free market policies through their publications, educational courses, and campus activism.

The Institute for Humane Studies (IHS) was established by F. A. Harper. Known as "Baldy," Harper had been the economist at the FEE before leaving in 1958 to set up his own think tank. The IHS was founded in 1961 in California. Originally located in Menlo Park near San Francisco, the institute moved to Fairfax, Virginia, in 1985 as it began an association with George Mason University (where Buchanan's and Tullock's public choice program was based after it moved from the Virginia Polytechnic Institute). During the late 1980s the IHS was run by John Blundell, in another of the many examples of transatlantic cross-fertilization between these neoliberal institutions. The IHS listed its main areas of work as providing scholarships, fellowships, conferences, formal teaching, consultation services, publications, book distribution to scholars, and a library.[59]

The IHS worked closely with Hayek, who, like Russell Kirk, Leo Strauss, Eric Voegelin, and Albert Jay Nock, had in *The Constitution of Liberty* emphasized the importance of the "Judeo-Christian ethic." The Judeo-Christian ethic was something that the IHS also "recognized as a time-tested distillation of human revelation and experience."[60] The institute's focus on the religious foundations of Western civilization was close to the attitudes of Popper and Mises and was one of the main preoccupations bringing neoliberals together with other conservatives in the 1950s and 1960s. An IHS booklet from the 1960s that told the story of the institute directly quoted Hayek's ideas about the need for a neoliberal intellectual and political strategy:

The process of thought revolution, whether good or evil, has been described by many careful students of history. Professor F. A. Hayek summarizes it this way:

"Experience indicates that once a great body of intellectuals have accepted a philosophy, it is only a question of time until these views become the governing force of politics."[61]

The institute invited Hayek to America as a visiting scholar in 1977, the year in which it also held a conference on Austrian economics. In 1980 the institute launched a Hayek Fund for scholars. Like the FEE, the IHS saw itself primarily as an educational institute that would help keep ideas of the free market and individual liberty alive.

Other important organizations in a similar vein in the United States were the American Economic Foundation and the Liberty Fund. The AEF was founded in Cleveland in 1939 by Fred G. Clark to promote free market ideas. It moved to New York City in the 1940s, and by 1963, Hayek and Antony Fisher, the British economist Graham Hutton, and the British advertising executive John Rodgers, then head of J. Walter Thompson, had all served on its board. They were accompanied from the United States by Friedman, Mises, Russell Kirk, Richard Mellon Scaife, William F. Buckley, Jr., and Henry Hazlitt. The organization wound down after Clark's death in 1973, however, as its membership numbers fell. The Liberty Fund was established in Indianapolis in 1960 by another businessman, Pierre Goodrich, to spread libertarian ideas through publications, events, courses, and the sponsorship of students and scholars. It runs reputable workshops on aspects of political and social philosophy, usually with an aspect of individual liberty or the life of a theorist of freedom as the theme. It has specialized in publishing new editions of classic texts by authors such as John Locke, Adam Smith, David Hume, James Madison, Alexander Hamilton, and Lord Acton, as well as Hayek, Friedman, Mises, Buchanan, and Tullock. It has also produced a series of interviews and intellectual portrait DVDs that have included important British and Australian neoliberals such as Peter Bauer, Ralph Harris, Arthur Seldon, and Alan Walters. Think tanks such as the IHS and the Liberty Fund saw themselves as providing what the supposedly mainstream liberal establishment, the academic institutions attacked by William F. Buckley in *God and Man at Yale*, would never offer to conservative and libertarian scholars: a source of funding and resources for their academic study and institutional bases where the universities would not.

The Second Wave: Free Market Think Tanks in the 1970s

A second major wave of think tanks was established in the 1970s as the post-war settlement died. The Centre for Policy Studies was founded in Britain in 1974 to be an additional policy arm of the Conservative Party in the wake of the collapse of Edward Heath's Premiership. Set up by Alfred Sherman under the patronage of Sir Keith Joseph and Margaret Thatcher, the CPS drew on the ideas of Hayek and Friedman, to promote a new economic policy agenda that would address the trade union "problem" and the scourge of inflation. Unlike most of the other think tanks, which regarded themselves as independent of political parties, the CPS was tasked explicitly with the exploration and development of new ideas for the Tory leadership. A former communist, Sherman developed the CPS into the prime motor, along with the IEA, behind Thatcher's overhaul of Conservative Party policy in opposition during the 1970s. Sherman was an outspoken and forceful personality. Eventually he began to criticize what he saw as Thatcher's timidity in office. However, she always credited him with playing a central role in the policy successes of the government especially in terms of Thatcher's strategy in opposition, and the CPS remained an important generator of Conservative policy ideas.

The IEA and, to a lesser extent, the CPS were crucial in bringing the thought of Hayek and Friedman to wider public attention in Britain. Their work provided a "public platform" for these "academic dissenters" and influenced important journalists such as Samuel Brittan, William Rees-Mogg, and the future chancellor, Nigel Lawson, wrote Jock Bruce-Gardyne, a Conservative MP and journalist, in the *Telegraph* in 1978.[62] The IEA, like the CPS later, was also highly influential among Conservative Party politicians. Geoffrey Howe, Nigel Lawson, Norman Lamont, and Leon Brittan, home secretary under Thatcher and brother of monetarist economic commentator Samuel Brittan, all attest to the significance of the IEA in rekindling free market ideas during the 1960s and 1970s.[63] At a dinner to celebrate the thirtieth anniversary of the institute, Margaret Thatcher echoed Reagan's sentiments about the Heritage Foundation quoted at the beginning of this chapter:

> Anyone who dared to challenge the conventional wisdom of the post-war concensus [sic] was derided, pilloried, criticised, frowned upon, and looked down upon as being either reactionary, pitiful, or ignorant. . . .

The IEA dared to challenge that. You did not say, as so many others do, "what can a few people do among so many?" . . . You set out to challenge, to change public sentiment . . . once you, with your courage, gave expression to other views others followed . . . what we have achieved could never have been done without the leadership of the Institute of Economic Affairs.[64]

The institute was the single most important organization promoting neoliberal ideas in the 1960s, when it was considered to be on the lunatic fringe—they were seen as "Nutters," according to Leon Brittan—of British politics.[65]

In the United States, the Heritage Foundation and the Cato Institute were the most prominent of the new wave of think tanks to emerge during the 1970s. The Heritage Foundation saw itself as conservative. It was founded in 1973 by Paul Weyrich and Ed Feulner. Feulner became president in 1977 and grew the organization through his links to the Republican Party and the wider conservative movement. He studied at the LSE in the 1960s and was also an intern at the IEA. Feulner arrived in Britain in 1965, armed with a letter of introduction from Milton Friedman to the director of the IEA, Ralph Harris. He was taken on as a research assistant on a project looking at the power of the British Trade Union Congress being undertaken by John Lincoln. According to Feulner, "it was a real time of intellectual ferment, both in policy and in politics," and working at the IEA was a boon because it afforded him the opportunity to attend their events and come into contact with some of the intellectual stars that surrounded the institute.[66]

According to Feulner, Hayek was "approachable" and about to reenter the academic and intellectual mainstream at this time in the mid-1960s.[67] Feulner also encountered the ideas of Peter Bauer at the LSE, whose work was beginning to "blow away [the work of the development economist] Walt Rostow" and his views on international aid and development. Bauer's reputation was really based on his advocacy for free markets rather than being a brilliant economist. According to Keith Tribe, this "was why he became Thatcher's favourite economist."[68] Bauer argued that aid was counterproductive because it got into the wrong hands and inhibited the introduction of free markets. Markets had to be unleashed, according to Bauer, in order for developing countries to be incentivized properly to improve their economic performance and to generate enough wealth to catch up with richer countries. Feulner spent two terms at the IEA absorbing the ideas of all these neoliberal thinkers and saw the experience as an invaluable inside view of the workings of a think tank on which he was able to draw when he came to head the Heritage Foundation.

On completion of his doctorate, Feulner moved into policy work in the United States and initially worked on Capitol Hill as an assistant to the Republican congressman Philip Crane and as staff director for the Republican Study Committee. This was a research unit for Republican congressmen and senators to brief them on legislative developments so that they might better generate a common view. He was joined there in the mid-1970s by Madsen Pirie and the brothers Eamonn and Stuart Butler, all recent graduates of St. Andrews University in Scotland, who later started the Adam Smith Institute in London in 1977. The Heritage Foundation had a similar though nonpartisan aim: to provide briefings and policy advice to congressmen, executive branch staffers, academics, and journalists. It was funded by the beer magnate Joseph Coors, and Feulner was on the board from the start, though it was initially run by Weyrich, subsequently a tireless conservative policy commentator and activist. Feulner, who also became a member of the Mont Pelerin Society, had been invited to head the about to be created Manhattan Institute, but was advised by friends to take over the Heritage Foundation, an already established organization, instead.[69]

According to Feulner, the Heritage Foundation's aim was different from the IEA's in that it tried to pass the "briefcase test." Heritage briefings were meant to provide a primer on a particular issue that a congressman could digest on the train home in an accessible form that fit into his briefcase.[70] Heritage's focus was on the issues that would unite conservatives from all of the different strands of the movement, the libertarians, neoconservatives, the religious and Christian conservatives, and traditional conservatives—in this sense he believed in William F. Buckley's fusionism. For example, Heritage was the link between Hayek and Ronald Reagan. Reagan acknowledged his debt to Hayek in a letter from 1984 to Eamonn Butler, thanking him for a copy of his book on Hayek:

> You may be certain that I share your admiration for Dr. Hayek, who has played an absolutely essential role in preparing the ground for the resurging conservative movement in America. In a real sense, Ed Feulner and I—along with many, many others—are his legatees, so it is

encouraging to see your scholarly work give his ideas the attention they deserve.[71]

The Heritage Foundation was crucial in the American context in bringing together neoliberal thinkers and their ideas with Republican politicians.

After Reagan's election victory, Heritage provided the administration with a thousand-page edited tome, *Mandate for Leadership* (1980), which offered detailed proposals for every major policy area by Heritage Foundation policy researchers and contributors. The foundation claimed on its website that nearly two-thirds of these proposals were realized during Reagan's tenure in office.[72] The Heritage Foundation also collected information on sympathetic national and international conservative policy academics, journalists, and activists through the development of its resource bank. The idea was to make the foundation a "hub of the conservative movement."[73] As William E. Simon, treasury secretary under Nixon and Ford, put it, the "foundation started the Resource Bank to help policy experts from across the country and the world to play a greater role in Washington policymaking." The Heritage Foundation's *Guide to Public Policy Experts* contained information on more than two thousand policy specialists and four hundred institutions.[74] The foundation helped cement and expand the transatlantic network through a properly resourced tool that connected conservative and neoliberal experts and thinkers.

The Cato Institute, founded by Ed Crane in 1977, was of a different character from the Heritage Foundation. It was libertarian rather than conservative. Crane was a young businessman whose main influences were Hayek, Friedman, and three American libertarian women authors, Isabel Patterson, Ayn Rand, and Rose Wilder Lane.[75] Ayn Rand in particular was influential among various neoliberal policymakers—Alan Greenspan, for example—through her novels, *The Fountainhead* (1943) and *Atlas Shrugged* (1957).[76] In 1974, Crane took time out from his day job in investment to chair the new Libertarian Party and run Roger McBride's Libertarian presidential campaign in 1976 and Ed Clark's California gubernatorial campaign of 1978. He was persuaded to leave his job permanently to set up a new think tank after he hit it off with billionaire businessman Charles Koch, who had also been involved in McBride's presidential bid.[77] Koch had taken over his father's business, the energy conglomerate Koch Industries, in 1961, and returned it to profitability.

Koch was also a major philanthropist, a member of the Mont Pelerin Society (like McBride, and later Crane as well), and a supporter of neoliberal causes. He funded a scholarship in his name at the IHS. Crane had been aware of the success of the AEI and the Brookings Institution, and thought that a libertarian think tank "would have a lot of leverage" in the market for political ideas.[78] Koch offered additional persuasion by promising to match the salary Crane was earning and agreeing that Crane could run the Cato Institute from San Francisco.

With the help of Murray Rothbard (an American Austrian school economist, former student of Ludwig von Mises, and fellow Mont Pelerin Society member), Crane started the Cato Institute in the Bay Area of San Francisco in 1977. As Crane tells it, "Charles [Koch] was a lot smarter than me, he knew that I myself would eventually move the think-tank back here [to Washington, D.C.] which I did in 1981."[79] Cato was also influenced by the British IEA and the ideological crusades of Antony Fisher. Though Fisher was not directly involved in its establishment, the Cato Institute worked very closely with Fisher's Atlas Foundation, the international umbrella organization for neoliberal think tanks that Fisher had set up. Crane suggests that the Cato Institute is the "closest clone of the IEA of all the free market think-tanks" in the United States. Hayek and Friedman also worked closely with Crane and Cato. The institute established a biennial Prize for Advancing Liberty in Friedman's name. Peter Bauer, the British development economist, won the prize in 2002. Hayek became a distinguished fellow there in 1985. Hayek joined the editorial board of Cato's *Policy Report* in 1979. Cato also reprinted two IEA monographs by Hayek, *Full Employment at Any Price?* (1978) and *A Tiger by the Tail* (1979). The title of the second was changed for the American audience from *Unemployment and Monetary Policy: Government as Generator of the "Business Cycle."* The change had been agreed with John Wood, the deputy director of the IEA.[80] The Cato Institute and the Heritage Foundation promoted the ideas of Hayek, Friedman, and other neoliberals to new and younger audiences in Washington, D.C., in the 1980s and 1990s. Institute members and leadership also expanded the neoliberal network and provided it with much greater organizational and financial clout in the United States.

In Britain, the London-based Adam Smith Institute was another important think tank to emerge in the 1970s. Madsen Pirie and Eamonn and Stuart Butler had studied together at St. Andrews University, which was something of a nest of neoliberalism in the 1950s, 1960s, and 1970s. Future Thatcherite ministers John MacGregor, Michael Fallon, and Michael Forsyth all attended St Andrews, and Ralph Harris taught there before he left to run the IEA. Pirie and the Butler brothers graduated in the early 1970s and subsequently worked together in Washington, D.C., with Ed Feulner on the Republican Study Committee in the mid-1970s. The group originally conceived of the institute as an academic transatlantic organization that would arrange for student exchanges and courses in a similar vein to the ISI or the Liberty Fund.[81] However, its purpose changed once it began. Pirie and now just Eamonn Butler (Stuart had moved to the United States to work for the Heritage Foundation) realized they could gain traction in the British press for their ideas. They were heavily influenced by Buchanan's and Tullock's public choice theory and wanted to "devise policies that would work" with the grain of vested interests to make the reforms stick.[82] According to Pirie, the institute was intended to provide a positive "policy counterpart to public choice," through its methodology of "micropolitics," which marked an attempt to move a free market agenda forward in policy spheres such as health or public administration incrementally. The idea was that each set of small-scale reforms would alter the policy framework slightly but would provide an improved foundation for the next set of market-based reforms, and so on and on. It was based in a belief that people feared radical or revolutionary change and that they were far more likely to accept a gradual process of improvement.[83]

As with so many others, the ASI was originally established with the help of battery chicken farmer Antony Fisher. The ASI, like the Heritage Foundation, consciously built the neoliberal network. Eamonn Butler wrote to Hayek in 1978, telling him of their latest projects:

> The Monthly Bulletin is just a first step in a long-term project, the Adam Smith Institute Freedom Resource Centre. The centre is building a computerised file of individuals and organisations working to further the free society, and eventually it will be possible for other groups and individuals to obtain details of their co-workers on the basis of specialty, field of interest, availability and many other useful items of information.
>
> . . . As you can see (or may know) the Institute is not a campaigning organisation, but an educational one, intended to improve the flow of

ideas about free market and social institutions. One of its specialities is in bringing to Britain the positive lessons of free enterprise in the United States, and in taking to America the lessons of socialism in Britain.[84]

Hayek joined the international advisory board of the ASI in February 1979.[85] The ASI influenced the Thatcher governments' policies during the 1980s through its work on privatization and "contracting out," the use of private contractors in the delivery of local government public services, an idea the ASI imported from state governmental practice in the United States. It was also partially responsible for proposing the Community Charge, or poll tax, a local taxation scheme suggested by one of its writers, Douglas Mason, in his report, *Revising the Ratings System* (1985).[86]

The Manhattan Institute (known first as the International Center for Economic Policy Studies) was also established in 1977. The Manhattan Institute became prominent during the 1980s for its promotion of Charles Murray's study of postwar social policy, *Losing Ground,* which suggested that the policies of the Great Society and the War on Poverty had been counterproductive and had led to a culture of dependency among the poor and indigent.[87] The institute's president, William Hammett, sent copies of the book to congressional Republican leader Bob Dole and to Thatcher's No. 10 Downing Street Policy Unit. Dole was tentative in his reply, stating, "I enjoyed it very much. I agree with much of what he states in the early chapters, but I am not certain I fully understand how he would correct some of the problems."[88] At No. 10, David Willetts, future Conservative MP and minister, received it, hailed it as "thought-provoking," and suggested an informal meeting to discuss its contents.[89] The Manhattan Institute, like the Cato Institute, was inspired by the IEA, and Fisher was again instrumental in its foundation. It focused on bringing thinkers, writers, and experts together through publications and events in New York City. Both Hayek and Friedman were involved in its early activities, and the institute holds an annual Hayek lecture.

Another breed of think-tanker, aside from the directors and presidents, were thinkers who provided a serious intellectual cutting edge. These thinkers popularized ideas and made them both accessible and applicable to policy and politics. Arthur Seldon, editorial director of the IEA, is the best example of this type of individual. Seldon vigorously defended the rigor of the institute's approach when he thought it had been slighted. In 1975, he chastised Hayek in a missive that reveals some of the nuances of these neoliberal organizations:

> [Can I correct] what may be a misapprehension. When you were here some months ago, you praised the Institute as being successful in publishing simplified versions of liberal economic writing. That is part of our work, but I think our main purpose has been to apply to current and coming economic problems and policies the best economic thinking which in our opinion comes from economists who appreciate micro-economic analysis without ignoring macro-economic aspects where they are relevant.
>
> In this work we have certainly sponsored economists in new applications of economic theory, and I think we can claim even to have pioneered studies into neglected studies [*sic*].[90]

Hayek apologized profusely in his reply, "if I ever have given the impression that I regard IEA as a mere popularising propaganda institution"; he highlighted the comparison with Leonard Read's Foundation for Economic Education:

> Indeed my constant difficulty when talking formally or informally about it is not to offend old friends like Leonard Read by saying too plainly how infinitely superior I regard it compared to such propaganda efforts as the Irvington setup [FEE] which aims at providing better arguments to the already converted—a meritorious but to me neither very interesting nor very effective effort. What I admire the IEA for is exactly for sponsoring and doing original work of great importance.[91]

Hayek then spoke of Seldon's personal role at the IEA with contrition and affection for both Seldon himself and the organization: "in private conversation I have said again and again almost in the words what you say in your letter. I am sorry if I have never said this to you since I am also fully aware that the scientific side of the work of the Institute is mainly your work—or more correctly, due to your inspiration." Hayek's attritional tone is tangible and his affection for both Seldon and the IEA is clear in this letter. Seldon was primarily responsible for the IEA's intellectual credibility and its reputation for independence, something he fought for tenaciously when it was called into question by critics.

Others, such as Murray and Stuart Butler, were academic policy wonks. Butler began in Britain at the ASI—which explicitly aimed to move ideas back and forth between Britain and the United States—with his brother Eamonn Butler and Madsen Pirie, but moved to Washington, D.C., to work at the Heritage Foundation and rejoin Ed Feulner, as we have seen. Butler brought with him Geoffrey Howe and the British socialist urban planner and geographer Peter Hall's idea for enterprise zones, which subsequently became the centerpiece of the Reagan administration's urban policy (see discussion in chapter 6). Butler eventually became a U.S. citizen, worked at the Heritage Foundation, and settled permanently in Washington, D.C.—an example of the brain drain from Britain to the United States in the 1970s, according to his brother Eamonn.[92]

Alongside the think tanks were American foundations and business funders of free market scholars and institutes such as Joseph Coors, Charles Koch, and Richard Mellon Scaife. Several other important funds included the Earhart Foundation, the William Volker Fund, and the Relm Foundation, which grew out of it. The WVF was instrumental in bringing Hayek to Chicago from the LSE in 1950. It was set up by the anti–New Deal businessman William Volker himself in 1932, with the leadership assumed by Harold Luhnow in 1944. Luhnow was also responsible for helping Hayek get the Mont Pelerin Society off the ground.[93] He also ensured that the WVF funded Mises' salary at New York University and Hayek's at the University of Chicago. Both Friedman and Hayek were regularly consulted in the 1950s and 1960s about who should receive scholarships and grant money from these large foundations. Hayek recommended Antony Fisher for help with his various think tank projects. Murray Rothbard was supported by the WVF. British academics and policymakers were funded to come over and work in American universities. The British-based American conservative philosopher Shirley Letwin, for example, was nominated by Hayek in 1955 for funding from the Earhart Foundation. Milton Friedman suggested British economist Stanley Dennison, the only person allowed to read the proofs of Hayek's *Road to Serfdom* before publication, for a grant from the WVF in 1958. At the time, Dennison was one of the few anti-Keynesian voices at Cambridge University.[94] Writing to the WVF's Richard Cornuelle, who later became an adviser

to Nixon and Reagan, Friedman suggested that Dennison was an "absolutely first rate person both intellectually and personally" but that he had
"allowed himself to be involved in administrative posts that have left him altogether too little time and energy for scientific work. . . . Dennison is one
of the few people in England who has maintained a constant nineteenth-
century liberal policy position in the face of a generally hostile intellectual
atmosphere. He has exercised an important influence in this direction on
the Cambridge student body."[95] This is typical of the sort of recommendations that were solicited and provided by trusted advisers such as Friedman
and Hayek.

Both the U.S.-based Relm Foundation and the Earhart Foundation
were regular supporters of meetings of the Mont Pelerin Society throughout the 1950s and 1960s.[96] Indeed, the difference in the funding capacities
of the Americans compared to the British is shown in a letter from Leonard
Read to Hayek from 1970 inviting him to give a talk to the FEE on inflation.
Read told Hayek that he should "by all means make the trip first-class both
ways."[97] American affluence was due to the willingness of businessmen to
fund neoliberal organizations and causes. At the same time, the Mont Pelerin Society bound many of these people and institutions together and gave
them the sense of being part of a larger movement, which they clearly felt.
As George Shultz put it, the society brought together "like-minded people,
who nevertheless argued with each other, and often started from different
premises."[98] The international network of neoliberals created a sense of fellowship that was sustained by the Mont Pelerin Society, the Atlas Foundation, and the constant communication between the American and British
think tanks.

The neoliberal conception of freedom as rooted in the free market underlay the goals, statements of aims, and purposes of these funds, organizations,
and think tanks. Cosmopolitan, transatlantic, and international in their outlook, there was a process of cross-fertilization that carried on, imperceptible
to the wider political classes or the public, that nevertheless shored up the
intellectual infrastructure of neoliberalism. The favored medium of the think
tanks was the written word, in the form of pamphlets, research reports, and
publications. A memo from the FEE, undated but probably from the early
1950s, to "Liberals of the British Isles and the Continent of Europe" discusses
the "Interchange of Liberal Literature:"

While our effort is directed mainly to persons within the United States, it is obvious that liberalism knows no national boundaries. The interchange of ideas and literature between liberals from all countries is now imperative.

Exchange controls prevent the "free purchase of liberal literature to the country in which it is produced."

We feel that it is consistent with the purpose of the Foundation to make available, within our means, to liberals in other countries, such books and publications, produced in America, as may be requested.

There may be other forms of service which we are in a special position to perform as an aid in the promotion of liberal ideas. Please feel at liberty to so express yourself.

In return, and this is all, we hope that you will apprise us of any works which you think may be valuable to our effort or which should be considered for distribution in America.[99]

Another example of typical transatlantic exchange comes when Ralph Raico, another of Mises' former students, writes to Hayek to tell him about the launch of the Cato Institute's new journal:

[Launch of "Inquiry" will be] a counterpart to The New Republic and National Review. Naturally we would like to establish contact with various writers in England and on the Continent who could either report on the local situation or provide us with articles of a more general scope. . . . As you may gather from the enclosed description, our main purpose will be to establish a dialogue between libertarians and those who in the United States are called "liberals"; so we would not want anyone who was too obviously "Tory." Writers with a strong and broad commitment to personal liberty would be most valuable from our point of view. I need hardly say that any assistance you could give us along these lines would be most appreciated. By the way, we are adequately funded and pay authors at competitive rates.[100]

The ideological entrepreneurs who ran these think tanks shaped their intellectual agenda and output and promoted detailed policy prescriptions that challenged the liberal and social democratic orthodoxy. These ideas were then pushed through the transatlantic network of institutions and individuals. A good example was the proposal of a U.S. constitutional amendment to limit taxes. James Buchanan and Milton Friedman provided prominent and vocal ballast to the supporters of the tax revolts that rose up across the United States during the 1970s, most prominently through the campaign for Proposition 13 in California in 1978. Tax was always a central preoccupation of Friedman's, and during the 1970s his ideas for tax reform—his universal support for tax cuts and his proposal of a negative income tax—received wide attention. Friedman argued that public expenditure was the most unwelcome sign of the expansion of government power. For Friedman, it was therefore much more important to reduce taxation than to reduce deficits.

Proposition 13 was a proposal to introduce a constitutional limit in California on property taxation of 1 percent, as well as requiring two-thirds majorities for the passage through the state legislature of other tax increases, including income tax. The Heritage Foundation Policy Review published an article by Friedman in 1978 on the tax issue in which he argued,

> There is an important point that needs to be stressed to those who regard themselves as fiscal conservatives. By concentrating on the wrong thing, the deficit, instead of the right thing, total government spending, fiscal conservatives have been the unwitting handmaidens of the big spenders. The typical historical process is that the spenders put through laws which increase government spending. A deficit emerges. The fiscal conservatives scratch their heads and say, "My God, that's terrible; we have got to do something about that deficit." So they cooperate with the big spenders in getting taxes imposed. As soon as the new taxes are imposed and passed, the big spenders are off again, and then there is another burst in government spending and another deficit.[101]

This quotation illustrates the logic of Friedman's suspicion of fiscal conservatism without tax cuts. It was a position that enabled supporters of Ronald Reagan's presidency to parry criticisms of budgetary irresponsibility. Friedman's argument for tax cuts could produce a certain laxness in relation to deficits, a position that many, especially in Britain, disagreed with. Nigel Lawson, for example, argued that Friedman was "too relaxed" about deficits because when it becomes accepted that they do not matter, the pressures on public spending greatly increase.[102]

The transatlantic network of neoliberal think tanks, foundations, funds, sympathetic businessmen, and policy experts described above worked tirelessly to promote its agenda throughout these thankless decades. Although these efforts largely fell on deaf ears in the political mainstream and among the general public, the subtle shifts in the ideological armory of the Right engendered through the promotion of scholarships, publications, and events were perceptible to the perspicacious observer. Neoliberal ideas about the power of free markets and the dangers of government entered the minds of some important and influential individuals in the media and the political parties, who in turn spread the word. Leading neoliberals and their ideas succeeded in the creation of an alternative ideological infrastructure that was able to take advantage when economic and political events took a turn for the worse in the early 1970s. The groundwork that had been laid by these organizations and individuals enabled them to capitalize on the crises when they came and to deliver a set of readymade policy proposals to those in power and in need of new responses to the economic problems of stagflation.

Neoliberal Journalists and Politicians

Many influential journalists and politicians were persuaded by the neoliberal ideas and insights that were peddled and promoted by the think tanks. One tireless journalist in the United States was William F. Buckley, Jr., the founder and editor of the *National Review,* which he edited between 1955 and 1990. Buckley was not strictly a neoliberal, though he shared many of their major preoccupations, in particular a strong commitment to the free market. Buckley was the grand architect of fusionism, the attempt to unite traditional and religious conservatives and libertarians in one camp.[103] Buckley promoted many neoliberal concerns and proposals in his *National Review* and on his long-running television show, *Firing Line.* Friedman, who wrote a weekly column in *Newsweek,* was a good friend of Buckley's and an admirer of Buckley's many newspaper articles. In reply to Buckley's letter asking him about his burgeoning journalistic career, Friedman said, "I have been enjoying it very much." He mentioned that his load was incomparable to Buckley's as it was "so relatively light," and that he was impressed by Buckley's prodigious output, which he thought "[stood] up, steadily and regularly, to an extraordinary standard."[104] Buckley's efforts to counter the dominant liberal political establishment had a lasting impact through his work both as a journalist and as a political adviser to and friend of Barry Goldwater and Ronald Reagan.

In Britain, the IEA did a sterling job as one of the only voices in favor of neoliberal policies during the 1950s and 1960s before the CPS and the ASI joined them in the 1970s. The IEA advocated for free markets, deregulation, trade union and labor reform, and the reform of rent control and housing policy. Ralph Harris and Arthur Seldon frequently published articles in the national press publicizing their authors' research. The most important journalists to pick up neoliberal economic ideas, especially Chicago school monetarism, were Samuel Brittan of the *Financial Times*, William Rees-Mogg of the *Times*, and Peter Jay of the *Times* and the BBC. These writers were convinced of the failures of Keynesian demand management and "fine-tuning." Jay in particular, the son of Labour Party cabinet minister Douglas Jay, president of the Board of Trade under Wilson, was a close adviser to Prime Minister James Callaghan during the economic crises of the 1970s and became Callaghan's ambassador to the United States in 1977. He was responsible for Callaghan's famous speech to the Labour Party Conference in 1976 that sounded the death knell of Keynesian demand management as the guiding policy framework in Britain (see full discussion in chapter 6). Sympathetic and convinced journalists were especially important in changing the climate of opinion on economic issues in Britain in the 1960s and 1970s. They gave credibility to some of the ideas coming out of the neoliberal think tanks that would not have been taken seriously otherwise. In the case of Jay and Samuel Brittan, they also showed that party political affiliation was not important to whether the ideas should be adopted or not.

Arizona Republican senator and presidential opponent of Lyndon Johnson Barry Goldwater and the former New Deal Democrat actor, union leader (he was head of the Screen Actors Guild), Republican governor of California, and U.S. president Ronald Reagan were among the first politicians to promote neoliberal ideas in the United States. Despite losing the 1964 presidential election to Johnson by the greatest margin in a generation, Goldwater was a trailblazer of the New Right. He employed Friedman as an economic expert, and William S. Baroody, Sr., of the AEI was his principal political adviser. Despite losing to Lyndon Johnson by a crushing margin of 61 percent to 39 percent and carrying only six states in the Deep South, Goldwater pushed strictly libertarian and free market policies, and his legacy was to radicalize the grass roots of the Republican Party.[105] His defeat has often been seen as the high-water mark of New Deal and Great Society liberalism, but his nomination actually marked important shifts in U.S. politics. The successful attempt by conservatives to draft the Arizona senator over the Eastern liberal Nelson Rockefeller represented for Rick Perlstein "the unmaking of the American consensus."[106] Goldwater's nomination showed that the Republican Party had moved in a radically different direction after the moderation of Dwight D. Eisenhower's presidency. The party was being taken over by a different range of interests located away from the old sources of wealth and influence on the eastern seaboard and toward the South and West, a development that would soon be reflected in its policies. It was no accident that the biggest hit of the Republican Convention that year was Ronald Reagan.

Like many conservative Republicans, and like his close friend, President John F. Kennedy, Barry Goldwater was a fiscal conservative and an avid cold warrior and foreign policy hawk. He supported Eisenhower's limited civil rights legislation of 1957 and 1960 but, although he was not racist himself (he worked closely with the NAACP in his native Arizona), Goldwater voted against Johnson's comprehensive 1964 civil rights bill on the basis of states' rights—the rights of the states to autonomous self-government—and the unwarranted extension of federal power. Mary Brennan, too, has seen the 1964 campaign as the result of a decision reached by many conservatives in the early 1960s that the Republican Party was the only viable vehicle for their ambitions.[107] Ed Crane of the Cato Institute has argued, in an interview with the author, that despite Eisenhower's election in 1952, the real change in neo-liberal fortunes occurred when Goldwater's *The Conscience of a Conservative* (1960) became the most popular political book in the United States. According to Crane, "Hayek would have expected" a reaction to the overweening liberalism of Roosevelt, Truman, Kennedy, and Johnson:

> that you would have a philosophical backlash when you have had a radical change in the nature of society and culture, one that was emphasizing individualism and then was radically changed into dominant

central government in all aspects of people's lives—because the *Conscience of a Conservative*, although not actually written by Goldwater—he signed off on it—was really an attack on the New Deal.[108]

Goldwater's success signaled that henceforth, the conservatives controlled the Republican Party agenda, which ensured a rupture between the Republican and the Democratic Parties and their outlook toward the legacies of Roosevelt and Johnson. This did not happen immediately, as Nixon's uncomfortable contortions would illustrate. But Crane is probably not exaggerating, politically at least, when he suggests that through the insurgency that his presidential campaign inspired, "Goldwater had started a movement."[109]

Ronald Reagan first came to political prominence through the speech he delivered at the Republican Convention at Cow Palace in San Francisco that nominated Goldwater in 1964. A master of political communication, Reagan became governor of California in 1966. He began to develop a homespun politics that drew heavily on radical neoliberal individualism. Business should take more responsibility in the exercise of political power rather than the other way around, Reagan argued, "politics is too important to be left to the politicians."[110] In a speech to the Institute of Directors in London in 1969, he suggested that business succeeded despite government interference because of "the virility of the free enterprise system." Quoting Ludwig von Mises, Reagan urged that business "recognize its obligation to participate in public affairs," by which he meant "more than just campaign contributions and attendance at rallies." Instead, Reagan advocated deep penetration of government by the "expertise and management skill of the private sector." It is easy to see here some of the roots of what George Soros has called "market fundamentalism."[111]

George Shultz later became Reagan's chairman of the President's Economic Policy Advisory Board in the White House and his secretary of state. Shultz earned a PhD from MIT in 1948 and served as a faculty member, working on labor issues. He took a leave of absence to serve as senior staff economist for President Eisenhower's Council of Economic Advisers before moving to the University of Chicago Business School in 1957 to become professor of industrial relations. Chicago was "the most intense intellectual environment I have ever experienced," according to Shultz.[112] He became dean of the University of Chicago Business School in 1962 before entering politics in the Nixon administration, where he served as labor secretary, director of the Office of Management and Budget, and treasury secretary.[113] Shultz was another early member of the Mont Pelerin Society who straddled the worlds of academia and politics, and his experience illustrates the ability of the neoliberal network to bring together influential decision makers and expose them to discussions of policies and ideas.

In Britain, politicians such as Keith Joseph and Margaret Thatcher, who, as we have seen, together established the Hayekian CPS with Alfred Sherman in 1974, became convinced of neoliberal ideas through the journalism of Peter Jay in the *Times* or Sam Brittan in the *Financial Times*. Former journalist Nigel Lawson and Conservative MP Norman Lamont, both later chancellors of the exchequer, were also converted either through the articles of Jay and Brittan, or through reading Friedman and Hayek's books or IEA pamphlets, or by attending events at the IEA and the CPS.[114] Again, the impetus in Britain came from the perceived economic breakdown of Keynesianism that seemed to be taking place in the early 1970s.

Joseph, Thatcher, and Howe were all scarred by the experience of Edward Heath's government of 1970–74. In Britain, the excesses of trade union power and the unions' ability to increase public sector wage settlements and thus fuel inflation became the single most important rallying cry for Conservatives, who felt that Heath's government had betrayed its radical agenda. This free market program was supposedly set out at the Selsdon Conference, the shadow cabinet conference, in 1970.[115] Joseph made the most significant policy speech of Thatcher's period of opposition, "Monetarism Is Not Enough."[116] He argued that the trade unions—the labor market supply—had to be reformed, together with the institution of a monetarist economic policy if Britain was to recover. Joseph, thought of as the philosopher-king of the new Conservatism of the 1970s, was responsible for reintroducing Thatcher to the work of Hayek and Friedman (she claimed to have already read them).[117]

Nigel Lawson, when still financial secretary to the treasury, claimed that neoliberalism was essentially conservative in a speech he made in 1980:

> To the extent that new Conservatives turn to new sages—such as Hayek and Friedman—that is partly because what those writers are doing is avowedly reinterpreting the traditional political and economic wisdom of Hume, Burke and Adam Smith in terms of the conditions

of today; and partly because, as specialists in economics (although Hayek in particular is a great deal more than that) they are of particular interest in an age in which, for better or worse, economic policy has achieved a centrality in the political debate which it never enjoyed in, say, the golden age of Disraeli and Gladstone. . . . The essential point is that what we are witnessing is the reversion to an older tradition in the light of the failure of what might be termed the new enlightenment. This is important, politically, not in the sense of some kind of appeal to ancestor-worship or to the legitimacy of scriptural authority: it is important because these traditions are, even today, more deeply rooted in the hearts and minds of ordinary people than is the conventional wisdom of the recent past.[118]

Friedman and Hayek themselves disagreed with this view. Hayek wrote a famous essay titled "Why I Am Not a Conservative," in which he declared himself to be a Burkean Whig.[119] In a similar vein, Friedman wrote to the British monetarist journalist and financier Tim Congdon in 1979: "I do not want to keep things as they are; I want to change them drastically." Friedman argued that liberalism's traditional meaning "of and pertaining to freedom" was closer to "the core of our fundamental philosophy," although, he concluded, "I flinch but seldom object when I am called a conservative."[120] Both Hayek and Friedman understood that their ideas had found a home in the Conservative Party in Britain and the conservative movement, whose vehicle was the Republican Party, in the United States.

Breakthrough?

Neoliberals were perceived as "eccentric right-wingers" by the economic and policy mainstream for much of the postwar period, according to the public choice theorist and Nobel Prize winner James Buchanan, writing to Hayek in 1963. But "this does not especially bother us," he added.[121] By the 1970s, however, the political climate was different. Neoliberalism was on the verge of a breakthrough. Still very much in the minority at the start of the decade, by 1980 neoliberal policies were at the core of the manifestos for government of both Ronald Reagan and Margaret Thatcher. The economic crises of these years—the collapse of the Bretton Woods international monetary system, stagflation across the Western world, the virtual collapse of labor relations in Britain, two oil crises, and the failures of prices and incomes policies—transformed the prospects of transatlantic neoliberal politics.

Neoliberal thought had been expertly promoted by the intellectuals and entrepreneurs who made up the web of transatlantic institutions and organizations that were beginning to be able to influence policymakers in London and Washington, D.C. The story of how these ideas became part of the political programs of Thatcher and Reagan, and before them the Labour and Democratic Party administrations that preceded, is one that is often assumed to have been inevitable. It has been told as a heroic story of the power of ideas and the force of individual personalities.[122] But despite the efforts described in this chapter, much in the end was the result of historical accident and a particular alignment of circumstances in the 1970s and early 1980s. This messy historical reality is visible in how neoliberal ideas broke through in the fields of economic strategy and moderate-income housing and urban policy, issues to which we now turn.

5

✳

Keynesianism and the Emergence of Monetarism, 1945–1971

The tide is turning, if it is, not because people like myself have preached the fallacy or the erroneous elements in Keynesian thinking, but because demand management has obviously been a failure. Because, far from achieving a nirvana of steady high levels of employment with stable prices, it has managed to achieve the worst of both worlds: high inflation and high unemployment....
The role of thinkers I believe is primarily to keep options open, to have available alternatives, so when the brute force of events make a change inevitable, there is an alternative available to change it.

—Milton Friedman, *The Money Programme*, April 21, 1978

The neoliberal breakthrough came in the seemingly unlikely realm of technical economic policy. The long postwar boom, often dubbed the Golden Age of capitalism, continued through the 1950s and 1960s, when politicians and publics alike believed they understood how to effectively manage capitalism using the tools of demand management developed by John Maynard Keynes and especially as expanded by the next generation of Keynesian economists. The tide had not yet began to turn in favor of the free market. That would not happen until the crises of the 1970s forced a change in policy direction. But an important set of ideas did emerge from the transatlantic neoliberal network during the 1950s and 1960s that would pave the way for a much larger challenge to the dominance of New Deal liberalism and social democracy from a neoliberal philosophy based on the free market.[1]

This body of thought centered on the restatement of the quantity theory of money by Milton Friedman. Friedman became associated with a powerful critique of the Keynesian ideas that, in varying degrees, had been the guiding light of U.S. and British economic policy in the postwar years. His ideas, famously set out in his address to the American Economic Association (AEA) in 1967, influenced many critics of an economic order that appeared to have completely broken down amid the collapse of the international monetary system based on fixed exchange rates in 1971, a system that had been jointly designed by Harry Dexter White and Keynes at Bretton Woods in 1944. But the monetarist explanation of why Keynesian policies had stopped working—at its simplest, the idea that inflation was a monetary phenomenon—would also provide sensible cover, after the events of the 1970s, for the wholesale adoption of a free market creed during the subsequent administrations of Margaret Thatcher, Ronald Reagan, and beyond.

It was in the seemingly narrow and technical arena of economic strategy, then, that the transatlantic neoliberal ideological and political movement first entered the mainstream policy agendas of the Conservative and Republican Parties and, just as important, the policies of the Labour and Democratic Parties. Monetarism's first political foray came in Britain, not through Friedman but with the machinations of then Conservative financial secretary to the treasury Enoch Powell in the late 1950s. In the United States, Friedman and other Chicago school economists threw down the gauntlet in the 1960s, and by the end of the decade, monetarist ideas were gaining traction among growing numbers of the political and technocratic elite, precipitated by the first signs of monetary crisis, inflation, and, in Britain, rising labor unrest. At the dawn of the 1970s, Friedman and his supporters seemed to offer a plausible set of remedies just as faith in Keynesian tools was about to collapse under the weight of years of stagflation.

Pure theory did not mix easily with the temporal imperatives of politics and elections. As the former British chancellor of the exchequer Nigel Lawson put it, economic history was often "more useful than theory."[2] There was also much confusion about what monetarism actually was, how to measure money, how to determine the aspects of Keynes that worked and those that did not, and, finally, whether monetarism and "supply-side" reforms— tax cuts, labor market reform, and market-based antipoverty strategies, for example—were in conflict. In the end, both Keynesianism and monetarism suffered from many of the same problems, primarily a lack of accurate economic information and measurement. But in the late 1960s and 1970s, Friedman's monetarism and its variants seemed to offer the clearest alternative to the perceived failures of economic management revealed by the disasters of the seventies. This was due in part to the force and skill with which the case was argued and promoted by transatlantic neoliberals in both Britain and the United States.

Keynes and Keynesianism

John Maynard Keynes towered over economic policy in the twentieth century. It is important, however, to differentiate between Keynes the man, his own ideas, and the ideas of his followers in the postwar period.[3] Keynes died prematurely in 1946, exhausted by his efforts to negotiate a loan from the Americans. His intellectual legacy was defined by a flexible approach to both economic theory and practical politics. He famously stated that "in the long run we are all dead," by which he meant that economic policy should serve people and their needs rather than the long-term requirements of economic theory. According to Keynes, "economists set themselves too easy, too useless a task if in tempestuous seasons they can only tell us that when the storm is long past the ocean is flat again."[4] This attitude lay at the heart of his debates with Hayek during the 1930s.[5] Keynes thought that democracies could not tolerate—indeed, as the experience of the 1930s had demonstrated, might not survive—a repeat of the perils of large-scale unemployment. Consequently, he turned his wits to the development of a set of economic proposals to attack and prevent economic depression. The big question for supporters and critics ever since has been whether Keynes's ideas worked outside the circumstances of the 1930s and 1940s. (Some, of course, never acknowledged that they worked even in this context.) Keynes himself, chameleon-like, constantly changed his mind—he famously responded to Hayek's detailed critique of his *Treatise on Money* by saying that it no longer represented what he believed anyway—and was wedded only to what worked.

According to Robert Skidelsky, author of the best and most authoritative biography of Keynes, he was the "last of the great English Liberals."[6] His work represented an "attempt to restore the expectation of stability and progress in a world cut adrift from its nineteenth century moorings." According to Skidelsky, Keynes "brought in the State to redress the failings of society, not because he loved it, but because he saw it as the last resource. His genius was to have developed an analysis of economic disorder which justified forms of state intervention compatible with traditional liberal values."[7] To this end, Keynes devoted his academic life and his political and civil service career to the development of an approach to economic policy that was at once more scientific and pragmatic.

Keynes went up to King's College, Cambridge University, from Eton in 1902, originally to study mathematics. He was convinced by Alfred Marshall, one of the fathers of neoclassical economics, to study economics. Marshall was an important figure in early twentieth-century microeconomics, and Keynes was influenced by his methods. As Roger Backhouse and Bradley Bateman have suggested, Marshall "used formal theory, but because his ideas were rooted in an evolutionary understanding of human nature and of social organisation, he remained skeptical about it, holding that the world was too complex for mathematical models." Instead his methods were akin to those of a historian in that they "derived not from statistical evidence so much as from careful observation," though at worst they approached "casual empiricism." Backhouse and Bateman have pointed to an important paradox in Keynes: "his ideas fuelled the formalisation of both macroeconomic theory and econometrics, but at the same time he remained profoundly skeptical of both developments."[8]

As we saw in the opening chapters, Keynes believed in the capacity of the educated, enlightened expert (in contrast to Ludwig von Mises' pejorative characterization of the bureaucrat) to solve the worst social, economic, and political problems. Given the right information, the best decisions would be made by those most able to interpret the data. In this sense, as could be seen in his debates with Hayek, Keynes retained a faith in a technocratic elite as the guardian of social progress. The logical consequence of this position was that economic theories and dogmas had to be adjusted to particular situations; they were not inviolable. For this reason, Keynes clashed with the Austrian theorists, whose belief in immutable economic law was unshakable. This was why the neoliberal critique of economic policy in the postwar period focused on Keynes, his theories, and his legacy, along with the New Deal and social democratic approaches to government and administration. The Bretton Woods monetary system was also attacked. Though many of the criticisms of what became known as Keynesianism were reconcilable with the core ideas of the man himself, many others were not.

Aside from his general importance as an economic theorist and architect of the Bretton Woods Agreement, Keynes's position was crucial to the development of neoliberal economic analysis in three ways: first, his belief in the value of government intervention; second, his invention of macroeconomic policy analysis; and third, because of his legacy as it was interpreted and enlarged by his followers after his death. The first was his theoretical justification for an approach to policy that became popular in the 1930s, especially in the policies of the Roosevelt administration during the New Deal.[9] This was the use of government and the power of the public purse to alleviate the worst effects of economic downturns. According to Keynes in *The General Theory of Employment, Interest and Money* (1935), it was critical to raise consumer demand in a depressed economy to boost production. This stimulus would kick-start the economy, as government expenditure and investment—even at the expense of increased public debt—would fill the void in demand left by the decline in private spending. Government planning of demand in the economy was central to recovery for Keynes. For example, one important form of government intervention was public works, which Keynes first advocated as a way to cure unemployment in 1924.[10] Roosevelt's strategy to beat the Great Depression had at its core the provision of jobs through government spending and the subsidy of infrastructure and arts projects. The Works Progress Administration and the Tennessee Valley Authority were vibrant examples.

As David Laidler has argued, this approach to economic reconstruction contrasted sharply with the ideas of the Austrian school economists and suggests one important reason why, after 1929, Keynes's ideas trumped those of economists such as Friedrich Hayek and Ludwig von Mises, who argued that government intervention through fiscal and monetary expansion was inflationary. "Austrian theory, as it was known, yielded nihilistic policy conclusions. It argued that credit creation by the banking system enabled firms to command the production of investment goods without any voluntary act of saving on the part of households, that this command could only be sustained at the cost of ever-rising inflation, and that when the process came to its inevitable end in economic crisis, the economy would be burdened with stocks of unfinished capital equipment and hence unable to satisfy demand for consumption goods." Laidler continues, "this imbalance could only be righted over time by labour force growth and depreciation of the capital stock." Efforts by governments to speed up the process did not work because "expansionary monetary impulses had caused the problem in the first place, so more of the same was the last thing needed, the capital stock was already overexpanded," and "there was no point in taking measures to stimulate consumption expenditure when the economy was already unable to meet existing demands."[11]

The Austrian analysis provided an account of the Great Depression that focused on government failure, in contrast to the generally presumed failures of capitalism of the 1930s. The echoes of such debates—between government and market as the cause of recession—have been heard time and again as boom turned to bust in subsequent economic cycles. The Austrian account was riddled with weaknesses. According to Laidler, they "treat logical possibilities as if they were logical necessities." But it was "rigorous economic theory (by the standards of its time), and it also provided intellectual respectability to arguments for a 'hands-off' policy towards the Depression that were extremely popular in the financial community, and conservative political circles more generally, on both sides of the Atlantic."[12] Keynes provided a breath of fresh air for those optimists who wanted economic and social change. Keynes's ideas seemed to arm politicians and public officials with a workable set of tools with which to deliver the reform of capitalism they desired in the wake of its seeming collapse. They appeared to offer power and control. As will be seen, Friedman provided a slightly different explanation of the Great Depression, based on the failures of the Federal Reserve's stewardship of monetary policy, but one that shared many of the Austrians' premises.

The second important aspect of Keynes's canon in terms of the development of neoliberalism after World War II was his invention of macroeconomic analysis—something that actually created the ground on which the monetarists erected their countertheory. Classical and neoclassical economics had always assumed that supply and demand would tend toward full employment equilibrium in the long run. Keynes, however, believed both that this was untrue and that it defined a laissez-faire approach that brought with it unacceptable social and economic costs. For him, the economy ought to be managed according to the large-scale relationships that were in operation, which in turn influenced the many economic decisions of individual actors in the marketplace. The relationships he had in mind were among money, tax, credit, debt, and expenditure.

In his *Tract on Monetary Reform*, published in 1923, Keynes began to develop his ideas for economy-wide phenomena. As Skidelsky has put it, the "central policy proposal of the *Tract* was that monetary policy should be used to stabilise the price level," and its "central theoretical claim was that this should be accomplished by trying to stabilise the 'demand for money' for business purposes." In other words, if the supply of credit could be determined by policy, "then, according to the quantity theory of money, the price level can be whatever the monetary authority decides." The central claim of the *Tract on Monetary Reform* was radical. According to Skidelsky, "by varying the amount of credit to the business sector, the banking system could even out fluctuations in business activity." Keynes had "identified a controllable single variable—the supply of credit—capable of determining the level of prices and amount of activity in the economy as a whole," which marked "the start of macroeconomics."[13]

Keynes understood that economies could be in equilibrium—balanced between supply and demand—even without full employment, a proposition thought to be impossible by classical and neoclassical theorists, who had assumed that economies were always in full employment equilibrium or moving toward it through the combined effect of the economic actions of self-interested utility-maximizing individuals. As the *Washington Post* put it, "the novelty of his thesis, at least so far as the academic establishment was concerned, was that there is no inherent tendency for free enterprise economics to achieve high levels of employment."[14] Keynes argued instead that wages and prices in advanced economies were sticky, by which he meant that they responded slowly to economic shocks such as changes in overall supply and demand.

This realization, for Keynes, created a problem of underemployment since it meant that a fall-off in demand was less likely to result in lower wages (given the presence of trade unions) than in a rise in unemployment. Keynes always wanted to rescue capitalism. According to Nigel Lawson, "his approach was a means of rescuing the free market idea from, on the one hand, the huge problems which had occurred in the 1930s, and on the other hand, from the socialist idea, which he didn't believe in."[15] Unemployment was the major problem he attempted to solve through the regulation and management of macroeconomic policy. Keynes thought governments could help solve this problem through intervention, either through tax cuts or through greater public spending, which would have an effect on aggregate demand. Skidelsky has shown that this focus enabled Keynes to pinpoint the major weakness of Austrian theory, namely, its lack of a theory of expectations. Hayek "claimed that only subjective valuations count as causes: total quantities can exert no influence on individual decisions." Unlike Hayek, "Keynes understood that collective expectations entered into individual valuations, and that by controlling aggregates, governments can influence individual expectations."

Seen in this light, Friedman never disavowed macroeconomics. He operated within a framework that had been set up by Keynes. As Skidelsky has pointed out in his article on Keynes and Hayek, the inflation targets that the Federal Reserve and the Bank of England pursued in the 1990s and 2000s were based on the management of expectations, something that had been advocated by Keynes in the *Tract*.[16] Keynes's development of a theory of macroeconomic demand management had a profound influence on the way economists and policymakers alike viewed economic strategy. But his analysis was fundamental to *both* the "Keynesian" *and* the monetarist approaches to economic policy after 1945. The monetarists, however, used his frame of reference to reach different conclusions about how economies should be managed.

The third, and for this study most relevant, dimension of Keynes's thought was his legacy, and especially the uses to which his ideas were put in British and U.S. economic policy in the postwar years by Keynesian economists and advisers. As we have seen, Keynes himself was skeptical of economic information and forecasting. He believed that government management of aggregate demand would never be exact but that it would be a significant "improvement on laissez-faire."[17] His followers, however, went much further. The crux of the successful management of economies according to Keynesian principles, as followed by postwar Keynesian economists, was a belief in the accessibility of good economic information, which would enable policymakers to make the correct adjustments in their policy planning. This would lead policymakers to the possibility of fine-tuning economic policy in such a way as to ensure full employment, with the accepted associated cost of a higher but manageable rate of inflation.

In a paper published in 1958 on unemployment and wage rises in Britain, the New Zealand economist William Phillips was the first to posit a curve (subsequently known as the Phillips Curve) suggesting an inverse correlation between unemployment and inflation: as unemployment levels were kept low, inflation would rise.[18] But this would occur only in the long term. This relationship in the American context was explored in a highly influential article by Paul Samuelson and Robert Solow in 1960.[19] The suggested remedy, from Samuelson and Solow in particular, was to pursue Keynesian policies that would maintain full employment at a particular rate of inflation through the manipulation of the budget and expansion and contraction of the money supply according to whether the economy was growing or slowing. This acceptance of inflation was characteristic of Keynesian policy in Britain and the United States in the 1950s and 1960s, though of course, at this time inflation was relatively becalmed owing to continuous economic growth and full employment.

Keynes himself, however, was very conscious of inflation as a potential and actual problem. For example, he argued during the war that if government increased its spending without taking steps to reduce private consumption, inflation would result. In *How to Pay for the War* (1940) and the 1941 budget, of which Keynes was the prime author, Keynes sought methods to finance the British war effort in a noninflationary manner.[20] In the former, he argued for higher taxation for the rich and deferred pay for the poor as a way of ensuring domestic wage and price stability. Friedman was influenced by both and gave the ideas they contained "great play in his first two articles on inflation (1942, 1943)."[21] According to George Peden, Keynes felt that the 1941 budget was revolutionary for public finance. It did indeed "set the pattern for subsequent budgets," and Keynes felt that "its logical structure and the limited acceptance of the principle of postwar credits [which would be saved for spending after the war was won]" were the parts he most influenced. The 1941 budget "marked the adoption of Keynes's macroeconomics in the context of controlling inflation, but its application to the political commitment to full employment came later in the war [in the government's 1944 white paper on employment]."[22] Peden argues that Keynes's association with deficit finance, when his wartime activities are taken into account, was a myth. Certainly, his concerns during this period reveal a flexibility when faced with new or different circumstances. They also illustrate the problem with attempts to pin Keynes's own ideas to the mast raised by the subsequent generation of economists who professed allegiance to his theories.

Monetarist ideas would later slowly seep through as the economic problems associated with Keynesian fine-tuning, summed up in the phrase stop-go, manifested themselves. But they were very much on the margins during the 1950s and 1960s. Conservative prime minister Harold Macmillan's most trusted economic adviser and Keynes's official biographer, Roy Harrod, for example, wrote to him in 1957 of monetarism:

> The idea that you can reduce prices by limiting the quantity of money is pre-Keynesian. Keynes spent half his energy inveighing against precisely that idea. Hardly any economists under the age of 50 would subscribe to it. If it were supposed that the Conservatives were associated with any such idea, that might drive many of the middle-of-the-way economists into the ranks of Labour, and, what is more, [Hugh] Gaitskell [the Labour Party leader] would probably succeed in galvanising them all into lambasting and ridiculing the policy. I do sincerely hope that no government speaker would use words implying that the government subscribes to such an antiquated doctrine.[23]

This was typical of the attitude of mainstream economists, as well as the politicians that they advised, at the time. It was an attitude born of practical necessity as well, for Keynesian ideas seemed to offer hope to those in power that they possessed a raft of techniques to respond to economic problems. Harrod's reproach was also indicative of the general attitude of educated opinion in Britain and the United States and was largely due to a belief that it was essential to maintain full employment even if a certain amount of inflation came with it. The levels of unemployment that could be tolerated seem minuscule now, ranging from 1 to 4 percent.[24] The low levels fueled critics, who believed that a higher level of unemployment was necessary for the labor market to operate effectively. The assumption of the validity of full employment as the highest priority was first challenged politically in Britain in the debates about the budget of 1958 by Chancellor Peter Thorneycroft and his treasury team of ministers.

"A Little Local Difficulty": Enoch Powell's Monetarism

An early test of the Keynesian consensus was the crisis that led to the resignations from the Conservative government of Chancellor Peter Thorneycroft
and his ministers, Financial Secretary Enoch Powell and Economic Secretary to the Treasury Nigel Birch, who advocated tight finance and control
of the money supply in place of the government policy of full employment
at under 3 percent. Thorneycroft outlined the case for monetarism, which
Enoch Powell had driven into him, in a paper circulated to the cabinet in
late 1957:

> I have come to the conclusion that the continual increase in wages and
> prices rests in the last resort on the belief in the country that the Gov-
> ernment will always make enough money available to support full, and
> indeed over-full, employment, whatever the heights to which wages
> and prices rise. Until we show that this cannot be counted on, we shall
> make no progress. The policy of appeals to employers and unions for
> restraint, which has been tried for 10 years by our predecessors and
> ourselves has been shown to be ineffectual under existing conditions
> of demand.[25]

Macmillan instead preferred a traditional Keynesian deflation. He cited
two theories about inflation, those of Roy Harrod, on the one hand, and of
Friedrich Hayek's sometime friend Lionel Robbins on the other (relations
between the two had become professionally distant because Robbins disagreed with Hayek's interpretation of the Great Depression, while personally,
too, their relationship had become strained over Hayek's treatment of his first
wife).[26] He wrote in his cabinet paper on inflation, "there is a feeling among
supporters that the thing to do is to have a row with the trade unions." But
that, Macmillan went on, would only "have dealt with the symptoms, not the
cause of the disease." He concluded that "the only practical thing to do is to
reduce demand" in typical Keynesian fashion.[27]

In January 1958, Thorneycroft, Powell, and Birch resigned because they
wanted £50 million of public expenditure cuts beyond what the cabinet was
willing to agree on. The *Spectator* reflected scornfully on what had happened
in its leader from January, 10, 1958:

Mr. Thorneycroft and his junior ministers have been represented as abruptly deserting their posts, as having resigned over a mere 50 million, and having wanted to slash the social services because of rigid adherence to a formula. The reasons that have been given for their departure are self-contradictory and untrue. For all the loud talk of Mr. Butler [Rab Butler, the Home Secretary] and others it is difficult to disagree with Mr. Birch who said of "the battle of inflation" that "we were fighting to win and they were not".[28]

For Macmillan's government, the fight against inflation was secondary to the goal of full employment. Macmillan was typical of the breed of Tory who had experienced the nightmares of the Great Depression and war and felt that everyone ought to have basic economic security by right. His political creed was marked by a commitment to a "middle way" that included a mixed economy and welfare state.[29]

It is remarkable that Thorneycroft, Powell, and Birch took their stance at a time when inflation was paltry, at about 3 percent, by comparison with the later standards of the 1970s. But Powell in particular was convinced of the need for a different strategy. Indeed, the *Economist* at the time suggested that the resignations were due to an administrative "amour proper" rather than from the important principle of reducing the "proportion of national income absorbed by government expenditure."[30] That "amour proper" was the concern with inflation, something that ran counter to the prevailing intellectual and policy atmosphere, which was gathering around a belief that unemployment should not rise above 2–3 percent.

The immediate consequences of the resignations were negligible. The government continued without fuss—Macmillan famously dismissed the resignations as "a little local difficulty"—although it would have to institute a pay freeze after the 1959 election, which harmed its popularity with the public.[31] But after this early monetarist challenge, Labour and Conservative governments continued to pursue Keynesian policies for almost another twenty years. The argument was whether to tolerate the risk of greater unemployment entailed in the restriction of the money supply and public expenditure. The answer, for governments of both parties, was no. Powell himself reflected on the affair in a letter to his former boss Thorneycroft after they had both left the government:

The Conservative Party is now almost pathological in its concern with 2.8% unemployment—a level barely sufficient at this season to be healthy—and has less than no interest in the level of government expenditure. It feels confident that whatever that level, substantial remissions of taxation can be relied on, and its only anxiety about expenditure is whether the government is spending enough. As for inflation, even the stock exchange and the bankers have quit worrying about that for the present at least.[32]

The low level of unemployment the government was willing to tolerate illustrates the belief among policymakers that it was possible to fine-tune the economy precisely. Peter Jay tells an anecdote that sums up the attitude of the policy elite very well:

I was appointed, when I was junior at the Treasury, in about 1962, to be secretary on a little committee setting up a training programme for Assistant Principals who were the kind of high-flying young Treasury officials at the starts of their career. The result was that there was a thing called the Centre for Administrative Studies set up in Regent's Park and I was then sent as a kind of guinea pig on the first course, and there we were, a fine bunch of high-flying young men and women (I can't think there were very many women, but anyway . . .). And the chief sort of economic forecaster and guru at the Treasury, a man called Wynne Godley came to talk to us and he proposed to discuss the question, "What is full employment?" (We were all committed to full employment of course—every government had been since the 1944 Employment Policy White Paper and since the 1946 Employment Act in the United States). But, what was it? Because it can't be 0% unemployment, and if you were going to make budget decisions about how much money you were going to have to inject to achieve the objective you had to have some idea of what it is rather than just some sort of emotional feeling about high employment? He proposed a number, and I remember, to this day, I mean, we, the bright young men of the future, including the future Cabinet Secretary and all sorts of things, fell upon him with horror and disgust and rage and said that what he was proposing was wicked and immoral and vile and reactionary and cruel and unkind and every other word we could think of. And that anything above another figure which we named was just inhumane and intolerable and not to be contemplated. The figure which he gave for the desirable, or the target level, for unemployment was 1 3/4%. The figure we gave was 1 1/4%. We regarded this as a profound ideological rift and most people did. There was a figure called Professor Frank Paish who proposed 2 1/2%, who was regarded as, more or less, a Nazi![33]

This was the conviction and the climate Powell challenged during the 1958 monetary policy episode. It was also the belief that Friedman would later fundamentally discredit, in the eyes of many, as inflation became seemingly intractable during the 1970s.

Powell continued to be the standard-bearer on the right of the Conservative Party throughout the 1960s. He consistently argued for free market policy solutions to social problems and gave voice to those who opposed the broad consensus between the two parties on the welfare state and demand management. He was also notorious for his warnings of the consequences of immigration into Britain from countries of the former empire and the Commonwealth. This made him an unfortunate bedfellow with many racists on the far right. Powell was also a member of the Mont Pelerin Society, and through its activities, Milton Friedman became a firm admirer of Powell. He lauded Powell's steadfast advocacy of monetarist and free market ideas. For example, he commented in a letter to William F. Buckley in 1970,

> The real reason for writing this letter, however, is different [from congratulating him on his performance against J. K. Galbraith on his television show, *The Firing Line*]. It is to comment on your column on "Enoch Powell." I think you have been misled by the British intellectuals. Their views on Enoch Powell have about as much resemblance to reality as the views of American intellectuals on Nixon and Agnew.
>
> I have met, talked with, and participated in meetings with Enoch Powell on a number of different occasions. He has a better and deeper understanding of economic principles, and a clearer conception of the relation between economic and personal freedom, than any other major political figure I have ever met. And even this is to put it too mildly. Broaden the field as widely as you want, and I have met few men who

have as sophisticated an intelligence on these matters as Powell. It is
precisely his intellectual qualities plus his unpopular views that turn
the intellectuals against him. I do not share his views on immigration,
but I have read his speeches on the subject and not one of them seems
to me to qualify as racist by however broad a definition of that term you
choose to use.[34]

Powell's final speech of the 1970 election campaign, wrote Friedman, "impressed me as one of the greatest political speeches I have ever read."[35]

Powell was an extremely influential figure with British Thatcherite Conservatives, many of whom have described his speeches during the sixties (he
was an energetic constituency speaker who toured the country to spread
his message) as having a formative influence on them. According to former
chancellor Geoffrey Howe, a chairman of the Bow Group in the 1950s, for
example, "[Powell] was a frequent speaker at the kind of meetings we went
to. He was a rather esoteric speaker, to Conservative Area Council meetings,
you could listen with amazement without understanding what he was saying, I say with amazement but by being impressed with the academic style."[36]
Powell took strong free market positions that went against the grain of mainstream Conservative opinion. Norman Lamont, for example, remembers
being a "left-wing centrist Conservative" in the 1960s and hearing Powell
speak, "denouncing French planning at Cambridge. I remember him denouncing incomes policies. I remember him denouncing overseas aid." But,
according to Lamont, at the time he found "all these things rather baffling
and rather against common sense. But, you know, of course, a decade later,
I was rather agreeing with quite a lot of them."[37] John Hoskyns, the head of
Margaret Thatcher's Policy Unit, thought that Powell, though a "wild card,"
was a "very brilliant man" who was "thinking outside of the box."[38] According
to Hoskyns, "you realised that he had read the tea leaves about thirty years
before anyone else had."[39]

Powell was, like Friedman, a vociferous critic of the Bretton Woods system. Indeed, Powell scoffed at the whole idea of a monetary system:

It sounds very grand and very imposing. Anything called "a system" is
immediately assumed to be systematic, that is, to be logical and rational. Surely the most irreverent of iconoclasts is bound to bow down in

awe before something called the world monetary system. Quite apart from the name of the idol, the international priesthood are persons of the utmost respectability and what the Romans used to call gravitas. When they gather from the four corners of the earth to offer propitiatory sacrifices to the god peoples of the world tremble.[40]

Powell argued against fixed exchange rates and exchange rate controls, which he thought meant that gold was treated like "a dangerous drug." "A system which necessitates absurdities is itself absurd," he maintained.[41] In a speech to the Mont Pelerin Society, Powell outlined the effects of the system as he saw them:

> Thus the fixed external parity of the pound sterling [with the dollar] has become a powerful engine for the extension of government control over the individual. The mechanism works as follows: the balance of payments moves into deficit at the fixed parity of the currency; although the government has been debauching the currency and intends to continue doing so [by printing too much money]. The blame is attributed to the behaviour of the citizens and not of the government; therefore the balance of payments "crisis" results in more control being imposed on the citizens; the balance of payments, nevertheless, continues in deficit again after an interval—probably (though not necessarily) because the government continues to debauch the currency; therefore it follows that the citizens have not been subjected to sufficient control and that the controls must be intensified. This vicious cycle is no mere imagination or jeu d'esprit. It is what the British people have lived through six or seven times since the idea of freeing sterling was abandoned around 1955.[42]

He argued that Britain was subordinated, through the fixed exchange rate system, to American power and the strength of the dollar. Powell concluded that "the jamming of the international price mechanism by fixed exchange rates is the most serious threat to the maintenance or restoration of free institutions."[43] The Institute for Economic Affairs (IEA) sought to push Powell on policy matters, for he was their preferred choice as prime minister in the event of a challenge to Edward Heath as Conservative Party leader in the early

1970s. Heath was leading the country to "destruction," according to Ralph Harris, the IEA's director, who in 1973 requested a meeting with Powell to discuss "priorities for policy when the time comes."[44]

Powell himself did not like the United States and did not even visit the country until 1968, then aged fifty-six. He was also apparently less keen on Friedman than Friedman was on him. In response to a suggestion that he meet with Friedman in 1974, Powell replied, "I am sorry that the apparent imminence of a general election here makes any prospect of meeting and hearing you in Brussels or London very uncertain."[45] This may have been true, but the coolness of the response, at a time when Friedman's fame was at its height and two and a half months before the general election, perhaps indicates a certain half-heartedness on Powell's part. In a speech to the U.S. Chamber of Commerce in 1965, Powell spoke in detached and humorous terms of the United States:

> I will begin with an admission. I have never crossed the Atlantic. For me therefore, the existence of inhabited lands on the other side of the Ocean is information at second hand, a matter of hearsay and report, though I hasten to add that I regard the evidence as so strong and circumstantial as to be for practical purposes conclusive.[46]

He went on to bemoan both the influence of John Kenneth Galbraith, the Harvard-based Keynesian economist and adviser to both President Kennedy and President Johnson, and the idea of America itself. He suggested that Galbraith provided ammunition to anticapitalist Britons, who could say, "why, even an American" believes in taming the market:

> Yet to some of us it is a sign that, if we could once but lay the myth of America as the perfect unblemished archetype of the capitalist free society, we might yet draw help and inspiration from her example, and comradeship and courage from her citizens.[47]

Powell's stance toward the United States softened when he found he could earn large sums presenting his now fashionable economic ideas in the late 1960s and 1970s.[48] His fundamental anti-Americanism, however, remained until the end of his life. Despite this, Powell is important as a member of the transatlantic network that produced and promoted neoliberal ideas through his links to the IEA and the Mont Pelerin Society.

Powell and his ministerial colleagues presented monetarist arguments at a time, 1957–58, when the British political class was deaf to their logic. Macmillan and most of his ministers were patrician Tories who believed in a form of social democratic settlement: the mixed economy and universalist welfare state as a guarantee against a reappearance of the horrors of the 1930s. The time was not yet ripe for a monetarist, and by extension neoliberal, breakthrough.

American Economic Policy in the Sixties

American economic policy during the 1960s was dominated by the avowed Keynesianism of Presidents Kennedy and Johnson and their economic advisers, Walter Heller, James Tobin, Gardner Ackley, Arthur Okun, and John Kenneth Galbraith. Theirs was a strategy based on keeping unemployment at or near 4 percent, a little above the British Conservative commitment, through the stimulation or deflation of the economy through tax cuts and the direction of the money supply. The 4 percent figure was the famous fiscal rule advocated by the American Committee for Economic Development in an influential statement from 1947.[49] This approach was challenged unsuccessfully by the presidential campaign of Barry Goldwater in 1964. But, as in Britain, this was the high-water mark of Keynesian economic policy, and Goldwater's fiscal conservatism and visceral dislike of social welfare and spending were out of tune with mainstream American opinion. As the sixties progressed, the U.S. economy experienced economic growth and a boom in public expenditure and consumption through the Great Society and War on Poverty programs and the escalation of the Vietnam War.

At the center of the Kennedy administration's economic plans were large tax cuts to stimulate demand. Despite consistent growth (aside from a brief recession toward the end of the Eisenhower years) and balanced budgets during the Truman and Eisenhower presidencies of the 1950s, Kennedy's advisers were worried about the return of recession or worse. Another depression had been feared ever since the 1930s. Their preemptive solution to this perceived threat was a massive stimulus based on tax cuts for both individuals and corporations, combined with increased government spending. As Thomas Karier has put it, the size of the stimulus was important: Keynesian theory enabled the calculation of the "precise size of the required fiscal stimulus" through the "so-called multipliers described in Keynes's book [*The General Theory*]. If the multiplier was two, an additional billion dollars of government spending would ultimately create $2 billion in additional national output."[50] Thus, Kennedy's economists thought they could judge the requisite levels of expansion needed to prevent any possible downturn. Karier provides a clear description of the method:

> Keynesians believed that monetary policy should reinforce fiscal poli-
> cy, as for instance when it became necessary to pump up the economy
> during a recession. All the Federal Reserve had to do was increase the
> amount of money in circulation and interest rates would fall. The lower
> rates would in turn encourage investment and consumer spending. Or
> if necessary, to slow the economy down to fight inflation, the govern-
> ment could reduce the money supply, raising interest rates and discour-
> aging spending. The key to successful monetary policy, in their view,
> was to coordinate it with fiscal policy so that they either both acceler-
> ated economic activity or they both slowed it down.[51]

The Kennedy-Johnson policy was fine-tuning in action. It was linked to the function of the international monetary system, too, as the United States, like Britain, had to stave off the threat of balance-of-payments crises. For example, in the early 1960s, gold drained out of the United States at such alarming levels that the Federal Reserve was forced to prop up the falling demand for dollars.[52]

Friedman argued for an alternative that would avoid these repeated balance-of-payments problems in his advice to Goldwater. Goldwater stood as a staunch fiscal hawk, and his campaign can be considered a founding mo-ment for the nascent conservative movement in the United States. The Re-publican convention in San Francisco in 1964 also marked the launch of Ron-ald Reagan's political career when he delivered a rapturously received speech in support of Goldwater's nomination. Friedman was close to Goldwater's top adviser, William Baroody, Sr., who ran the American Enterprise Institute, and was in frequent contact with Goldwater, offering economic advice over the years leading up to his nomination. It was one of many close relationships between Friedman and senior Republican leaders.

As for Powell, a particular concern of Friedman's that emerges from his advice to Goldwater was the inimical effects of exchange controls on freedom. For example, in 1960, Friedman wrote to Goldwater about his flirtation with the idea of placing restrictions on the sale of gold and on the amount of dollars that tourists might take out of the United States. It is worth quoting Friedman's comments at length for an illustration of his belief that such controls represented the thin end of a totalitarian and communist wedge, beliefs that echoed the totalitarian fears of the Austrian neoliberals, Mises and Hayek:

> Such a measure [exchange controls] is a direct restriction on individual freedom, no less so if done in the name of saving dollars than if done, as the Russians do, to keep their citizens from contact with the rest of the world. It is the first step toward full exchange control, one of the few really modern devices invented to enable the state to control its citizens. To the best of my knowledge, sweeping direct control of foreign exchange transactions was invented by Schacht and first introduced by Germany in 1934. Almost without exception, wherever introduced it has been a prelude to a wide range of further direct controls over personal and business transactions. Hardly any other type of control is so insidious in giving rise to similar misshapen progeny. This type of cure—if it can even be called one—is far worse than the alleged disease. In promoting it, you are—unwittingly, I know—giving aid and comfort to the enemies of everything you and I hold most dear.[53]

After this admonishment, Friedman went on to argue that in his view, only certain options were available that were consistent with individual liberty in a free democratic society:

> There are only two resolutions of the gold drain that are consistent with a free society. One is a full-fledged Gold Standard which would involve submitting our internal monetary policy to its discipline, including following a policy of internal deflation if that be required. This would be an excellent solution if followed by the major Western countries. But we do not now have such a system. And given the kind of political in-

terventionism rife in the rest of the Western world, it would be undesirable for the US alone to act as if we did.

The only other satisfactory resolution is the application of free market principles to exchange rates, namely, the suspension of any fixed price for gold, and the adoption of floating exchange rates, which is to say, a system under which the price of the dollar in terms of other currencies is determined in the market by private transactions and could vary from day to day (this is the system Canada has been following with great success for a decade). The problems we are currently facing with gold and the dollar are of the same class as those that arose under rent control or still arise with wheat. If the government pegs a price, there will inevitably be a shortage (as under rent control and currently with gold) or a surplus (as with price-fixing of wheat or after the appreciation of gold in 1934). The correct remedy for wheat and also for gold is to eliminate government price fixing.[54]

(The applicability of the gold standard—the full convertibility of currency into gold—to the international monetary system was one of the doctrinal issues on which Friedman disagreed with Hayek and the Austrian school economists.) Friedman also argued against exchange controls in his 1962 book, *Capitalism and Freedom*, in which he made the case for free markets as a counterpoint to Soviet communism in the Cold War.[55]

Friedman also vigorously defended free trade to Goldwater. He argued that tariffs and quotas were totally unjustified:

> As libertarians, our strategic objective is free international trade. [exception may be the USSR]. The so-called practical objections that are urged, notably lower wages abroad, are mostly based on a misunderstanding of the operation of a price-system and are not valid objections to free trade either in principle or in practice.[56]

He argued that the United States should unilaterally remove restrictions on international trade as Britain had done in its nineteenth-century heyday when its prosperity had been based, according to Friedman, on policies of free trade and laissez-faire under Gladstone and Disraeli. Pushed for an answer on which were better, tariffs or quotas, he opted for tariffs, as they were impersonal and fixed, and therefore required no bureaucratic interference. This preference for predictable rules over discretionary power echoed the ideas of Henry Simons and is another example of the sort of economic policy preferred by later policy technicians such as Paul Volcker in the United States and Geoffrey Howe and Nigel Lawson in Britain.[57]

The Kennedy-Johnson policies were supplemented by Johnson's War on Poverty and Great Society programs. Goldwater's defeat left the path open for a large-scale experiment in government intervention to tackle society's worst problems. This was, of course, combined with the stealthy and subsequently open-ended escalation of the conflict in Vietnam. As the decade wore on, the fabric of the Keynesian policy began to fray. Central to the public criticism of the Democrats' priorities was the emergence of Milton Friedman as a powerful public intellectual.

Milton Friedman's Monetarism

The most consistent, systematic, and significant alternative economic strategy to Keynesian demand management and fine-tuning was the monetarism developed by Milton Friedman.[58] It offered a deceptively simple and painless proposition: by keeping a steady hand on the monetary tiller, the worst extremes of economic fluctuation would be evened out. Friedman's free market neoliberal philosophy has already been discussed. But Friedman himself always distinguished between his belief in individual liberty and the market from his scientific work on economic processes. It was the technical insights contained in Friedman's analysis of demand management and its failures that mainly explains his influence among public policymakers in the 1970s.

Friedman's arguments, despite remaining controversial among most economists, initially attracted people from across the political spectrum, not just those on the right. Friedman argued that the error in Keynesian policies was based on an underestimation of the importance of a stable supply of money. Where Keynes had emphasized fiscal policy and expansive money as a route out of economic downturns, Friedman and his followers marshaled an impressive amount of evidence to show that the mismanagement of money was most often responsible for prolonged slumps, including the Great Depression of the 1930s. In this sense, through his concept of the natural rate of unemployment, Friedman made a similarly "hands-off" argument about the role of government and public authorities in economic management as the Austrians had. Although much of the economics profession came to accept the limits of the Keynesian consensus, it was Friedman who gained the most prominence among politicians and policymakers, in part because he had correctly predicted the onset of stagflation in his AEA address in 1967.

Friedman put forward the evidence for the importance of a stable monetary policy most comprehensively in his *Monetary History of the United States*, written with Anna Jacobson Schwartz, in 1963.[59] In this famous book, Friedman and Schwartz presented copious amounts of empirical material to show that the operation of monetary policy was the prime mover in the booms and busts of recent U.S. history. The authors claimed that the Great Depression of the 1930s was caused by the Federal Reserve's overly tight contraction of the money supply after the Wall Street crash of 1929. This was made worse, according to Friedman and Schwartz, by Roosevelt's introduction of many kinds of economic regulations and price controls, after 1932, in an effort to alleviate the worst effects of the crisis. This thesis clearly contradicted Keynes's analysis in the *General Theory* (though Keynes had presented a similar analysis in *A Treatise on Money*) and suggested an alternative reason for the Great Depression than capitalism's pernicious potential, that of government and regulatory failure.

Friedman summarized his view of Keynes's arguments in the *General Theory* in his seminal and hugely influential address to the AEA in 1967:

> Keynes offered simultaneously an explanation for the presumed impotence of monetary policy to stem the depression, a nonmonetary interpretation of the depression, and an alternative to monetary policy for meeting the depression and his offering was avidly accepted. If liquidity preference is absolute or nearly so—as Keynes believed likely in times of heavy unemployment—interest rates cannot be lowered by monetary measures. If investment and consumption are little affected by interest rates—as Hansen and many of Keynes's other American disciples came to believe—lower interest rates, even if they could be achieved would do little good. Monetary policy is twice damned. The contraction, set in train, on this view, by a collapse of investment or by a shortage of investment opportunities or by stubborn thriftiness,

could not, it was argued, have been stopped by monetary measures. But there was available an alternative—fiscal policy. Government spending could make up for insufficient private investment. Tax reductions could undermine stubborn thriftiness.

The wide acceptance of these views in the economics profession meant that for some two decades monetary policy was believed by all but a few reactionary souls to have been rendered obsolete by new economic knowledge.[60]

Friedman believed that the centrally important role of monetary policy had been forgotten in the widespread acceptance of Keynes's views by the economic profession. Friedman pointed out that, having been thought of as crucial in the 1920s, monetary policy had been deemed insignificant in the postwar period. However, by 1967, when Friedman was speaking, he suggested that "the pendulum may well have swung too far, that, now as then, we are in danger of assigning to monetary policy a larger role than it can perform, in danger of asking it to accomplish tasks that it cannot achieve, and, as a result, in danger of preventing it from making the contribution that it is capable of making."[61]

So, what was money capable of doing? Like Powell, Friedman was a believer in Irving Fisher's "quantity theory of money," which in fact had a long history, going back to the Polish polymath Nicolaus Copernicus, the sixteenth-century French political theorist Jean Bodin, the Enlightenment philosopher David Hume, and the British liberal theorist and political economist John Stuart Mill. Updating Fisher, he argued that the money supply was the most important economic policy instrument in the establishment and maintenance of the stability of markets. But this was only if its limitations, especially as pursued by Keynesian economists, were properly understood:

From the infinite world of negation, I have selected two limitations of monetary policy to discuss: (1) It cannot peg interest rates for more than very limited periods. (2) It cannot peg the rate of unemployment for more than very limited periods. I select these because the contrary has been or is widely believed, because they correspond to the main unattainable tasks that are at all likely to be assigned to monetary policy, and because essentially the same theoretical analysis covers both.[62]

For Friedman, these misunderstandings stemmed from a confusion about the potential short-term versus long-term effects of expansionary or contractionary monetary policy in terms of both interest rates and employment. For example, "The *initial* impact of increasing the quantity of money at a faster rate than it has been increasing is to make interest rates lower for a time than they would otherwise have been. But this is only the beginning of the process not the end."[63] Expanding the money supply creates three effects: more spending, rising incomes, and higher prices. These effects combined would reverse the downward pressure on interest rates and fuel inflation, according to Friedman. Finally:

> A fourth effect, when and if it becomes operative, will go even farther, and definitely mean that a higher rate of monetary expansion will correspond to a higher, not lower, level of interest rates than would otherwise have prevailed. Let the higher rate of monetary growth produce rising prices, and let the public come to expect that prices will continue to rise. Borrowers will then be willing to pay and lenders will then demand higher interest rates—as Irving Fisher pointed out decades ago. This price expectation effect is slow to develop and also slow to disappear. Fisher estimated it took several decades for a full adjustment and more recent work is consistent with his estimates.[64]

He continued:

> As an empirical matter, low interest rates are a sign that monetary policy *has been* tight—in the sense that the quantity of money has grown slowly; high interest rates are a sign that monetary policy *has been* easy—in the sense that the quantity of money has grown rapidly. The broadest facts of experience run in precisely the opposite direction from that which the financial community and academic economists have all generally taken for granted.[65]

(A Keynesian would have said that low interest rates were a sign that demand had been too low, and the reverse in the opposite case.) Because of these effects and their time delay, according to Friedman, interest rates are notoriously bad at predicting whether monetary policy is tight or loose. Instead, "it is far better to look at the rate of change in the quantity of money."[66]

Friedman also pointed to the same kind of process in the rate of unemployment, which in his view cast doubt on the viability of the Phillips Curve and the popular full employment policy in Britain and the United States. According to Friedman, "monetary growth, it is widely held, will tend to stimulate employment; monetary contraction, to retard employment. Why, then, cannot the monetary authority adopt a target for employment or unemployment[?]" For the same reasons as with interest rates, the differences between the short-term and long-term effects of such a policy:

> Thanks to [Swedish economist, Knut] Wicksell, we are all acquainted with the concept of a "natural" rate of interest and the possibility of a discrepancy between the "natural" and the "market" rate. The preceding analysis of interest rates can be translated fairly directly into Wicksellian terms. The monetary authority can make the market rate lower than the natural rate only by inflation. It can make the market rate higher than the natural rate only by deflation. We have added only one wrinkle to Wicksell—the Irving Fisher distinction between the nominal and the real rate of interest. Let the monetary authority keep the nominal market rate for a time below the natural rate by inflation. That in turn will raise the nominal natural rate itself, once anticipations of inflation become widespread, thus requiring still more rapid inflation to hold down the market rate. Similarly because of the Fisher effect, it will require not merely deflation but more and more rapid deflation to hold the market rate above the initial "natural" rate.[67]

Thus Friedman, unlike the Austrians, built on Keynes's foundations by incorporating expectations, inflationary ones, into his macroeconomic theory. Just as with interest rates, there is a similarly "natural" rate of unemployment. According to Friedman, this had been artificially suppressed through the misunderstanding of the long-term effects of monetary policy:

> To avoid misunderstanding, let me emphasize that by using the term "natural" rate of unemployment, I do not mean to suggest that it is immutable and unchangeable. On the contrary, many of the market characteristics that determine its level are manmade and policy-made. In the United States, for example, legal minimum wage rates, the Walsh-Healy and Davis-Bacon Acts, and the strength of labor unions all make

the natural rate of unemployment higher than it would otherwise be. Improvements in employment exchanges, in availability of information about job vacancies and labor supply, and so on, would tend to lower the natural rate of unemployment. I use the term "natural" for the same reason Wicksell did—to try and separate the real forces from monetary forces.

But the central point about the natural rate of unemployment was that it was hard to know what it actually was. "The "market" rate will vary from the natural rate for all sorts of reasons other than monetary policy"; thus, if monetary authorities decide to respond to sporadic variations, it will be like a random walk:[68]

> To state this conclusion differently, there is always a temporary trade-off between inflation and unemployment; there is no permanent trade-off. The temporary trade-off comes not from inflation per se, but from unanticipated inflation, which generally means, from a rising rate of inflation. The widespread belief that there is a permanent trade-off is a sophisticated version of the confusion between "high" and "rising" that we all recognize in simpler forms. A rising rate of inflation may reduce unemployment, a high rate will not.[69]

Instead of the Panglossian belief in the power of government and public officials to control the economy with the precision of a computer programmer, Friedman thought that economists and publics alike ought to accept much more modest goals for monetary policy—as a guarantor of a stable market economy rather than as an engine of full employment.

Monetary growth set the terms for everything else in the economy. Rather than target full employment, Friedman suggested that the most important and persistent economic problem was inflation, which he saw as a form of invisible taxation driven by government's lax willingness to print more money. As he put it,

> money has one feature that these other machines [those that facilitate more efficient industrial or agricultural production] do not share. Because it is so pervasive, when it gets out of order, it throws a monkey

wrench into the operation of all the other machines. The Great Contraction [the Great Depression] is the most dramatic example but not
the only one. Every other major contraction in this country has been
either produced by monetary disorder or greatly exacerbated by monetary disorder. Every major inflation has been produced by monetary
expansion—mostly to meet the overriding demands of war which have
forced the creation of money to supplement explicit taxation.[70]

(There is an obvious link here to the U.S. situation in Vietnam.) Friedman
argued that governments and central banks should ensure a constant and predictable level of monetary growth to "provide a stable background for the
economy":[71]

> Our economic system will work best when producers and consum-
> ers, employers and employees, can proceed with full confidence that
> the average level of prices will behave in a known way in the future—
> preferably that it will be highly stable.[72]

In particular, Friedman argued that the belief that full employment could be
maintained at the cost of a limited amount of inflation was a dangerous chimera. Instead, he showed that such a policy would only suppress inflation
in the short term at the cost of much larger inflation further down the line,
which would have a concomitantly damaging effect on jobs, wages, and economic stability.

Friedman's AEA address created a major stir and became one of the most
important economic statements of the twentieth century. His arguments
were noticed across the Atlantic in Britain by notable commentators and
economists such as Peter Jay, Samuel Brittan, and Alan Walters. These figures
were crucial for the spread of monetarist ideas in Britain. Norman Lamont,
for example, states that he picked up on Friedman's ideas through Walters's
IEA pamphlet, *Money in Boom and Slump* (1970), which was an application
of Friedman's ideas to the British economic experience.[73]

The AEA address provided a piercing critique of the failures of Keynesian demand management as well as Friedman's suggested remedy, which
appeared simple and seductively painless. *Monetary History* performed a different though related task. It provided the empirical data that showed the

essential importance of the money supply, and its control by the monetary authorities, in the economic history of the United States. The book was criticized for Friedman's and Schwartz's selective use of evidence, and for Friedman's dismissal of Keynes. For example, Harry Johnson, the Canadian monetary economist and a colleague of Friedman's at the University of Chicago who also worked at the London School of Economics, thought that Friedman had accepted large parts of the Keynesian revolution without proper acknowledgment.

As this exchange of letters makes clear, a defensive Friedman attempted to point out the distinction between the parts of Keynes he accepted and those he did not:

> As is implicit in the above, your statement that "to admit interest rates into the demand function for money is to accept the Keynesian revolution and Keynes' attack on the quantity theory" seems to me simply wrong. Certainly, Irving Fisher was entirely aware of the effects of interest rates on velocity and so were most of the classical writers. In my theoretical essay, "The Quantity Theory of Money—A Restatement", I certainly emphasize the role of interest rates in the demand function for money without in any way accepting either the Keynesian revolution or Keynes' attack on the quantity theory. I believe you are confusing two things: admitting interest rates and admitting the special liquidity trap for which [sic] Keynes gave to the demand function in deep depression. Admitting the latter is indeed to accept the Keynesian attack on the quantity theory. Admitting the former has no such implications.[74]

But Johnson countered with a list of refutations in which he suggested that Friedman was reluctant to acknowledge the importance and relevance of Keynes for his own work on macroeconomic history and theory:

> (b) This [to admit interest rates into the demand function for money]
> could be argued to be the fundamental impact of the Keynesian rev-
> olution. I think it is silly to identify Keynes with the liquidity trap,
> which so far as I remember he stated only as a possibility; the debate
> over the liquidity trap, so far as my knowledge goes is an American is-

sue about the 1930's and has become a sort of testing area or focus for fiscal versus monetary policy advocates or more bluntly for the liberal-Keynesian-Democrats versus the radical-anti-Keynesian Republicans. Rather it seems to me that Keynes's real impact was in introducing the conception of a simple macro-economic general equilibrium system in which monetary and real variables interact, in place of the classical dichotomy. I think that the main appeal of that model is for short-run analysis, and I know that it will give classical results on classical assumptions; nevertheless, monetary theory as largely understood and taught now is formulated in terms of this kind of system, though after Patinkin and others we formulate it in terms of the goods, money, bonds, and labor markets instead of the way Keynes did it.[75]

He continued:

(d) I don't need instruction on Irving Fisher and the other classical writers; your restatement of the Quantity Theory does manage quite skilfully to avoid mentioning Keynes's contribution to the theory of demand for money, and any suggestion even that he existed (so far as I can recall), but what it amounts to is relieving the quantity theory of responsibility for explaining prices, which quantity theorists had discredited themselves by claiming to be able to do in the past.[76]

At issue was Friedman's interpretation of Keynes, the significance of the difference between what Keynes himself would have said given the conditions of the 1960s and 1970s and the cruder interpretation and expansion of his ideas by Keynesian followers in both the United States and Britain, which Friedman attacked. The idea of fine-tuning was an extrapolation of Keynes's ideas rather than those of the man himself. As we have seen, Keynes was skeptical of economic and financial information and, consequently, of the capacity for such precision in economic policy. This has been a long debate, and it would appear that given the evidence of the 1941 budget, as well as Keynes's ideas about the importance of inflation and his responsiveness to new realities, he may well have agreed with some of Friedman's analysis, though probably not with his solutions.

Johnson also criticized Friedman's and Schwartz's methods and aired a common complaint about the ideas of neoliberal theorists, who based their arguments so often on assumptions of rational self-interest, as if humans lacked other crucially important motivations:

> [T]his ad hoc approach naturally irritates all readers I know who have absorbed the notion that a model should be a model—i.e., should try and incorporate the main relationships at work, not simply one dominant or allegedly dominant relationship supplemented with casual remarks.
>
> [...]
>
> What annoys us all about all this, I think, is your habit of insisting that the simplest possible models of each type should be tested against each other in this fashion, whereas the rest of us (especially the empirically inclined, now) take the view that if we need to construct more complex relationships to explain reality better, that is what we should do.[77]

The temptation for Friedman (and others, such as James Buchanan, Gordon Tullock, and George Stigler) was to downplay or ignore the parts of the story that didn't fit into their explanatory frame. British economist, fellow member of the Mont Pelerin Society, and collaborator with the IEA, Peter Bauer also queried the Chicago and Virginia models' application to politics and government with which Stigler, Buchanan, and Gary Becker, in particular, were associated in their development of public choice theory:

> Another matter on which I would welcome further comment from you is that of the usefulness of economic modes of reasoning in explaining political behaviour. I am not disputing the usefulness of this method in certain contexts of political behaviour. But, I feel that it is more limited than you, Gary Becker and others admit.[78]

A talented communicator, Friedman was the master of the snappy catch-phrase, asserting, for example, that inflation was always and everywhere a monetary phenomenon. Eamonn Butler of the Adam Smith Institute (ASI) believes that much of the credit for the transatlantic breakthrough of neoliberal politics can be put down to Friedman's efforts. According to Butler and his colleague, Madsen Pirie (who are both obvious fans), there were

> fortunately, folk like Ed Feulner at Heritage [Foundation], and these sorts of people, the American Enterprise Institute over in the United States and the IEA and ourselves here [at the ASI], had actually been working through the times when socialism was in the ascendancy to think out these policies and, you know, some of which, many of which, were regarded as incredibly off the wall at the time but are now very mainstream. . . .
>
> [Madsen Pirie interjects] But, the alternative was ready. . . .
>
> [Butler continues] But the alternative was ready, that's right. . . .
>
> [Pirie again] We didn't just say, "oh look, the liberal consensus has collapsed, what on earth are we going to do now!?" No, we already had ready what we were going to do. . . .
>
> [Butler again] And, I think actually, I mean Milton Friedman should get a lot of the credit for that because he just kept going and he was just such a fantastic communicator and you know, he spoke to all these meetings and events and so on and he deserves a lot of the credit for [the change in intellectual and political climate].
>
> [Pirie] And intellectually coherent and indeed commanding.[79]

Friedman worked assiduously to spread his ideas through the transatlantic, indeed international, network of neoliberal think tanks, especially the IEA in Britain and the AEI, the Heritage Foundation, the Hoover Institution, and the Cato Institute in the United States. But his ideas were also picked up in the mainstream media through his appearances on television shows such as *Meet the Press*, in the United States, and *The Money Programme,* in Britain (see the next chapter). The deceptive simplicity with which his ideas and slogans could be grasped accounted in part for their political appeal. But such simplification also risked the possibility of misunderstanding.

Friedman's ability to communicate complex economic ideas raises an interesting question about the relationship between economic theory and policy. Policymakers' use of theory is fraught with problems arising from their need for quick, simple solutions and their need to compromise with electoral and constituency concerns. Theorists, on the other hand, believe their ideas will work only if they are tried purely and properly. Neoliberalism was a particularly powerful theory, almost a faith, for true believers in the free market and its possibilities. Friedman's monetarist analysis and market solutions grabbed people's attention as a ready-made and plausible alternative strategy when the economy began to unravel under the weight of stagflation. Friedman was not the only one who saw the primary economic policy problem as shifting from full employment to the control of inflation. But whether non-monetarist and even former Keynesian economists had understood this or not was irrelevant because the Keynesian economic elite had by then lost credibility with the public and with policymakers. Friedman instead was able to offer a solution with a set of policy prescriptions that could immediately be put into effect. Technical policy ideas burst the dam of Keynesian dominance, and Chicago neoliberal philosophy rushed through. Friedman's monetarist macroeconomics, and other ideas such as George Stigler's theory of regulatory capture, for example, opened the door to the eventual breakthrough of neoliberal politics. The result from the 1980s onward was a surge of the free market faith into all manner of policy areas in both Britain and the United States. But why did the long boom come to an end?

The Gathering Storm

As Peter Jay explains,

> There was real intellectual evolution going on in the postwar period, there was certainly in the Anglo-Saxon world, something which thought of itself as a kind of Keynesian consensus, a great deal more optimistic and self-confident than Keynes himself had ever been about the possibilities, (though he was a very self-confident man) but he would not have made the claims for what demand management could do which were made in his name. I think the events of the 1960s and 1970s largely undermined that.[80]

The strategy pursued by Kennedy and Johnson in the 1960s began to break down after 1968.[81] As Thomas Karier has put it, that year marked the end of the Keynesian experiment with expansionary stimulus, the external deficits of the late sixties have "been blamed on increased spending for the Vietnam War," but although that was important, domestic fiscal irresponsibility—there were no spending cuts or tax rises—was also to blame. "The influence of Keynesian advisers had waned sufficiently by 1968 so that their policy recommendations were being routinely ignored. Despite the resounding success of their experiment, politics regained control of the federal budget."[82] Karier argues that the Keynesian approach was largely responsible for the continued growth of the U.S. economy during the 1960s. But, he observes, the election of Nixon marked the beginning of the slow dismantling of these policies.

In conclusion, it is apt to return to Keynes's biographer, Robert Skidelsky, who sees the outcome of the Keynesian experiment somewhat differently. He has reflected on the demise of the Golden Age of the 1950s and 1960s and argues that it was "the breakdown of the Keynesian strategy of boom control which proved fatal."[83] Skidelsky suggests that the United States was responsible for setting the inflation rate for the whole of the fixed exchange rate system owing to the position of the dollar as the strongest currency:

> The fiscal conservatism of the Truman-Eisenhower years was dubbed non-Keynesian by the generation of Keynesians who came into power in the 1960s. But this was a misreading of the Keynesian revolution. Setting tax rates to achieve an employment target consistent with a low rate of inflation was properly Keynesian; it marked a radical departure from pre-Keynesian fiscal orthodoxy which paid no attention to the "state of trade." Ironically, the real contribution of Keynesian policy to the golden age was not to stimulate aggregate demand. It was to keep inflation under control by methods which did not bring about the collapse of the secular boom.[84]

But as American fiscal restraint disappeared in the 1960s, Keynesian economists who advised President Kennedy thought that economic recession was imminent. They felt that more stimulus was necessary as they feared the economic and political power of the Soviet Union. This set the scene for the Kennedy-Johnson tax cuts, the War on Poverty, and the Great Society programs of the mid- to late 1960s:

The American economist Robert Triffin invented the famous "Triffin paradox": the world needed the growth in reserves which only dollars could provide; but, in splaying convertible dollars round the system, the US government was not only igniting world inflation but undermining confidence in its own currency. The unfolding of the 'paradox' might have been postponed had America not got involved in the Vietnam War. But vast military overseas coming on top of the 'Great Society' programmes, started a haemorrhage of gold from Fort Knox in the late 1960s.

But, as Skidelsky continues,

> Once inflationary expectations got built into the global system, fiscal policy was disabled. Raising taxes could no longer be used to fight inflation, since unions would ask for higher wage increases to compensate for reductions in take-home pay; reducing taxes to stimulate the economy would only ratchet up prices. When the US's short debt came to exceed its gold reserves, it was forced to suspend dollar convertibility into gold and float the dollar in 1971. The Bretton Woods system collapsed, inflation was let loose, and the long boom ended.[85]

The main consequence of this slow process, in terms of economic strategy in Britain and the United States, was to discredit the Keynesian economists and advisers; their ideas, it appeared had proved incapable of adjustment to the flaws in the system. The reputation of the Keynesian policy elite collapsed as a result. This unfolded slowly during the 1970s and, from the perspective of the time, with unpredictable results.

6

✳

Economic Strategy

The Neoliberal Breakthrough, 1971–84

> The supposed profound differences between governments and parties which
> the 'sports commentator' school of political writer delights to invent bear al-
> most no relation to the reality and continuity of the substance of government
> policies and actions. It will be noted that all the virtues of financial 'realism'
> and monetary discipline which have since become associated, whether as vir-
> tues or vices, with the post-1979 government [in Britain] were in fact strongly,
> centrally and officially celebrated as key elements in the economic strategy of
> the previous government.
>
> —PETER JAY, *The Crisis for Western Political Economy*

Economic crisis led to the breakthrough of transatlantic neoliberal politics
in the 1970s. As Britain and the United States experienced stagflation—the
combination of high unemployment, high inflation, and low or no growth—
political leaders and policymakers, for the first time since World War II, cast
around for serious alternative economic policies to Keynesian demand management. The end of the Bretton Woods international monetary system, two
oil price shocks in 1973 and 1979, the Vietnam War, the Watergate break-in
at the Democratic Party headquarters in Washington, D.C., at the behest of
senior figures of the Nixon administration and with the president's complicity in its cover-up, Britain's International Monetary Fund (IMF) loan of 1976,
the virtual collapse of British industrial relations, and the failure of the prices
and incomes policies that were supposed to fight inflation in both countries
all created a policy vacuum into which neoliberal ideas flowed. The preceding

chapters have shown how a transatlantic network of people, institutions, and money was primed with an alternative set of diagnoses and prescriptions to sate the desire of political leaders for a new approach. Just as in 1932 or 1945, the 1970s were a rare moment when the pieces of the political and economic jigsaw were strewn all over the place, in need of painstaking rearrangement.

The success of Milton Friedman's monetarism and the application of versions of it to economic policy in both Britain and the United States after the mid-1970s had greater consequences beyond the technical details of monetary and fiscal policy.[1] Monetarist ideas seemed to offer an alternative way of running an advanced economy, one based on a return to purer free market economics. However, this hope largely rested on a conflation of monetarism with a theoretically separate set of arguments about the supposed superiority of markets over government intervention in the economy. The importance of freeing markets—through liberalization, lower taxes, deregulation, and privatization—became known as supply-side reform, so called in contradistinction to Keynesian demand management. An early example of this trend toward free market solutions at the macroeconomic level was the move from fixed to floating exchange rates after 1971, something that had been advocated by Friedman since the 1950s. Another example, at the microeconomic level, was the growing acceptance in the wake of George Stigler's ideas (described in chapter 3) of the failures of government regulation. Similarly, politicians sought to foster greater private sector involvement and ownership in key areas of social policy such as housing and urban policy in order to open up, so the theory went, market opportunities for poor and disadvantaged groups both in terms of the delivery of services and in terms of job creation (see chapter 6). Market mechanisms were to be an alternative to public provision, benefits, and subsidies. These supply-side policies have been retrospectively allied to the monetarist analysis of the failures of demand management by observers of the programs of the Conservative and Republican administrations of Thatcher and Reagan. In fact, they should be seen as distinct.

The trend toward a new macroeconomic strategy was actually firmly bipartisan in the 1970s. The Labour Party under Prime Minister James Callaghan and Chancellor of the Exchequer Denis Healey (and arguably even earlier for a brief moment under the chancellorship of Roy Jenkins in the late 1960s) was a reluctant convert to a form of monetarist financial discipline by 1976.[2] Equally, after an expansionary beginning, Democratic president

Jimmy Carter, a fiscal hawk by nature, appointed Democratic Party economic policy technocrat Paul Volcker to replace the more conventionally Keynesian G. William Miller as chairman of the Federal Reserve in 1979. Volcker was later reappointed by President Ronald Reagan in 1983. He reformed the Fed's operation of monetary policy through the introduction of monetary targets and held in place high interest rates for three years to defeat the "Great Inflation" that scarred the late 1970s. Jimmy Carter, too, launched the first significant efforts at deregulation of the airline industry, of transportation, and of parts of the financial sector. This ripple of deregulation would turn into a tidal wave that washed away controls from large segments of the economy in the last two decades of the twentieth century. It is often forgotten that this movement began in earnest during the Carter years.

This transformation in economic policy occurred incrementally through a particular constellation of circumstances during the 1970s. The dominance of the market in social and economic policy enabled by Reagan's and Thatcher's later electoral successes was far from assured in the late 1970s. The Labour and Democratic Party leaderships had by this time been convinced of the technical economic case against Keynesian demand management and fine tuning, at least as it had been practiced by British and U.S. policymakers. The Labour Party had even tried and failed to reform the trade unions in 1969. What followed after 1979 and 1980 was therefore by no means inevitable. The late 1960s and early 1970s brought a succession of economic shocks that undermined the postwar international monetary system and pushed the world economy into stormy waters. The final stage in the shift in economic strategy in Britain and the United States, the reason neoliberal ideas found a receptive audience, was the force of these events.

The Slow Collapse of the Postwar Boom, 1964–71

In Britain, the Labour Party under Harold Wilson defeated Alec Douglas-Home's Conservative government (Home had replaced Macmillan as prime minister in 1963) and was elected with a small majority in 1964. The Labour government moved further in the direction of the indicative planning, on the French *dirigiste* model, begun under Conservative chancellor Reginald Maudling.[3] Planning bodies such as the National Economic Development

Council (known as "Neddy") and its regional counterparts (the little "neddies") were established under the Conservatives in 1961. Influenced by the French Economic and Social Council, Wilson created the Department of Economic Affairs in 1964, headed by his deputy, George Brown, as a second economic department in charge of planning to rival the power of the Treasury. The idea was to bring government, industry, and the unions together to tackle economics problems and plan for long-term economic growth.[4]

Milton Friedman bemoaned the trajectory of British economic policy, especially Maudling's and Wilson's drift toward increased government planning, to British economist and fellow member of the Mont Pelerin Society Peter Bauer in 1966. He wrote, "[it] is discouraging to see what has happened in Britain. I had been hopeful that just as Britain led us into the present direction of policy so she might lead us out but that hope seems now to have little basis."[5] Bauer replied that the "performance of the Conservatives [in the 1964 election] was lamentable" and suggested that the party seemed "to be completely out of touch with the world of ideas." He was eager to talk about the election and its implications when they next met.[6] They would meet at the next society meeting. These types of discussions illustrate an awareness of, and fellowship felt between, the correspondents of each other's ideas and developments in their respective countries—the sense of a shared struggle. George Shultz has described how Mont Pelerin Society meetings, and the connections between members in different countries that they fostered, provided an opportunity to share "what works and what doesn't work."[7] The transatlantic network functioned almost like a kind of Neoliberal International.

Just as Lyndon Johnson's landslide in 1964 had for American New Deal liberalism, the Labour Party's successful reelection in 1966 with an increased majority of ninety-six appeared to indicate the lasting success of British social democracy. However, by 1967, just as in 1924, 1931, and 1949, the Labour government was mired in economic turmoil as a result of financial crisis, this time because of its failure to prevent a devaluation of the pound sterling. Chancellor James Callaghan was left with no choice but devaluation after a run on the pound in the currency markets. It was the latest of many balance-of-payments crises that littered the postwar years.[8] The Labour Party's dire reputation for economic competence was further damaged when the whole edifice of the government's policy crumbled. In a dry run for what would happen in 1976, the new chancellor, Roy Jenkins (Callaghan had offered to resign but was instead persuaded to move to the Home Office), was forced into a period of fiscal and budgetary austerity for the last three years of the Labour government after accepting a loan from the IMF in early 1968. Jenkins's financial and fiscal discipline briefly brought the return of a trade surplus, although a small deficit had returned by the 1970 election, which the Conservatives, under Edward Heath, unexpectedly won.

Perhaps the single most important economic issue in both the United States and Britain at the end of the sixties was the instability of the international monetary system. There was not always agreement among members of the Mont Pelerin Society over the best way to run international monetary policy. Hayek argued for the gold standard as the best means of imposing the external financial discipline needed to maintain fiscal and monetary restraint (though he later came to advocate a version of free banking through competing currencies in a pamphlet written for the Institute of Economic Affairs in 1976).[9] Friedman thought this was a good idea in theory, but, he argued, it would not work unless all major Western countries followed suit, something he thought highly unlikely.[10] While Lionel Robbins, for example, was undecided on the matter. Robbins stated no objection to occasional adjustments in exchange rates and suggested to Friedman that "what divides us apparently is the question of perpetual freedom versus fixity." Robbins questioned whether floating exchange rates were, as Friedman claimed, the "essentially liberal solution":

> Now I do not say that forcible interference with private freedom of contract is necessarily illiberal. My particular brand of liberalism is content to judge these things on their merits. I only want to claim that the argument for free exchanges should be judged on its own grounds and not buttressed by any special presumptions regarding the virtues of the free market.[11]

Friedman argued that the case for floating rates rested on the merits rather than on liberal ideology.

The Bretton Woods system collapsed because of the expense of the Vietnam War, the decline in American gold reserves, and the continued expense of Lyndon Johnson's antipoverty programs. In 1971, President Nixon was forced to float the dollar and suspend the convertibility of the dollar into

gold. Thus began an experiment with wage and price controls that was deeply
unpopular with neoliberal economists and commentators. The controls were
ostensibly introduced to combat rising inflation, but they also proved an electoral boon to Nixon because they helped him present the public image of a
president firmly in charge in the midst of an international economic crisis.[12]
In 1972, Britain followed the United States' example and floated the pound.[13]
The fixed exchange rate framework, which had held the international economy together since 1945, was dead.

In the end, Friedman's preferred market-based solution to the monetary
system came about less through his own advocacy and more because of
global economic forces. As Friedman himself put it,

> For twenty-five years and more I and others like me preached the vir-
> tues of floating exchange rates. It had absolutely no effect on anybody.
> Nobody was persuaded by it. Until the brute force of events produced
> exchange crises. The Bretton-Woods fixed exchange rate system was
> obviously obsolete, it could not be maintained. People are very stick-
> in-the-mud. All of us hate change, we like to go on the way we are going,
> we only change when we're forced to. But when the time came that you
> had to change, that the old fixed rate system fell down, the fact that we
> had been talking about floating exchange rates, had been discussing its
> virtues, analyzing the problems it would raise and how it would work,
> meant that there was an alternative ready there to be picked up.
>
> In the same way as the increasing burden of taxation, as the increas-
> ing reaction against successive regulation makes itself felt, the fact that
> there have been thinkers around who have been outlining free market
> alternatives will mean that those are now in the realm of the possible.
> They will be around to be picked up. In my opinion that is the real role
> of the thinker, not to produce the fundamental change.[14]

Friedman admitted that events and crises forced a change in policy. But it was
crucial that those alternative policies had been developed and promoted, and
lay ready to be applied by pressurized leaders when the time came.

The second major issue to emerge as a serious problem at the end of the
sixties was inflation. In the United States, Nixon pursued a short-lived anti-
inflation strategy, based on Keynesian fine-tuning, on taking office in January

1969.[15] But, as with the British Conservative governments of the 1950s and 1960s, as well as during Edward Heath's brief premiership in the early 1970s, the battle against inflation remained an explicitly secondary goal to that of full employment. Kenneth Cole, the deputy assistant to the president for domestic affairs, wrote to Nixon in November 1969:

> Our strategy should be focused on achieving full employment and stable economic growth without extreme shifts in economic policy but with the objective of a balanced budget or small surplus at full employment. The basic economic objective of full employment should not be treated as secondary to the goal of achieving a moderate budget surplus.
>
> It is also important to decide if the current monetary policy is consistent with the longer run plan for economic policy. The present course of monetary policy seems to be of the extreme sort pursued under the "old" strategy and could contribute to the kind of instability we are presumably trying to avoid. To put the point bluntly, Dr. McCracken's [Nixon's chairman of the President's Council of Economic Advisers] memorandum argues for more stable long-run fiscal and monetary policies while we actually continue to follow in monetary policy the extreme swings that characterised the policy in the last few years. It is important to give more consideration to the process by which we expect to accomplish the transition from the present policy to the more moderate long-run policy.[16]

Nixon's White House followed Keynesian prescriptions—the president famously declared, "we are all Keynesians now"—despite the exhortations of Milton Friedman and the monetarists to adopt a different strategy.[17] Nixon's concern about reelection in 1972, following disappointing results in the 1970 mid-term elections, led him to an inflationary expansion that, like the "Barber Boom" in Britain (when Heath's chancellor Antony Barber presided over an unsustainable bout of loose monetary policy in 1972–74), had lasting consequences for the future of moderate politics in the United States, especially in the Republican Party. According to the historian Allen Matusow, by avoiding the problem of tackling inflation and maintaining and increasing spending on Vietnam and the social programs of the New Deal, the Great Society, and the

War on Poverty, Nixon missed an opportunity to address the fundamentally changed economic climate.[18] The result was a recession in 1969, followed by a move toward expansionary policies, which prepared the ground for the stagflation of the 1970s.

Friedman occasionally advised Nixon. For example, he and George Stigler visited the White House in June 1971 to discuss the economic situation.[19] Both were also present as invited guests, along with William Baroody of the American Enterprise Institute, at a state dinner at the White House organized for British prime minister Edward Heath's visit in December 1970.[20] Friedman was definitely not a significant influence on the administration's economic strategy however. Mainstream political opinion during the Nixon years was still skeptical of monetarist alternatives. Nixon's most important economic advisers were Council of Economic Advisers chairman Paul McCracken; George Shultz, who was successively labor secretary, director of the Office of Management and Budget, and treasury secretary; and Herbert Stein, who succeeded McCracken in 1972 (another important figure was the Federal Reserve chairman, Arthur Burns.) Instead, Friedman's correspondence with Nixon's staff leaves the impression of a relatively powerless observer. He nevertheless kept up a steady stream of commentary on the economic situation throughout the 1970s, which he sent to members of the Nixon and Ford administrations.

In 1970, Friedman warned Nixon of what he saw as the adverse effects of an unpredictable and unstable monetary and budgetary policy. Despite his lack of influence and his disagreement with the president's inflationary approach, Friedman clearly felt himself a close supporter of the administration:

> The deepening recession will clearly affect adversely our political fortunes in this Fall's election. As this becomes clearer, there will be, and no doubt already is, strong pressure to pull out all the stops in the effort to reverse the economic trend—to take off the restraints on spending, to let the deficit become much larger, to encourage the Fed to expand the money supply more rapidly.[21]

This is exactly the direction that Nixon and his advisers, out of a mixture of cynical opportunism and philosophical confusion, chose to pursue after the elections. Friedman was seen as one alternative voice in economic policy debates rather than as a unique authority. Consequently, his input was limited. For example, Paul McCracken wrote to Nixon of the problem of the adminis-tration's tight monetary policy in 1969:

> Milton Friedman fears that this degree of severity courts the risk of a recession. There is, on the other hand, a pervasive view in the business and financial community that "Washington" will not persevere in bat-tling inflation, so decisions can be made as if inflation will continue un-abated. Any overt easing of monetary policy would thus be interpreted by many as a signal that we are off to the races again.[22]

This passage is an indication of both the relative seriousness of the administra-tion's concern with inflation in its first years and also of a Keynesian belief in deflation, as opposed to Friedman's ideas about the importance of the money supply. As we have seen, Friedman was pushing his simple and optimistic message, that a stable operation of monetary policy and a controlled expan-sion of the money supply would right all ills, while the Nixon administration practiced a Keynesian contraction of monetary and fiscal policy according to events and forecasts. But Keynesians themselves were pessimistic about what such a policy would bring in terms of unemployment, hence the "alternative" of wage and price controls.

Friedman wrote to Nixon that "a drastic easing [of monetary policy] would be catastrophic." He continued, the "longer-term economic effect would be to make the '70's an even more inflationary decade than the '60's, with still higher interest rates, and with spreading and deadening controls nearly inevi-table." Friedman argued that the "political effect would be to trade a negligible improvement in 1970 prospects for a sharp deterioration on 1972 prospects [highlighted, probably by Nixon, as "correct"]."[23] His prediction was remark-ably prescient, as the 1970s did become a far more inflationary decade and Nixon pursued the measures that Friedman feared. Friedman's prescription instead would have been "to stick with the present policy of moderate expan-sion, to put primary emphasis on stopping the inflation, and to accept the recession as an unavoidable price of prior mistakes—the inflationary mistake of 1964–68 and the deflationary mistake of the last half of 1969."[24]

Friedman advocated a tight monetary policy characterized by a gradual and predictable growth in the supply of money to get inflation under control.

He acknowledged that more unemployment was unavoidable if this course was followed, but he thought such an approach was essential. He counseled the president

> that the ground be laid now, that statements be avoided like the one reported in today's Wall Street Journal—"White House officials emphatically denied that the Administration will let the jobless rate drift so high or so long." This promise cannot in fact be redeemed. The emphasis should rather be on the determination to stop inflation, even at high costs in unemployment, and on the measures you have already proposed to ameliorate the effects on the unemployed.
>
> The nation is heavily in your debt for the political courage you have displayed in the battle against inflation and in particular in resisting the easy yet false path of direct price and wage controls. Success is in sight, but it will require continued determination and political courage to reap the reward of the policies followed so far.[25]

Quite aside from the economic merits of such arguments, no politician, least of all Nixon, likes to hear such recommendations.

Alan Greenspan, then the chairman of his own economic consultancy firm called Townshend-Greenspan, agreed with Friedman's prognosis. He argued that wage and price controls—which were increasingly seen as the solution to inflation by policymakers and Keynesian economists—would not "have any restraining effect on inflation." "Moreover," Greenspan continued, "to the extent that they are successful in temporarily suppressing some price and wage levels" they "only build up a back-log of subnormal wage and price levels which must ultimately break through, worsening an already difficult problem."[26] Friedman's consistent advocacy of a strict reboot of monetary policy, even if it meant the inducement of recession, marginalized his influence over the administration's economic policy. Nixon's response to Friedman's position, drafted by Paul McCracken, made it clear that Friedman's advice was held at arm's length:

> As I am sure you understand, the tolerances within which our economic policy must be managed are exceedingly narrow. What we must try to achieve is a modestly more expansionist combination of policies that

will enable us to make further progress toward dampening the inflation without, at the same time, producing such a weak economy that responsible economic policy will be politically jeopardised.[27]

McCracken's emphasis is still on the capacity of the administration to make minor and frequent adjustments to produce the desired outcomes in terms of inflation and growth—to pursue demand management—something that Friedman believed was impossible and dangerous.

Stagflation and Wage and Price Policies

There were similarities between the approaches of the Nixon administration and the governments of Harold Wilson and Edward Heath in Britain, especially after the collapse of the Bretton Woods system. Both accepted full employment as their primary economic goal. Both pursued forms of wage and price controls (or prices and incomes policies, as they were known in Britain). Both used Keynesian tools of fiscal and monetary expansion and contraction. Despite these similarities, American observers of British policy in the White House looked on the British experience of experimentation with prices and incomes policies in the mid- to late 1960s under Chancellor James Callaghan with a distinct lack of enthusiasm and sometimes scathing criticism.[28]

A 1970 White House policy paper commented that incomes policy in the UK was "generally viewed as a failure so long as it was voluntary" and, though partially successful when mandatory during 1966–67, the policy "could not be maintained, however, and whatever was accomplished during the freeze was shortlived."[29] Peter G. Peterson, the assistant to the president for international affairs, wrote to Treasury Secretary John Connally in June 1971 that the "UK Strategy Against Inflation" was "worth scanning as an example of something that has failed."[30] Fusionist and New Right journalist William F. Buckley's comment on the economic situation in Britain was no less damning:

England is paying the high cost of an economics of illusion, which chimera socialism builds on. In America we don't go in very much for nationalized industries, mostly because we escaped the doctrinaire liturgy of European Socialism. But we laze our way over in the same direction in our own way, and we are coming on to crises not dissimilar to England's.[31]

But after 1971 the administration was forced into a similar approach. At the same time as announcing that the convertibility of dollars into gold would end, a typically opportunist Nixon declared a raft of temporary economic controls, including a ninety-day wage and price freeze and exchange controls, on August 15, 1971. Wage and price controls had been tried on a voluntary basis during the Kennedy years, but Nixon was the first to introduce them as statutory measures.

Friedman was fully supportive of the decision to float the dollar, but he was steadfast in the face of rumors that the administration would compromise on currency "freedom." He outlined what he saw as the dangers of a partial or complete return to fixed exchange rates to Connally at the end of 1971. He suggested that such a step "would snatch defeat from the jaws of victory." Friedman argued that "European central bankers, their fellow travelers in the New York financial community, and the Eastern European–oriented journalists are trying to conjure up the spectacle of crisis, world recession, trade war and all the rest unless there is a prompt agreement on a new structure of fixed exchange rates." According to Friedman, these were simply "scare tactics directed at fooling us into entering once again into unwise commitments that will give foreign countries unjustified power over us." He affirmed his strong support for "what the U.S. should have done years ago: put foreigners on the same basis as U.S. citizens with respect to the dollar." The response of the currency markets, Friedman maintained, was "excellent" because "flexibility has replaced rigidity." He concluded that "we do not need and should not seek specific commitments from other countries about exchange rates"; instead, "what we must avoid is making any such commitments ourselves."[32]

Friedman, like Enoch Powell in Britain, had long argued that the Bretton Woods system obstructed the proper free market operation of currencies and had powerful and inimical domino effects across the economy. In his view, the fixed rate system necessitated an unacceptable and needless level of control of people's freedom as well as having a distorting effect on market activity. Friedman's attitude to economic wage and price controls was different. He initially supported Nixon's policy as a short-term expedient that might help break inflationary expectations and also aid the president's political prospects.

George Shultz, like Friedman, was opposed to controls in general, but he articulated the rationale behind the administration policy in a speech to the National Press Club. He argued that "we applied controls at the time when they have the best chance of having a positive impact." According to Shultz, the "fundamental preconditions are well in place so as to make it possible for controls to add a finishing touch—to break inflation psychology, to reinforce the declining rate of inflation and speed it on its downward course."[33]

Nixon's measures were meant to address a temporary emergency, the breakdown of the Bretton Woods international monetary system and the resultant currency market instability. In this context they gained Friedman's reluctant acquiescence, although he thought the accompanying economic controls would not have a significant effect on inflation. He continued to warn of the danger of an inflationary spiral resulting from too much monetary expansion. He wrote to Connally that "it is almost literally incredible that there should be such a chorus of commentators complaining that not enough is being done to stimulate the economy." Friedman argued that any administration effort to pursue a more expansionary policy "would produce an inflationary situation in 1972 that would be a major obstacle to the re-election of Mr. Nixon and the continuation of policies on which we have been embarked."[34]

Friedman's warnings went unheeded. The respected British economic commentator and journalist for the *Financial Times* Samuel Brittan wrote to Friedman about Nixon's introduction of import controls:

> Your interpretation of the Nixon surcharge as a tactical step backward in order to move two steps forward, may be justified. But having been at the IMF meeting, I must report that there is something of a credibility gap among other countries. Although some people accept that the surcharge is a negotiating weapon, there are others who believe that the surcharge et al are domestically popular and doubt the sincerity of Connally's posture. My own instincts are to believe that people mean what they say.[35]

Brittan's trust was confounded when the administration successively reimposed wage and price controls and encouraged an expansive monetary policy on the part of the Federal Reserve. In the end, a temporary policy, the wage-price freeze, intended to last only three months, continued throughout

1971–74. Friedman's response was to call on Shultz to resign in 1973 as it became apparent that the controls would be extended again.[36]

Friedman explained his opposition to wage and price controls to Brittan in 1975, commenting on the British "dilemma":

> I have no doubt that the controls are ultimately far more dangerous than inflation. I have always argued that open inflation is nothing like so dangerous as suppressed inflation. My problem is a different one. I am not sure you have the alternative available to you. So long as inflation is proceeding at a rapid pace, I fear it will be impossible to end controls. The public pressure to restore them will be overwhelming. Hence, I fear that the only effective policy is one which combines measures directed at reducing inflation with measures directed at abolishing controls.
>
> As you may know, I do not share the views of people who regard wage and price controls as effective shock tactics for reducing inflation. Hence, if there really were an alternative, I would unquestionably opt for abolishing controls and letting inflation rip.[37]

For Friedman, wage and price controls were a fundamentally misguided means of tackling inflation that misunderstood the short- and long-term effects of policy on the macroeconomic forces of inflation and employment. Instead of government "price fixing," Friedman continued to believe that only a stable monetary policy would work for the long-term banishment of inflation at a reasonable level of unemployment.

In 1974, President Nixon resigned over the bungled burglary of the Democratic headquarters in the Watergate building in Washington, D.C., and subsequent coverups. He was replaced by Gerald Ford, whose brief interregnum lasted until his election defeat by Jimmy Carter in November 1976. Nixon's resignation came on top of rising inflation, the replacement of his vice president, Spiro Agnew, for criminal corruption, the first oil shock of 1973, as well as the end of the Bretton Woods Agreement. The chairman of the Federal Reserve, Arthur Burns, wrote to Nixon in the summer of 1973, before the first oil crisis struck, about the general malaise:

What is ailing people? The dominant factor appears to be the sharply accelerated pace of our inflation. Most people—Americans and foreigners, businessmen and consumers, investors and working men— have no use for Phase III [of Nixon's post-1971 economic policy]. They seem to regard it as a mistake, and some regard it as a downright disaster.

The thinking and feeling of people is never compartmentalized. When they are in an anxious mood, one worry reinforces another— whether or not they know or understand what they are worried about. Thus, many people, besides being concerned about inflation, are worried about the devaluation of the dollar, the deficit in our foreign trade, the decline of stock prices, the rise of interest rates, fraud on the stock exchanges, booming profits, shortfalls in government integrity, the Watergate affair, etc. Of late, questions have been raised in the press about your leadership, about your interest in the problems that concern people, about your absorption in foreign affairs, about your attention to domestic issues, and so on.

All this is affecting the state of confidence. In fact, as I see it, this country is now in danger of being buffeted by a crisis of confidence. This sort of problem clearly requires a political approach. It requires strong leadership on your part. It requires visible proof to the American people that you care about their concerns, that you are doing something real in their interest, that you intend to continue to do more as needed, and that if one policy doesn't work you will be ready to move to another in an unceasing effort to protect and advance their welfare.[38]

The letter affords a powerful insight into the toxic atmosphere surrounding the president and his policies toward the end of his humiliated administration. The description of events and policies is ironic, given subsequent Republican attacks on Jimmy Carter about the crisis of confidence and leadership in the United States.

Friedman revealed his own sympathies on the Watergate issue, as well as the events surrounding the administration, in a letter to Republican congressman Philip Crane after the November mid-term elections of 1974:

Needless to say, I am delighted that you survived the recent holocaust and saddened as you are by the number of our friends who did not. It is hard even for an inveterate optimist like myself to pluck much cheer out of the present situation. I am reduced to hoping that overweening power, like pride, goeth before a fall.[39]

At the same time as Nixon's role in the Watergate burglary cover-up was agonizingly revealed, the first oil crisis flared in 1973. The Organization of Petroleum Exporting Countries (OPEC) cartel decided to raise oil prices and place an embargo on supporters of Israel, and the United States in particular, during the Yom Kippur War. This crisis led to widespread fears over the West's energy dependence on the Middle East. The shock fueled inflation by forcing price rises across the parts of the economy most dependent on oil for their operations. OPEC's move was a direct result of the collapse of the Bretton Woods system. Most currencies floated and stabilized at new, higher levels in relation to the weakened dollar. This meant that the oil-producing countries received less in real terms as oil was priced in dollars. The effects of the oil shocks (there was a second oil shock in 1979) are much debated, but it is clear that they stoked the economic downturn and also increased inflation.

The Heath Interregnum and the Neoliberal Alternative

In Britain, Edward Heath's Conservative Party was elected in 1970. Heath was a Conservative of the old school who believed in the efficacy of the state. According to his parliamentary private secretary Douglas Hurd (who was later home and foreign secretary under Margaret Thatcher and John Major), he believed "an efficient, well-led state could do substantial things in Britain":

> He rejected, in 1970, a compulsory incomes policy and then, as it were, fell into one, but the falling into one wasn't contrary to his basic beliefs. On the contrary, he did feel that, properly led, competent civil servants could make policies work even outside their normal sphere, so that you've got people like Geoffrey Howe deciding what the right price for toothpaste was. I mean it was a ludicrous thing. But, he did believe that . . . with an emphasis on free enterprise, the state was a good

performer. . . . It had been a good performer in France and he saw no reason why it couldn't be in Britain.[40]

There was an echo of Keynes in Heath's outlook. His was the idea of the enlightened technocratic elite pursuing the best policies in the larger interests of the nation. In opposition, Heath had flirted with a more radical free market agenda, and he was accused by right-wingers of several policy U-turns—on prices and incomes, on privatization (or "denationalization," as it was then known), on the unions, on financial management to battle inflation—which rowed back from the program that was supposedly outlined at the shadow cabinet conference at Selsdon Park in 1970. As the political historian Anthony Seldon suggests, "the Heath Government is intriguing in part because it promoted elements of both the old and the new worlds and was trapped uneasily as one paradigm was beginning to lose its hold, but the other model had yet to secure intellectual credibility or popular backing."[41]

The Heath period saw opinion among the political elite on economic policy begin to change. As Seldon recounts, "Douglas Allen [former cabinet secretary and permanent secretary to the treasury] has said that up to about 1972 the general body of opinion in the treasury was Keynesian. From about 1973, we were beginning to think that more attention should be given to the money supply."[42] Friedman, meanwhile, was considered an oddity in Britain in the late 1960s and 1970s. Heath wrote a handwritten comment in response to the suggestion of a meeting with Friedman by his friend, R. A. Allen, the vice chairman of Longman Publishers: "It would be very interesting to hear his views but if it was known he had come here would people think we had succumbed?"[43]

Heath's attempts to wrest control of the economic situation were curtailed by continued balance-of-payments crises, a failure to curb union powers despite the first comprehensive labor reform legislation (the Industrial Relations Act of 1971), and a huge inflationary boom. The combined effect drove a cycle of boom and bust epitomized by Chancellor Antony Barber's deliberate pre-election relaxation of monetary policy, known as the "Barber Boom." As economist and former British treasury official Alec Cairncross has put it, "It was . . . the workings of the monetary system in the early 1970s that converted many to monetarism."[44] At the same time, despite Heath's attempts to reform the trade unions, increased labor militancy caused the country to come to a virtual standstill. According to Hurd, Heath had wanted to help make the unions respected and responsible "contributors" to British society.[45] Instead, Heath was forced to declare a three-day week as the economy appeared to nosedive, to conserve electricity in the wake of strikes by the coal miners in 1973. He finally called an election in February 1974, asking of the country, who governs?

Heath was defeated in two elections in 1974—in February and in the subsequent election, called in October by Harold Wilson, who was finally installed for a second stint as prime minister with a wafer-thin majority of three seats. The prices and incomes policies of both Heath and Wilson, whose Labour Party won power on the basis that it was best able to deliver a "social contract" between the trade unions and government, were showing signs of bankruptcy. Friedman gave his view of the accumulated economic problems of stagflation in Britain and the United States to Hayek in early 1973:

> As I read it over again, your premonitions about accelerating inflation assumed even greater relevance than they did when I heard them at Mont Pelerin. In Britain the situation is truly frightening when you have a Government supposedly entering off its commitment to disbanding economic controls and promoting a restoration of a price system moving in the opposite direction to an even greater extent than the Labour Government ever did. In the United States, superficially it looks as if we are moving toward the dismantling of controls, but on a deep review I am very unsure that that will be the outcome. Inept monetary policy seems to have built in a danger of accelerating inflation which I fear will force a restoration of more wide-sweeping and stringent controls. I trust my fears will not be realised.[46]

Britain was unable to avoid the economic downturn. In 1975, Heath was challenged for the leadership of the Conservative Party and was surprisingly defeated by Margaret Thatcher, who had been his education secretary in 1970–74. Thatcher and her closest colleagues, Keith Joseph and Geoffrey Howe, signaled through their establishment of the Hayekian Centre for Policy Studies in the aftermath of Heath's defeat that they would develop a new economic policy program. Their primary focus was to be the trade union "problem." Meanwhile they sat back and watched the travails of the Labour Party in power.

In both Britain and the United States in 1974, inflation and unemployment were on the rise, and commentators saw political crisis as a real possibility to go with economic stagflation. The events of the early 1970s had created an economic climate that brought the fundamental assumptions of politicians and experts alike into question. The alternatives were finally being taken seriously after many years when the transatlantic neoliberal network had appeared to be whistling in the dark. Economic crisis had fostered an environment conducive to new ideas.

Sympathetic journalists and politicians were the most important conduits for the monetarist and free market ideas of the transatlantic network in Britain in the 1960s and 1970s. These individuals ensured that the neoliberal alternative reached a wider audience. Among the journalists, Samuel Brittan and Peter Jay, the economics editor of the *Times* who became James Callaghan's (Wilson's successor as prime minister in 1976) ambassador to the United States between 1977 and 1979. From the mid-1960s, and against the tide, they promoted the economic strategies suggested by Friedman and the Chicago school.

Samuel Brittan had been taught by Friedman at Cambridge in 1957, when Friedman was a visiting professor at the university. Friedman remembered Brittan "very vividly" as "one of the very small sample of Cambridge Students whom I could inspect with anything like sufficient detail."[47] Peter Jay was introduced to monetarist ideas by American friends, and he also read Friedman's work, especially his address to the American Economic Association (AEA) in 1967 and his *Monetary History of the United States* (written with Anna Jacobson Schwartz and published in 1963).[48] They were joined by others, such as economist Alan Walters, who wrote on the importance of the money supply in Britain for the IEA.[49] As the former civil servant and member of Margaret Thatcher's Policy Unit, Andrew Duguid, put it,

I do think that both [Brittan and Jay] were very important. Peter Jay, who had these articles in *The Times* in which he would put, he would convey, thoughts and ideas that he picked up from somewhere else to a different audience, so he was a channel of communication and Sam

Brittan as well because he used to write so many think-pieces and ev-
erybody in government read those pieces. You know, it would be on
the lips of everyone at lunchtime, what has Sam written today sort of
thing. . . . So he was very influential. They were two really important
sources for the transmission of ideas in the direction of Britain [from
the United States].[50]

Nigel Lawson, Geoffrey Howe, and Norman Lamont have all testified in interviews with the author to the important and influential role played by both
journalists in helping to shift opinion in Britain in the 1970s away from traditional Keynesian techniques.[51]

Brittan and Jay became convinced of the case for monetarism as a solution
to stagflation and what was known at the time as "the British Disease" of the
"sick man of Europe."[52] Neither could be classified as political conservatives.
Instead, they had become convinced of the economic case against demand
management. Jay, for example, wrote that the assumption of popular Keynesianism that the idea to "put more spending power into people's pocket,
whether by cutting taxes, increasing government spending or easing credit
conditions through monetary policy" was harmful and wrong.[53] Instead,

the economic realities were unhappily different. The belief that outside the narrow range of the Phillips curve, the regulation of spending power (known as 'demand management') uniquely affected price
levels or uniquely affected employment levels, according to whether
the pressure of demand was above or below the full employment zone,
was false in the long-term and therefore dangerously misleading in the
short-term.[54]

He went on:

The truth was that in the short-term—for the first year or two—
demand management mainly affects the real volume of spending, output and so employment while in the longer run it only affects the price
level. The notion inherent in the popular understanding of Keynes that
an economy would be indefinitely under-employed through deficient
demand without prices eventually being forced down sufficiently to

clear markets, including the labour market, was a dangerous misunderstanding of the unhappy experiences of the 1930s.[55]

Thus Jay articulated the main components of Friedman's case against fine-tuning.

Brittan also advocated monetarist policies as a response to the failures of Keynesian demand management in a report written for the recently founded Centre for Policy Studies (CPS). Brittan had by this time become, alongside Jay and his colleague at the *Times*, William Rees-Mogg, a leading advocate of monetarist ideas as a solution to Britain's economic woes. Alfred Sherman, director of the CPS, commissioned Brittan to write on the problems of demand management. Despite writing for the CPS (which was explicitly meant to provide new policy ideas to the Conservative Party), Brittan was not a Tory.[56] Brittan's pamphlet, *Second Thoughts on Full Employment Policy*, was satisfying for Sherman, who was clearly pleased that he had got such a respected and independent voice to present the case.

In the introduction to Brittan's pamphlet, Sherman himself emphasized the apolitical and technical nature of the case against full employment policy:

> Any Government, whatever the colour of its politics, must try to contain inflation in the interests of the national economy and of all classes. Inasmuch as it transpires that deficit financing to expand demand has been a major cause of accelerating inflation, and hence has undermined full employment in the long run by weakening the economy, anyone committed to sustaining a high level of employment, prosperity and economic advance, must question these policies.
>
> There is nothing quintessentially right-wing in wishing to have coherent, consistent policies. It would be truer to say that by an historical accident, the left in this country happens to have been frozen into attitudes adopted in the nineteen thirties. That is surely carrying conservatism too far. They are bound to break away from their fixation sooner or later and come to grips with reality.[57]

In the pamphlet proper, Brittan suggested that Milton Friedman "removed the scales from my eyes—not by his more technical views on money, but by his analysis of the effects of demand management on unemployment."

Brittan referenced the 1967 AEA address, but went on, "It did not take Milton Friedman to make me understand the connection between capitalism and freedom, and why true libertarians, radicals and iconoclasts should be on the side of capitalism, although not necessarily of capitalists."[58]

Brittan's main focus in *Second Thoughts* was on the effects of the Keynesian goal of full employment and the belief that it was possible to manage it with little inflationary cost. He described the relationship between the international monetary situation, inflation, and employment:

> One of the most important influences on the real value of money wages is the "equilibrium" terms of trade, that is the terms of trade prevailing when the exchange rate is neither overvalued nor undervalued and overseas payments are in balance without drawing on the reserves or official overseas borrowing. The large deterioration in the prevailing terms of trade (and even greater in the equilibrium terms) following the 1972–4 commodity boom and the oil price explosion is an outstanding example. This led to a reduction in the real wage at which a given level of employment could be provided. Resistance to the required reduction in real wages was bound to lead to a rise in the unemployment rate, however hard British Governments tried to postpone the issue by overseas borrowing and income transfers from other groups to manual workers. It is extremely difficult to believe that the behaviour of trade unions has not increased this resistance and therefore raised the unemployment rate.[59]

But more than the international context, Brittan's analysis centered on the problematic influence of demand management on the labor market in Britain.

Both Jay and Brittan saw the connection in Britain between demand management and the trade unions, whose power, after the demise of the Heath government, was seen as a crucial economic issue in the problem of inflation. Brittan wrote to Friedman in 1973 that the impact of the "ultra-Keynesian" intellectual climate in Britain was to give the unions a "perfect get-out clause for neglecting the interests of the unemployed, as high unemployment rates can always be blamed on inadequate government policies."[60] In other words, the unions, by pushing ever higher wage claims, were irresponsibly fueling the inflationary cycle and helping sustain the very conditions that made their members' jobs more vulnerable.[61]

The labor issue was one of Friedrich Hayek's biggest concerns, possibly because of his commitment, as a citizen, to the British economic and political scene. Chancellor of the Exchequer under John Major during the early 1990s, Norman Lamont became an MP in 1972 and remembers that it was Hayek who focused the attention of Conservatives on the power of the unions in Britain in the 1970s. Until then, Lamont's focus had been on how to deal with inflation. He described the shift in thinking on economic matters in the Conservative Party in the early seventies in an interview with the author, which is worth quoting at length:

> The big issue was the means to control inflation and I think that is often underestimated today. There was a real belief in this country and in America, to some extent, that in order to control inflation you had to control the price of bread, you had to have price controls and wage controls and the idea that you could control inflation by interest rates and the money supply, to some people, just appeared unbelievable and I think that was the big early battle. It was the first battle that I got engaged in, in the early seventies when I was both a Member of Parliament and working in the financial services and I myself had become completely convinced that our failure to use monetary means was the real cause of our inflation. . . . I gradually absorbed the ideas of Friedman. . . . It was that rather than the supply-side revolution, rather than privatisation, or abolition of exchange controls, or all the things that came later. That was the first thing I became aware of.
>
> DSJ: How did you become aware of it?
>
> NL: I became aware of it, first of all, because I was very conscious of the very high inflation we had getting towards 20% during the Heath Government and one was desperate for action to be taken on the money supply. There were fierce arguments in the Conservative Party and among Members of Parliament and the then Prime Minister, Edward Heath, who refused to acknowledge that this was remotely relevant, the money supply. We were just told the velocity of circulation blah blah blah, you know, don't be so simplistic. It was first of all a battle in the Heath Government and then when Heath lost the election, Keith Joseph was the person who, through his Preston speech ["Inflation is caused by governments," delivered in Preston on September 5, 1974], made this into a great issue. It was a remarkable, landmark speech,

drawing on Hayek and Friedman. Of course, I think the relevance of Hayek was on the trade unions. The need for trade union reform was a second issue coming along the road. What Hayek had argued was that monetarism, really, was not enough. And you had to have measures for a more evenly balanced labour market, a properly functioning labour market. That was the second big issue.[62]

Joseph's speech was heavily influenced by Hayek's and Friedman's ideas. But it was Hayek rather than Friedman who raised the problem of the labor market in Britain through his IEA pamphlets, *Tiger by the Tail* (1972, also published in the United States by the Cato Institute) and *Full Employment: At Any Price?* (1975).

Brittan debated with Milton Friedman the potential causes of inflation in Britain in the mid-1970s. Friedman believed that inflation was a strictly monetary phenomenon. But Brittan argued that in Britain, inflation may have been, at least in part, caused by the unions and their power. According to Friedman,

> I have always argued that it is hypothetically possible that a growth in union power would produce a degree of unemployment which, given a Government committed to a full employment policy, would in turn lead to inflationary monetary and fiscal policies in an attempt to wipe out the unemployment. This has always seemed to me a hypothetical possibility. My problem has been to know when and whether it is a real possibility. The only case I do know of is the one I have cited in the late 1930's in the United States.
>
> Except for such an episode and occasion, it does seem to me that we really can leave the unions out of account in the analysis of policy with respect to general inflation and general levels of employment. We cannot leave unions out of account in the analysis of the efficient use of resources. As you know, I believe that unions do immense damage denying workers opportunities, by falsifying relative prices and denying consumers opportunities. But that is, of course, a different subject.[63]

But Brittan maintained in his reply that the unions could cause inflation and also force unemployment up because "people's attitude to these matters in the UK is governed by the ultra-Keynesian intellectual climate":

The general belief accepted, at least until very recently, even by the vast majority of professional economists, is that the Government can determine the general level of employment and capacity utilisation, although perhaps at some cost in terms of inflation. This gives the union leadership a perfect get-out for neglecting the interests of the unemployed, as high unemployment rates can always be blamed on inadequate government policies; and the Government normally obliges by printing yet more money and increasing still further the budget deficit.[64]

Brittan argued that union power had increased during the 1960s and early 1970s to such an extent that governments and leaders were now convinced that union leaders had the power to bring the nation's economic life to a halt. This was unprecedented, according to Brittan, because union leaders had only recently become fully conscious of their power.

Friedman questioned the scientific rigor of such an analysis. For Friedman, the proposition that union power had lain dormant was not falsifiable (in Popperian terms) because it was tantamount to saying that "anything may happen at any time."[65] Thus it lacked any concrete content and was essentially meaningless speculation. However, unperturbed, Brittan countered with:

But there does seem to be, at least in the British situation, a large range of unpredictability within which "anything may happen at any time" depending to a large extent on the accident of personality and political manoevering [sic]. What then happens becomes validated by monetary expansion in the way you yourself outlined.[66]

He then reflected on the potential uses of union power:

The most interesting analytical point seems to be whether there is any use for the concept of "unused but potential power." One can make the proposition that power will always be used tautological, e.g. [British economist John] Hicks's monopolist who uses his power to lead "a quiet life" rather than to gain an above normal cash rate of return. But I doubt if, as an empiricist, you would want to look at matters in this way. For if monopoly power is used but in a wide variety of different ways, are we scientifically anywhere unless one can state the circumstances in which it will be used in one form rather than another.[67]

The effect of Brittan's and Hayek's intervention in the debate on industrial relations and inflation was to make clear a linkage between the failures of demand management and the power of trade unions in Britain. Friedman was less convinced of the relationship, although he always maintained that unions had a kind of monopoly power that distorted the labor market by artificially keeping unionized wages high and pushing up unemployment.

Jay, Brittan, and Friedman all saw a real possibility of political crisis in the vicious cycle of inflation and unemployment of the 1970s in Britain. Jay reached

> the depressing conclusion that the operation of free democracy appears to force governments into positions (the commitment to full employment) which prevent them from taking the steps (fiscal and monetary restraint) which are necessary to arrest the menace (accelerating inflation) that threatens to undermine the condition (stable prosperity) on which political stability and therefore liberal democracy depend. In other words democracy has itself by the tail and is eating itself up fast.[68]

Writing to Brittan in 1975 just as Thatcher was elected leader of the Conservative Party, Friedman shared his worry about whether Britain could avoid the fate of Chile, whose democracy had been overthrown by the military dictatorship of Augusto Pinochet in 1973. He predicted that the "destruction of its democratic society," were it to occur in Britain, would come "from the left" rather than the authoritarian right.[69] Friedman speculated whether the direction that the UK had taken would lead to a new form of dictatorship due to the amounts of national income being consumed by the government:

> I wonder therefore whether even in your present situation it may not be that a shock treatment either already is or shortly will be the only effective means of facing up to your inflation problem. Of course, even if the inflation problem were fundamentally faced up to, even if you were back on a 2 or 3 per cent per year rate of inflation with reasonable levels of employment, the basic problem of the fraction of income being taken by government and its tendency to drive you in a totalitarian direction would remain. Once you have gotten to the point where close

to 60 per cent of a nation's income is being spent by the government, is it possible to reverse? That is surely the question for the future.[70]

To Friedman in 1975 it appeared an open question in which direction Britain would turn and what the outcome would be.

The Left Turns to Monetarism
1: Callaghan, Healey, and the IMF Crisis

In retrospect, Friedman's fears of a new totalitarianism from the left were exaggerated, but a political crisis duly arrived in Britain with the events that led to the Labour government going to the IMF for a loan in December 1976. The two years of Harold Wilson's second premiership between February 1974 and April 1976, when he resigned, were marked by rapidly increasing inflation and ever higher wage claims from the trade unions. This was compounded by Labour's expansive social commitments, pressure on which was increased by the rising cost of living and union demands. The Labour Party was even more vulnerable to the trade union "problem" because it had been narrowly elected in February and October 1974 in part owing to its claims to better manage the social contract between government and the unions than the Conservative Party.[71] The party had also adopted the so-called "alternative economic strategy" (AES) when in opposition. The AES was an ambitious program based on an expansion of socialist-style workers councils, import quotas and tariffs, and the increased nationalization of industry.[72] Despite being adopted as official Labour Party policy by the left-wing-dominated party conference, the plan was never implemented in office. But the failure of Wilson or Callaghan, who succeeded Wilson as prime minister in May 1976, to make any serious attempt to introduce the AES was a constant source of friction between the leadership and the party's left, led by Energy Secretary Tony Benn.

The government, like Edward Heath's Conservative predecessor, was soon overtaken by events. In 1975 and 1976 inflation rose above 20 percent, peaking at 26.9 percent in August 1975. In 1975, Chancellor Denis Healey presented the first postwar budget in which full employment was not the highest priority. The introduction for the first time, by Healey in 1976, of monetary targets and cash limits—a fixed amount of cash available in advance of pay negotiations—on spending arguably marked the Labour government's conversion to a version of monetarism. Inflation had replaced full employment as the primary economic goal and, as James Cronin has put it in his study of the Labour Party in the postwar period, "the Treasury was itself in the process of a conversion that would take it away from a lukewarm attachment to Keynesian demand management to a fixation on the size of the public debt—symbolised by the Public Sector Borrowing Requirement (PSBR)—and, finally, to monetarism."[73] High inflation and the increased number of jobless in the setting of a reduced tax take and a rising PSBR prompted Callaghan and Healey to go to the IMF for a loan because they feared the government and country were on the verge of financial collapse, a worry that was subsequently revealed to have been much exaggerated. This was the final step in the slow process whereby the Labour leadership abandoned its commitment to Keynesian demand management—in fact, it was just five ministers, Healey, Callaghan, Joel Barnett (chief secretary to the treasury and Callaghan's right-hand man), Reg Prentice (the minister for overseas development), and Edmund Dell (the trade secretary), who took this position in the cabinet debates.[74]

Peter Jay was the prime influence behind Prime Minister James Callaghan's speech to the Labour Party Conference in 1976, where he sounded the death knell of Keynesianism in Britain:[75]

> We used to think that you could spend your way out of a recession and increase employment by cutting taxes and boosting government spending. I tell you in all candour that that option no longer exists, and in so far as it ever did exist, it only worked on each occasion since the war by injecting a bigger dose of inflation into the economy, followed by a higher level of unemployment as the next step.[76]

Callaghan and Healey managed to get reluctant left-wingers and moderates such as Tony Crosland (who became the key swing vote) in the cabinet to back the stringent conditions attached to the loan. But, unsurprisingly, Callaghan's efforts were hampered by the machinations of the Conservative Party opposition. German chancellor Helmut Schmidt asked Callaghan in a telephone call on November 2, 1976, whether he knew that Keith Joseph,

Thatcher's ideological inspiration and political partner, was "very strongly . . . trying to influence people in Washington against you." Joseph's activities in Washington, D.C., were another indication of the influence of the transatlantic neoliberal network. Schmidt said of Joseph that "he has very good established contacts in every quarter in Washington, and bears some influence there."[77]

Schmidt was probably thinking of William Simon, Ford's treasury secretary and a strong advocate of monetarist and neoliberal ideas. Simon wrote a popular book about his time in the Nixon and Ford administrations titled *A Time for Truth*, which had a foreword and preface by Hayek and Friedman.[78] The book, which popularized neoliberal free market philosophy, was published in association with *Reader's Digest* and became a bestseller in the United States in the late seventies. Foreign Secretary Tony Crosland, writing from Washington, D.C., told Callaghan that Americans held two positions on helping the British get a loan from the IMF:

> The first would be to respond as helpfully as possible to the PM's message to the President, augmented by what I had just said about HMG's determination to carry on with present policies. The second would be to argue that the US would only be contributing to Britain's policies in the longer-term by making things too easy for us [by helping the British get the loan with lower spending cuts] in our short-term difficulties.[79]

Crosland attributed the second position to Simon, who felt that the Labour government was not serious about its responsibilities to cut spending and attack inflation.

According to Edmund Dell, a participant in the cabinet debates, there was a pitched battle between the ministers of the hard left, led by Tony Benn, who supported the AES, and moderates, led by Crosland.[80] Healey stood firm for the fiscal and monetary restraint demanded by the IMF. Benn advocated holding out, and a resort to protectionism through the imposition of import controls. Crosland believed that the crisis was overblown and the demands of the IMF for cuts were too steep. He argued that the government had already done enough to restore economic growth. Instead, according to Crosland, the government should weather the storm and wait for the coming economic upswing. This might have worked. Almost as soon as the loan was secured, the economic indicators began to show that the economy was in ruder health than had been thought, the result of Healey's tough policies during 1975–76.

Harvard economist John Kenneth Galbraith supported a straight Keynesian line. He believed the IMF loan was necessary and told Callaghan that he had met with Henry Kissinger in Washington, D.C., to press the British case. He made clear to Kissinger that "Britain is facing the problems of all the industrial countries but as usual is a bit ahead on the timetable," and he emphasized "the broad imperative of the mixed economy."[81] Galbraith wrote a policy paper for Callaghan which suggested that "the most important general need is for the Government to assume a far more confident and assertive posture" and to start "controlling" events rather than responding to them. But he saw a promising future as

> the funding loan will give a quick upward flip to sterling from people who will gamble on the long-run prospect as opposed to selling at the present low price. The increase in indirect taxation, reduction in the public deficit will reinforce this effect. Social expenditure for the most needy is protected. The prospective shift from monetary to fiscal restraint—to taxes instead of tight money—will aid investment and labor productivity, reduce the peculiarly intractable kind of unemployment that monetary policy causes.[82]

The treasury response to Galbraith's paper indicated changes in the thinking of the British economic policy elite:

(a) As one would expect, Prof. Galbraith's analysis is strictly in "old Keynesian" terms. There is no reference to monetary policy, as such. On the other hand there is nothing in Prof. Galbraith's paper to suggest that monetary policy is unimportant. It goes no further than the argument (which few of us would dispute) that it can be harmful to rely on severe monetary policy to make good the deficiencies of a lax fiscal policy.

(b) In arguing that there is "an excess pressure of demand" on real resources at the present time, Prof. Galbraith needs (I suggest) to be interpreted in a rather special sense. Certainly, there is at present excess demand, in relation to domestic production (in the sense that there is a balance of payments deficit). At the same time, there is a large margin of unused productive capacity. This surely suggests not only a weakness in demand management, but also a weakness on the supply side—a failure of British industry to compete in international markets. Hence the emphasis which we have placed in our recent strategy papers on both price competitiveness and (looking to the longer term) the industrial strategy.[83]

There was clearly an increased willingness to be critical of "old Keynesian terms," although the response did conclude by suggesting "there is much in common between the broad scope of Prof. Galbraith's approach and the Treasury's present strategy."[84] This may have been treasury-speak to assuage nonexperts, however.

Callaghan hedged and allowed a full debate of all these positions in cabinet. But the thrust toward a monetarist approach instead of Galbraith's Keynesianism continued. Callaghan evoked the threat of a left-wing takeover to ensure American support from Gerald Ford in the negotiations with the IMF. According to Dell, the idea that Britain would collapse into the hands of left-wing extremists led by Tony Benn was fanciful:

> At stake in the UK was the survival of the Labour Government, not the survival of democracy, let alone the survival of Western European democracy. The survival of the Labour Government could be secured by the simple device of persuading Callaghan to make up his mind. Eventually, this was achieved with little difficulty and less sorrow.[85]

Forecasts for growth had been too pessimistic. In fact, growth rose by 3 percent and unemployment fell by 1978—"one measure of successful economic management is independence of forecasting errors"—and the forecasts had once again proved incorrect.[86] Crosland was proved right too late.

Healey reflected on the problem of negotiating the muddy economic waters of the 1970s in his memoirs. He thought Keynesian and monetarist strategies were both flawed. According to Healey, the lack of reliable economic information was the most important reason why economics and economic theory had limited utility in the successful operation of economic policy, as he pointed out in his November economic statement of 1974:

Like long-term weather forecasts [economic forecasts] are better than nothing. . . . But their origin lies in the extrapolation from a partially know past, through an unknown present, to an unknowable future according to theories about the causal relationships between certain economic variables which are hotly disputed by academic economists, and may in fact change from country to country or from decade to decade.

Healey reflected, as the memoirs continued:

The most fashionable reaction to these uncertainties, which had made it so difficult to follow Keynesian prescriptions in managing demand, was to drop Keynes in favour of Milton Friedman, and rely simply on controlling the money supply. However, no one has yet found an adequate definition of money, no one knows how to control it, and no one except Friedman himself is certain exactly how the control of money supply will influence inflation, which is supposed to be its only purpose.

It is arguable, then, how much faith Healey had in a new monetarist strategy. The policies he introduced, such as monetary targets and the curtailment of spending to ensure the reduction of the PSBR, according to Kevin Hickson in his study of the crisis, were more "cosmetic" in order to restore and enhance confidence in the financial markets than representative of a damascene conversion to a new economic philosophy.[87]

Hickson argues that the crisis and the government's response were not monetarist because the government continued to rely on the Keynesian methods of prices and incomes policies and increased expenditure after the crisis had passed in 1977–79. But Hickson suggests that a transformation in economic strategy occurred before the IMF crisis, not after it. The crisis "did not result in a new approach to fiscal and monetary policy because public expenditure cuts, cash limits and monetary targets had already been introduced before December 1976, and the decision to abandon the historic commitment to full employment had already been taken." This amounted to "a shift in the overarching policy paradigm." Healey's letter of intent to the IMF "was therefore of symbolic importance since it was the public acceptance by the Government that it had abandoned the full employment commitment and the postwar consensus."[88] According to Peter Jay, a participant in the events through his role as an adviser to Callaghan, the government was forced to accept the monetarist critique of demand management:

> It is true that there was a flaw in the economic analysis, people on the left and right were beginning to perceive this flaw and problem and were trying to grapple with it. It is not difficult to find, mainly from things that were in the Callaghan leadership and Jimmy Carter leadership, things that were just as, indeed in some ways earlier and more profoundly, addressing those questions than anything that came out of the Neoliberal consensus. Therefore the attempt to tell the story as though it were a kind of story of ideological evolution, revolution or counter-revolution or something, seems to me to do great violence to the actual detail and particularity of history which is much more messy than that.[89]

As Jay points out, a similar process of adjustment to the new economic realities was unfolding in the United States during Jimmy Carter's presidency.

The Left Turns to Monetarism
2: Jimmy Carter and Paul Volcker's Federal Reserve

Jimmy Carter was elected president in 1976 at a moment when the economic certainties of previous years had all been called into question. He had the disadvantage of taking office after Gerald Ford presided over the worst recession since the Great Depression. Ford had applied typical measures to boost demand and reduce inflation, such as tax rebates and a voluntary price freeze, through his Whip Inflation Now campaign. Ford also refused a federal bailout to New York City in 1975 when the banks refused to continue to fund the city's debt, and the city was plunged into financial disaster. David Harvey has argued that the city's cave-in to the chafing conditions of the banks and financial markets, mainly in terms of cutting essential public and municipal services, became the prototype of the neoliberal approach. Harvey argues that the "structural adjustment" policies of the IMF in the 1980s and 1990s in relation to the developing world, for example, had their origins in the troubled resolution of the New York fiscal crisis.[90] "This practice of prioritizing the needs of banks and financial institutions and diminishing the standard of living of the debtor country had already been pioneered in the New York City debt crisis."[91] An alternative to Harvey's Marxist perspective is that the bases of public support for proper redistributive levels of taxation and the effective regulation of finance were steadily and systematically eroded by the successful rhetoric and relentless pro-market policies that were pursued by successive administrations, of whatever political stripe, after the mid-1970s.[92]

President Ford's tactics didn't work, and inflation continued to rise. As in Britain in the mid-seventies, the boundaries between Keynesian and monetarist approaches were sometimes blurred, and there was a definite lack of clarity about which represented the best policy direction. The confusion stemmed in part from the fact that Friedman's monetarism operated within the macroeconomic framework set up by Keynes. The difference was between those who emphasized fiscal policy and those who emphasized monetary policy as the most appropriate solution to the problem of inflation. As W. Carl Biven's study of Carter's economic policy suggests, it was "Carter's misfortune to come into office just as the consensus on macroeconomic policy was becoming badly fragmented." Two different Nobel Prize–winning economists gave President Carter totally opposite advice in 1977, for example.[93] Carter's economic program throughout his presidency reflected this fragmentation. Much maligned by conservatives, he nevertheless introduced and expanded deregulation, attempted to balance the budget after a shaky expansionary start, and appointed Paul Volcker to head the Federal Reserve and launch a profound shift in macroeconomic management.

A signal achievement, then, of the Carter presidency and one of the first supply-side reforms to be attempted was deregulation. This was unusual coming from a Democratic Party president. Carter sent Congress two deregulation bills, on trucking and the airlines. Airline deregulation was passed in October 1978. In 1980, three major deregulation bills passed through Congress: trucking; the Staggers Rail Act, which liberalized railroad freight; and the Depository Institutions Deregulation and Monetary Control Act, which gave more command over lending to saving and loans associations and mutual savings banks. This last act also abolished interest rate ceilings for banks. Carter's efforts at the liberalization of industry and finance must be considered significant. They began a movement toward deregulation in the United

States that continued until the financial crisis in 2007–10 among policymakers, especially in terms of the financial markets.

George Shultz argued, in an interview with the author, that Carter introduced the agenda of "economic deregulation" into the airline industry, trucking and some parts of the financial services sector.[94] He was strongly and directly influenced in this program by the Chicago neoliberal economist George Stigler (whose ideas are discussed in chapter 3). The administration's deregulation efforts were bipartisan, and the atmosphere of the time in Washington, D.C., fostered a significant appetite for reform across the political divide. Liberal Democratic senator Ted Kennedy, for example, was instrumental in pushing the agenda through Congress, and President Carter himself helped raise public awareness on deregulation through his personal leadership on the issue. The successful passage of these bills in the late 1970s was another example of the successful breakthrough into the political mainstream of a neoliberal policy insight. In this case it stemmed from Stigler and the public choice theorists James Buchanan and Gordon Tullock.

But inflation remained the central economic policy concern during the Carter presidency. It pushed close to 10 percent in 1977–78, and Carter tried several approaches to bringing it down. At first, the basic methods open to Carter were voluntary wage and price controls and using the soft power of the executive office in a series of exhortations to industry and consumers to keep prices down. The Federal Reserve, first under Arthur Burns, whose term was not renewed in 1978, and subsequently under G. William Miller, who became Carter's first appointment as its chairman, pursued a traditional Keynesian monetary expansion during 1977 and 1978. Carter and his economic advisers—Chairman of the Council of Economic Advisers Charles Schultze; Treasury Secretary Michael Blumenthal; and inflation czar Alfred Kahn—were increasingly concerned about inflation throughout 1978. Interest rates were high, and the money supply was growing fast. They tried to influence the Fed to tighten its monetary policy. At the end of 1978, formal guidelines on wages and prices were introduced. Soon after, the second oil shock struck to further fuel inflation and dampen domestic demand in the United States, which had to ramp up its production of goods and services to afford enough oil from the Gulf states.[95] At the same time, the American economy was experiencing a secular decline in productivity—a problem that burdened the administrations of Nixon and Ford and continued until the end of the 1990s. This fall in productivity was another major reason for the failure of Carter's policies.

Perhaps the single most important economic policy decision made by Carter was his appointment of Paul Volcker in August 1979 to replace Miller as chairman of the Federal Reserve, who moved to become treasury secretary. The appointment was precipitated by Michael Blumenthal's resignation as treasury secretary in July 1979. Volcker was a Democratic monetary economist with a background in finance and economic policy who had served in the Kennedy and Nixon administrations on monetary affairs before becoming chairman of the New York Federal Reserve in 1975. Thatcher's former British Chancellor and Foreign Secretary Geoffrey Howe described Volcker well:

> Towering over them both [Reagan's advisers, Don Regan and Beryl Sprinkel], intellectually as well as physically, was the immensely competent, cigar-smoking, lamppost-like figure of Paul Volcker, who as head of the Federal Reserve (a Carter appointment) was America's sheet-anchor of economic sanity throughout the decade.[96]

Carter was keen to have someone who would be independent and who would take the problem of inflation seriously. In Volcker, he got both in spades.

The Federal Reserve plays the central role in monetary policy in the United States. Biven explains the relationship between the quantity of money and interest rates:

> If interest rates are high, one would ordinarily conclude that the Fed is restraining growth in the quantity of money. The rate that the Fed manages on a day-to-day basis is the federal funds rate, the rate banks charge one another for overnight loans. The Fed does not set this rate administratively, but it can determine the rate through its role as the supplier of bank reserves. It controls reserves by buying and selling federal securities in the open market. If it sells, money to pay for the purchase is drawn from banks and their cash reserves are lowered. If reserves are reduced because of Fed sales, banks are forced into the federal funds market to augment reserves. The increased demand, interacting with a Fed-controlled supply, forces the Fed rate to rise.[97]

On October 6, 1979, Volcker announced a crucial change in the way the Fed operated monetary policy. He set a target for monetary growth. Biven describes the impact of Volcker's announcement:

> The Federal Reserve could target either interest rates or the quantity of money—in the lingo of the trade, the federal funds rate or the "monetary aggregates." The Fed can slow down the creation of new money, which is generated through bank loans to the public, by raising interest rates. Or it can more directly limit loans and new money creation by controlling bank reserves. The Fed has traditionally preferred to target interest rates, and for a specific reason. If the Fed uses interest rates as the policy variable, they tend to be more stable. Erratic behaviour of rates can be a critical problem for banks and other financial institutions, a problem that the Fed would like to minimize. Banks live in a world of interest rates; they lend money at one rate and attract funds into deposits at another. Fluctuating rates make it more difficult to maintain a profitable spread between the two. By exercising control through interest rates, the Fed can dampen instability in financial markets. There is a downside to this approach. "With the best staff in the world," Volcker has written, "and in all the computing power we could give them, there could never be any certainty about just the right level of the federal funds rate to keep the money supply on the right path and to regulate economic activity."[98]

Volcker chose monetary aggregates as the best measure to control the money supply and ensure that people would understand that he was resolute in his focus on inflation. The choice of monetary aggregates had a political side benefit, too. As Carter's chairman of the Council of Economic Advisers, Charles Schultze, put it,

> the genius of what Volcker did, during the period when you had to get the public used to this, was to adopt a system which came to the same thing, but in which he said we are not raising interest rates, we are just setting a non-inflationary path for the money supply, and the markets are raising interest rates. It enabled the Fed to do politically, during that transition period, what it couldn't have done in a more direct way.[99]

Carter strongly supported Volcker's approach. He refused the counsel of his advisers in the run-up to the election of 1980 to cut taxes. He refused any pre-election bonanzas out of his belief in balanced budgets. Volcker's stewardship, though detrimental to Carter's electoral prospects, "broke the back of the Great Inflation."[100] By September 1983, inflation was back down at just above 3 percent, from a high point of almost 15 percent in March 1980.

Any assessment of whether Carter and Callaghan pursued a monetarist strategy runs into the problem of a meaningful definition of what monetarism is. Is a concern with public expenditure and monetary policy as a means to tame inflation enough to warrant the term monetarist? Milton Friedman thought not. His judgment on Carter's and Callaghan's policies was damning in his appearance on *The Money Programme* on British television during the spring of 1978:

> In discussing whether the tide is turning [in favour of free markets and monetarism], it is necessary not only to distinguish this fundamental tide of collectivism [in Carter and Callaghan's policies] from the more superficial tide of demand management, but also to distinguish between what political leaders say, what the Government does and what is happening to the underlying tide of public and intellectual opinion.[101]

What are the manifestations of change?

> With respect to the pronouncements of leaders, there is no doubt that there has been a major change. I need not recall to this audience the remarkable statement by your Prime Minister at a Labour Conference in 1976 when he rejected out of hand the demand management policies that had been followed in Britain by Labour and Conservative governments alike in the postwar period. But his statement is not the only one. In January of this year, our President, President Carter, in his State of the Union message, took care to insert a paragraph about the limits of government. He said, and I quote "we really need to realise that there is a limit to the role and function of government. Government cannot solve our problems, it cannot set our goals, it cannot define our vision." A statement, needless to say, with which I think we all agree, and with

which almost the whole of the rest of the State of the Union message proceeded to disagree.[102]

The rhetoric was not backed by action, in Friedman's view. It was not enough to profess a conversion to a new economic strategy when the tenor of a government's policies pointed in a different direction. He noted that in Britain, "The remarkable statement of Prime Minister Callaghan rejecting fine-tuning has not prevented Chancellor Healey from engaging in fine tuning. It has not prevented him from announcing in his Budget that minor changes in tax revenue are going to enable him to achieve a change in the pattern of growth within Great Britain. So the talk is fine, but the performance leaves a great deal to be desired." It should be remembered that Friedman was speaking before Volcker's appointment and the change in the Federal Reserve's operation of monetary policy. But Friedman's criticisms can be framed differently. The approach of Carter and Callaghan is an example of governments of the left accepting the logic of the technical insights of Friedman and Stigler in terms of macroeconomic strategy or deregulation without also importing their neoliberal philosophies.

Friedman's verdict downplays the significance of the major shift that did occur, regardless of whether it met with Friedman's pure theoretical standards. As Healey stated in a speech to the Council on Foreign Relations in Washington, D.C., in 1979:

Almost the only uncontroversial statement about money supply is one on which Keynes and Friedman would agree: "No continued and substantial inflation can occur without monetary growth that substantially exceeds the rate of real growth." We can all say yes to that. And I think most people would agree that if monetary growth exceeds the rate of real growth as much as it did for two years under my predecessor, Lord Barber, galloping inflation is bound to follow. But beyond that all is uncertain. We do not know how monetary growth influences inflation, or with what time-lag. We do not know how to measure the relevant monetary growth or how best to influence it. And some economists still believe that changes in the velocity of circulation may make monetary growth an unreliable indicator in any case.[103]

The Labour government, under duress, had fundamentally changed its economic strategy to encompass financial discipline through tight control of public spending, monetary targets, and the commitment to fight inflation. In the United States, President Carter appointed Volcker, who was later eulogized as the savior of the American economy by President Reagan's admirers. In his State of the Union address that year, Carter proclaimed that government could no longer solve people's problems. The Left's reforms and realizations in the environment of the 1970s were as fundamental as those on the radical neoliberal right: the economic and political crises required new responses from those that had been the staple of governments since the 1940s. This was very different from an acceptance that the parties of the Right and their ideas were the natural alternative. Neoliberal philosophy, which did eventually find a home in the Thatcher and Reagan administrations, aimed instead to produce an ideological transformation that entrenched the market as the first and last port of call for public policy in the last third of the twentieth century.

Thatcherite Economic Strategy

The Labour government struggled toward its defeat after the "Winter of Discontent" of 1978–79. Callaghan had been expected to call an election in September 1978, when most commentators felt he would have won. Labour had been ahead in the polls at that stage, but its lead turned into a large deficit by the winter as Callaghan chose to go on and the country descended into a frenzy of strikes and labor unrest that came to characterize the Winter of Discontent. Healey tried to impose a 5 percent limit on public sector wage increases as an example to the private sector in the battle against inflation. This prompted a series of industrial actions across the country, which notoriously included even the gravediggers in Liverpool and refuse collectors in Westminster. By the new year, Labour was behind in the polls, and Callaghan's prospects had been transformed to that of an imminent loser. The government had lost its outright majority in 1976, which left it dependent on a series of pacts with minor parties such as the Liberals, nationalists, and the Ulster Unionists to stay in office. When the Scottish Nationalist Party withdrew its support after the defeat of devolution legislation in Parliament, Callaghan lost a vote of confidence in Parliament and was forced to call an election. The

Conservative Party, led by Margaret Thatcher, defeated the government and took office with a healthy majority of forty-three on May 4, 1979.

Thatcher's Conservatives had worked hard in opposition to develop an alternative program for government. Geoffrey Howe, Keith Joseph, James Prior, David Howell, John Hoskyns, Norman Strauss, and Alfred Sherman were the prime movers behind two major policy documents on economic policy in the late 1970s, both of which formed the basis for their policies immediately after 1979. *The Right Approach to the Economy* was the "Outline Economic Strategy of the Next Conservative Government" (1977).[104] It opened with a scathing analysis of the Labour Party's historical experience with economic policy:

> a flashback to 1950–51 is a salutary exercise; for it shows that Labour Governments always create the same kind of problems and frustrations—and that Socialists never really learn from their failures in the past. They may be pushed by events—or the IMF—into temporary conformity with the policies needed in a crisis. But their ideology remains unaltered—and next time in office they are at it again.[105]

The authors asserted their philosophy based on the individual and the free market and the report targeted inflation as the most pressing issue facing the country. It argued that monetarism, public sector pay restraint, and tight finance were the necessary prescription. Greater independence was also proposed for the Bank of England—something that Thatcher in office would grow leery of, owing to her commitment to the needs of lower-middle-class and middle-class mortgage-holders. A core aim was to keep control of the money supply:

> The country has now learned that government oils the wheels of this cycle [of monetary expansion followed by inflation and unemployment] if it prints money at an excessive rate and if it spends too much. If the united approach on keeping a tight rein on money supply is maintained, and if in the field of public spending we can properly distinguish what would be pleasing (and what could be postponed) from what is really necessary, then we shall have taken a fundamental step to get us out of our economic difficulties.[106]

The report went on to advocate a number of supply-side measures that included an end to Labour's "social contract," to be replaced by "improved" pay bargaining, tax cuts for both corporations and individuals, and a general commitment to "new forms of free enterprise."[107]

The second major policy document aimed to provide an economic strategy for the Conservative government that would ensure it was not pushed off course by the inevitable thunderstorms of power. The project was led by John Hoskyns, a former businessman whose frustrations had driven him to get involved in politics. Alfred Sherman, the director of the CPS, and Norman Strauss were also involved. Like many, Hoskyns admired "Sunny Jim" Callaghan and felt he might become a partner. He flirted with working for the Labour Party but soon came to the conclusion that the party leadership would not take the necessary reforms seriously.[108] Hoskyns would ultimately be appointed by Thatcher to head her Policy Unit at No. 10 Downing Street after the election of 1979. The result of the project was a strategy paper, never published, called "Stepping Stones" (1977). It was developed in secret because, according to Hoskyns, it was "assumed that there would be plenty of people in the shadow cabinet and shadow ministers outside it who would not be at all sympathetic to what we were going to say."[109] As Hoskyns puts it, there was a real need for a "sea change" in the Conservative strategy, "to change anything, you needed to change everything" about the way the economy and economic policy worked.[110]

At the time, despite Thatcher's election as leader, the Conservative Party was still dominated by the "wets," as they were disparagingly known—those like Ian Gilmour, Jim Prior, and Francis Pym who mostly accepted and supported the postwar consensus on the welfare state, Keynesianism, and a healthy involvement of the government in social and economic policy. The new strategy unveiled in "Stepping Stones," on the other hand, aimed to bring industrial relations within a framework of the rule of law by ending unlawful strikes, secondary picketing, curbing labor militancy, and, most important, abolishing the closed shop, whereby employment in a particular company or organization was dependent on membership in the relevant union. Such laws had already been passed in the United States after World War II with the Taft-Hartley Act of 1947. In Britain, however, trade union reform, despite the efforts of Barbara Castle at the end of the 1960s, had been unsuccessful. Most of the Tory party wets opposed the reforms.

The development of an alternative economic strategy also included a trawl of the best ideas from the neoliberal think tanks, especially the IEA, the CPS, and the Adam Smith Institute (ASI). The program that the shadow cabinet agreed on was radical in some respects but fell far short of the revolutionary plan with which Thatcher later became associated. The Conservatives had sensibly targeted the two most obvious and unpopular political challenges in Britain at the time. But they had not outlined any radical new ideas. In relation to monetarist economics, they were willing to embark on more stringent and swingeing cuts than their predecessors. They were also comfortable enough with free market economics, more than their Labour predecessors, to abolish exchange controls. But in the central area of macroeconomic strategy they had first restated and then followed neoliberal policy ideas that had already been adopted to some degree by their opponents.

The big exception was the trade union issue. Since the Winter of Discontent, this had become the most serious political problem. Although Barbara Castle and Harold Wilson had tried to reform the unions in 1969, the Labour Party was thoroughly discredited by the collapse of the social contract during the Winter of Discontent. The party had retreated into internecine civil war and a destructive flirtation with the Bennite Left, which resulted in a split and the formation of the Social Democratic Party by the so-called Gang of Four of Roy Jenkins, David Owen, Shirley Williams, and Bill Rodgers, all of whom had served in the Labour cabinet under Callaghan. The Liberal Party, meanwhile, appeared to be in terminal decline since the 1920s. For all these reasons, the Conservative Party emerged as the only party capable of making the case for trade union reform. But it is striking that during this early period, even among many Tories (including Thatcher's first employment secretary, Jim Prior), too radical a departure in policy was unpopular. Thatcher and her advisers waited until the miners' strike of 1984–85 before they fought the unions. Before confronting the emblematic miners, whose strikes had brought down Edward Heath's government in 1974, the Energy Department and the National Coal Board built up stocks of coal in readiness for a long and bitter struggle, which they eventually won.

What emerges clearly from interviews with former Thatcherite ministers was the unplanned nature of the most radical reforms of the 1980s. According to Norman Lamont,

I think a few people should be given praise, like Ian Gow, like Nick Ridley, they really argued for this [the supply-side revolution]. But my impression is that, initially, Mrs Thatcher, she liked it in her heart of hearts, but there was no indication she was going to do it [implement radical reform]. I mean the Conservative Party was never committed to doing it. But it did it. . . . You know, if one's being honest, all this happened gradually. All credit to Mrs Thatcher but it is quite, sort of, self-deceiving if people like myself pretend that we saw how this would all happen. We didn't. You know we followed, participated and supported. The one thing I was very enthusiastic about was always having a tight control of the money supply. That was one thing I had got to square one on which is more than most.[111]

Leon Brittan, brother of Samuel and a cabinet minister during the 1980s, also emphasized the gradual nature of the development of Thatcher's economic program.[112] Privatization, a key part of the supply-side program of the government later on, was also absent from the 1979 manifesto. As Lamont continues, the "privatisation idea wasn't there in the beginning and it just grew, initially it was the non-trading, recently nationalised part of the sector that was denationalised and the idea of going beyond the trading part of the sector to the utilities was, you know, quite startling."[113] The Thatcher government's strategy grew incrementally during her first administration. But it began from the base of the Labour Party's tempered introduction of monetarism. Lamont emphasized that "chance played a bigger part in it than people sometimes think."[114] The Falklands War, coming at a time of rising unemployment and recession, and the weaknesses of an internally riven Labour Party after 1979 are clear examples of the sort of fortune Lamont refers to.

The first major battle for the Conservative government was the attempted application of a strict monetarist approach to the public finances. The government, under Geoffrey Howe's leadership as chancellor, sought to deepen the Labour Party's turn to a tight financial policy. Nigel Lawson, the financial secretary to the treasury, who later replaced Howe as chancellor after the 1983 election, authored the Medium Term Financial Strategy, a policy that was meant to introduce rules and targets into monetary policy in a similar fashion to Volcker's reforms of the Federal Reserve's monetary policy in the United States. The purpose was to combat inflation through strict control of the money supply and was directly influenced by Friedman's monetary economics. But Lawson did not agree with Friedman about the merits of floating currencies.[115] Lawson and the Conservative government also thought it important to target the PSBR:

> Obviously, I was aware of what Friedman was writing and arguing and with the greater part of it I was wholly in agreement—his general approach to free market issues. But there were two things that I didn't agree with. One was his belief in free floating exchange rates and the other was his belief that budget deficits didn't matter, you didn't need to bother, that it didn't matter how big the budget deficit was, forget about that. I thought as far as the first was concerned, that, ideally, free floating is the best system. But starting from where we were, we needed, for a time, some external financial discipline because we have had these problems, this complete breakdown of financial discipline and that it would serve the purpose for a time. But, as I say, you know, ultimately I was philosophically and practically in favour of floating rates, I just didn't think that you could not take advantage of an external discipline to try and correct serious problems in the British economy. I also thought, for the same reasons, that you needed the discipline of bearing down on the budget deficit. Again in an ideal world, it may be, that you could take a much more relaxed view although I don't think anybody really, or very few people, thought you could be as relaxed as Friedman was about it. . . . Quite apart from the inflationary problem, it is clearly the case that, in practice, if you say that the budget deficit doesn't matter, you will get bigger and bigger increases in public spending which is undesirable. You need to have a budgetary discipline in order to bear down on public spending, in my opinion. It is a practical matter, these are practical politics, not economic theory. This is how things work in practice.[116]

Lawson here presents his view of the need for an anchor to keep the economy from floating off into loose money and unsustainable inflationary expansions.[117]

Friedman disagreed with the British emphasis on the PSBR. He presented a memo to the UK Treasury and Civil Service Committee in 1980 in which

he favored monetary targets but was skeptical of the role of targets for the
PSBR.[118] Friedman did come down in favor of the government's general approach, though:

> Higher government spending provokes taxpayer resistance. Taxpayer
> resistance encourages government to finance spending by monetary
> creation, thereby increasing monetary growth and hence inflation,
> which, as a by-product very welcome to legislators, raises effective tax
> rates without legislation. Government spending plus government in-
> tervention reduce output growth, thereby further raising inflation for
> any given rate of monetary growth. Slower growth also increases the
> burden on the community of any given level of government spending,
> exacerbating the resistance to explicit taxation.[119]

Both inflation and slow growth were worsened by the energy crisis of the
1970s, according to Friedman:

> Restraint in the rate of monetary growth is both a necessary and a suffi-
> cient condition for controlling inflation. Controlling inflation, in turn is
> a necessary but not sufficient condition for improving Britain's produc-
> tivity, which is the fundamental requirement for a healthy economy.
> That requires measures on a broader scale to restore and improve in-
> centives, promote productive investment, and give a greater scope for
> private enterprise and initiative.[120]

Friedman thought that inflation and slow growth were related in several ways,
mainly through "too big and intrusive a government."[121] He argued, as usual,
for a combination of monetarism and supply-side reform. An important act
that Friedman fully supported was the government's abolition of exchange
controls and the deregulation of credit markets, which came in a surprise decision in 1980.[122] According to Howe, "We sent out a message to the world
[through this measure] about our commitment to liberal economics as the
means of reviving Britain."[123]

Before long, the country was mired in a deep recession. The key early battle for the Conservative government had been driving through a tough slew
of measures to bring the deficit under control and create the conditions for

economic recovery in the famous budget of 1981. Taxes were increased and spending cut severely in one of the most austere retrenchments of the twentieth century. According to historian Richard Cockett, it "was undoubtedly a radical Budget, following through the suggestions of Hoskyns, Sherman and Walters, and shifting the burden of the Government's anti-inflationary policy from the monetary to the fiscal side."[124] This primary influence of Hoskyns, Sherman, and Walters is disputed by Howe, who has always claimed that the important content of the budget came from the treasury. Either way (or in combination), the budget was controversial among monetarists, who argued between themselves about whether the policy of tight finance and spending cuts had been too harsh and whether its fiscal focus had been properly monetarist.[125] Mont Pelerin Society member and British economist Alan Walters was brought over from his academic job in the United States at Johns Hopkins University by Thatcher to be her economic adviser in 1980. He brought with him a distinctly Friedmanite approach to economic and monetary policy. Walters believed that on entering office, the government had pursued too tight a monetary squeeze, which had made the resultant recession worse.[126] His arguments echoed Friedman's about the Great Depression of the 1930s in the United States. The government combined these harsh cuts with a plan to restore the competitiveness of British industry through a reorientation of the tax system to provide greater incentives for entrepreneurship.

The Conservative economic strategy rested on a form of monetarism. But it also came to include many other measures that were inspired by neoliberal theories. Lawson outlined what the new approach looked like in his Mais address, delivered in 1984, by which time he had taken over from Howe as chancellor:

> The conventional postwar wisdom was that unemployment was a consequence of inadequate economic growth, and economic growth was to be secured by *macro*-economic policy—the fiscal stimulus of an enlarged Budget deficit, with monetary policy (to the extent that it could be said to exist at all) on the whole passively following fiscal policy.
>
> Inflation, by contrast, was increasingly seen as a matter to be dealt with by *micro*-economic policy—the panoply of controls and subsidies associated with the era of incomes policy. The conclusion on which the present Government's economic policy is based is that there is indeed

a proper distinction between the objectives of macro-economic and
micro-economic policy, and a need to be concerned with both of them.
But the proper role of each is precisely the opposite of that assigned to
it by the conventional postwar wisdom. It is the conquest of inflation,
and not the pursuit of growth and employment, which is or should be
the objective of macro-economic policy. And it is the creation of conditions conducive to growth and employment, and not the suppression
of price rises, which is or should be the objective of micro-economic
policy.

Needless to say, this fundamentally important role reversal implies a
major change in the nature of the macro and micro policies themselves.
Instead of monetary policy simply accommodating increased budget
deficits (except when periodic sterling crises brought the process to
a temporary halt), fiscal policy has to be in harmony with declining
monetary growth. And instead of micro-economic policy consisting
of increasingly numerous forms of intervention and interference with
market forces, its role is now seen as removing controls and allowing
markets to work better.[127]

Lawson laid out how economic strategy had changed by the mid-1980s, but
it is important to remember the continuities between the Labour and Conservative approaches in terms of macroeconomic policy. Lawson's predecessor, Geoffrey Howe, gives an impressively level-headed judgment about the
development of monetarist policy in Britain in the 1970s and 1980s, which
he argued "was already an established part of Britain's economic policy and
of those of several other countries at the moment when Margaret Thatcher
and I moved into Downing Street." For Howe, this could not "be stated too
often, particularly to those critics in my party [the wets] who love to portray
our arrival in office as the start of an era of uncoupled dogma and unprecedented lunacy."[128] The major differences, and the real departure in economic
terms, between the Callaghan government and the Conservatives lay in
their radicalization of microeconomic policy through various market-based
supply-side reforms and their importation of market mechanisms into public service provision, something the Labour Party continued and deepened
after 1997.

Reaganomics

The Reagan presidential campaign was conducted in an atmosphere of economic and foreign policy crisis. As inflation raged and the Iran hostage affair undermined President Carter's credibility, Reagan promised a similar mixture of monetarist macroeconomic policy and supply-side reform as that proposed by Thatcher. There were two major differences between Reagan's Republican policies and those of the British Conservatives, however. The first was that the trade unions were not as important across the economy as a whole in the United States as they were in Britain. Their more limited role was rather felt in certain sectors and industries, a consequence of the Taft-Hartley Act of 1947, which had outlawed what the act termed "unfair labor practices."[129] The reduced power of the unions in the United States was also a reflection of the distinctive character of the American welfare state, which had been shaped by the decision by the major unions and the AFL-CIO after the war to pursue a strategy of benefits tied to jobs—the United States' distinctive private welfare state—instead of a universalist model like Britain's.[130] By contrast, in Britain the unions were seen as virtual governmental partners during the 1970s, most obviously in Wilson's social contract. The second major difference between the Reagan and Thatcher administrations' approach was that more of the U.S. economy rested in private hands, which meant that the development of a denationalization or privatization strategy, from the conservative perspective, was less pressing or necessary than it was in Britain. Nevertheless, even in these areas, the administration followed neoliberal principles influenced particularly by the ideas of Hayek, Friedman, Stigler, and Buchanan.

Ronald Reagan entered office in January 1981 planning to achieve four things in economic policy: increased deregulation and market liberalization, tighter control of the money supply, tax cuts, and cuts in public spending. Many of the major tenets of Reagan's program were outlined in the Republican Study Committee's critique of the Humphrey-Hawkins Act of 1978, an act that reaffirmed the U.S. government's policy commitment to Keynesian demand management. The report presented a summary of Hayek's philosophy of individualism and the merits of spontaneous markets compared to planning, and Friedman's monetarist analysis of stagflation.[131] Both men also had regular and frequent contact with the committee and its members.[132] Ed Feulner, who became president of the Heritage Foundation, was the committee's executive director in the mid-1970s.

The Humphrey-Hawkins Act, though it renewed the commitment to full employment, also introduced a requirement for the Federal Reserve to publish an annual report on inflation and monetary policy. The committee's report suggested some noninflationary alternative solutions:

1. Substantial and *permanent* across-the-board tax reductions for all individuals and businesses.
2. A reduction in government bureaucracy and regulation at all levels.
3. Adoption of a fiscal and monetary policy designed to stabilize the value of money. This is the only safeguard of *long-term* employment.
4. Removal of other specific obstacles to capital accumulation and investment, particularly the taxation on capital incentives. The capital gains tax should be cut back to 25 percent maximum, or completely eliminated. Capital losses should be fully deductible against gains.[133]

The report argued that the "four measures, alone, will produce great strides toward attracting capital, increasing productivity, securing long-term jobs, and most importantly, *trending all real income levels and living standards upward.*" All the major priorities of the incoming administration were present. The report argued for the notion that a rising tide lifts all boats, which became a crucial component of Reagan's economic philosophy. The force of this idea created space for an acceptance of inequality as an essential part of economic growth and social progress.

Similar strategies were outlined in two other major policy manifestos. The first was a Hoover Institution publication titled *The United States in the 1980s* (1980).[134] This tome included pieces on the economy by Milton and Rose Friedman (Milton's wife and the sister of fellow Chicago economist Aaron Director) and Alan Greenspan, as well as an essay on international aid by British economist and Mont Pelerin Society member Peter Bauer. Many of the authors, such as Friedman, Martin Anderson, and Greenspan, went on to work for the administration. According to Anneliese Anderson, the book represented a blueprint for Reagan's domestic policy.[135] The second book was the Heritage Foundation's *Mandate for Leadership: Policy Management*

in a Conservative Administration (1980, discussed in chapter 4).[136] This was
a thousand-page doorstopper written in haste, in time for Reagan's inaugu-
ration. The publication was meant as a policy manual and included articles
by Ed Feulner and twenty-seven other Heritage Foundation policy experts.
Many of its proposals were subsequently adopted by the Reagan administration, including the call for across-the-board tax cuts, something that had also
been promoted by the Republican Study Committee.

With monetary policy in the hands of Paul Volcker's Federal Reserve, the
administration concentrated mainly on supply-side reforms. Reagan's top economic advisers included the chairman of his Council of Economic Advisers,
Martin Feldstein; Treasury Secretary Don Regan; the chief economic adviser
to the Reagan presidential campaign, Jude Wanniski; Milton Friedman, who
sat on the president's Economic Policy Advisory Board; and Bill Niskanen,
another member of the Council of Economic Advisers, who later became
the chairman of the Cato Institute. Beryl Sprinkel, who replaced Feldstein
in 1983, and Alan Greenspan, who replaced Volcker as head of the Federal
Reserve in 1987, were also important influences on economic issues.[137]

As soon as he entered the White House, in January 1981, Reagan lifted
the remaining economic controls on oil and petrol that had been in place
since Nixon's administration and reduced taxes on their profits to address the
energy crisis. But two major events in Reagan's first year helped define the
president's economic program. The first was the air traffic controllers' strike
of the summer of 1981 during which the administration successfully busted
the union and fired all the striking workers. The second was the passage of a
series of large-scale tax cuts through Congress, a legislative progress that also
began in 1981. The top rate of taxation was reduced successively from 70 percent to 50 percent and later, in 1986, to 28 percent.

Reagan's tax cuts were based on a belief in the philosophy of limited government espoused especially by Friedman and the other neoliberals. They
were also guided by the ideas of economist Arthur Laffer, whose famous
curve suggested that tax take would rise as levels dropped because more people would pay taxes and fewer would attempt tax avoidance. The result was
supposed to lead to increased investment by rich people and thus, happily,
to more opportunity, a process also known as trickle-down or, in the words
of George H. W. Bush, as "voodoo economics." This idea was another example of a justification, presented in supposedly undeniably logical terms, for a

redistribution of wealth to the middle-class and upper-tier earners as a way of promoting economic growth for all. But the tax cuts were also born of a practical political commitment to the goals of the tax limitation movement of the 1970s. They became the centerpiece of what Martin Anderson has called Reagan's supply-side "revolution."[138] Anneliese Anderson, Martin's wife, who also worked in the Reagan White House, has suggested in an interview with the author that the focus on the supply side marked a "recognition that incentives mattered."[139]

In August, as the air traffic controllers' strike blazed, Reagan signed into law what were then the largest tax cuts in American history. It was a bipartisan bill supported by the congressional Democratic Party majority at the time. The bill contributed to the spiraling of the federal deficit, which expanded from $700 billion in 1981 to over $3 trillion by the time Reagan left office.[140] According to Anneliese Anderson, the size of the budget deficit by 1989 was the "greatest regret" of his presidency.[141] But many of his advisers and supporters did not worry about the size of the deficit, especially when it was a result of government tax cuts. Jack Kemp and Jude Wanniski were the proponents of this view.[142] Friedman always believed tax cuts were a good thing as they would increase individual freedom and reduce the size of government. For many other conservatives, the budget deficit had the desirable side effect of acting as a constraint on state spending on welfare and social policy.

The second major event at the start of Reagan's presidency was the Professional Air Traffic Controllers Organization (PATCO) strike of the summer of 1981. After many years of deteriorating working conditions and pay, PATCO announced a strike on August 3. In the preceding years, concern had mounted about the impact of the work on the controllers' health, so much so that President Nixon had established a panel in 1971 to investigate working conditions in the sector.[143] In one of the first domestic crises—the "first big test," according to Ed Feulner—of his presidency, Reagan and his advisers took an uncompromisingly harsh line.[144] Reagan immediately announced that the controllers would have to return to work within forty-eight hours or be summarily fired because the "strike was a peril to national safety."[145] The president invoked the Taft-Hartley Act to dismiss 11,345 workers on August 6. His logic was that the air traffic controllers had sworn an oath not to strike as part of their terms of employment, which they had subsequently reneged on. To the president, the issue was simply one of bad faith on the part of the controllers and risk to public safety.

PATCO was defeated by the administration's stance. George Shultz remembers that Reagan thought of the strike as a situation where his enforcement of constitutional principles had a big impact on foreign policy because it showed that he was serious about his radical reform agenda.[146] Such a belief belied the supposed straightforward view the president was alleged to have taken on the actions of the controllers. For some members of his staff and administration at least, there were larger political and ideological issues at stake in the outcome of the strike. The decision was a deliberate statement of intent, as well as a response to a set of unpredictable circumstances. As Anneliese Anderson has pointed out, Edwin Meese, joint head of the Reagan White House with James Baker, knew he had to act tough because the postal workers were next in line to strike.[147]

The PATCO strike also had international ramifications. The strong response by the administration to the strike provided encouragement to the Thatcher government's determination to weaken the strength of the trade union movement in Britain. According to Andrew Duguid, then inside the No. 10 Downing Street Policy Unit, Thatcher and her advisers "drew comfort" from Reagan's success, and the strike "emboldened thinking" about the upcoming confrontation with the miners.[148] The approach of the Conservative Party to the unions under Edward Heath, according to Douglas Hurd, had been that of trying to introduce a "regulatory process" to ensure that the unions became a respected part of the British economy. The Thatcher government instead sought a "liberating process."[149] Or, to put it more brutally, she wanted to eradicate the unions' special position of power in the British polity during the yearlong miners' strike of 1984–85. Norman Lamont describes the development of the government's tactics toward the miners:

[John Hoskyns] recounts a lunch I had with him, of which I have no recollection, but he says that I was very impatient that we weren't making any progress on trade union reform—that was something I and Michael [Howard, later Thatcher's Employment Secretary] were really hot enthusiasts for. According to that Hoskyns lunch, I slightly berated him for not getting on with it, for not doing anything, for drifting.

DSJ: Were you aware of Reagan and the air traffic controllers?

NL: Oh I remember that, yes.

DSJ: Was that an influence?

NL: I mean yes, that was a really tough stance. I mean I was very disillusioned when, you know, she was right and I was wrong, Mrs Thatcher gave in to the first Scargill-threatened strike [Arthur Scargill was the leader of the National Union of Mineworkers]. I just couldn't believe this and I think I said that to her. I was really annoyed about it. But, you know she had decided that we needed to buy coal stocks, she had really thought it through and she went on and subsequently, I mean it was an amazingly long-term strategy.[150]

Initially, Thatcher's attempts to reform the unions were hampered by the continuing strength of the Conservative Party wets, and especially Employment Secretary Jim Prior, who was firmly in the Heath mold. But when the confrontation came, with true believer Norman Tebbit at the helm, the miners were defeated. Her plans to destroy their power were sealed by the untroubled passage through Parliament of a sequence of laws throughout the 1980s.

Reagan and Thatcher both built on the new economic strategies that were in place by the late 1970s with a radical new economic philosophy governed by the neoliberal belief in the supremacy of the free market. Many of their most important advisers, government colleagues, and supporters were drawn from the transatlantic neoliberal network. The policy experiment with this philosophy had decidedly mixed short-term results even on neoliberal terms—high deficits, frequent recessions, and increased government spending on the welfare state and public services that neoliberal policymakers had professed a determination to reduce. The long-term effects were arguably even more problematic: a legacy of financial deregulation and the wholly inappropriate importation of free markets into the provision of public services such as health care provision, education, and housing. These policy areas were classic examples of market failure. It was rarely profitable to provide high-quality services for poorer people, which was the reason why the state had originally taken on such responsibilities. But the policy practice of the Thatcher and Reagan governments, as much as the discussion and research of neoliberal academics and activists, exhibited a reluctance to address these failures. The crudeness of postwar Chicago neoliberal economic theory left a painful imprint on the social fabric of Britain and the United States after 1980 through the economic policies of the Thatcher and Reagan administrations. In the understated words of Douglas Hurd, neither government had been able to solve the "social question."[151] More to the point, they had displayed very little interest in trying.

Conclusion

An intellectual free market revolution, driven and spread by a transatlantic network of writers and activists, might have been stillborn but for a series of economic crises during the late 1960s and 1970s. Instead, neoliberal ideas helped smash apart the policy consensus of the immediate postwar years and led to a change in economic strategy and policy. Norman Lamont has described the policies and ideas of the Reagan and Thatcher governments as "heroic." Yet, as Peter Jay points out in the epigraph to this chapter, the Labour and Democratic Parties' adoption of a new economic approach before the Conservative and Republican Party election victories renders such an assessment, viewed from any political perspective, inadequate.[152]

When Nigel Lawson outlined the economic strategy of the Conservative government, based as it was on monetary targets, in a speech called "The New Conservatism" in 1980, it perfectly described the move, begun under Labour, from Keynesian to neoliberal economic strategy:

> The economic policy of the new Conservatism has two basic strands. At the macroeconomic level, our approach is what has come to be known as monetarism, in contradistinction to what has come to be known as Keynesianism, although the latter doctrine is a perversion of what Keynes actually preached himself. At the microeconomic level, our emphasis is on the free market, in contradistinction to state intervention and central planning. While these two strands fit easily and harmoniously together, so much so that they are frequently confused, they are in fact distinct. It is quite possible to be a monetarist and a central planner.[153]

This quotation nicely illustrates the point that some neoliberal policy prescriptions for economic management—sound finances and trade union reform, for example—were perfectly compatible with political creeds other than Thatcherism or Reaganomics. In the 1970s, Carter and Callaghan signaled that the Left had also changed its economic approach. According to Lamont, "Denis Healey always denounces monetarism but he himself arguably introduced it."[154] Certainly, the economic insights of the transatlantic neoliberals had become embedded in the political agendas of many of those on the moderate left as well as the New Right by the end of the 1970s.

But, as we have seen, there were important differences between the particular policy insights of Friedman or Stigler and the larger neoliberal political philosophy of radical free market individualism promoted by Friedrich Hayek or the IEA. The technical contributions, and especially the critiques, provided by monetarism, Stigler's economic theory of regulation, or the public choice theory of Buchanan, Tullock, or Gary Becker were separate from the wholesale acceptance of market-based approaches to government and public policy to which many of these thinkers also subscribed. It is therefore possible to accept some of the conclusions of the scholarly work of these neoliberal theorists without embracing their interpretation of what the conclusions mean. Important analyses of the problems of demand management, regulation, and bureaucratic management might have been better separated from some of the policy conclusions of their authors and followers. Thatcher's and Reagan's political success enabled a free market ideology to spread. The wide adoption of this neoliberal theology brought with it a whole new set of problems, especially in terms of the neoliberal linkage of economic and political freedom, and its elevation of the market as the supreme area of human activity, development and growth. The obsession with the market corroded the idea of the public realm and ate into its foundations, something that had important implications for social policy, as we shall see.[155]

Despite the changes in Labour and Democratic Party policy in the 1970s, there is little doubt that the elections of Margaret Thatcher and Ronald Reagan reshaped the political and economic landscape. What might have been a limited adjustment to the way governments managed macroeconomic policy, with some necessary microeconomic reforms thrown in for good measure, became a fundamental move to a new political culture dominated by the free market. This latter idea helped breed a culture that led to financial disaster in 2007–10. The elevation of the market to an almost theological status was a development that should not be ascribed to a master plan on the part of either government or leader. Instead, the space within which a market-based economic strategy could be pursued and expanded came about through the successful and lucky political negotiation of recession and wars, the Falklands War of 1982 between Thatcher's Britain and Argentina's military junta and Reagan's unlawful invasion of Grenada in 1983. Equally, the electoral successes of Reagan and Thatcher would not have been possible without the relative political and philosophical weakness of the liberal and democratic left in the 1980s. Supporters and foes alike assume in retrospect an ideologically consistent agenda that never was. It is a view propagated partly through the memoirs of the participants themselves and also in the simplifications of journalists and commentators.[156] But by 1984, the path was clear for a radicalization of British and American politics as both Reagan and Thatcher were reelected with sizable increased majorities. Neoliberal ideas—free markets, deregulation, low taxes, limited government, flexible labor markets—reigned supreme.

The neoliberal contribution to the political changes of the last third of the twentieth century in Britain and the United States was massive. Neoliberal thinkers and activists helped shape the changed economic approach epitomized by Thatcher's and Reagan's governments. The new economic policy framework that emerged in the 1980s also governed the policies and ambitions of Bill Clinton, Tony Blair, Gordon Brown, and Barack Obama as well. Two essentially instinctive, talented, and pragmatic politicians came to power without a blueprint for free market revolution. Instead, as Jay suggests, their political victories allowed more sophisticated policy technocrats such as Reagan's Chair of Economic Advisers Martin Feldstein, Chancellor Nigel Lawson, Volcker's successor as chairman of the Federal Reserve Alan Greenspan, and Eddie George, the governor of the Bank of England in the 1990s, to embark on an economic experiment with a new form of macroeconomic management targeted on inflation. Arguably, a new consensus around the successful operation of macroeconomic policy through interest rates and some version of monetarist control of the money supply was confirmed by the policies of Clinton and Blair and their finance ministers, Robert Rubin, Larry Summers, and Gordon Brown. The long triumph of the market and the progressive destruction of the public sphere, however, were not the inevitable associated effects. They were chosen by successive policymakers beginning in the 1980s and continued to be remade in the agendas of the Labour Party and Democratic Party politicians, who confirmed their applicability during the 1990s. How this process worked out in an important arena of social policy—affordable housing and urban policy—is the subject of the final chapter.

7

✳

Neoliberalism Applied?

The Transformation of Affordable Housing and Urban Policy in the United States and Britain, 1945–2000

> Public housing (and subsidized housing) can thus, at best, be an instrument of assisting the poor, with the inevitable consequence that it will make those who take advantage of it dependent on authority to a degree that would be politically very serious if they constituted a large part of the population. Like any assistance to an unfortunate minority, such a measure is not irreconcilable with a general system of freedom. But it raises very grave problems that should be squarely faced if it is not to produce dangerous consequences.
>
> —Friedrich Hayek, *The Constitution of Liberty*

There was a slow transformation in affordable housing and urban policy between the 1960s and the 1990s in both the United States and Britain. Housing and urban policy for low- and moderate-income groups was one of the few social policy areas where the administrations of Margaret Thatcher and Ronald Reagan had a positive program to counter what they saw as a culture of dependency created by the welfare state. The problem of how to help disadvantaged people and poor communities was to be addressed through incentives, deregulation, and the creation and stimulation of opportunities in the private market. The state was to be responsible for a smaller core of services and housing stock in the most vulnerable neighborhoods and was to cater to a residual group of the most deprived people in society. But the majority of capable individuals and families would prosper instead as the forces of competition and private enterprise were unleashed in poorer areas.

The initial change in policy direction in the provision of affordable housing and the regeneration of the inner cities was a reflection of a new approach to urban problems among housing and regeneration experts about how best to attack the endemic poverty and nonexistent economic opportunities for vulnerable and disadvantaged groups in the blighted inner city. Later, the different approach to urban problems reflected the ideological thrust of neoliberal free market policies after Margaret Thatcher's and Ronald Reagan's election victories.

In the United States, public housing was never more than a last resort for society's poorest. In 1979, the year Thatcher was elected and one year before Reagan entered the White House, slightly more than 1 percent of households in the United States lived in public housing, with a further 2–3 percent living in federally assisted accommodation.[1] Public housing, despite early debates during the New Deal about its proper role, had never come to be accepted as an important social entitlement.[2] The shortage of affordable housing in the United States was addressed through rent subsidy and the development of a large-scale housing voucher scheme in the 1970s called Section 8 (appended to the U.S. Housing Act of 1937). Then, under the Reagan administration, attempts were made to replace urban renewal and slum clearance strategies with a new policy concept imported directly from Britain, the enterprise zone.

In the United States, support for public housing and housing assistance in the 1960s and 1970s, never very strong, drained away, especially among the middle classes, which, unlike in Britain, had never occupied public housing. After the 1960s, President Nixon's middle-class "silent majority" felt threatened by stagflation, labor militancy, inner-city violence, racial conflict, and the perceived excesses of Great Society liberalism.[3] Meanwhile, the public sector occupied a radically different space in the popular imagination in American politics, economy, and society than in Britain. Different attitudes were reflected not only in the size of the public sector—which was always proportionately tiny in the United States in comparison to Britain—but also in fundamental cultural and philosophical beliefs. The notion of the American Dream provides a clue to these differences. As journalist Jason Deparle put it in his study of the 1996 Clinton welfare reforms, "We live in a country where anyone can make it."[4] This commonly held American belief was underpinned by a belief in the virtues of homeownership and private property.

"Making it" for many Americans involved owning a single-unit, detached house with a garden in a leafy suburb far from the deprivations of the inner city. Alternative ideal conceptions of the lived urban experience such as urban theorist Jane Jacobs's famous idea of a public neighborhood where diverse groups of people lived harmoniously together in the city held little sway in much American media commentary and scholarly research on public housing, urban regeneration, and the city.[5] Instead, the categories through which housing has been understood and envisioned have, in conservative political terms, been dominated by an individualistic (and usually white) ideal of the detached single-family unit in the suburbs. This idealized vision has been at best complicated for African Americans, who have often been systematically excluded from its attainment by both open and covert means, leading to a remaking of the lines of segregation in American cities around suburban divisions.[6]

By contrast, in Britain, "council housing"—the term for local authority–funded public housing—had been meant to provide for the general needs of large swaths of working- and middle-class people at various times in their lives. In Britain, 25 percent of the population lived in public housing in 1979, with an almost further 5 percent living in social or assisted housing—accommodation run by housing associations for low- and moderate-income groups.[7] By 2003, homeownership rates in Britain had increased from 55 percent in 1980 to 68 percent.[8] Owner-occupation had become the overwhelmingly favored housing tenure, as it had always been in the United States. Britain attained homeownership parity with the United States largely by selling off public housing stock at discounted rates. This was done through one of the most enduring of Margaret Thatcher's privatizations, the pathbreaking Right to Buy policy, which was continued by Tony Blair's Labour government after 1997. Over two million families and individuals bought their own homes through the policy. But the best local authority housing stock was sold to tenants, and much of what was left in public ownership was allowed to fall into disrepair through an assault on local authority funding begun under Labour during the IMF crisis of the mid-1970s and deepened by the Conservative governments of the 1980s and 1990s. Thus, although the numbers living in public housing in Britain remained much higher than in the United States after the Conservatives left office, Britain had moved decisively in the direction of the American model.

One reason for this is that despite different approaches to affordable housing and urban policy in each country, there was a similar trend in both the United States and Britain, in terms of housing policy for the disadvantaged, toward more market-based approaches. The shift toward the market began during the 1960s and 1970s in both countries. But after the elections of Thatcher and Reagan, the influence of neoliberal ideas about the superiority of free market solutions began to be felt through, for example, the Right to Buy policy and enterprise zones. These new free market–based policies did not emerge out of nowhere. They were also inspired by a restatement of traditional liberal and conservative notions about the importance of the nuclear family, private property, and home ownership that had been around since John Locke, or even earlier. Neoliberals added an all-important ingredient to this older mix: an argument for greater efficiency.

Neoliberal theorists and policymakers argued that markets were the most *efficient* mechanism to deliver better social outcomes in housing and urban policy. Rather than the state providing ever more public housing or the government providing ever increasing handouts, neoliberal policymakers suggested that strong nuclear families were best led by responsible, self-sufficient individuals and cemented through incentivized local communities. Rent control should be abolished and the private rental sector set free, as George Stigler and Milton Friedman argued in one of the Foundation for Economic Education's first pamphlets, published in 1946. Later, during the 1970s, British Conservative politician Geoffrey Howe and socialist urban planner Peter Hall argued that vulnerable and desolate inner-city neighborhoods could be revived through the creation of opportunities for local initiative that would be generated through a system of tax breaks, deregulation, and the encouragement of private investment. This was the enterprise zone concept that Stuart Butler brought with him across the Atlantic when he moved from the London-based Adam Smith Institute (ASI) to the Heritage Foundation in Washington, D.C., in the late 1970s.

But as with economic strategy, it is important to recognize that the shift toward market-based policies had significant antecedents in the policies of the political parties of the Left, in the Democratic and Labour Parties during the 1960s and 1970s. The concrete failures of public housing in Britain and urban renewal and slum clearance in the United States, for example, prompted liberal and social democratic policymakers to consider alternative policy models. Successive Democratic administrations were instrumental in the development and implementation of the Section 8 housing voucher program in the United States, while in Britain, the Labour Party had begun to experiment with council house sales and Housing Investment Programmes (HIPs), whereby local authorities were given greater "autonomy" over shrinking budgets, prior to Margaret Thatcher's election in 1979. But while this policy experimentation by Labour Party and Democratic Party administrations was governed by a central commitment to public assistance in the provision of affordable housing, it had at its core different values from those of conservative and neoliberal policymakers with respect to the role of the state in urban regeneration and affordable housing.

The Thatcher and Reagan administrations were therefore able to build their radical alternative policy agenda of deregulation, lower taxes, and market liberalization in deprived communities on these foundation stones. The central difference between the early housing and urban policy innovation of the Labour and Democratic Parties and the subsequent ideas of their Conservative and Republican Party successors in Britain and the United States was the radical individualist philosophy inspired by Friedman, Hayek, and a new generation of policy experts influenced by them, operating in think tanks such as the Heritage Foundation or the ASI (and others, described in detail in chapter 4) or within government itself. A reduced role for the state was supposed to be supplemented with new strategies, epitomized by the privatization of public housing through the Right to Buy program, the expansion of housing vouchers to boost the private rental sector's role in the provision of affordable housing, and enterprise zones.

There is, then, a different shape, texture, and structure to affordable housing policy, urban policy, and the impact of neoliberal ideology on both these areas in the United States and Britain. But there are key themes in common in the trajectory of both countries' approach since the 1960s. First, underlying continuities in policy belie any total rupture perceived in the Conservative and Republican election victories of 1979 and 1980. The policy shifts represented by Thatcher and Reagan obscured a larger coalescence across the political spectrum around alternative market-based policy solutions. Second, despite this continuity, there was an ideological bent under Thatcher and Reagan toward radical free market solutions to the seemingly intractable problems of the inner cities. Third, the distinctive policies of the Conservative and Republican governments—vouchers, council and public housing sales, and enterprise zones—illustrated the neoliberal influence on policy in both countries. British policymakers, especially individuals such as Stuart Butler and Geoffrey Howe, influenced the Reagan administration. Subsequently, the policies of the New Democrats, especially the Clinton administration's Hope VI project, which created mixed-tenure housing estates, and also through Community Development Block Grants, influenced the New Labour governments of the late 1990s and 2000s. A consequence of these transatlantic policy transmissions was that Britain moved closer to the American-style provision of affordable housing and urban regeneration programs. Public housing was now targeted at the poorest, and increased home ownership rates had become the central policy goal. A new policy paradigm defined by the free market had emerged to replace that of collective public provision of housing.

Postwar Low-Income Housing and Urban Policy in the United States

In the United States, housing for poor and low-income social groups was provided by a flexible mixture of the public and private sectors during the twentieth century. The mix tended to wax and wane with the political complexion of the country. During the New Deal, Congress passed a series of acts that have guided the direction of affordable housing policy ever since. The Housing Act of 1934 established the Federal Housing Administration (FHA) and the Federal National Mortgage Association (known as Fannie Mae) to help finance mortgages and stimulate the release of credit through the federal assumption of homebuyers' risk. The Housing Act of 1937 created the U.S. Public Housing Authority (USPHA), which aimed to bolster the provision of affordable local government constructions that could be rented to poor citizens. It also provided funds for slum clearance. During the 1930s the provision of public housing assistance and construction was intended by many advocates to be a large-scale state intervention to guarantee basic living standards for the working as well as the indigent poor. In short, it was supposed to be more like council housing had become in Britain, a large-scale program to promote urban development and prevent poverty.[9]

The 1949 Housing Act created a division in the types of federal involvement in housing policy between various forms of tax incentives, favorable loans and mortgage arrangements, and infrastructure development, on the one hand, and the funding of public housing projects on the other. Part of President Harry Truman's domestic policy program known as the Fair Deal after World War II, the act provided for the construction of 800,000 new public housing units. But its main goal was the cheaper financing of mortgage loans to prospective homeowners. According to historian Delores Hayden, the 1949 act carried the stamp of architects such as Le Corbusier, whose conception of the ideal city was "a collection of residential towers in a park." This vision was influential with public housing authorities.[10] However, Hayden continued, "Subsidies were greatest for the FHA/VA [Veterans Administration] homeowner (suburban mortgage supports, tax deductions and highways, rather than direct housing construction and public transportation subsidies) while the public housing that was built was often cheap, nasty, and badly thought-out."[11]

Recent scholarship has shown that the distinctive development of American cities described by Hayden, and defined spatially by racial and class separations, was far from accidental. Cities were shaped by deep structural inequalities between and among blacks, whites, and Hispanics and with the complicity of federal agencies, which colluded with the prejudices of local people in Chicago, Detroit, Oakland, and the urban and suburban South.[12] Blacks have tended to occupy the most deprived inner-city neighborhoods as more affluent whites left in waves for the suburbs.[13] At the same time, the state has subsidized middle- and upper-class earners through the tax system. The federal government has also helped construct the landscape through the federal funding of infrastructure and highways, which has shifted the center of economic gravity from the old industrial North to the South and West.[14] State and county governments, sometimes with the support of federal judges, have facilitated and applied a legal framework that has excluded the poor and minorities through zoning rules about the social and racial makeup of areas and the practice of redlining (simply put, the exclusion of blacks from affordable housing finance, subsidy, and mortgages).[15]

The story of urban and suburban development has consequently been particularly troubled for African Americans. The main target of housing and urban policy during the 1950s and 1960s was often poor African Americans who had migrated from the South in large numbers to the inner cities of the North to look for jobs and opportunities during the "Great Migration" of the interwar period. The story of the African American migration cannot be divorced from the parallel narrative of the white suburban dream, which is the enduring theme of the history of American urban space in the twentieth century. Black efforts to share in this dream and to escape their disadvantage and ghettoization during the postwar years were obstructed at every step. Blacks were the victims of housing discrimination, segregation, lack of private investment, pollution, and political gerrymandering as they were increasingly confined to decaying inner-city neighborhoods, with whites moving out. According to Andrew Wiese, African American exposure to these subtle and unsubtle forms of prejudice imposed "a burden on everyone who lived in black neighborhoods and [limited] the empowering potential of black space."[16] Federal subsidies of the 1940s and 1950s through the FHA pushed segregated suburbanization. Wiese suggests that this was "rooted in a vision of metropolitan space in which white communities were seen as normative and African-American places were seen as aberrant, threatening and negatively valued."[17]

In the United States, the crucial period of suburban development was the middle of the twentieth century, when the federal government intervened to establish the single-family subdivision as the preeminent residential unit. The important public policy choices made between the years 1930 and 1970 firmly entrenched the conditions of endless sprawl in the United States. This sprawl had implications for the political and democratic culture of the nation. Beginning with Herbert Hoover's stuttering response to the Great Depression in the early 1930s and continuing during the New Deal, the federal government put in place an incentive structure that encouraged suburban development at the expense of other forms of public housing. The Home Owners Loan Corporation (HOLC) was set up in 1933 to refinance home mortgages and provide support to residents suffering from the threat of foreclosure. The key element of the HOLC was an appraisal system that ranked properties according to risk. The FHA took its lead from the HOLC in classifying properties, the origin of the now notorious practices of zoning and redlining. As Hayden shows, "their highest classifications were reserved for all-white, all-Protestant neighborhoods, and they refused loans in racially mixed neighborhoods."[18] Also built into the provisions of the FHA were recommendations for covenants, stipulations about the types of residences that would be allowed in a particular neighborhood, and loans for repairs that were small and inconsequential, which made purchase an easier option. The net effect was to encourage the growth of single-family households and a bias toward white suburbs.

Compounding this bias toward suburbanization was the New Deal approach to slum clearance, urban renewal, and public housing. The Wagner-Steagall Act of 1937 included a requirement that public housing only replace slums in a ratio of one to one, despite a massive shortage of affordable housing. Urban renewal programs such as the Greenbelt towns, authorized and overseen by agricultural economist and Roosevelt adviser Rexford Tugwell, were attempted, but these experiments were fairly small in scale. Ultimately, the 1930s witnessed the victory of the subdividers who promoted the detached home ideal over those who, like Tugwell, championed high-density public housing for poorer and disadvantaged groups. Opposition to the alternative of widespread, even universal, public housing provision was at base ideological and the outcome of the debates over the future of the city during the New Deal. As Hayden argues, the result was that a "very powerful coalition had formed [against public housing and in favour of suburban development], one with close ties to the Republican Party, but also a lobby the Democrats would not be able to ignore."[19]

Margaret Pugh O'Mara's insightful account of the relationship between the politics of the Cold War, the scientific establishment, and suburbanization provides an important example of some of the effects of these exclusionary shifts in U.S. social policy. O'Mara "examines the way in which federal expenditures on higher education and scientific research during the early Cold War encouraged the suburbanization of advanced scientific industry" at the expense of other groups.[20] She focuses on three case studies—Stanford University and the San Francisco peninsula, or Silicon Valley; the University of Pennsylvania in Philadelphia; and the Georgia Institute of Technology in Atlanta—to show the interlocking of state intervention and scientific research in the postwar period. According to O'Mara, a distinctive urban form that she calls the "city of knowledge" emerged in a deliberately planned way. Between 1940 and 1970, federal government spending on scientific research and development increased from $74 million to $15.7 billion. O'Mara shows how federal Cold War aims such as effective civil defense compounded the "shape and composition of American urban space."[21] For example, one justification for the large-scale federally sponsored highway building programs was the need for quick and easy evacuation in case of a nuclear attack. Quickly, the federal government saw a complementary relationship between urban renewal and defence.

Section 112 of the 1959 Housing Act, introduced during the Eisenhower administration, created incentives that would connect universities and colleges to urban renewal and slum clearance efforts. It was also crucial that the scientific research that might win the United States the Cold War was relatively secure, which pushed the necessity of suburban location for such facilities. Legislation such as the 1957 National Defense Education Act, the 1963 Higher Education Facilities Act, and the 1964 State Technical Services Act all increased the prominence and role of the research university and propagated a culture of science, which dominated the political discourse of the Cold War. Many scientists and members of the high-tech establishment believed they had been successful in their research efforts in spite of government. In fact, central government planning was central to the construction of the "metropolitan-military complexes" in the 1960s. However, O'Mara's work emphasizes the longer-term implications of this relationship between industry and government. By excluding minorities, poor people, and other undesirables and by channeling money and resources to affluent oases, public policy contributed to the decline of inner cities by consciously pursuing a suburban agenda.[22]

After 1949, then, attitudes toward government intervention in housing policy changed, as the latter was perceived—contrary to the financial realities—to be directed mainly at the lethargic and "undeserving" poor and dependent minorities rather than the affluent beneficiaries of tax breaks.[23] Unlike the subsidy of richer Americans through the tax system or the federal infrastructural investment that enabled suburban development, as political scientist Paul Pierson has argued, "extensions of government activity" in housing policy toward the poorest in the United States "have been hotly contested."[24] Public housing was lumped together with the much reviled federal program Aid to Families with Dependent Children, also known as welfare, in the angry critiques of conservative politicians, who argued that the welfare state undermined the bases of responsibility among the unemployed in poorer neighborhoods. But public policy also reinforced the outward growth of cities into the "exurbs" and even beyond, a unique sort of urban sprawl that was both fueled and compounded by a downward spiral in funding and support for proper public transport systems. Thus, for these structural

reasons, a divide was created in the United States between the marginalized
poor, unemployed blacks in the city or blacks and whites living at barely sub-
sistence levels in parts of rural America and the rest of the population. Certainly, there was not the fluidity between working- and middle-class groups
that shared public housing estates, often situated in the middle of cities alongside more affluent neighbors, that existed in Britain.

To some extent, the place of public housing in the composition of American housing tenures remained open throughout the 1960s as Presidents Kennedy and Johnson attempted to continue and deepen the reformism of the
New Deal. But gradually, policy experiments during the 1960s led to a different strategy for meeting the housing needs of the poor and closed off the
possibility of the large-scale public housing construction envisaged by Tugwell and other progressive Democrats. What emerged instead was a voucher
scheme for rent subsidy that became known as Section 8 (of the U.S. Housing
Act of 1937).The origins and passage of this housing legislation revealed the
political impossibility, by the mid-1970s, of mounting a sustained defense of
public provision of housing to low-income groups when wider public support had disappeared. The move to grant subsidies and allowances in place
of public housing construction anticipated the almost complete withdrawal
that would occur through the 1980s under Reagan. There had been advocates
of housing subsidies going back to the 1930s, so it would be a mistake to see
the advent of Section 8 provisions as a revolutionary moment. Instead, it was
emblematic of a gradual shift toward reliance on the market to solve what was
perceived as a central dimension of the urban crisis: the concentration of the
poor in blighted public housing.[25]

The model for what became Section 8 can be found in Lyndon Johnson's
successful push to introduce rent supplements and the Section 23 leasing
program in 1965. These small beginnings could have been missed at the time,
however, as Nixon presided over the greatest boom in housing construction
in U.S. history. As in many areas of policy, Nixon continued to push through
the legacy of Lyndon Johnson's quest for a Great Society and War on Poverty. For example, between 1967 and 1973, over half a million new public
housing units were built.[26] The link between the experiments under Kennedy
and Johnson with public-private partnerships and a lessening of the role of
the state in the provision of housing, on the one hand, and the more wholesale shift toward the market implied by Section 8, which was enacted by the

Nixon administration, on the other is shown in a renewed wave of bipartisan criticism of the state's ability to solve the worst social problems in the late 1960s and 1970s. The development of a new approach was brought about largely through the greater awareness of and disillusionment with the reality of life in many of the projects and, perhaps most important, the Department of Housing and Urban Development's administration of its programs.

The Kennedy administration's Housing Act of 1961 marked the beginning of an expansion of private sector involvement in the provision of affordable housing through Section 221(d)(3), which allowed direct government loans at favorable rates for new rental housing construction for moderate-income households, as well as other incentives to private builders. Three crucial initiatives followed in 1965. First and most important, Johnson established the Department of Housing and Urban Development (HUD), which placed housing firmly at the center of federal government activity. Second, Johnson proposed an adjustment to Kennedy's 1961 act so that the Section 221(d)(3) provision better served the poor and needy through federal funding of the difference between an appropriate rent and 20 percent of a tenant's income.[27] After much controversy and debate in Congress, dominated by the vociferous opposition of white southern Democrats to the prospect of faster desegregation and greater racial mixing, the plans were passed. However, partly to allay such fears, Congress included a stipulation that required HUD to get approval for sites from the local government authorities concerned—a sop to the racist South. This meant, of course, that integration was limited to areas where the local authorities were color-blind and there would be next to no building—no racial mixing—in the de facto segregated suburbs.[28] Third, HUD introduced Section 23, a program that enabled housing authorities to lease existing units from private owners and rent to low-income tenants at a subsidized rate. Section 23 was a precursor to the Section 8 Existing Housing Program, the voucher scheme that eventually became the principal means for providing publicly assisted housing by the 1980s.

Congress passed another housing act in 1968 at the end of the Johnson administration that experimented further with production-based innovations for affordable housing. As the historian Roger Biles has argued, the 1968 act "added other programs that sought to privatize low-income housing."[29] The act created Section 235, which provided subsidies to private builders for units aimed at purchases by moderate-income families, and Section 236, which was directed at rental housing. The income limits were set 35 percent higher than equivalent local public housing. As Galster and Daniell have pointed out, poorer people "were still to be served indirectly through filtering" (in filtering, the opposite process to gentrification, poorer people move into affluent and high-income housing stock). Much later, rent supplements were added to include more low-income groups.[30] The turn from direct loans for purchase to subsidy was motivated by immediate political and budgetary considerations because this type of assistance would not add so much expenditure in the short term to federal balance sheets because the outlay in each year was relatively less than the total amount. Section 235 was originally a Republican proposal, while Section 236 was proposed by the Johnson White House, which indicated there was now broad agreement between the different parties on the need to enhance the role of the private sector in housing production for low- and moderate-income families.

After Nixon's election in November 1968, George Romney, former governor of Michigan, became HUD secretary. Romney, an advocate of increased private sector involvement in the provision of housing to low-income groups, facilitated the growth of production of new household units under Sections 235 and 236, leading to the approval of 1.6 million units by 1970. But a series of scandals emerged around the new programs as HUD relaxed its inspection requirements. According to Biles, this was particularly "disastrous in cities like Detroit and Philadelphia where corrupt real estate agents lured home buyers into shabbily constructed or poorly renovated housing."[31] As a result of these problems, the administration's policies and the administration of the programs came under increased scrutiny by Congress, the glare of which slowly created the conditions for Section 8.

First, in the face of the costs of Section 235 programs and the scandals associated with their shortcomings, the chairman of the House Banking and Currency Committee, Congressman Wright Patman, initiated a congressional investigation into Section 235 practice in ten major cities in September 1970. The report noted,

A disturbing number of situations where real estate speculators purchased properties at a minimal cost and, after repairs which, if made, were cosmetic in nature, resold to the section 235 purchaser, with FHA

(Federal Housing Authority) approval, sometimes double in price within days or a few months after purchase.[32]

Escalating maintenance costs squeezed purchasers, and the FHA was forced to foreclose on many units. About one in fifteen units were in default and had to be taken over by HUD.[33] It was also revealed that FHA agents had been taking kickbacks from landlords. On January 14, 1971, Romney suspended the program. Section 236 also came to be viewed with skepticism because it had not helped fix the entrenched problems of inner-city neighborhoods. Developers were incentivized to build close to where they felt demand existed, which tended to further concentrate the worst-off and compounded the social problems of concentrated poverty. Zoning laws in affluent areas meant that building housing for low-income groups in these neighborhoods was blocked. The program thus became stigmatized in much the same way as public housing.

In March 1971, John J. Sparkman, chair of the Senate Committee on Banking, Housing and Urban Affairs, instigated an investigation of the Nixon administration's requisitioning of $1 billion earmarked for housing and other programs. Although the suspension of the funds was part of a larger campaign to cut public expenditure, it showed that housing policy was losing approval in the administration. Romney had stated publicly in 1970 that he desired a "basically new housing approach to federal housing assistance."[34] The explosion by dynamite of the Pruitt-Igoe project in St. Louis in the summer of 1972 was a symbolic moment that helped drive the new policy. After an expensive attempt to save the project failed, it was spectacularly destroyed, with its demise widely covered by the national media. Some $5 million of public money had seemingly been publicly wasted, further discrediting the administration's housing policy. Romney subsequently resigned from office after Nixon's reelection in 1972, stating, "my experience in public service has convinced me that inherent limitations in our political processes make the achievement of fundamental reform too dependent upon a crisis."[35] In December 1972, Nixon announced an end to new projects. It was to last eighteen months, and Congress took until August 1974 to come up with a legislative answer to the housing problem. The result was a major reform of U.S. housing policy.

In 1968 the Kaiser Committee had been commissioned by the Johnson administration to look into existing housing programs, partly in the wake of the urban crises and disturbances of the mid-1960s. The committee proposed a move toward experimentation with housing allowances. Important members of the incoming Nixon administration picked up on this recommendation, and plans for the implementation of allowances were made by the administration in 1970. The first experiment was carried out in Kansas City in a joint venture between HUD and the housing authority. Malcolm E. Peabody, Jr., the deputy assistant secretary for equal opportunity at HUD, adjudged the program to have been a success. On the basis of the preliminary findings, the administration sponsored a provision for a national experiment that was inserted into the Housing and Urban Development Act of 1970. Section 501 of the act ordered the secretary of HUD to "undertake on an experimental basis a program to demonstrate the feasibility of providing families of low-income with housing allowances to assist them in obtaining rental housing of their choice in existing standard housing units."[36]

In the autumn of 1973, the administration pushed ahead with plans for the introduction of housing allowances despite the demonstration projects not having yet reported their findings. On September 19, 1973, Nixon told Congress that "direct cash assistance" for low-income families was the right approach. He argued that tackling the problem in this way would "give the poor the freedom and responsibility to make their own choices about housing—and it would eventually get the Federal Government out of the housing business."[37] This scheme echoed the sentiments of Milton Friedman's advocacy of direct cash subsidies and vouchers in education. At the same time, Nixon continued the rental supplement programs ongoing since Johnson's presidency by ending the bar on the old Section 23. However, Nixon's sudden support for housing allowances was also a product of bipartisan opinion. For example, Democratic presidential candidate George McGovern had also called for a housing allowance program during the 1972 presidential election. The Housing Assistance Payments Plan, the product of deals in both houses of Congress, later known as Section 8 Existing, came into being with the passage of the 1974 Housing Act. Over the following year, the number of households assisted through the program was almost 300,000. The passage of Section 8 legislation is usually seen as marking the retreat of the federal government from large-scale funding of public housing construction. But it also indicated the emergence of a bipartisan consensus over the need to address the problem of low-income housing differently. This consensus was manifest before Ronald Reagan's election in 1980.

For a variety of reasons, then—federal support for predominantly white suburban development, the closing off of the option of large-scale public housing provision after 1949, the experimentation with and development of new forms of public-private partnerships in housing during the 1960s, and the eventual creation of Section 8—the trajectory of housing policy aimed at low- and moderate-income groups in the United States moved away from public provision and toward a reliance on the state subsidy of the private rental sector through housing allowances or vouchers. In place of the high-rise projects, which were perceived to have fostered and compounded urban crisis of the late 1960s, a mixture of federal government policies under successive Democratic and Republican administrations from Eisenhower through Kennedy and Johnson to Nixon and Ford aimed to encourage a private housing market for the poor in the inner cities. Whatever the intentions of the architects of these policies, the overwhelming fact of market failure and the structural inequalities in affordable housing provision prevented the worst urban problems of African American ghettoization, poverty, and segregation from being overcome.

Postwar Low-Income Housing and Urban Policy in Britain

After World War II in Britain, council housing construction boomed during the 1950s and 1960s, as it had after World War I. Public housing was seen by policymakers of both parties as a crucial weapon in the battle against "poverty and ill health and in the development of a more equal society with greater equality of opportunity."[38] By the century's end, support for public housing had slipped among the public amid perceived tensions between indigenous and immigrant communities, sensationalized and stoked by the press and populist politicians, coupled with a perception that architectural failure and planning hubris had created "sink estates" where alcohol, drugs, and unemployment were rife.[39] But support for public housing also declined as a result of a sustained policy assault by Conservative politicians and their advisers after 1979, many of whom had been influenced by the kinds of argument made by Friedrich Hayek and Milton Friedman on the dependency culture fostered by the welfare state of which, in Britain, housing was a central component. The Right to Buy program—the sale of council houses to their tenants at discounted rates—was the first and most popular of the Thatcher government's landmark privatizations, and after the 1980s, a residualized council sector began to be seen as a last resort for the "elderly, the unem- ployed, female-headed households and those with no other choice."[40]

The preponderance of council housing in the UK was partly the historical legacy of a strong centralized state. Since the early twentieth century there had been an assumption that local authorities had a proper role in the plan- ning and delivery of housing provision, as when, after the Great War of 1914– 18, the Liberal prime minister David Lloyd George proclaimed a commit- ment to build "homes fit for heroes" for the returning soldiers. Housing in London, for instance, was the most important domestic issue in the interwar period, second only to unemployment during the Great Depression of the 1930s. The annihilation of inner-city housing stock through the bombing of the Luftwaffe during World War II also required massive rebuilding. Housing construction consequently became a priority for the 1945 Labour govern- ment and was championed especially by the minister of health (the Health Ministry covered housing at the time) and founder of the National Health Service, Aneurin (or Nye) Bevan.

Large-scale construction of housing units continued through the 1950s and 1960s under successive Labour and Conservative governments—Harold Macmillan, the future Conservative prime minister, for example, committed to 300,000 new homes a year during his time as housing minister in the early 1950s. The Conservative governments of the 1950s, unlike their Labour predecessors, placed greater emphasis on encouraging the private sector to build new homes as well as those built by local authorities.[41] At the same time, the early 1950s also saw a relaxation of the prevailing standards for local authority–constructed council housing from the generous specifications out- lined by the wartime Dudley Committee (1944).[42] The policy of encourag- ing the private sector instead of local authorities to build new houses would be continued by Edward Heath's Conservative government after 1970. The Heath government also sought to encourage existing private sector landlords to rent to low-income groups through the Housing Finance Act (1972). This act led to the creation of a rent allowance program for low-income private rental tenants at exactly the same time that, in the United States, Congress authorized its experimental housing allowance program.[43]

Housing became a particularly explosive issue in the 1960s in the context of rising tensions between local populations and new immigrant arrivals, and as a result, just as in the United States, support for public housing began to drain away. Although there was no equivalent structural racial divide in Britain, the place of public and social housing at the heart of the British welfare state ensured there was often deep conflict over its provision and distribution among different groups in society.[44] Until the 1960s in Britain, working-class demands on the state for improved housing, made through the Labour Party, local pressure groups, and trade unions, tended not to be defined by racial issues. To be sure, racial antagonism brewed beneath the surface, and sometimes exploded in violent struggle; blacks and Asians were deliberately discriminated against by landlords, neighbors, and local residents; and new waves of immigration, first from the former empire and subsequently from the European Union, caused widespread resentment and undermined, or sometimes paradoxically reinforced, particular "white" or English notions of Britishness and conjured fears of takeover and foreign domination. Equally, the reality of the physical design of high-rise council estates such as those in Notting Hill or Elephant and Castle combined with intracommunity tensions to have a negative effect on wider support for public housing and the larger welfare state by the 1970s.

Paranoid white fears of immigration were coupled with what British historian David Feldman has called a conservative pluralism prevalent in the political and state establishment, an attitude that contributed to a sense of disconnection between poorer white working-class communities and elites that helped fuel support for Enoch Powell after his famous "Rivers of Blood" speech in Birmingham on April 20, 1968. Powell was seen as one of the few prominent national political leaders to give voice to widespread white working-class sentiment. The conservative pluralism Feldman speaks of existed on the basis of acceptance of cultural difference as a "strategy of incorporation and governance" and was as evident as any concurrent belief in the promotion of assimilation as the appropriate response to diversity.[45] According to Feldman, the historical policy responses of the British state to the separate nations of Britain, Scotland, Wales, and Ireland, to different religious groups, including Jews, Catholics, and other non-Conformists, and even in the governance of the colonies were often guided by a toleration "embedded within state institutions."[46] This expedient British establishment form of tolerance was later subverted, in housing policy terms, at the moment of the rise of multiculturalism in Britain by the policy of selling off council housing stock to tenants. As the public resources available to local authorities for the housing of those in need shrank, and the definition of need itself in relation to public housing also shriveled in the face of alternative policies favoring home ownership, tensions among whites, blacks, and Asians increased. This subversion of the public space for tolerance that was occupied by council housing, which accelerated during the 1980s, had unpleasant and unpredictable consequences, such as the rise to prominence of far-right groups like the National Front in the 1970s, or more recently the British National Party.

In this context of postwar social and racial politics, the election of Harold Wilson's Labour government in 1974 continued the subtle change in the direction of affordable housing policy in Britain in the 1970s, as in the United States, toward a focus on home ownership and rental allowances (seen, e.g., in Heath's 1972 Housing Finance Act). The Labour governments of the 1960s and 1970s, as much as their Conservative counterparts, made home ownership the central aim of government policy. Partly out of fiscal necessity, Labour helped drive the new policy by embracing a cynical decentralization of shrinking local government budgets.

Wilson first entered office as prime minister in 1964 with the professed aim of constructing half a million new homes a year between 1964 and 1968. Events swiftly overtook this ambition because the Labour governments of the 1960s and 1970s, as we saw in the last chapter, became subject to severe financial pressures brought about by devaluation in 1967, the collapse of the international monetary system, rising inflation, and unemployment. Public expenditure cuts were perceived as crucial to economic stability, and in 1968 and 1969, funding for 16,500 planned local authority homes was cut as part of a larger austerity package. The impact of tightening central government capital spending on housing construction, first under Labour and then under Heath's Conservative government, had a cumulative effect. The result was the Labour government's 1974 Housing Act, legislation that authorized experimentation with a bids and allocations system for capital spending on housing.[47] Pilot councils (local authorities were responsible for funding council house construction in Britain) were tasked with drawing up detailed local expenditure plans and made to bid for funds from the central government. The IMF crisis of 1975–76 exacerbated the problem of funding and resulted in a series of harsh measures that further adversely affected housing, while amounts available to councils to spend were cut.

In the shadow of the IMF crisis, the Labour government began to set out a new direction for housing policy in its green paper published in 1977. The government, disingenuously, had drawn strength from the fact that the UK had reached a notional surplus in household units. There were supposedly slightly more vacant houses than people looking for places to live. The Housing Services Advisory Group stated in its assessment of housing requirements in 1977:

> By 1976 the serious housing shortage which existed at the end of World War Two had been converted into a crude surplus of some 0.5m units. The proportion of households known to be sharing dwellings had diminished from around 14% to less than 6%; the occupation density had similarly been reduced; and the quality of housing stock had been improved. The number of unfit houses fell from 1.8m in 1967 to an estimated 0.9m in 1976, and the number of fit dwellings lacking one or more amenities reduced from 2.4m in 1967 to 1.6m in 1976.[48]

This complacent picture was only half the story. As the pressure group Shelter (founded by the Reverend Bruce Kenrick in 1966) argued, there is always a need for around 4–5 percent of homes to be vacant at any one time to ensure proper levels of social mobility between different income groups across the country.[49]

Council housing had begun to lose some of its public support in the 1960s and 1970s partly through the rising tensions between different communities, but also because of the design failures associated with the high-rise estate. As social historian John Burnett has suggested, "the high-rise flat was clearly an episode which did not fulfil the expectations of its proponents and never commanded the widespread affection, or even approval, of users."[50] Although at its peak in 1966, high-rise builds accounted for just 26 percent of new council house construction, estates such as the infamous Ronan Point block in Newham in East London, which partially collapsed in 1968, began to attract strident opposition among the public, policymakers, and even the architectural profession, for all of whom the high-rise blocks had been the realization of an ideal. The Labour Party responded to falling support for council housing, for example, in its National Executive Committee (the party's ruling body) statement from 1978:

> While these form only a tiny part of the total public housing stock, there is no doubt that conditions on such estates cause considerable hardship to the tenants concerned, and can be exploited politically to foist a second-rate image onto public housing as a whole.[51]

High-rise, badly lit, concrete estates built with the best intentions had often turned into hellish concrete jungles that provided ammunition for enemies of state provision.

The difficulties associated with high-rise council estates arose at a time—the late 1960s and 1970s—when Britain's economic state was worsening. Many of the worst design faults required demolition and massive reinvestment to be corrected, things for which there was not enough appetite in the midst of economic crisis and other higher social priorities. In 1977 and 1978, Labour did produce a new policy for housing to address the public disquiet over public housing estates. The government devised a strategy based on devolving more decisions to local authorities. The aim was to encourage greater autonomy and choice for those with local expertise. As a sign of the times, it was telling. For example, Labour's 1977 green paper on housing opened with a disavowal of the central government's role:

> The powers of Central Government in housing matters are inevitably limited. They must set the legislative framework and distribute resources available for investment. They can provide a subsidy system . . . which is consistent with national housing policy and reflects local needs they can advise and persuade. But the real effectiveness of the public sector's contribution to the solution of our housing problems depends on the way in which national policies are applied on the ground—on the energy and foresight of the members who take the local decisions.[52]

To this end, Labour proposed that councils develop Housing Investment Programmes, which expanded the bids and allocations experiment that had been under way since the 1974 act, to all capital spending on housing. This meant that all councils now had to compete for smaller pieces of a smaller central government funding pie.

The government, led by Secretary of State for the Environment Peter Shore, claimed that its proposal for HIPs had four distinct advantages: they would control expenditure and allow flexibility, they would increase local discretion over spending decisions, they would create incentives to create cost-effective measures, and they would allow a more comprehensive approach to local housing needs.[53] The idea was that authorities would bid for the amount of money they thought they needed through the development of local strategies. Central government would then allocate resources on the merits of the bids as they saw them and redistribute to areas of greatest need. Labour sought to maintain a rhetorical commitment to housing equality, as is shown, for example, in a policy paper that outlined its priorities in 1978: "The reforms which we seek aim to open up public housing to all who choose to rent, to extend to public tenants the rights and freedoms of the other housing tenures, and to achieve parity of esteem between the tenures."[54] But the problem, of course, was that less money would be available for building, repairs, and maintenance. In fact, the HIPs ended up augmenting central government power by expanding central control over local authorities, and also provided cover for large cuts—something that continued apace under the Conservative administrations of the 1980s.[55]

In both the United States and Britain, then, there is much evidence of continuity between the policies of the 1970s and the 1980s. Former Department of Industry and No. 10 Policy Unit civil servant Andrew Duguid has argued that the housing policy of the Conservative Party after 1979 was not at first ideological and would likely have been continued had Labour been reelected.[56] This is a matter of opinion, of course, as different pressures would surely have been brought to bear on any reelected Labour administration. It is highly unlikely, for example, that the Right to Buy policy would have become a flagship policy under Labour as it did under Thatcher. But it is probable that council house sales would have continued. Despite a clear radicalization after 1980 in both Britain and in the United States, a new approach had been revealed in the development of Section 8 in the United States and the trend in Britain in the 1970s toward encouraging private sector involvement in affordable housing provision and the limited withdrawal from public housing implied by budgetary austerity and the nascent policy of council house sales. Policy toward affordable housing and urban renewal had changed before Reagan and Thatcher.

Jimmy Carter and the Limits of Government

In the United States, the Carter administration (1977–81) continued these trends. Carter confirmed the move away from the construction of public housing, in part because of the worsening economic stagflation that engulfed the United States during the late 1970s. Section 8 had originally been split into three subprograms—Section 8 Existing, to open up access to existing housing stock through a voucher scheme (this later became the housing subsidy program that is usually associated with the name Section 8), Section 8 New Construction, for new builds, and Section 8 Substantial Rehabilitation, for the restoration of existing stock. The administration now reined in the growth of the Section 8 Existing program as well as the Section 8 New Construction program. Some 170,000 new household units were built under the Section 8 New Construction program in 1976, with 175,000 additional households receiving subsidy under the Section 8 Existing program.[57] By 1980, only 92,554 new units had been built and just 38,740 additional units had been subsidized.[58]

Carter remained sympathetic to the principles of decent housing for all, and in particular to support for those on low and moderate incomes, but under his administration, HUD (now led by former U.S. ambassador to Luxembourg and the first African American to enter the presidential line of succession, Patricia Roberts Harris) emphasized targeting resources at the most vulnerable, and greater efficiency and management instead of expanded new construction or large-scale redevelopment of affordable housing. The federal role in affordable housing was to be carefully circumscribed. As historian John Bauman has argued, the "Carter administration represented an early milestone in this retreat from Neo-Keynesian economic solutions." The Neo-Keynesians had "preached that large-scale government spending programs such as Urban Renewal, Model Cities, and public housing fuelled economic growth that produced jobs and general prosperity," but Carter "challenged what he saw as the Great Society 'excesses' of the 1960s without surrendering his compassion for the dispossessed" by openly advocating the smaller government of his Georgian roots. Bauman points out that "Carter denied that government could 'solve our problems . . . it cannot eliminate poverty, or provide a bountiful economy, or reduce inflation, or save cities, or cure illiteracy, or provide energy.'"[59] But the new reticence over government provision provoked a new crisis of affordability for low- and moderate-income families just when Carter imposed fiscal retrenchments to balance the budget. The housing boom that began under Nixon continued in the first years of the administration. But the worsening inflation and unemployment created a serious problem for many of those in greatest need of assistance.

Carter's National Urban Policy, announced in 1978, emphasized targeting resources at the poorest and a reduced role for the state. The report lists guiding principles, including a greater "flexibility" of approach to different local problems, greater prioritization according to "community need," "reinforcement," and "preservation" of existing neighborhoods, and greater involvement of the private sector. In relation to the role of the federal government, the tone is strict:

> Federal resources are limited. A fundamental reassessment of existing programs is necessary to ensure their future efficiency and effectiveness. To achieve maximum return on the Federal resources available, states and localities should be assisted and encouraged to use them to attract and support other public and private investments in the community. Used alone, Federal aid will never be sufficient to meet community needs. Used in conjunction with other funds, it can play a critically important catalytic role.[60]

The Carter administration's policies, then, continued the trends established under Nixon and prepared the ground for Reagan's more drastic retreat after 1980. Carter's strategy was also similar to that pursued by the Labour Party in Britain, which, as we have seen, in its experiments with HIPs attempted decentralization of housing decisions to local authorities at the same time as their funds were being cut. The Carter administration's strategy also opened the way for the creation of inner-city urban enterprise zones during the Reagan administration by fostering an atmosphere conducive to local experimentation with partnerships with the private sector.

As a counterpoint to its support for fiscal austerity, the Carter administration introduced an all-important corrective reform: the Community Rein-

vestment Act. The act, passed in 1977, ensured that poorer groups, especially
African Americans and other minorities, had access to proper credit facilities
and housing finance from banks. In particular, the act tackled the infamous
practice of redlining, whereby banks would rate neighborhoods according to
the supposed risk of default by its residents.[61] This practice often became a
cover for the continued racial segregation of American cities because black
neighborhoods were usually given poor ratings, making it almost impossible for residents to obtain mortgages to buy property in certain, usually
suburban, neighborhoods. The practice was made even more unacceptable
to liberal reformers in the administration because predominantly white areas
would receive lower ratings when blacks moved in, exacerbating the already
heightened tensions, even outright revolts, associated with racial mixing
within and between different neighborhoods and communities.

The Community Reinvestment Act forced banks to lend to individuals and
businesses in low- and moderate-income neighborhoods in the inner city, as
well as in the affluent and mainly white suburbs. It was made a condition of
their operation that banks offer loans in any areas where they were chartered
to do business. The new finance mandated through the act led to the successful regeneration of areas such as the Northside Manchester neighborhood
of Pittsburgh, where, according to historian Thomas Hanchett, "community
activists used Community Reinvestment Act dollars to spark noticeable revitalization."[62] The Community Reinvestment Act was an example of a Democratic Party–led attempt at increasing the provision of affordable housing
to poorer communities despite the federal budgetary constraints of the late
1970s. It was an important reform because it helped eradicate a painful and
unjust form of housing discrimination that stained the record of increased
legal equality and civil rights in postwar America.

Property-Owning Democracy and Individual Freedom:
Housing and Neoliberal Ideas

It is necessary at this juncture to return briefly to neoliberal ideas and their
relationship to other conservative ideas, less because they were influential
on the policies and governmental practices just described than because the
writings of Friedrich Hayek and Milton Friedman, for example, had a powerful influence of some of the key architects of the policies of the Reagan and

Thatcher governments that followed. Against the background of postwar housing policy, a new set of ideas about low-income housing, urban policy, and poverty came into view, one that clashed with the presumptions of the New Deal in the United States and the social democratic settlement in Britain but meshed with traditional conservative philosophical concerns about private property and urban space.

Neoliberal policies such as public housing privatization and enterprise zones did not enter a vacuum. Rather, they emerged to sit alongside typical conservative notions about the importance of home ownership such as British Conservative prime minister Anthony Eden's concept of the "property-owning democracy." As Anthony Eden stated in his address to the 1946 Conservative Party Conference,

> there is one principle underlying our approach to all these [social] problems, a principle on which we stand in fundamental opposition to socialism. The objective of socialism is state ownership of all the means of production, distribution and exchange. Our objective is a nationwide property-owning democracy . . . whereas our opponents believe in State capitalism, we believe in the widest measure of individual capitalism. I believe this to be a fundamental principle of political philosophy. Man should be a master of his environment and not its slave. That is what freedom means. It is precisely in the conception of ownership that man achieves mastery over his environment. Upon the institution of property depends the fulfilment of individual personality and the maintenance of individual liberty.[63]

Eden's concept of the property-owning democracy was the leitmotif of Conservative Party housing policies in the postwar period. It receded somewhat during the governments of the 1950s, becoming more an aspiration than a political reality as Winston Churchill, Anthony Eden, and Harold Macmillan pursued council housing construction as part of their accommodation with the core elements of the British welfare state. However, the idea returned under Heath, and successive Conservative politicians have subscribed to the idea up to the present day. In particular, Margaret Thatcher and her successor, John Major (1990–97), expanded the notion to become that of a share-owning democracy during their campaigns to promote the privatization of British Telecom (1984), British Gas (1986), British Airways (1987), water (1989), electricity (1990), British Energy (1996), and British Rail (1996). The power of the neoliberal emphasis on the supremacy of free markets was plain in these efforts, but they also reinvented Eden's conviction that private property was the bedrock of a successful society.

In the United States, Democratic president Harry Truman's announcement of the priorities of the 1949 Housing Act in his State of the Union address illustrated a clear focus on the private sector even at the peak of the dominance of New Deal liberalism. "Private enterprise" was always expected to be the primary vehicle for the construction of affordable housing:

> The housing shortage continues to be acute. As an immediate step, the Congress should enact the provisions for low-rent public housing, slum clearance, farm housing, and housing research which I have repeatedly recommended. The number of low-rent public housing units provided for in the legislation should be increased to 1 million units in the next 7 years. Even this number of units will not begin to meet our need for new housing.
>
> Most of the houses we need will have to be built by private enterprise, without public subsidy. By producing too few rental units and too large a proportion of high-priced houses, the building industry is rapidly pricing itself out of the market. Building costs must be lowered.
>
> The Government is now engaged in a campaign to induce all segments of the building industry to concentrate on the production of lower priced housing. Additional legislation to encourage such housing will be submitted.
>
> The authority which I have requested, to allocate materials in short supply and to impose price ceilings on such materials, could be used, if found necessary, to channel more materials into homes large enough for family life at prices which wage earners can afford.[64]

But the act, part of Truman's Fair Deal, had unexpected effects. It facilitated the new high-rise projects that were developed in the 1950s and 1960s, the equivalent of the estates that had proved unpopular in Britain. As in Britain, these projects turned into a target for critics of welfare and public housing after the 1960s who believed that such neighborhoods were nests of crime, social and family dislocation, and dependence. Arguments over the social impact of "the projects" could be found in the work of neoliberal writers, especially Friedrich Hayek and Milton Friedman. Others, such as housing policy analyst and future adviser in the Reagan White House Martin Anderson, launched an assault on key government programs such as slum clearance and urban renewal in his book, *The Federal Bulldozer* (1964).[65] Anderson argued that the urban renewal program tended to hurt those it was most meant to help by being too slow and too costly and failing to meet its objectives of providing a decent living environment for all because it inevitably privileged the interests of some. Early critiques such as Anderson's formed the basis for a crescendo of criticism that followed the perceived failings of Lyndon Johnson's Great Society and War on Poverty campaigns of the 1960s, while the ideas of Hayek and Friedman also influenced the next generation of policymakers, those who rose to prominence in the Reagan and Thatcher administrations.

There were murmurings in the 1940s and 1950s of a neoliberal market-based alternative to the dominant public housing, urban renewal, and slum clearance strategies. In the United States, for example, Milton Friedman and George Stigler wrote a pamphlet for the Foundation for Economic Education titled *Roofs or Ceilings*, published in 1946, which argued for the abolition of rent control.[66] In Britain, young Conservatives involved with One Nation and the Bow Group (described in chapter 4) began to argue for a return to market solutions in social and economic policy. They included the young Geoffrey Howe, who also advocated the abolition of rent control in a report published by the Bow Group in 1956.[67] Howe posed the central question as one of a choice between state and market:

> There are two major interrelated issues here, the first largely economic and the second largely political: the first is whether or not the provision of housing can and should be regulated by reference to the free market; and the second is whether we wish to rely predominantly on private or on public enterprise to meet the nation's need for housing.[68]

Although not written about the problem of low-income housing specifically, Howe's pamphlet on rent control argued that rent restrictions distorted housing supply by artificially keeping rents low. Such a market distortion, in his view, led to a lack of incentives for landlords to properly maintain their properties, which in turn exacerbated the shortage of affordable rents and allowed the deterioration of existing stocks.

Friedrich Hayek developed the outlines of a policy program that met the strict criteria he argued had to be met for the protection of individual liberty in *The Constitution of Liberty* (1960). He included a chapter titled "Housing and Town Planning," along with chapters on other major social and economic policy issues, including education, social security, the unions, taxation, and monetary policy. Hayek acknowledged the importance of community in urban space for the creation and sustenance of neighborhoods when he stated that "the usefulness of almost any piece of property in a city will in fact depend in part on what one's immediate neighbors do and in part on the communal services without which effective use of the land by separate owners would be nearly impossible."[69] But Hayek went on to argue that government interventions in the housing market to help the poor and disadvantaged failed the people at which they were aimed and fueled even worse problems further down the line.

According to Hayek, any attempt to interfere with the price mechanism was liable to lead to misdirected investments that were unsustainable. This was a typical neoliberal trope; indeed, it is a standard of all policy criticism to argue that particular efforts are misdirected and harmful. But for Hayek and the Austrian school, inaction was vastly better if it meant less interference with market processes. As Hayek put it,

> We must not overlook the fact that the market has, on the whole, guided the evolution of cities more successfully, though imperfectly, than is commonly realised and that most of the proposals to improve upon this, not by making it work better, but by superimposing a system of central direction, show little awareness of what such a system would have to accomplish, even to equal the market in effectiveness.[70]

Efforts to help the poor and "combat particular evils have made them worse."[71] According to Hayek, it was much better to allow the market to deliver affordable accommodation through the efficient allocation of resources under the price mechanism.

Hayek reserved particularly harsh comments for what he saw as the follies of public housing. He thought that the market distortions of government involvement in the construction of council or public housing created a vicious loop which had a series of deleterious effects on the market. These effects meant ever-greater expense and fostered the famed culture of dependency:

> Efforts to reduce the cost of housing for the poorer sections of the population by public housing or building subsidies have come to be accepted as a permanent part of the welfare state. It is little understood that, unless very carefully limited in scope and method, such efforts are likely to produce results very similar to those of rent restriction.
>
> [The] limitation of public housing to the poorest families will gener-ally be practicable only if the government does not attempt to supply dwellings which are both cheaper and substantially better than they had before; otherwise the people thus assisted would be better housed than those immediately above them on the economic ladder; and pres-sure from the latter to be included in the scheme would become irre-sistible, a process which would repeat itself and progressively bring in more and more people.[72]

As the epigraph to this chapter illustrates, Hayek believed that public hous-ing and assistance ought to be firmly limited to the poor to avoid the inevi-table entrenchment of an entitlement program such as Social Security in the United States. Hayek knew that when the middle class is co-opted into uni-versal social provision, as with Social Security or the British National Health Service, for example, such government intervention becomes comprehen-sive, permanent, and, in Hayek's view, a threat to individual liberty. The ori-gins of the neoliberal strategy of a "residualization" of the public sector so that it becomes merely a refuge for the poor and most vulnerable while the market delivers for the rest of society is evident in Hayek's argument.

Milton Friedman echoed Hayek in his own chapter, titled "Social Welfare Measures," in *Capitalism and Freedom* (1962). Friedman proposed direct cash assistance in place of government programs. According to Friedman, it was much better to provide a direct cash subsidy:

> Public housing is proposed not on the ground of neighbourhood ef-fects but as a means of helping low-income people. If this be the case, why subsidize housing in particular? If funds are to be used to help the poor, would they not be used more effectively by being given in cash

rather than in kind? Surely, the families being helped would rather have a given sum in cash than in the form of housing. They could themselves spend money on housing if they so desired.

Public housing cannot therefore be justified on the grounds either of neighbourhood effects or of helping poor families. It can be justified, if at all, only on grounds of paternalism; that the families being helped "need" housing more than they "need" other things but would themselves either not agree or would spend the money unwisely.[73]

Friedman also suggested, like Hayek, that the best intentions and efforts of public policy were futile because they made the situation worse rather than better:

Far from improving the housing of the poor, as its proponents expected, public housing has done just the reverse. The number of dwelling units destroyed in the course of erecting public housing projects has been far larger than the number of new dwelling units constructed. But public housing as such has done nothing to reduce the numbers to be housed. The effect of public housing has therefore been to raise the number of persons per dwelling unit.[74]

The main problem with government construction of public housing was that the motivation and support behind the policy was "diffuse and transitory." As a result, according to Friedman, it became dominated by special interests.[75]

Friedman argued that the public housing projects exacerbated the worst forms of social and familial breakdown associated with poorer and disadvantaged neighborhoods more explicitly than Hayek. Advocates of public housing had believed that decent living conditions would have a positive effect on juvenile delinquency or even eliminate it. On the contrary, Friedman argued that

the program in many instances has precisely the opposite effect, entirely aside from its failures to improve *average* housing conditions. The income limitations quite properly imposed for the occupancy of public housing at subsidized rentals have led to a very high density of "broken" families—in particular, divorced or widowed mothers with children. Children of broken families are especially likely to be "prob-lem" children and a high concentration of such children is likely to be increase juvenile delinquency. One manifestation has been the very ad-verse effect on schools in the neighborhood of a public housing project. Whereas a school can readily absorb a few "problem" children it is very difficult for it to absorb a large number. Yet in some cases, broken fami-lies are a third or more of the total in a public housing project and the project may account for a majority of the children in the school. Had these families been assisted through cash grants, they would have been spread much more thinly through the community.[76]

Though Friedman himself holds back from judgment or criticism of the way poorer people lived their lives, the associations that he employs would become a staple of conservative welfare reformers in subsequent decades. The phrases "dependency culture," "welfare moms," and "broken families and communities" trip readily off Republican and Conservative politicians' tongues in Congress or Parliament. Friedman's ideas, especially for vouch-ers as the best means of providing assistance to those in need, would trickle slowly into policy debates in the 1960s and 1970s, drip-fed by the neoliberal network of think tanks and politicians into the political mainstream.

The slow move to create housing vouchers in the United States to replace public housing began in the mid-seventies with the creation of the Section 8 Existing program of housing subsidy. More broadly, as we will see, Hayek's and Friedman's ideas had influenced urban policy analysts such as Stuart Butler, an originator of the idea of urban enterprise zones to regenerate the inner cities.

The Reagan Administration

The Reagan administration completed the federal government's withdrawal from public housing during the 1980s. President Carter had continued the shift toward an increased role for the private sector in addressing housing needs. Reagan, like Thatcher, went much further. As we have seen, during the 1970s, HUD came under increased pressure over the management of its housing programs. In an assessment of HUD's performance in the adminis-tration of the Section 8 program, the U.S. General Accounting Office, a congressional supervisory body, criticized the department harshly. The report described HUD as inefficient, not sufficiently aware of its responsibility to keep down costs, and, most damning of all, not successful at getting federal aid to those most in need of it. HUD issued a firm rebuttal of the charges and, in a question that reflected the choice at hand for U.S. policy direction in 1980, asked whether "a program which combines a production subsidy for new housing with a rent subsidy to enable low income families to live in that new housing [is] too costly and troublesome to be politically and socially desirable."[77] To this question, the incoming Republican administration answered a resounding yes. Public provision and subsidy were to come under ever greater scrutiny by policymakers for their value to the taxpayer.

The most important and comprehensive elaboration of President Reagan's approach to housing was his Commission on Housing's report, published in 1982. It echoed many of the contemporary themes in British Conservative Party policy under Margaret Thatcher (see below). The key principles, laid out at the beginning, were:

fiscal responsibility and monetary stability in the economy,
encourage free and deregulated housing markets,
rely on the private sector,
recognize a continuing role of government to address the housing
    needs of the poor,
direct programs toward people rather than structures, and
assume maximum freedom of housing choice.[78]

The same commitment to choice, private markets, economic and fiscal responsibility, and providing for individuals rather than institutions is in evidence here as in the British Conservative policy statements of the time. However, the core policy proposal was for a program of housing payments or vouchers. According to neoliberal policy analyst Stuart Butler, who had moved from Britain to work at the Washington, D.C.–based Heritage Foundation in 1979, these were "techniques to give people market power that didn't have it before, to function in a market."[79]

The report identified affordability for the poorest as the greatest housing problem in the United States, and the Section 8 New Construction program, which had been in operation since the housing act of 1974, was criticized for being too inefficient and expensive. There was an adequate supply of good-quality housing, the report found, but people could not afford it. Instead of an expansion of the Section 8 New Construction program, the report pointed out,

> The primary national need is not for massive production of new apart-ments for the poor, but for income supplements that will enable low-income families to live in available, decent housing at a cost that they can afford. . . . The primary purpose of Federal housing programs should be to help people not to build projects.[80]

Friedman's arguments were now government policy. To this end, the balance of Section 8 would be redirected toward its existing housing assistance pro-gram, while a conversion to vouchers was encouraged for most tenants.[81] In addition, the administration proposed adding a housing component to the existing Community Development Block Grant mechanism so it could bet-ter target limited resources at the poorest, who were in greatest need. Os-tensibly, the idea behind the block grants was to decentralize housing policy decisions in similar fashion as the British Labour Party's HIPs in Britain. In a survey carried out by the U.S. General Accounting Office, the report sug-gested that many local officials were aware of the hidden traps behind such a policy:

> Block grants for housing would give local governments greater discre-tion and flexibility in designing and implementing housing programs. Many local housing officials do not want these increased responsibili-ties if federal funding decreases.[82]

The problem, of course, was that this was exactly what the administration planned—to cut funds. Between 1981 and 1989 HUD's share of the total U.S. budget fell from 4.59 percent to 1.31 percent.[83]

In 1988, the MIT Housing Policy Project published a series of reports that exposed some of the fallacies and failures of the Reagan years. Housing policy analyst Anthony Downs, author of one of the most incisive of these reports, criticized the administration in diplomatic terms in a report that outlined an alternative strategy for housing policy. However, if the tone was polite, the content was unforgiving. First, Downs pointed to the problem of a lack of investment:

> Any national Housing Policy that effectively copes with the nation's major housing problems—especially those of low-income households—will require large-scale government subsidies of both new housing construction and the incomes of poor households. There are no inexpensive ways to solve the nation's housing problems.[84]

He pointed to the need for 200,000 more affordable households each year to meet the chronic housing shortage in the United States, as well as maintain five million existing units and ensure that existing contracts under Section 8 were renewed. Second, the most pressing current problem remained affordability, he argued, which, as we have seen, was Reagan's top priority six years earlier. Third, Downs suggested that the increased presence and distress of the homeless, whose numbers and visibility had grown during the course of the 1980s, were reaching a crisis point. Allowances, vouchers, or supplements to the least well-off, Downs insisted, ought to be the policy priority when government funds were scarce. Resources should be diverted from other types of prospective homeowners such as first-time buyers. He also pointed to the persistence of racial discrimination and segregation in housing. A renewed commitment to provision for low-income groups was essential if the most severe social and economic problems of inequality and deprivation were to be reversed.

MIT housing policy experts Langley Keyes and Denise DiPasquale also argued, in another report published by the MIT Housing Policy Project that year, that affordability had not been adequately addressed by the Republican administrations. They pointed out that only 28 percent of those eligible for assistance under the various programs had actually received help. In fact, the affordability crisis had got much worse because use restrictions on subsidized housing under Section 8 and other programs were expiring, which meant that housing stock was at risk of being lost and not replaced. Ageing public housing, meanwhile, required massive investment to remain viable, and low-rent private stock was being lost to "demolition and condominium conversion."[85] In sum, the Reagan administration had succeeded in driving back what remained of the government commitment to the public provision of affordable housing. But the affordability crisis had not been solved by the turn to the private sector. In fact, the opposite had occurred.

Council House Privatization: The Right to Buy Scheme

Under Labour, and throughout the 1970s, local councils had been able to sell off housing stock at their discretion where demand existed.[86] The earliest examples of council house sales occurred in the interwar years, but advocates were "prominent" by the mid-1960s.[87] By the 1970s there were two very separate issues at play in relation to council housing. The first was the image problem created by the high-profile failures of the high-rise estates. Second, and partly as a response to the first issue, there was a larger policy question about how best to prioritize increased home ownership. The Conservative policy in the 1970s became more radical than Labour's quiet toleration of council house sales in government had been.

By the time of Thatcher's election as party leader in 1975, the Conservative Party was beginning to move toward a wholesale advocacy of council house sales to local authority tenants as of right. For instance, Conservative policy analyst Angela Killick, writing for the Tory think tank the Bow Group, argued in 1976:

> Many Socialists vehemently object to selling council houses. They argue that if a council tenant buys his house the stock of rented accommodation is reduced by one. They seem to overlook that simultaneously the demand for rented accommodation is also reduced by one so there is no net effect, except that one person now has the tenure of his choice.[88]

Killick also called for 70 percent ownership rates and less centralization, with more autonomy returning to local communities. She dismissed the problem of homelessness as usually being a temporary or foreign phenomenon. In these respects, she anticipated the policies of Thatcher's governments. Killick also raised, in a position typical of the Conservative Party at the time, the "fundamental and political point of what the role of local authorities should be in housing, and whether that role should be reduced or redirected."[89]

While pamphlets and reports from Conservatives such as Killick indicate the more expansive thrust of right-wing thinking vis-à-vis the sale of council housing, her concern for increased decentralization reveals a further dimension of continuity between the policies of Labour's 1977 HIP strategy and the Conservatives. In repeated policy statements from the 1980s, the Conservatives proposed similar ideas to devolve power and decision making from local authorities to local communities or arrogate them back to central government. First, in 1980, the Conservatives announced plans to introduce a tenants' charter, which set down rights for tenants living in public and social housing. Second, homeownership was maintained as the central plank of government housing policy, as it had been since the 1960s under both Labour and Conservative governments. Third, the Thatcher government actually witnessed an expansion of central control of local authorities through rate capping—rates were the local property taxes in Britain at the time—and the large-scale transfer of housing assistance from local housing authorities to individuals through the introduction of a program of housing allowances. This marked the national roll-out of experiments with rental allowances that had continued through the 1970s under Labour. The Conservatives therefore expanded and consolidated these trends and covered them in a thick coating of ideological paint.

Thatcher's policy of council house sales was seen as the key element in the establishment of former Conservative prime minister Anthony Eden's cherished ideal, the transformation of Britain into a "property owning democracy." The slogan was used by Thatcher and her ministers and became central to the way in which policies such as the Right to Buy program were marketed and presented to Parliament and the British public. Housing featured prominently in the 1979 Conservative Party manifesto. Though ostensibly a rejection of ideological motivations, the opening passage is nevertheless an apocalyptic affirmation of the Conservative Party's break with the policies of social democratic consensus that had characterized the politics of Conservative governments from Winston Churchill through Harold Macmillan to Edward Heath:

For me, the heart of politics is not political theory, it is people and how they want to live their lives. No one who has lived in this country during the last five years can fail to be aware of how the balance of our society has been increasingly tilted in favour of the State at the expense of individual freedom. This election may be the last chance we have to reverse that process, to restore the balance of power in favour of the people.[90]

The 1979 manifesto included a page and a half on housing under the heading "Helping the Family." Criticizing Labour policies of nationalization, the state ownership of industry, it stated that "to most people ownership means first and foremost a home of their own."[91] A number of policies were intended to encourage a rise in homeownership. In the context of its wider economic policy plans for large tax cuts, the Party planned to introduce shared purchase schemes that would help first-time buyers get mortgages through part payment in anticipation of greater future earnings.

In another echo of a key tenet of Conservative philosophy, reduced public spending, the manifesto argued that as "it costs about three times as much to subsidise a new council house as it does to give tax relief to a home buyer, there could well be a substantial saving to the taxpayer."[92] The manifesto underlined the interconnection of housing policy and larger economic policy. Housing policy was to be linked to a program of cuts in public expenditure and borrowing, another departure that represented the dominance of neoliberal economic orthodoxy at the heart of Thatcher's approach to social policy. As Peter Malpass and Alan Murie have suggested, a "policy built on ideology and electoral calculations also served to contribute massively to the government's taxation and monetary objectives."[93] Finally, the manifesto focused on the proposed expansion of the sale of council houses under the Right to Buy program, the flagship policy of the Conservative Party's platform of 1979. The Conservatives proposed to make the Right to Buy scheme near universal and available at discounted rates according to the length of a tenant's occupancy.[94] The party also proposed to make 100 percent mortgages available to tenants to buy their houses. Independent social housing associations were also encouraged to sell to their tenants. Another important development was the already mentioned tenants' charter, which would give council house tenants "new rights and responsibilities." The final element of the Conservative housing policy was to "make better use of our existing stock of houses."[95] The Conservatives' housing policy prioritized four key areas: increasing rates of homeownership, the encouragement of repairs and improvement of existing stock, the subsidization and incentivization of the private sector, and the concentration of public resources on those in greatest need.

During the parliamentary debates on the 1980 Housing Bill, the Conservative minister for housing and construction John Stanley declared it the "the most far reaching and fundamental piece of housing legislation of the postwar period."[96] He went on, the "Right-to-Buy and the tenants' charter are among the most important social advances that have been made this century."[97] However, these claims were accompanied by a concerted government attack on the predominantly Labour-controlled local authorities. The strategy was to break Labour's local authority housing dominance and hopefully win over a new constituency whose loyalty would be transferred to the Conservatives. The government did not just make arguments *for* the legislation. Stanley contrasted his party *against* the Labour Party, which felt it had to oppose the policy. He attempted to cloak the opposition's arguments against the Right to Buy program in terms of its attachment to state socialism:

> I noticed the recent comments of Mr. Rose, a 60 year old Labour supporter, who has been prevented from buying his council house in Birmingham. He has lived in that house since 1944. I thought that he echoed the feelings of a great many people when he said:
>
> > "I have supported Labour since I was old enough to vote but now I am disgusted with the party. I feel totally let down. . . . There is nothing wrong with a working man owning his own house."
>
> Mr Rose is absolutely right. There is nothing wrong with a working man owning his own house. What is wrong is the Labour Party's policy of denying people the opportunity to do so.[98]

The manifesto, too, had criticized the previous Labour Government and Labour local authorities for obstructing the potential for people to "buy their own homes." The use of language in these attacks on Labour is illuminating. Strictly speaking, council houses were a crucial part of the local public sector's assets and revenue. They were nearly all occupied by renters, so it was deliberately misleading to suggest they belonged to the tenants. More accurately, housing policy was to be the government's first major privatization of the public sector. The policy was less based on any solid policy evidence about quality, quantity or needs than founded on a theory about the superiority of the market. Arguably, the Conservatives actively pursued a policy aimed at the residualization of the public sector in Britain so that it would occupy a position similar to that witnessed in the United States.

Despite the overall trend of Britain moving in the direction of the United States in terms of housing policy, the influence went the other way with two specific policy proposals, the Right to Buy policy itself and enterprise zones. The Reagan administration supported congressional efforts by the congressman for western New York, Jack Kemp, the future President George H. W. Bush's HUD secretary, to introduce a kind of right-to-buy initiative in the United States. He picked up the idea from Britain when he visited in the early 1980s. Madsen Pirie, of the Adam Smith Institute, explained that Kemp wanted to watch a pre-season American Football game played in London by the Denver Broncos and "wanted to use the opportunity to justify the trip." Pirie and his brother Eamonn, the joint heads of the ASI, were asked to set up a meeting on housing to share ideas. The event was a mixed success, according to Pirie, because "ostensibly he was coming over to study British council house sales but in fact his speech consisted of, as I recollect from memory, giving the arguments why something should be done for poor people in public housing," which, he continued, meant that the "audience of experts grew slightly restless because they all knew this and they wanted to hear about methods and techniques and they didn't get it."[99] By attempting to imitate Thatcher's policies, Kemp hoped that a million people would buy their first homes through the scheme. Kemp's legislative package coupled the sale of public housing, in another echo of the Conservative approach, with greater local autonomy and management for tenants.

The Right to Buy policy was a very good example of a failed transatlantic import from the British context to the United States that was propagated by neoliberal politicians and think tanks. According to Heritage Foundation vice president Stuart Butler, although the idea did not really translate very well to the United States, it was part of a larger discussion policy discussion in the early 1980s about how to run public housing. Butler recounts that "there was a documentary done [by the Heritage Foundation] specifically on British Telecom which included the sale of public housing and Jaguar and so on, which we'd show on the Hill [Capitol Hill, the seat of the U.S. Congress]." Butler continued that the Heritage Foundation's leaders "were very much involved in showing in detail how it was done and that certainly did have an impact very much on the way people looked at it," and he concluded "there was a lot of clear interaction" between British and U.S. policymakers on housing policy during the 1980s.[100]

For Butler, Kemp's tenant-management legislation was more successful in the American context. Butler argued that debates about giving tenants more control and ownership over their communities exposed some of the more patrician and patronizing attitudes of liberal Democrats:

> There was tenant-management legislation in the 1980s which was led by conservatives—Dick Armey and Kemp was involved in that and so on. They were fighting for changes in the public housing laws to permit tenants to own on the floor of the Congress, with the Democrats, you know, saying that inner-city people aren't able to look after them, to handle these things. One thing I was involved in was actually bringing in from local public housing projects, people to sit in the gallery to jeer at the Democrats. This was all very targeted to change the whole discussion of housing and also urban policy which was successful for a long period. There has been a certain amount of going back because, you know, you now have these ideas [for urban regeneration] where you build a ball park if you're in Washington and so on, convention centers . . . has made something of a comeback, but nothing to the degree that was conventional wisdom in the sixties of, you know, just massive [slum] clearances . . . where you build high hotels and a convention center and you do this and pretend that you've turned a neighborhood around.[101]

Thus, for Butler, despite its failure in the U.S. context, both the Right to Buy scheme and the tenant-management scheme helped change the debate around urban policy, which had, up to that point, been based on strangely people-free programs such as urban renewal and slum clearance. These were the policies attacked in the *Federal Bulldozer* (1964) by Martin Anderson, who by the early 1980s was Reagan's chief domestic policy adviser.

Britain's Right to Buy policy after 1979 was pushed to a large and varied group of council tenants of different social classes, many of whom earned decent wages and could afford to buy their homes. Many council houses were desirable detached houses in attractive neighborhoods; others, such as Tachbrook Estate or parts of Churchill Gardens Estate in London's Pimlico, were prize-winning flats in prime locations. The situation in the United States was very different, for the public housing population was already outcast, containing as it did large groups of single-parent families, the unemployed, and elderly people, and most U.S. public housing was in high-rise projects in the inner city. According to Stuart Butler, the appeal of tenant-management schemes in the United States rested on a stronger tradition of local community-based organizations:

> In Britain, if you look at the big high rises, built in the fifties and sixties, in London, I don't know whether it [Right to Buy] has been that successful there either and you certainly can't say it's changed the neighborhood in that sense. Here we were talking about more of that kind of housing so it's very difficult. But tenant-management has been a little different. That is not, of course, what Thatcher did. But that has been a different thing and it's much more in line with the general pattern in the US for community-based organizations. It is essentially the co-op model but that was built on a much stronger tradition here in low-income neighborhoods of strong neighborhood-based organizations, particularly church-based organizations which is, you know, really much less common in Britain. To the extent that it has been successful, it has been around that. But we didn't have the large blue collar, decent housing that, you know, you could really quickly move over and have big changes [in housing tenure] that you had in Britain. That was never a real possibility. What we have of course, instead, unfortunately, is sub-prime structures. But that is a very different strategy. But that would be more comparable actually in the sense of the group of people being aimed at which you could do through council-house sales at a discount in the UK.[102]

Britain's good-quality public housing relative to that in the United States was largely a result of the building programs of the interwar period and then the postwar 1945–51 Labour government, characterized by Nye Bevan's insistence on the high specifications for new construction, which were proposed for all public housing by the Dudley Committee during World War II. These standards were then superseded by the specifications, now proposed for all homes, public and private, set out by the Parker Morris Committee's report in 1961, made mandatory by the Labour government in new towns in 1967 and for local authorities in 1969. The Parker Morris standards were abandoned under Thatcher in 1981. The British experience was also instructive in terms of the mixture of housing tenure and social class. Consequently, it was harder for large groups of people to become as marginalized as they were in the United States. For all these reasons, as Michael Katz has pointed out, "In the end, during Kemp's four years as secretary [1989–93], HUD sold only 135 units to tenants."[103] The policy had failed in a country where public housing itself had become an endangered species.

Transatlantic Transmissions: Reagan's Enterprise Zones

A more successful example of transatlantic policy exchange than the sale of public housing was the enterprise zone. The policy idea originated in Britain and was successfully imported into the United States by Stuart Butler of the Heritage Foundation. It became the centerpiece of Reagan's urban policy and provided a positive agenda for the Republicans on poverty and deprivation to go with his administration's plans for tax and spending cuts. Enterprise zones were based on a new conception of deregulation, reliance on business investment, and experimentation with new forms of public-private partnership. But the central element was to incentivize the private sector to invest in neighborhoods that had been left behind. The market was to provide an infusion of the profit motive to revive the entrepreneurial spirit believed to be latent in the worst parts of America's inner cities.

The idea for enterprise zones in Britain came from the urban planner Peter Hall in the late 1960s. Hall co-authored a piece in the British magazine *New Society* in 1969 that suggested a bonfire of controls as a way of releasing the energy and vitality of blighted communities.[104] The authors proposed

> a precise and carefully controlled experiment in non-planning . . . to seize on a few appropriate zones in the country, which are subject to a

characteristic range of pressures, and use them as launchpads for Non-Plan. At the least, one would find out what people want; at the most one might discover the hidden style of mid-20th century Britain.[105]

Inspired by the experience of Hong Kong and Singapore, Hall thought that such an approach might work as a "last-ditch solution" in certain parts of especially postindustrial cities and urban areas.[106] By the late seventies, according to Hall, the idea's time had come, as economic expansion had long been replaced by stagflation and chronic unemployment, especially in the worst parts of British cities. He outlined the main features of the "Non-Plan" in an article in which he later reflected on the experience of enterprise zones in Britain:

> This radical solution would include three elements. First each area would be completely open to immigration of entrepreneurs and capital—meaning no immigration controls. Second, it "would be based on fairly shameless free enterprise"; "Bureaucracy would be kept to the absolute minimum." Third, residence would be based on choice, because the area would effectively be outside the United Kingdom's normal legislation and controls."[107]

Hall launched his idea in a major speech to the Royal Town Planning Institute in Chester in June 1977.

The policy was taken up by the Conservative Party, whose leaders were excited to be able to find such an idea from someone like Hall, perceived to be on the left of the political spectrum. Keith Joseph, Thatcher's closest ally in charge of policy and research when in opposition and a cabinet minister after 1979, initially championed enterprise zones, declaring, at an event at the ASI in 1978, that there would be a series of pilot "demonstration projects," where the "queen's writ shall not run."[108] But the idea was given real impetus by the shadow chancellor, Geoffrey Howe, who backed the enterprise zone concept enthusiastically in a speech in the Isle of Dogs, part of London's former industrial east end, in the same year. Howe repeatedly pushed the plan on Margaret Thatcher in a series of letters before the party adopted it as their policy before the election in 1979.[109] Enterprise zones were introduced in 1980. Peter Hall wryly describes the legislation:

The official scheme, which came out of the Local Government Planning and Land Act 1980 and the Finance Act 1980, allowed Local Authorities, New Towns, or Urban Development Corporations to prepare
an Enterprise Zone scheme for a site in their area, within which there
would be a mixture of fiscal benefits and administrative simplifications
for ten years from designation. Specifically, these zones would enjoy
a simplified land-use planning regime with minimal conditions like
health and safety; new and existing commercial and industrial enter-
prises would be exempt from rates (property tax) and from a tax (later
rescinded everywhere) on development of land; they could also off-
set expenditure on buildings against Corporation Tax. There would be
greatly reduced requirements for industrial training and for statistical
reporting.[110]

Many of the most radical elements of Hall's original plan, though, had been
omitted, such as "the free migration of labor, the encouragement of immigrant entrepreneurs, the general freedom from mainstream legislation including removal of protection under the Employment Protection Acts." Eleven
sites were originally sanctioned in the first round in 1980–81, including, most
famously, London Docklands, with a further thirteen coming in the second
tranche in 1983–84.[111] According to Hall, it was an exercise in how to turn a
radical idea into something harmless.[112]

As we have seen, public policy, the racist machinations of many local communities and public and private institutions, and the flight of business and investment had made large areas of the urban United States untouchable. Many
inner-city neighborhoods were effectively considered no-go areas by affluent
whites, while for very different reasons prosperous suburbs were very often no-
go areas for blacks. For example, President Jimmy Carter's *National Urban Policy Report* from 1980 pointed out that blacks were disproportionately concentrated in the city despite the general trend of people leaving for the suburbs. In
every region (Northeast, North Central, West, and South) blacks scored badly
in the index of suburbanization.[113] The official view was articulated in graphic
terms in President Reagan's Commission on Housing report of 1982:

Public housing programs designed to help the big-city poor had suffered visible failures: huge structures rose above the cityscapes like

faceless warehouses, and with the passage of time the communities clustered within them were demoralized, blighted by crime, and frustrated by the failure of their expectations.[114]

A more accurate description of what had happened to public housing since the 1930s has been suggested by Delores Hayden. As "public housing became reconceptualized as a publicly funded resource for coping with the needs of the most desperate city-dwellers, public neighborhoods inevitably became treated as storage facilities rather than communities."[115] Inner-city public housing and their majority poor, predominantly minority ethnic, populations were stuck in a web of racism, segregation, business and other powerful interest groups and an often hostile array of government agencies.

Stuart Butler brought the enterprise zones idea with him to the United States as a new way of tackling these seemingly insoluble issues when he moved from the ASI in London to work for the Heritage Foundation in 1979. It was another way of changing the terms of discussion surrounding urban problems:

Enterprise zones . . . challenged orthodoxy about how you get urban development, everything from the "Model Cities" and the Urban Renewal, or as they used to call it, "negro removal." That was the term they used in the early seventies because that's what it was, I mean, literally tearing down and rooting people out. That's what they did in Detroit. . . . This is what was going on.[116]

How did enterprise zones in the United States come about? In the British context, enterprise zones were conceived as a way of injecting new life into areas that, for the most part, had fallen into disuse and dereliction owing to abandonment and the flight of old heavy industry. In the United States, Butler imagined a means of revitalizing run-down residential neighborhoods. According to Butler, he was inspired by Hayek and urban theorist Jane Jacobs in his application of the British version to the context of the United States:

The basic idea in Britain was to take derelict parts of cities, places like the East End of London, bombed-out areas, where really there weren't a lot of people living and to make them clear away, in some cases literally clear away what was there and say: why don't we just basically clear away the regulations, the impediments and taxes and encourage business to come in and just turn these places around. What Peter Hall was saying, because he was the "unplanning planner" . . . got a lot of interest, and Geoffrey Howe had taken this on and I said OK, well, let me take that and turn it into something different, something which is not quite the same. I'd go to somewhere like the South Bronx, which is not like the East End of London, it's not an area which is bombed-out. . . . No! There are lots of people there.[117]

Butler's focus was on how to tap into the entrepreneurial spirit that he claimed already existed in these neighborhoods. Instead of creating a zone for business to come into and develop, he wanted to foster new kinds of partnerships that would help people living there become fruitful contributors rather than, in some cases, out-and-out criminals.

Rather than make it an industrial sort of strategy. No, let's look at what it would take to get the sort of informal economy that's there, you know, people doing things for cash, people doing shady things, sometimes criminal things and let's create an environment where it becomes much more attractive for people, say, who are working off cars and running a chop shop, you actually open a garage repair shop and it will do well because you know how to do this stuff—you know, go legit . . . Let's take the ground floor of a public housing block and make it literally a shop and let the guy just set up shop and go legit. You know there are rules, things like, you know you are not allowed to mix commercial with residential, well, we'll change that. There's a tax lien on this building, you know, no one can do anything unless they pay a hundred thousand dollars in taxes, you know, while the place is deteriorating. Let's just wipe—let's just start all over again. So, that was my innovation. I took an idea and Americanized it and I think that is the key to how a lot of these things work. You take something and, you don't import it perfectly. You bring it in and alter it.

He wanted to create an atmosphere in these neighborhoods that built on and opened up the potential spontaneous power of individuals allied to untrammeled market mechanisms. For Butler, this drew on Hayek's critique of planning and belief in the vibrancy of markets, which he connected with Jacobs's ideas about public neighborhoods. He explains,

> The other thread in the whole enterprise zones thing was Jane Jacobs and her analysis of American cities which I had read and been completely convinced by. I got around to seeing this in practice, again, very Hayekian, unplanning, think about waves of change in a city. You know, don't think about what it is going to look like and try to build it from scratch so that you've got it in mind what it's going to look like in twenty years' time. No, set in motion dynamics—you don't know who is going to run the corner store ten years from now, but allow a corner store to be developed. So intellectually, I called it the equivalent of the western movement in America. If you look at pioneering and the history of that, you have this idea of the frontier. Things change when people interact with different circumstance, and over time things develop. I'm very much an American, my PhD is in American history, so I applied that notion, I applied that sort of idea that when you think of a city, you should think of waves of change all affected by how people react to what is the frontier. So, intellectually it had Hayekian roots and American roots.

Butler's ideas influenced conservatives such as Jack Kemp in Congress. But the idea also had a bipartisan feel, as it was jointly sponsored in the House of Representatives by Democratic congressman Robert Garcia and was supported by a number of local black community organizations.

The enterprise zone plan was successful in policy circles in the United States. Butler describes the process by which enterprise zones gained support beyond the academics and policy experts of the Heritage Foundation:

> I did a paper for Heritage in late '79, just laying out, would this be a good idea. [Jack] Kemp, in particular, picked up on this and then I started to talk to other people and traveling around the country and the administration and Reagan, when he ran in 1980. This essentially was his urban policy with housing vouchers for low-income people, both market mechanisms. He went to the South Bronx and was photographed there with Kemp, I think. I worked with the administration,

and they developed legislation that got very close to passage and then eventually became law in a more diluted way under Clinton. We had state enterprise zones created starting in Connecticut—again, it wasn't a pure version. But, one thing is, like a lot of these policy ideas it is not only the specific policy but it led to a change in the way people thought about inner cities, and this was very interesting to Americans because you have conservatives dealing with black inner-city organizations and saying, these people can actually—I mean, you don't have to remove these people. I mean this was counterintuitive to the pigeonholing press. It was just neat and interesting and bizarre as was the sale of public housing because we had exactly the same issue with that.[118]

The Reagan administration supported the Kemp-Garcia bill through Congress, but despite the White House's backing, the legislation failed to pass a Democratic Party–dominated Congress. It was defeated narrowly. However, many states introduced their own versions of enterprise zones, beginning with Louisiana in 1981, and during the Clinton administration a version of the idea was enacted, entitled Hope VI.

Hope VI, Urban Regeneration, and the Third Way

The Hope VI housing program, begun in 1993, illustrated the accommodations with the new, neoliberal-influenced housing policies begun under President Reagan, made by the Democratic Party led by President Bill Clinton. Similar community development and mixed-tenure experiments in Britain, such as the idea of "stakeholder housing," illustrate that a similar process occurred as Labour party leader and prime minister Tony Blair pursued a "Third Way" initiative in housing policy in the 1990s. The Third Way represented an attempt by left or liberal policymakers, led by Clinton and Blair, to accommodate the free market and the goal of social justice.[119] They were often criticized as nebulous or meaningless but affordable housing and urban policy offer an example of a concrete attempt by Third Way policymakers to respond to the supposed successes of the free market during the 1980s.

In 1988, the National Housing Task Force, appointed by Congress, produced a report that highlighted the huge division in the United States between the haves and the have-nots. It struck a discordant note with the policy outlook of the Reagan and Bush administrations in its call to arms. America was very rich, it argued, and yet inequality was stretching the bounds of acceptability for a civilized and compassionate society. The report explicitly rejected the laissez-faire policies of the 1980s. The "housing problems of the poor," it stated, "are beyond solution by the market system alone and have fallen outside the focused attention of society."[120] Returning to the commitments of the 1949 Housing Act, the task force argued that while most—two-thirds—of Americans had enjoyed the benefits of a vast amount of federal assistance in the acquisition of their homes, a large minority, especially blacks, had been left out. It recommended what it called a "Housing Opportunity Program" to "foster and stimulate state and local initiatives to develop, renovate, and conserve low-income housing."[121]

The members of the MIT Housing Policy Project already mentioned, Downs and Keyes and Di Pasquale, also argued in the same year as the congressional report appeared that social policy needed to be holistic, with its various dimensions joined up, to achieve the aim of a decent and affordable place to live for everyone. In a sign that the terms of the agenda for housing policy for low- and moderate-income groups, and as a response to the findings of its National Housing Task Force, the Democratically controlled Congress established the National Commission on Severely Distressed Public Housing in 1989. The commission concluded that public housing "systematically created neighbourhoods of isolation, alienation and fear, devoid of any meaningful community social interaction."[122] The commission estimated that of the 1.3 million public housing units in the United States, roughly 86,000 qualified as seriously distressed and required a comprehensive approach to deal with the endemic problems that existed on these developments. The commission's conclusions led to the enactment of Hope VI, or Urban Revitalization Demonstration Program, by Congress in the autumn of 1992, just before Bill Clinton's election as president. The program's stated objectives were as follows:

> To improve the living environment for residents of severely distressed public housing through the demolition, rehabilitation, reconfiguration, or replacement of obsolete projects (or portions thereof);

to revitalize sites on which such public housing projects are located and
   contribute to the improvement of the surrounding neighborhood;
to provide housing that will avoid or decrease the concentration of very
   low-income families; and
to build sustainable communities.[123]

Congress appropriated $5 billion for the program, which was supposed to fund local housing agency plans covering five hundred units with grants of up to $50 million. The general aim was to demolish the worst high-rise, high-density projects and replace them with mixed-income, low-density developments that would foster community building and social capital. The idea was to reduce concentrated poverty, and under Clinton, the program developed a "New Urbanist" feel. According to housing policy analyst Edward Goetz,

> The new urbanism informs both community design and architecture. In the realm of landscape design, the emphasis is on narrower streets, sidewalks, parks, and public gathering places, and a street layout that integrates residents rather than isolating them. Identifiable, clearly demarcated (and therefore defensible) space (such as lawns marked by hedges or small fences) also produces greater watchfulness of outdoor areas.[124]

Key to the approach encouraged by HUD during the 1990s was the balancing of rights and responsibilities in local communities, a key dimension of Third Way thought.[125] Consequently, there was a complementary push to attack some of the cultural problems associated with poverty and deprivation by emphasizing personal responsibility in, for example, efforts to drive out drugs and other forms of criminal behavior from public housing and the new Hope VI developments.

In tandem with Hope VI, the Clinton administration encouraged Community Development Corporations (CDCs), which had first emerged in the late 1960s. CDCs are nonprofit groups that band together to revitalize low- and moderate-income communities by providing job opportunities and affordable housing. President George H. W. Bush acknowledged the contribution of such organizations in 1990 with the passage of the Low-Income Housing Preservation and Resident Homeownership Act, which set aside money for nonprofits. CDCs are usually composed of a mix of "citizens, clergy and businesspeople" and operate through public agencies and local institutions. Urban historian Alexander Von Hoffman has described them thus:

> The small inner-city organizations would do almost anything to improve the desperate situation of their neighborhoods. They pressed the government to provide the city services that had been withdrawn. They organized crime watches and coordinated community policing with the local precinct. Many built new homes or took over and fixed up old buildings, threw out drug dealers, renovated apartments, and rented to low-income tenants. Some groups helped to start or expand businesses. Others set up programs for childcare, job training and drug rehabilitation. Some groups introduced medical clinics to their neighborhoods. A few even operated schools.[126]

Many such organizations were funded under Hope VI. However, behind these initiatives was the objective of bringing in private philanthropy and investment. Through the Local Initiatives Support Corporation, a nonprofit body that aimed to revitalize urban neighborhoods and was supported by the Ford Foundation, CDCs also managed to benefit from selling tax credits via the Low-Income Housing Tax Credit, making them enormously attractive to potential investors. The buzzwords were partnership and revitalization. The 1990s saw an explosion of CDCs, with, according to Van Hoffman, more than four thousand founded since 1990. In mid-decade, CDCs were producing around sixty thousand dwellings a year.[127]

The British Labour Party's policy in the 1990s toward low- and moderate-income groups, like those of Clinton and the new Democrats, was structured around the themes of partnership, sustainability, diversity, and choice. Initially, the government released £1.3 billion through the Capital Receipts Initiative in the first three years of the government, to be directed toward regeneration of existing estates and developments.[128] This was augmented by a further £3.9 billion devoted to local authorities to tackle the backlog of renovation work and improvements necessary in many of the 1.5 million council homes that remained under local authority control. There was also a focus on "joined-up" delivery of housing and related services through the better management of social policy objectives. To this end, the Labour Government established a Housing Inspectorate to supervise standards in service provision. This holistic approach was evidenced in the four themes of Labour's new policy agenda: to tackle the problems of social exclusion, to improve the quality of investment strategies, to improve service delivery to consumers, and to promote public-private partnerships in housing delivery.

Between 1997and 2000, the Labour government, in a conscious echo of Hope VI and other Clinton-era housing policies, sought to develop an agenda that combined mixed-tenure, low-density public housing with support services. But this program did not initially have the resources and investment to take off beyond a change in emphasis, as the new government was committed to the strict Conservative Party spending plans that had been put in place by Chancellor Kenneth Clarke. However, the future thrust of Labour policy was clear: it would be built according to principles similar to those witnessed in the United States. The government's white paper, *Planning for the Communities of the Future*, stated, "the government is committed to creating mixed communities, wherever appropriate, rather than areas of exclusively high-cost or low-cost housing."[129] But as Ben Jupp put it in 2000, "the rhetoric certainly runs far ahead of actual practice."[130]

Conclusion

There is much evidence of policy continuity between the Democratic Carter administration and James Callaghan's Labour government and their Conservative and Republican Party successors, which complicates any simple idea of revolutionary change after 1979. What certainly changed was the tone and ideological focus of government policy under Thatcher and Reagan. Even where legislation had clear antecedents in the actions of previous administrations, the programs of the new regimes were stridently proclaimed. Where previous policies had been based, according to President Reagan's 1982 Commission on Housing, on "a common belief that all problems would be solved if only the government would set the right goals and enforce the right policies," now the report triumphantly asserted "an entirely different belief: that the genius of the market economy, freed of the distortions forced by government housing policies and regulations that swung erratically from loving to hostile, can provide for housing far better than federal programs."[131] From now on, in terms of American and British housing policy, the assumption would be that "nothing works unless the private sector works."[132]

By the late 1980s and early 1990s, important policy changes had occurred as a result of the influence of neoliberal ideas in the realm of affordable housing and urban policy. A new set of policy paradigms about the superiority of markets in the generation of positive social outcomes had been set in place, if not yet permanently, then at least forcefully. The Labour Party, in opposition throughout the 1980s and 1990s until 1997, was forced to accept that council house sales had been popular and successful, at least for those who had benefited from the cheap rates, which by 1990 meant more than a million people.[133] In the United States, the Democrats were on the defensive, and public housing advocates, as in Britain, were notable for their absence. First, the case for low taxes had marginalized those who had argued for large-scale housing construction in the 1980s. Second, the residualization of public housing had been completed in the United States and was arguably well under way in the UK as well. Third, the emphasis on home ownership had been accepted as central to housing policy strategies. In the United States, this aim had always been present, although by the late 1980s home-ownership rates had stalled for the first time in seventy years as a result of the affordability crisis.[134] Finally, the focus on the private sector and the market as a necessary engine driving housing policy was firmly established on both sides of the Atlantic, propagated through the transatlantic neoliberal network that was described in chapter 4.

The evidence for such a transformation is seen in the response of the Democratic and Labour Parties, in the administrations of Bill Clinton and Tony Blair during the 1990s, and their attempts to construct a Third Way in housing policy. The approach of HUD under Henry Cisneros and Andrew Cuomo, Clinton's two appointees as secretary, revealed three principles of what has been termed the Third Way—of the application of the market to social policy, balanced with social justice objectives. First, in the combination of resources and money with crackdowns on drugs and crime, the administration pushed an agenda that was based on the balance of rights and responsibilities, which was supposed to temper the stark reliance on the market. Investment and revitalization efforts were explicitly connected to personal responsibility and self-sufficiency on the part of beneficiaries. In this way, Hope

VI was aligned with the administration's primary social policy goal after 1994 of welfare reform. Second, at the core of Clinton's housing policies, drawing on themes that had been present in Democratic Party thinking since the ideas of maximum feasible participation and community action that underlay Lyndon Johnson's War on Poverty, was the idea of collaborative partnership, with a strong emphasis on the involvement of the private and voluntary sectors. Partnership working had also been a theme in Republican pronouncements on housing assistance, especially under President George H. W. Bush, and in many ways Clinton continued with an approach that crossed party lines by the 1990s. Finally, the requirement built into Hope VI that projects should provide an associated web of social services targeted to residents, as well as fitting in with the Welfare-to-Work policy agenda, marked the recognition of a holistic and community-based approach to the provision of housing that, as we have seen, had emerged in the late 1980s. These three areas, taken together, illustrate the dimensions of what Clinton and Blair came to call a Third Way approach to low- and moderate-income housing policy. The New Labour government after 1997 pursued similar approaches.

Whether the Third Way amounted to anything more than an accommodation with the market-dominated reforms of the 1970s and 1980s is open to doubt. In the United States, Clinton did not challenge the basic direction that had been taken by successive administrations since Johnson's Great Society toward forms of subsidy for poor householders to rent in the private sector. In the UK, the Blair government did not renew the state's commitment to construct large numbers of new affordable homes. Instead, in both countries the parameters of housing policy for low- and moderate-income families remained strictly limited to the revitalization of existing stock and subsidy for private rental. If the policies of Clinton and Blair could be said to have added anything distinctive, it was more rhetorical than real. Their policy language incorporated the ideals of community and sustainability, and while the limited successes of a program like Hope VI implied a potential for improvement, it is clear that such an improvement would not come without huge investment and a willingness to deal with *all* of the poorest citizens. It is equally true that the willingness, among politicians and public alike, did not exist.

Whatever attempts were made by Republican and Conservative administrations to encourage the private sector to provide low-income accommodation in the for-profit rental sector clearly failed. Reliance on market-based solutions did not resolve the severe problems of homelessness, poverty, and health in many communities on either side of the Atlantic. There was a resultant crisis of affordability in the United States and in Britain. Without state intervention to ensure the right level of provision according to need, this crisis worsened as the 1990s wore on. The role of the state in housing had changed fundamentally and was understood to have changed by 2000. Empowerment and rights and responsibilities were to be combined with markets and public/private/voluntary sector partnerships in mixed-tenure neighborhoods. The state's role had become that of an enabler and facilitator of people and communities within the strict limits of what governments could supposedly afford. The neoliberal faith in the market, epitomized by the ideas of Stuart Butler, had tempered the collectivist impulse in British and American social policy.

Conclusion

The Legacy of Transatlantic Neoliberalism

Faith-Based Policy

Neoliberalism transformed British, American, and global politics. At the dawn of the twenty-first century, the triumph of the free market was almost universally accepted by mainstream politicians, public officials, and civil servants. More important, the distinctive neoliberal brand of free market individualism had prevailed over alternative forms of managed market-based capitalism.

Neoliberalism was a radical form of individualism that was first generated before World War II in a reaction to New Liberalism, Progressivism, the New Deal, and the onset of Nazi and communist totalitarianism. Together, these strands were called "collectivism" by neoliberals. In 1947, economists surrounding Friedrich A. Hayek came together to form the Mont Pelerin Society. After this founding moment, neoliberals in Britain, Europe, and the United States responded to the large-scale social, political, and economic catastrophes of the interwar years and the onset of the Cold War by deepening and broadening their ideological project of countering the New Deal and social democracy with a creed based on free markets, deregulation, and limited government. Among publics and policymakers alike, the collective traumas of depression and war had fostered a strong belief in the necessity of welfare states and neo-Keynesian economic policies to curb the excesses of capitalism. After the 1960s, the trend in Britain and the United States toward bigger government and greater economic intervention continued at just the moment when the structural conditions that had supported their growth began to disappear. Consequently, the appropriateness of demand management and higher welfare spending as policy responses to the problems of the 1970s were called into question.

In the last third of the twentieth century, waves of globalization engendered a process of deindustrialization in many British and U.S. cities. Old industries such as coal mining and shipbuilding declined, and after a painful transition, new service-sector jobs sprang up in their place. In 1913, industry accounted for 44.8 percent of total employment in Britain and 29.3 percent in the United States. By 1984 the figure was 32.4 percent in Britain and 28 percent in the United States; those employed in services had meanwhile risen from 38.4 percent to 68.7 percent in the United States, and from 44.2 percent to 65 percent in Britain over the same period.[1] The new jobs tended not to be unionized, offered fewer benefits, and often paid barely minimum wage. Despite these drawbacks, such jobs were celebrated by free marketeers in the name of "flexible labor markets." At the same time, governments of the Left and Right enabled the globalization of capital through financial deregulation.

Between the 1950s and the 1980s, the GDP had more than doubled in Britain and almost doubled in the United States.[2] But during the last two decades of the century, inequality (the gap between rich and poor), poverty, and homelessness all increased.[3] Unemployment seemingly disappeared as a major problem in the immediate postwar years but returned with a vengeance after the 1970s. Inflation also reemerged before being cowed, in the United States at least, by the uncompromising policies of central bankers and pliant politicians in the early 1980s. In Britain, unemployment and inflation returned during another deep recession by the time Thatcher was forced from office in October 1990. During the 1980s and 1990s, large parts of the welfare state survived the ambitions of both the Thatcher and the Reagan administrations to cut them down.[4] In fact, government spending proved tenacious over the entire postwar period. It increased in the United States from $39 billion in 1949 to $1.3 trillion in 1990, and in Britain from almost £3.5 billion to £158 billion over the same period.[5]

In response to these shifts, neoliberal policy technicians such as Alan Greenspan and Nigel Lawson built on the electoral successes of their politically talented leaders and pushed forward an agenda based on a conviction that markets would free the individual from harmful interference by governments. Market-based reforms were supposed to produce greater efficiency by unleashing the power of human initiative. Markets would cost less and produce better social outcomes. This was because they better fitted real human motivations—self-interest and the individual pursuit of happiness. The trade unions therefore became an inimical force in society, in the neoliberal view, whose main effect was to "distort" the labor market. The citizen was really a consumer whose wants and needs—including the fundamental human needs of housing, health care, education, and pensions—could be satisfied better through the release of market forces.

The result was a conflation of technical policy analysis with ideological assertion, built on the assumption of the superiority of market mechanisms in dealing with any given policy issue. The larger philosophy of markets was forcefully packaged by the ideological entrepreneurs of the transatlantic neoliberal network. When the economic crises of the 1970s seemed to prove the breakdown of the postwar Keynesian settlement, therefore, neoliberal ideas were waiting in the wings. In Milton Friedman's words, "the role of thinkers I believe is primarily to keep options open, to have available alternatives, so when the brute force of events make a change inevitable, there is an alternative available to change it."[6] The neoliberal network was ready. A genuinely transatlantic enterprise, the network had by the 1980s become increasingly international through the efforts of such organizations as the Atlas Foundation and the Mont Pelerin Society. It connected think tanks, businessmen, academics, journalists, and politicians. Some think tanks, such as Ralph Harris's and Arthur Seldon's Institute of Economic Affairs, saw themselves as serious research establishments developing new policy applications for free market neoliberal ideas. Others, such as Leonard Read's Foundation for Economic Education, reproduced neoliberal ideas in cruder form and pitched them into the political mainstream.

The dynamic but above all cosmopolitan nature of neoliberal ideas ensured they would spread beyond their origins in interwar Vienna, Freiburg, and London. As Ed Crane, the president of the Cato Institute, put it, liberalism more easily transcends borders, while conservatism tends not to.[7] During its second phase, after 1945, neoliberalism moved from its specific anti-totalitarian and anti–New Deal roots to become a successful transatlantic political movement defined by a simple message: the superiority of markets over all forms of government intervention, or collectivism. My account has differed from others in treating neoliberalism as both an intellectual and a political movement for concrete social and economic change. It has moved beyond the characterization of neoliberalism either as a specific intellectual movement of the 1930s and 1940s or as an impersonal and global hegemonic force, to focus on how it developed and broke through politically.

More prosaically, transatlantic neoliberal politics successfully transformed the commonsense assumptions of policymakers in Britain and the United States when confronted with social and economic problems, especially in the years after Margaret Thatcher left office. A number of pronouncements became commonplace across the political spectrum, in the Democratic and Labour as well as the Conservative and Republican Parties: Consumers vote with their feet by buying some things and not others. Value for money is effectively delivered through the discipline of the market to satisfy consumer wants. An equilibrium is achieved through the price mechanism, which also acts as Hayek's information processor, guiding the activities of disparate sellers and producers. In other words, the market allocates resources to their most efficient and productive use. Efficiency can only be achieved through the incentives that are built into markets, which therefore should become the deliverer of all public systems as well as private companies. Incentive structures, profit and loss, and customer satisfaction are the values that should drive public service, just as they drive private enterprise. These nostrums have not only guided social and economic policy in Britain and the United States since 1980. They have also been exported to many other countries since the collapse of the Berlin Wall in 1989.

The third phase in the history of neoliberalism saw these basic ideas extended into international trade and development so that "structural adjustment" to market discipline became the holy grail for the economists and policymakers of the IMF, the World Bank, the WTO, and other regional and global institutions. This colonization of international institutions by neoliberal ideas carried with it the logic of Milton Friedman's claims about the link between economic and political freedom. As Anneliese Anderson, an adviser to President Reagan, has said, "The Pope [John Paul II] argued that economic liberty was essential for people to be free in other ways."[8] The success of Solidarity in Poland, alongside the pope's support for free enterprise, marked the beginning of an embrace of the market gospel in the former Soviet bloc countries. Outside Eastern Europe, a belief in the connection between economic and political liberty united leaders as diverse as Reagan, Thatcher, the German chancellor Helmut Kohl, the French finance minister and president of the European Commission Jacques Delors, and the Chinese paramount leader Deng Xiaoping.

That neoliberal politics was able to effect so much was indicative of the simple power of a firm faith in markets as the best means of allocating resources. But this commitment to markets was rarely subjected to detailed empirical examination and criticism. The skepticism of mainstream professional economists toward the claims of general equilibrium theory or rational expectations, for example, was largely ignored. Yet as the social inequalities, growing poverty, and deprivation that had been characteristic of the nineteenth century returned to Britain and the United States after more than a hundred years of rising average incomes, politicians and officials operated as if under a spell cast by Karl Popper's unwanted "Godhead," the free market.[9] They found it increasingly impossible to think differently about economy and society.

Parallelisms: The Place of Transatlantic Neoliberal Politics in History

It might have turned out differently. Labour and Democratic Party leaders pioneered the introduction of key neoliberal insights in the 1960s and 1970s. President Jimmy Carter, Chairman of the Federal Reserve Paul Volcker, Chancellor of the Exchequer Denis Healey, and Prime Minister James Callaghan moved to a different kind of macroeconomic management in the 1970s. Their governments championed forms of deregulation. Experimentation with private sector involvement in housing and urban policy began even earlier, in the 1960s (particularly under Kennedy and Johnson in the United States). Under different circumstances, either administration might have been reelected at the end of the 1970s. If the Labour Party had entered the 1980s with Denis Healey as a moderate leader, or if the Falklands War had not happened, Labour might have recovered to benefit electorally from the deep recession the Conservative economic strategy had induced. If the second oil shock had not struck before the Iranian hostage crisis, Jimmy Carter may not have been unfairly characterized by the sense of "malaise."[10] Luck and historical contingency played central roles.

In assessing the historical significance of transatlantic neoliberal politics, two central legacies are most important. The first is the neoliberal theory (and practice) of the state. As has been commonly noted, despite the rhetoric of rolling back the state, it actually required energetic government action to recast the balance between state and market in favor of the latter. In the years after Margaret Thatcher and Ronald Reagan were elected, a shift occurred from limited changes in policy and macroeconomic management to the wholesale adoption of a new governing political philosophy based on the neoliberal faith in free markets. Clearly, changes in policy were necessary in the late 1970s, and as we have seen, Carter and Callaghan changed their economic approach by cutting spending and prioritizing inflation. But whatever the intentions of the Conservative and Republican policymakers who followed, the general effect of the neoliberal philosophy of unbridled markets ended up as an unvarnished triumph for some sections of society at the expense of others: there were winners and losers. The poor and disadvantaged often lost out while the middle- and upper-tier earners gained through lower income taxes and personal subsidies such as mortgage interest tax relief, relentless deregulation, and privatization of state assets and nationalized industries, and through "trickle-down" supply-side economics and business-friendly policies.

The rise of a neoliberal theory of the state had serious implications for government and the public sphere. Hayek's criticisms of state planning illustrated the potentially hubristic folly of paternalist political and civil service elites. He argued that positive outcomes in public policy too often rested on the good fortune of having talented and benign political leaders and public officials rather than on any robust value in the systems of government themselves. If either of these features was lacking, and often even if they were not, Hayek suggested, the results were likely to be unsatisfactory at best. Milton Friedman's cogent attack on the claims of Keynesian demand management undermined faith in government's ability to manage the economy successfully through macroeconomic manipulation, though it has to be said that his own prescription, monetarism, was similarly flawed. The "profit-maximizing" public choice theory of Stigler, Buchanan, and Gordon Tullock damaged confidence in bureaucratic management and government regulation. The idea that the deficit didn't matter, propagated by Friedman and applied first by the Reagan administration and then by George W. Bush's big-government conservatism in the United States, clashed with people's basic financial instincts. A post-Watergate belief that governments and officials were corrupt dovetailed with popular movements underlining a general loss of trust in politicians and political institutions: the tax revolts in the United States in the 1970s, the collapse of industrial relations in Britain, and widespread disillusion with the urban unrest and violence that scarred the end of the 1960s. The end result was a broad breakdown of the characteristic mid-twentieth-century belief in the efficacy and moral superiority of government and collective action.

Yet the neoliberals did have a theory of the state. It was certainly far removed from the New Deal or the British welfare state, but it was nevertheless prominent and essential. For neoliberal thinkers, the starting point lay in the traditional areas of security, defense, and the protection of the citizenry. But it went beyond these basic requirements, necessary in all societies. The central function of the neoliberal state was the proactive construction and protection of the conditions for the market economy.

Early neoliberalism, in particular that of German ordoliberals, the Chicago economist Henry Simons, or Friedrich Hayek in *The Road to Serfdom*, was united in the belief that the state had crucial economic and social functions. For these early thinkers, the state was to be more than the night watchman of laissez-faire economics. Instead, the role of the state was to police and prevent monopoly, to supervise monetary policy responsibly, and to address the social question by providing a social safety net, all within the tight framework of a rule of law that protected private property rights. The social safety net was necessary to protect the vulnerable from the harshest effects of market capitalism, and also to ensure that the working and lower classes accepted the status quo. The recognition of such important responsibilities for government crucially stemmed from the lessons learned from the Great Depression and the experience of the rise of totalitarianism in the 1930s and 1940s. According to these early writers, the strong but limited state existed to enforce the conditions for the competitive order of the free market.

This reasonable and nuanced view of the appropriate balance between government power and the economic freedom of individuals in the marketplace was, however, slowly eroded. In the neoliberal thought of the second Chicago school—that of Friedman, George Stigler, Aaron Director, and Gary Becker—conceptions of the function of the state changed in the important areas of monopoly, trade unions, and regulation. At the same time, James Bu-chanan's and Gordon Tullock's Virginia school public choice theory under-mined the basis for a public sector that was defined by public service rather than by self-interest and profit (in this sphere, the particular interests of the bureaucrat or bureaucracy supposedly displaced the public interests of citi-zens whom they were supposed to serve). These writers argued that market mechanisms should be introduced into areas that had previously been thought of as separate and distinct from the imperatives of private enterprise. The con-sequence of this sparse view of the need for government was the importation of market mechanisms across many different policy spheres, as evident in the internal market of the National Health Service introduced by Thatcher's gov-ernment or the increasing prominence of proposals for voucher schemes for education or social security privatization in the United States.

The second major historical feature of neoliberal politics was the political and ideological movement embodied in a transatlantic network, whose suc-cess also revealed the potential power of a new form of political organization: the think tank. It is hard to know exactly how to characterize this movement or to assess whether it was driven from above or below. Its success was un-doubtedly the result of the policy activism of the ideological entrepreneurs and their organizations, described in chapter 4. According to Anneliese An-derson, the growth of think tanks was a direct result of the expansion of the government activity of the 1930s and 1940s.[11] Think tanks had existed before, notably the Fabian Society in Britain (founded in 1884) and the Brookings Institution in the United States (founded in 1916). As we have seen, Hayek sought to emulate the Fabians through his organizational strategy for a neo-liberal intellectual international to counter the dominance of "collectivism." The neoliberal Right built a dazzling array of think tanks in Britain and the United States in the postwar years. Subsequently, they built them all over the world. Crucially, as Kim Phillips-Fein has shown, these efforts were often funded by those who ran such powerful symbols of American capitalism as DuPont, General Electric, and General Motors.

It is important to avoid hyperbole about the role of think tanks, just as it is important to discount the claims of narcissistic politicians, but there is no doubt that the think tank was the preferred vehicle of neoliberal thinkers, especially Hayek, Friedman, Stigler, Buchanan, Tullock, Ludwig von Mises, Peter Bauer, and Alan Walters. These intellectuals mastered the new medium, while the men who ran the think tanks became sophisticated and strategic promoters of policies to politicians and decision makers. It is also striking that think tanks were intellectually, strategically, and organizationally heterogeneous. Some focused on the need to communicate the message to new audiences, others focused on generating innovative policy ideas or attempted to build databases of contacts and connections in order to increase the influence of the movement, while still others pursued all these aims. They tended to be interdisciplinary, most famously the Mont Pelerin Society, which embraced a wide range of scholars: historians, economists, philosophers, social scientists, and journalists. This variety added unprecedented flexibility as well as intellectual dexterity to the armory of neoliberalism.

It would be inaccurate to describe transatlantic neoliberal politics as anything but an elite-driven movement. Its main proponents were academics, politicians, and journalists. Its characteristic forms of political activism required money from rich businesspeople and foundations. The movement sought directly to influence policymakers and decision makers at the top of politics and government through publications, lectures, events, targeted mailings, research, and advisory work. Yet despite its elite profile, both in the United States and Britain, neoliberals found a simple political language that chimed with the fears and aspirations of a large part of the population of both countries. This political language was a vibrant replacement for the idiom of the New Deal and social democracy, which by the 1980s had grown stale. In the United States, neoliberal ideas about low taxation and limited government tapped into the popular tax revolts, most obviously in the campaign for Proposition 13 in California, for which Milton Friedman became a vocal cheerleader. The simple script of individual opportunity and free enterprise reified staple American ideals of individualism, just as the campaigns of suburban communities against busing had appropriated the language of the civil rights movement for their exclusionary demands. In Britain, Thatcher's Right to Buy scheme proved a masterstroke in its perfect harmony with the aspirations of the working and lower-middle classes. Parties of the center left, the Labour Party and Democratic Party, struggled to find a language that could counter this heady neoliberal brew, until Bill Clinton and Tony Blair reformulated the foundations of their political parties around the key elements of the new political settlement.

The legacy of transatlantic neoliberal politics is therefore powerful. It offers an example of a highly disciplined and effective political movement. It also illustrates the power of ideas in influencing political and social outcomes, as if further evidence were needed. The transatlantic neoliberal network proved Hayek and Friedman right in their belief that a change in the "climate of opinion" would lead to profound political and economic change as well. Some of the most powerful insights of these thinkers did help to address pressing social and economic issues by increasing homeownership or stabilizing persistently high inflation. But such successes were not so numerous as to make the effect of transatlantic neoliberal politics anything better than ambivalent.

Neoliberal political success brought with it a number of consequences. There was a newfound acceptance of inequality as a necessary and unavoidable evil. There was a cumulative squeeze of the public sphere—of the space for generously funded, comprehensive, and universal public services, and for collective industrial action and communal activity, of shared public spaces and institutions. A general assumption took hold among policymakers and publics, encouraged by the neoliberal interpretation of Adam Smith's concept of the invisible hand, that self-interest could mean selfishness. Greed, and less pejoratively profit, were to be celebrated. The provision of assistance to the poorest suffered as the public listened to arguments about the "escalating" costs of welfare. That this came during a period when middle- and upper-tier earners benefited more through the tax system from state subsidy than those deprived groups had ever done was rarely mentioned.[12] There was in fact a redistribution from the poorest to the wealthy over the course of the 1980s, and this continued in the 1990s under Bill Clinton and Tony Blair.[13] Whether these were intended effects (they probably weren't, in most cases) is less important than the fact that neoliberal policies tended to affect the most vulnerable members of society in the harshest ways.

The Apotheosis of Neoliberalism?

All of us might miss the consequences of pushing the ideological case too far.

—GEOFFREY HOWE, interview, 2007

The apotheosis of the neoliberal faith in free markets came with the financial crisis of 2007–8. The crisis was the direct result of a culture that had endowed the free market with a divine status it has never merited. The idea that markets were self-regulating mechanisms whose inherent incentive structures made them fireproof was widely held, most famously by the former chairman of the Federal Reserve, Alan Greenspan. This belief was based on the view that the self-interest of financial institutions would effectively substitute for the rigorous external regulation of financial markets because it would prevent banks from overexposure to high-risk strategies. This idea lay at the heart of the policy failures that led to the credit crunch, the worst recession since the Great Depression. It was a calamity that graphically illustrated the limits of what the journalist John Cassidy has called "utopian economics," the unthinking and uncritical acceptance of the logic of the free market.[14] Commentators were divided over how to apportion blame for the meltdown, and three major reasons for the crash were suggested.

The first was the irresponsible behavior of the bankers themselves. The crisis was triggered when it became clear that the balance sheets of most of the major financial institutions of Wall Street and the City of London were stuffed full of toxic and worthless assets based in subprime mortgage liabilities. Simply, this meant that such assets that had been grotesquely overvalued. The banks had been seduced by the claims of the mathematical economists who worked for them that it was possible to construct models that would eliminate uncertainty and herald the perfect management of risk between their various activities. This fantasy led to the creation of fanciful and deceptively packaged financial products such as credit default swaps, collateralized debt obligations, and other mortgage-backed securities whose value it was impossible to assess.

The models, and the products on which they were based, far from eliminating risk, actually concealed the real worth of these assets. They led banks, inappropriately capitalized, to leverage their balance sheets to scandalously astronomical levels, approaching thirty to one in some cases, in the pursuit of ever greater profits. The mortgage-backed securities were rated by credit agencies such as Standard & Poor's, Moody's, and the Fitch Group. These rating agencies, which gave AAA ratings to the riskiest assets of all, were paid for by the very companies that required the ratings. The whole edifice disintegrated when traders, driven by a herd mentality, realized that the major banks and insurance companies were overexposed, and this realization precipitated selling and a market crash. Banks collapsed one by one, Northern Rock and HBOS in Britain, Bear Sterns, and then, devastatingly, in September 2008,

Lehman Brothers. Citibank, Morgan Stanley, and even the supposedly gold-plated Goldman Sachs teetered on the brink before policymakers and tax-payers came to the rescue through the Bush administration's Troubled Asset Relief Program.

A second major reason for the crisis, especially popular with conservatives, was the supposed policy failures of the Carter and Clinton administrations. The accusation was that the Democrats had encouraged cheap money and mortgages for people who could not afford them. First, the Community Reinvestment Act of 1975 forced banks to lend money in low- and moderate-income neighborhoods. Then it was alleged that, from 1995 onward, Fannie Mae (the Federal National Mortgage Association) and Freddie Mac (the Federal Home Loan Mortgage Corporation) were mismanaged by policy-makers in the Department of Housing and Urban Development (HUD), who relaxed the restrictions on mortgage availability for low-income people who could not afford mortgages. This approach to fostering homeownership among poorer people, it was suggested, coupled with the cynical practice of "bait and switch" by unscrupulous lenders, became the means through which people were encouraged to refinance their loans by leveraging their homes for the sake of liquid cash. The dreadful result of predatory lending and sub-prime borrowing was a culture of living beyond means, fueled by fantastical notions of endless prosperity. (It should be noted, however, that a majority of subprime mortgages were offered by private lenders, not Fannie Mae or Freddie Mac.)

The third and most important reason for the financial crisis was the di-rect result of neoliberal policies. The deregulation of the financial markets stripped away the safeguards that had progressively been put in place since the New Deal in the United States and Britain, especially the separation be-tween retail and investment banking that was enshrined in the U.S. Glass-Steagall Act (1933). Financial deregulation began in the United States during the Carter administration with the Depository Institutions and Monetary Control Act (1980), which relaxed financial restrictions on banks and broad-ened their lending powers. In Britain, Thatcher and her chancellor, Geoffrey Howe, abolished exchange controls as one of the government's first actions in 1979. Deregulation continued in the 1980s with Reagan's liberalization of the financial sector through measures such as the Garn–St. Germain Depository Institutions Act (1982), which allowed banks to offer adjustable-rate mortgages. It continued in Britain also with Thatcher's "Big Bang" deregulation of the City of London between 1983 and 1986. Finally, the process was accelerated by Bill Clinton's, Tony Blair's, and Gordon Brown's preference for "light touch" regulation in the 1990s.

Financial deregulation was an extreme manifestation of the neoliberal faith in markets. It was a mantra universally followed by Republicans, Conservatives, Democrats, and Labour Party politicians alike. The successful fight against the "Great Inflation" of the 1970s waged by Paul Volcker during the 1980s was superseded in the 1990s by Alan Greenspan's monetarist "fine-tuning," the loosening or tightening of interest rates according to whether forecasts were good or bad. The supposedly stable operation of monetary policy was meant to have ushered in a "Great Moderation" of low inflation, high employment, and quietly simmering prosperity. The ludicrous nature of these claims was exposed by the events of September and October 2008. Clinton's main advisers had to take their share of the blame for the crisis. Robert Rubin and Larry Summers allowed the repeal of the Glass-Steagall Act through the passage of the Gramm-Leach Act (1999). They also refused to heed the advice of the former chair of the Commodity Futures Trading Commission, Brooksley Born, to regulate the emerging derivatives markets in 1998.

These policy failures illustrated beyond doubt that the faith in markets had become divorced from reality. The success of transatlantic neoliberal politics for thirty years following the elections of Thatcher and Reagan indicated a convergence between the United States and Britain in economic policy terms. The countries converged around a beguiling belief in markets. The dramatic crisis of 2007–8 seemed to offer a challenge to the neoliberal worldview. But instead, policymakers attempted to row back as quickly as possible to what they saw as the safety blanket of a pre-2007 status quo. Radical new thinking about the world economy was absent. There was no new Keynes in sight. The original Keynes was the best the mainstream liberal Left could muster to criticize the out-of-control culture that was revealed on Wall Street and in the City of London. Worse, this greed seemed to have infected the rest of society. The conservative (and Conservative) Right had become harder, more uncaring, and had regressed in its economic outlook to a pre–Great Depression policy of savage cuts, which seemed to ignore even the lessons of the neoliberal economists themselves.

Both the Conservative-led coalition government elected in Britain in 2010 and the congressional Republicans who vanquished Obama's Democrats in the 2010 midterm elections argued that deficits, which had mainly been generated by the bank bailouts and the fallout from the financial crisis, had to be eradicated as quickly as possible. This approach ignored the logic of both Keynesians and monetarists, whose emphasis on expectations suggested the need for a stimulus of either a fiscal or a monetary nature, in the context of an ideological desire to reduce public expenditures. The argument in the 1960s had been whether a little more unemployment or a little more inflation should be tolerated. The argument now became whether there should be 25 percent or 40 percent cuts in government spending. Discussion of the prospects for growth was a secondary concern to Conservative and Republican policymakers.

There were two further signs of the tenacious endurance of the neoliberal faith in markets. One, suggested by Mark Lilla in an article titled "The Tea Party Jacobins," was the growth in the modern United States of a destructive and ignorant politics of protest, characterized by a disturbing tendency to speak and listen only to itself and according to its own standards of evidence and proof. This was epitomized by the Tea Party movement, which grew out of opposition to President Obama's health care reforms. The Tea Party was facilitated by a television and media network, Fox News, owned by Rupert Murdoch. It was led, and goaded, by Glenn Beck, Michele Bachmann (whose favorite economist was apparently Ludwig von Mises), and Sarah Palin, all of whom were apparently immune to the normal constraints placed on leaders by expert knowledge and the need for a proper understanding of world affairs. Lilla pointed to a sort of "wisdom of the crowds" dystopia fostered by concentrated media ownership.[15] In Britain, too, Rupert Murdoch sought complete ownership of Sky television to go with his dominance of the market for newspapers and printed media. His bid collapsed in 2011 amid the scandalous journalistic standards of his top title, The News of the World. In the twenty-first century, the problem of corporate monopoly, which had exercised the original neoliberal writers, had once again reared its ugly head. Neoliberalism in the revised Chicago version of Friedman, Director, and Stigler, however, did not recognize this problem.

Further examples of the continued dominance of the neoliberal commitment to markets were the radical policy proposals of the Conservative-led government in Britain. In place of a cautious program born of their failure to win an electoral majority in the election of 2010, Prime Minister David Cameron and his ministers outlined a radical overhaul of both health and education policy. In health care, the government passed a bill to transfer responsibility for budget allocation to GPs (local general practitioner doctors), in the process risking the introduction of clinical decision making based on profit rather than on care needs. The public outcry was so severe that the government was forced to water down its proposals, but its intention had been very clear: the complete marketization of health care in Britain.

In education, under the banner of choice, the Conservatives, supported by their Liberal Democrat governmental partners, aimed to relax nationally supervised standards by allowing parents to operate and run their own local schools. Even more radically, the government planned virtually to privatize university funding by almost abolishing teaching grants to the humanities, leaving only science subjects publicly funded. In the absence of the American tradition of philanthropy and well-funded public state universities, the British government's approach could only be seen as a completely new experiment in a market for higher education, unlike the systems that existed in any other developed country. These developments all pointed to a political culture on both sides of the Atlantic unable to escape a fantasy world in which free markets solved everything.

Reason-Based Policymaking

The lesson of this book is that it must be possible to return sanity to important political and economic debates. We ought to be able to learn the lessons of the management of inflation as well as those of the New Deal, to learn the limits of markets as well as their virtues. Inflation targets should exist alongside a properly regulated banking sector whose riskiest operations are treated for what they are: high-level gambling. This means they should be kept as far away as possible from the crucial social functions of banking, such as lending, basic pension provision, and saving.

Attempts to rebalance the scales have been scorned. Because of market failure, the financial system spiraled beyond Greenspan's "irrational exuberance" and into personal tragedy for many ordinary families and state-sponsored financial assistance for the banks. These were the terrible effects of uncritical deregulation and market liberalization, bred by the Chicago faith in untrammeled markets. But such failures were outweighed in conservative accounts by a still pervasive moral view that anyone willing to work hard and apply his or her ingenuity would be able to succeed, even in a new world dominated at the bottom by the service sector and at the top by the super-rich. The moral distinction between the deserving and undeserving poor had returned at a moment when Anglo-American political conversation had lost the perspective that makes possible discussion of the morality of the undeserving rich. The fact that some people are not well equipped to survive the harsh environment of a globalized economy—the poor, disadvantaged, or badly educated, for example—was glossed over in a vacuous political language of freedom and economic opportunity. This was a language that had been expertly developed by neoliberal thinkers and politicians.

The neoliberal vision of globalization was that a system based on individual freedom, free markets, and the opportunities provided by "flexible labor markets" would substitute for universal high-quality publicly funded education and health care systems, more efficient and cheaper privatized alternatives. The citizen was nothing more than a consumer. But neoliberals, at least from the time of the second Chicago school after 1945, abandoned any attempt to account for the possibility, let alone likelihood, of market failure in key social policy areas such as education, housing, or health. The losers were labeled, by conservative politicians on both sides of the Atlantic, welfare moms, dole-scroungers, or indigent free riders. At the same time, the language of profit, efficiency, and consumption replaced that of citizenship, solidarity, and service. In the United States, Obama's health care reforms were prevented by the Tea Party nihilists from including any kind of public option capable of reducing the sometimes corrupt and universally escalating costs of private health care. Dominated by the free market gospel, the irony of this brave new world was that it produced everything conservative politicians hated: insecurity, social, sexual and cultural changes, violence, and the collapse of community.

The end of ideological conflict—the disappearance of the fundamental division between collectivism and capitalism—has been lamented for the accompanying loss of certainty and of tribe-like belonging and loyalty. But perhaps what is needed is a greater acknowledgment of the point of political ideas. They are meant to improve people's lives, and so must be changed and amended in response to evidence. Faith, even a secular faith in individual liberty as expressed through free markets, should never drive the application of a model inflexibly, impervious to real social and economic problems. Reason-based policymaking needs to return. The mundane reality of incremental reform and regulation to meet urgent human needs depends on it.

Notes

✳

Introduction

1. J. M. Keynes, *The General Theory of Employment, Interest and Money* (London: Macmillan, 1936).

2. M. Friedman, "Neo-liberalism and Its Prospects," *Farmand* 17 (February 1951): 89–93.

3. See R. Van Horn and P. Mirowski, "The Rise of the Chicago School of Economics and the Birth of Neoliberalism," in *The Road from Mont Pelerin: The Making of the Neoliberal Thought Collective*, ed. P. Mirowski and D. Plehwe (Cambridge, MA: Harvard University Press, 2009), 139–81.

4. See J. Williamson, "What Washington Means by Policy Reform," in *Latin American Adjustment: How Much Has Happened?*, ed. J. Williamson (Washington, DC: Institute for International Economics, 1989), chap. 2.

5. See chapter 1 in K. Popper, *The Open Society and Its Enemies* (London: Routledge, 1945).

6. See chapter 3 in J. Shearmur, *Hayek and After: Hayekian Liberalism as a Research Programme* (London: Routledge, 1996).

7. In *Thatcher's Britain* (London: Simon and Schuster, 2009), for example, Richard Vinen has argued that *The Road to Serfdom* "merely provided a convenient philosophical polish on things that Thatcherites wanted to do for reasons that had little to do with Hayek's thinking" (7). Michael Howard, former Conservative Party leader and Thatcherite minister, in an interview with the author, echoed such skepticism about the influence of neoliberal ideas, claiming that it was the economic reality of Britain in the 1960s and 1970s that had led to "Thatcherism."

8. R. Turner, *Neo-Liberal Ideology: History, Concepts and Policies* (Edinburgh: Edinburgh University Press, 2008).

9. See especially Hayek's epic political philosophical trilogy, *Law, Legislation and Liberty,* 3 vols. (Chicago: University of Chicago Press, 1973, 1976, 1979).

10. The "Manchester school" was a term first coined by the British Conservative prime minister Benjamin Disraeli.

11. See the work of Philip Mirowski, Dieter Plehwe, Rob Van Horn, Ben Jackson, and Angus Burgin, especially the chapters by Van Horn and Mirowski, in Mirowski and Plehwe, *The Road from Mont Pelerin*; B. Jackson, "At the Origins of Neo-Liberalism: The Free Economy and the Strong State, 1930–1947," *Historical Jour-*

nal 53, no. 1 (2010): 129–51; and A. Burgin, "The Radical Conservatism of Frank Knight," *Modern Intellectual History* 6, no. 3 (2009): 513–38.

12. See R. Cockett, *Thinking the Unthinkable: Think-Tanks and the Economic Counter-Revolution, 1931–1983* (London: Fontana, 1995). Cockett uses "The Heroic Age" as the subtitle of chapters 7 and 8.

13. G. H. Nash, *The Conservative Intellectual Movement in America* (Wilmington, DE: Intercollegiate Studies Institute, 1996).

14. See, e.g., R. Perlstein, *Before the Storm: Barry Goldwater and the Unmaking of the American Consensus* (New York: Hill and Wang, 2001); S. Heffer, *Like the Roman: The Life of Enoch Powell* (London: Weidenfeld and Nicolson, 1998); J. Campbell, *Margaret Thatcher*, 2 vols. (London: Pimlico, 2004, 2007); M. Thatcher, *The Path to Power* (London: HarperCollins, 1995) and *The Downing Street Years* (London: HarperCollins, 1993); R. Reagan, *An American Life: The Autobiography* (New York: Buccaneer Books, 1995). Also, N. Lawson's *The View from No. 11* (London: Bantam Press, 1992) stands out as one of the most intelligent and comprehensive of the genre.

15. The "Chicago boys" were young, Chicago-trained economists who led the Chilean military junta's economic reforms in the 1970s and 1980s. See M. Skousen, *The Making of Modern Economics: The Lives and Ideas of the Great Thinkers* (New York: M. E. Sharpe, 2001), 394. On the Chilean experience, see J. G. Valdés, *Pinochet's Economists: The Chicago School in Chile* (Cambridge: Cambridge University Press, 1995). See also K. Fischer, "The Influence of Neoliberals before, during, and after Pinochet," in Mirowski and Plehwe, *The Road from Mont Pelerin*.

16. D. Harvey, *A Brief History of Neoliberalism* (Oxford: Oxford University Press, 2005).

17. A. Glyn, *Capitalism Unleashed: Finance, Globalization, and Welfare* (Oxford: Oxford University Press, 2006), esp. chap. 1.

18. N. Klein, *The Shock Doctrine: The Rise of Disaster Capitalism* (London: Allen Lane, 2007).

19. See Mirowski's review of Harvey's *Brief History of Neoliberalism* in *Economics and Philosophy* 24 (2008): 111–17.

20. P. Pierson, *Dismantling the Welfare State: Reagan, Thatcher and the Politics of Retrenchment* (Cambridge: Cambridge University Press, 1994); Monica Prasad, *The Politics of Free Markets: The Rise of Neoliberal Economic Policies in Britain, France, Germany and the United States* (Chicago: University of Chicago Press, 2006).

21. Although I should add here that I anticipate that future research will uncover more links than have surfaced to date. Tim Weaver at the University of Pennsylvania undertakes a detailed examination of the history of enterprise zones in Britain and the United States in his thesis, "Neoliberalism in the Trenches: Urban Politics and Policy in the United States and Britain, 1976–2000." See also Jim Cooper's thesis for the University of Aberystwyth titled "Mutual Impact? Intellectual Transfer between the Thatcher and Reagan Administrations in Domestic Policy."

22. See, e.g., S. Jenkins, *Thatcher and Sons* (London: Penguin, 2006).

23. See S. Hall, *The Hard Road to Renewal: Thatcherism and the Crisis of the Left* (London: Verso, 1988).

24. See, e.g., J. Stiglitz, *Globalization and Its Discontents* (New York: W. W. Norton, 2002).

25. P. Krugman, "Who Was Milton Friedman?," *New York Review of Books*, February 15, 2007.

26. See chapter 1 of Jamie Peck's *Constructions of Neoliberal Reason* (Oxford: Oxford University Press, 2010).

Chapter 1: The Postwar Settlement

1. On the history of Social Security and America's welfare state, see M. Katz, *In the Shadow of the Poorhouse: A Social History of Welfare*, 2nd ed. (New York: Basic Books, 1996), and *The Price of Citizenship: Redefining America's Welfare State* (New York: Metropolitan Books, 2001); D. Beland, *Social Security: History and Politics from the New Deal to the Privatization Debate* (Lawrence: University of Kansas Press, 2004); and E. Berkowitz, *America's Welfare State: From Roosevelt to Reagan* (Baltimore, MD: Johns Hopkins University Press, 1991). On the United States' lack of universal health care, see J. Quadagno, *One Nation Uninsured: Why the U.S. Has No Universal Health Care* (Oxford: Oxford University Press, 2005).

2. "Never again" was a famous political catchphrase in the 1940s. It is also the title of Peter Hennessy's history of Britain in the postwar years, *Never Again, Britain, 1945–51* (London: Vintage, 1993).

3. Though, of course, this was limited in important respects in the United States. Blacks, for example, were to remain excluded from many of the provisions of the GI bill. On this, see I. Katznelson, *When Affirmative Action Was White* (New York: W. W. Norton, 2005).

4. G. Soros, "The Financial Crisis: An Interview with George Soros," *New York Review of Books*, May 15, 2008.

5. All figures for the United States are taken from B. R. Mitchell, *International Historical Statistics: The Americas, 1750–2000* (London: Palgrave, 2003), and for Britain from B. R. Mitchell, *International Historical Statistics: Europe, 1750–2000* (London: Palgrave, 2003). For government expenditure in Britain, see pp. 821–23. For the United States, see p. 667.

6. Mitchell, *International Historical Statistics: The Americas*, 682.

7. Mitchell, *International Historical Statistics: Europe*, 844.

8. R. Skidelsky, "Hayek Versus Keynes: The Road to Reconciliation," in *The Cambridge Companion to Hayek*, ed. E. Feser (Cambridge: Cambridge University Press, 2006), 95.

9. See D. Kynaston, *Austerity Britain, 1945–51* (London: Bloomsbury, 2007), 467–69.

10. On the New Deal and its limits, see A. Brinkley, *The End of Reform: New Deal Liberalism in Recession and War* (New York: Vintage, 1996).

11. On blacks and the welfare state, see, e.g., R. Lieberman, *Shifting the Color Line* (Cambridge, MA: Harvard University Press, 1998), and J. Quadagno, *The Color of Welfare: How Racism Undermined the War on Poverty* (Oxford: Oxford University Press, 1994). On women, see, e.g., L. Gordon, *Pitied, But Not Entitled* (Cambridge, MA: Harvard University Press, 1994), and S. Michel, *Children's Interests/Mothers' Rights* (New Haven, CT: Yale University Press, 1999).

12. See P. Hennessy, *Having It So Good: Britain in the Fifties* (London: Penguin, 2006).

13. For a useful introduction to this period, see P. Clarke, *Hope and Glory: Britain in the Twentieth Century* (London: Penguin, 1997). For a more detailed treatment, see J. Harris, *Unemployment and Politics: A Study in English Social Policy, 1880–1914* (Oxford: Clarendon, 1972).

14. On the origins of the welfare state reforms of Attlee's governments, see P. Addison, *The Road to 1945* (London: Jonathan Cape, 1975). See also Clarke, *Hope and Glory*; Hennessy, *Never Again*; and Kynaston, *Austerity Britain*.

15. J. Harris, *William Beveridge: A Biography* (Oxford: Oxford University Press, 1997), 3.

16. On grassroots conservatism and the Cold War, see L. McGirr, *Suburban Warriors: The Origins of the New American Right* (Princeton, NJ: Princeton University Press, 2001), and Gregory Schneider, *Cadres for Conservatism: Young Americans for Freedom and the Rise of the Contemporary Right* (New York: New York University Press, 1999). On the Republican Party, see M. Brennan, *Turning Right in the Sixties: The Conservative Capture of the GOP* (Chapel Hill: University of North Carolina Press, 1995).

17. On these urban struggles in Detroit, see T. Sugrue, *Origins of the Urban Crisis* (Princeton, NJ: Princeton University Press, 1998), and in Chicago, see A. Hirsch, *Making the Second Ghetto: Race and Housing in Chicago 1940–60* (New York: Cambridge University Press, 1998).

18. One of the most significant pieces of recent scholarship on this is Matthew Lassiter's discussion of the "southernization" of the suburban United States, *The Silent Majority: Suburban Politics in the Sunbelt South* (Princeton, NJ: Princeton University Press, 2006). Lassiter argues that "the widespread tendency to attribute the conservative shift in American politics to a top-down 'Southern strategy,' launched by the Republican Party in order to exploit white backlash against the civil rights movement, misses the longer-term convergence of southern and national politics around the suburban ethos of middle-class entitlement" (7).

19. On this, see also D. Carter, *The Politics of Rage: George Wallace, the Origins of the new Conservatism and the Transformation of American Politics* (Baton Rouge: Louisiana State University Press, 2000).

20. On black immigrants' experiences in Britain, see, e.g., *Empire Windrush: 50 years of Writing about Black Britain* (London: Phoenix, 1999). On the right-wing anti-immigrant backlash and its figurehead, see Simon Heffer's biography of Enoch Powell, *Like the Roman* (London: Weidenfeld and Nicolson, 1998).

21. See Kynaston, *Austerity Britain.*

Chapter 2: The 1940s

1. F. Denord, "French Neoliberalism and Its Divisions," in *The Road from Mont Pelerin*, ed. R. Mirowski and D. Plehwe (Cambridge, MA: Harvard University Press, 2009), 48.

2. "Statement of Aims," 8 April 1947, available in full at www.montpelerin.org/montpelerin/mpsGoals.html. R. Max Hartwell's *A History of the Mont Pelerin Society* (Indianapolis: Liberty Fund, 1995) provides the best insider's account of the society and its history and origins.

3. Indeed, as Ben Jackson points out in his article, "At the Origins of Neoliberalism: The Free Economy and the Strong State, 1930–47" (*Historical Journal* 53, no. 1 [2010]: 129–51), it was less the case that early neoliberals such as Hayek and Popper wanted to roll back the state, though this was desirable. Instead, they wanted a strong state that would ensure the establishment and maintenance of a competitive order. Seen in this way, the neoliberal agenda becomes one of transformation of the role of the state to a new purpose: the protection of free markets.

4. Mises engaged in, for example, the famous "socialist calculation debate" with socialists such as Oskar Lange over whether it was possible for modern industrialized societies to continue were they to be reorganized along socialist lines. Hayek, following his failure to dent Keynes's theories in the early 1930s, had mounted an attack on central planning through his 1936 paper, "Economics and Knowledge," followed by a series of articles that culminated in the publication of *The Road to Serfdom* in 1944. Popper, since his move to New Zealand in 1937, had been a little more isolated, but it was during this period that he wrote his two major contributions to these debates, *The Open Society and Its Enemies* and *The Poverty of Historicism.*

5. F. A. Hayek, *The Road to Serfdom* (London: Routledge, 1944, 1949), 184.

6. Ibid., 190.

7. Karl Popper to Friedrich Hayek, 14 March 1944, box 305, 11–17, Karl Popper Papers, reel 326, reproduced from the Hoover Institution, London School of Economics Archives (hereafter "Popper Papers").

8. On Popper, see A. O'Hear, *Karl Popper: Biography, Background, and Early Reactions to Popper's Work* (London: Routledge, 2004); G. Stokes, *Popper: Philosophy, Politics, and Scientific Method* (London: Polity Press, 1998); and M. H. Hacohen, *Karl Popper: The Formative Years, 1900–1945: Politics and Philosophy in Interwar Vienna* (Cambridge: Cambridge University Press, 2002). On his political thought, see also J. Shearmur, *The Political Thought of Karl Popper* (London: Routledge, 1996).

9. Shearmur, *Political Thought of Karl Popper*, 19.

10. M. Friedman, "The Methodology of Positive Economics," in *Essays in Positive Economics* (Chicago: University of Chicago Press, 1966), 3–43.

11. L. Mises, *Human Action* (New Haven, CT: Yale University Press, 1949).

12. Friedman to Hayek, 11 September 1975, box 20, folder 19, Hayek Papers, Hoover Institution, Stanford University, Palo Alto, CA (hereafter "Hayek Papers").

13. Ibid.

14. Popper to Hayek, 26 April 1943, Popper Papers.

15. Popper to Hayek, 26 October 1943, Popper Papers.

16. Hayek to Popper, 4 December 1943, Popper Papers.

17. Hayek to Popper, 12 July 1943, Popper Papers.

18. Popper to Hayek, 26 October 1943, Popper Papers.

19. Popper to Hayek, 15 March 1944, Popper Papers.

20. Popper to Hayek, 11 January 1947, Popper Papers.

21. Quoted in "The Future Is Open: A Conversation with Sir Karl Popper—Adam Chmielsewski and Karl Popper," in *Popper's Open Society after Fifty Years,* ed. I. Jarvie and S. P. (London: Routledge, 1999), chap. 2, 36.

22. Henry Simons's and Milton Friedman's work from this period is discussed in chapter 3.

23. Hayek to Bruce Caldwell, 29 September 1984, box 13, folder 30, Hayek Papers.

24. K. Popper, *The Open Society and Its Enemies,* 2 vols. (London: Routledge, 1945), 1:xvii.

25. Ibid., 1:4.

26. Ibid., 1:53.

27. Ibid., 1:146.

28. Ibid., 1:107.

29. Ibid., 1:108.

30. Ibid., 2:34.

31. Ibid., 1:xix.

32. Ibid., 1:14.

33. Ibid., 2:117.

34. Hayek to Popper, 29 January 1944, Popper Papers.

35. Popper to Hayek, 14 March 1944, Popper Papers.

36. Popper, *Open Society,* 2141.

37. Ibid., 2:142.

38. Ibid., 2:143.

39. Ibid., 2:144.

40. Ibid., 2:260.

41. Ibid., 1:167.

42. Ibid., 1:171.

43. Ibid., 2:202.

44. Ibid., 2:271.

45. Popper to Hayek, 28 May 1944, box 44, folder 1, Hayek Papers.

46. For a sympathetic account of Mises, see I. Kirzner, *Ludwig von Mises: The Man and His Economics* (Wilmington, DE: ISI Books, 2001). Eamonn Butler has written a useful introduction to his thought, *Ludwig von Mises: A Primer* (London: Institute of Economic Affairs, 2010). See also P. Boettke and P. Leeson, eds., *The Legacy of Ludwig von Mises: Theory and History* (Cheltenham: Edward Elgar, 2006). There is also a wealth of material about Mises, his life, and work available at the Mises Institute's website, www.mises.org.

47. L. Mises, *Bureaucracy* (New Haven, CT: Yale University Press, 1944), 83.

48. Machlup would also later join the Mont Pelerin Society.

49. Lawrence Fertig (1898–1986) was an American libertarian advertising executive and journalist who worked for the *New York World-Telegram* and the *New York Sun*.

50. Mises, *Bureaucracy*, iv.

51. Hayek had originally planned to call the Mont Pelerin Society the Acton-Tocqueville Society. He wrote to Popper that Lord Acton and de Tocqueville should form the "agreed foundation from which such a common effort may start." Hayek to Popper, 28 December 1946, Popper Papers.

52. Mises, *Bureaucracy*, 4.

53. Ibid., 6.

54. Ibid., 71.

55. Ronald Reagan, like Tony Blair later, was an advocate of importing successful business leadership into government and the public services. See chapter 4.

56. Mises, *Bureaucracy*, 49.

57. Ibid., 48.

58. Ibid., 60.

59. Quoted in the PBS documentary, *The Commanding Heights*, 2001.

60. Mises, *Bureaucracy*, 61.

61. Ibid., 63.

62. See, e.g., Friedman's interview with Charlie Rose, 26 December 2005, available at www.charlierose.com/search/?text=milton+friedman, and the author's interview with Nigel Lawson, June 2007.

63. Their classic analysis, *The Calculus of Consent* (Ann Arbor: University of Michigan Press), which built on Duncan Black's early research, was published in 1962.

64. Mises, *Bureaucracy*, 19.

65. Ibid., 66. It is interesting to see Mises argue this point here, for it is exactly the same approach that the rational expectations schools in economics and political science use when they suggest the predictable and rational nature of economic and other forms of human behavior. The models adherents construct run into problems when they encounter behavior that does not fit within the range of the model—hence the recent rise of behavioral economics, which seeks to address some of these shortcomings in traditional economic approaches by factoring in other influences and motivations, including rational irrationality. See, e.g., G. Akerlof and R. Shiller,

Animal Spirits: How Human Psychology Drives the Economy, and Why It Matters for Global Capitalism (Princeton, NJ: Princeton University Press, 2009).

66. Mises, *Bureaucracy*, 68.

67. Ibid., 76.

68. Ibid., 9.

69. "Pork barrel spending" refers to the practice of congressional representatives' inserting lumps of funding for local pet projects into legislation as a condition for their support of a bill.

70. Mises, *Bureaucracy*, 102.

71. Ibid., 103.

72. Ibid., 95.

73. Hayek, *Road to Serfdom*, 17.

74. There have been a couple of useful biographies of Hayek. The most complete history of his life and thought is by Alan Ebenstein, *Friedrich Hayek: A Biography* (London: Macmillan, 2001). An intellectual biography by Bruce Caldwell was published in 2005: *Hayek's Challenge: An Intellectual Biography* (Chicago: University of Chicago Press). The best survey of Hayek's work as an economist, political theorist, and philosopher is probably *The Cambridge Companion to Hayek*, ed. Edward Feser (Cambridge: Cambridge University Press, 2006). Jeremy Shearmur's book, *Hayek and After: Hayekian Liberalism as a Research Programme* (London: Routledge, 1996), focuses on Hayek's methodological utility. John Gray has written an essay on Hayek's philosophical importance that appeared as a pamphlet titled *F. A. Hayek and the Rebirth of Classical Liberalism* (Arlington, VA: Institute for Humane Studies, 1982), and a book, *Hayek on Liberty* (London: Routledge, 1984). Eamonn Butler has also written a useful introduction to Hayek, *Hayek: His Contribution to the Political and Economic Thought of Our Time* (Middlesex: Maurice Temple Smith, 1983); see also A. Gamble, *Hayek: The Iron Cage of Liberty* (London: Polity Press, 1996). On his economics, see G. R. Steele, *The Economics of Friedrich Hayek* (Basingstoke: Palgrave Macmillan, 2007), and P. Boettke, ed., *The Legacy of F. A. Hayek: Politics, Philosophy and Economics*, 3 vols. (Cheltenham: Edward Elgar, 1999).

75. Hartwell, *A History of the Mont Pelerin Society*, 18. Cannan's edition of *The Wealth of Nations* was published by Methuen in 1904.

76. Hayek returned to Freiburg in 1963 before moving to Salzburg in 1968. Margaret Thatcher made him a Companion of Honour in 1983, the highest award a British civilian can receive.

77. Airgraph, Popper to Hayek, 28 May 1944, Hayek Papers.

78. Hayek, *Road to Serfdom*, 13.

79. See the postscript, "Why I am not a Conservative," in F. A. Hayek, *The Constitution of Liberty* (Chicago: University of Chicago Press, 1960).

80. Hayek, *Road to Serfdom*, 14.

81. Popper to Hayek, 7 February 1944, Popper Papers.

82. Hayek to Popper, 29 January 1944, Popper Papers.

83. Popper to Hayek, 14 March 1944, Popper Papers.

84. Popper to Hayek, 9 December 1943, Popper Papers.

85. Hayek to Popper, 29 January 1944, Popper Papers.

86. Popper to Hayek, 7 February 1944, Popper Papers. In this letter Popper goes on to float an intriguing theory about the history of ideas:

> The parallelism you mention between Comte and Hegel is very striking; even in the "indirect" manner of their influence, which you mention at the end of your article on Comte. I wonder whether the contrast between continental and British thought (Cp. Ec. vol. VIII, p. 319, n.1) in some respects I think that Burke fits better the continental series, and Kant the British; cp. Kant's smashing criticism of Herder) may not be due, in part, to the fact that the industrial revolution was autochtonous in England, and heterochtonous in Germany (with France somewhat intermediate); thus evolutionist philosophy, which seems to be partly a reaction to revolutionary changes, broke out more violently, and in a more metaphysical or other-worldly style, in those countries in which the change was imported, as it were, from another world, and was felt as such. (This is just such an idea, and not to be taken seriously! Still, I should like to hear how it strikes you. I hope you don't mind if I allow such immature thought to kreep [sic] into a letter to you!

87. Despite their frequent disagreements, Hayek and Keynes were friends. For example, when the LSE was evacuated to Cambridge during the war, Hayek stayed with Keynes.

88. Keynes to Hayek, 28 June 1944, box 30, folder 19, Hayek Papers.

89. Hayek, *Road to Serfdom*, 5.

90. Ibid., 79.

91. C. Murray, *Losing Ground: American Social Policy, 1950–1980* (New York: Basic Books, 1984), and D. P. Moynihan, *The Negro Family: The Case for National Action* (Washington, DC: U.S. Department of Labor, Office of Policy Planning and Research, 1965).

92. Hayek, *Road to Serfdom*, 60.

93. Ibid., 71.

94. Ibid., 24. On Saint-Simonianism, see F. A. Hayek, *The Counter-Revolution of Science: Studies on the Abuse of Reason* (Indianapolis: Liberty Fund, 1980).

95. Hayek, *Road to Serfdom*, 26.

96. Ibid., 162.

97. Ibid., 165.

98. On ordoliberalism, see the next chapter. For an effective analysis, see R. Ptak, "Neoliberalism in Germany: Revisiting the Ordoliberal Foundations of the Social Market Economy," in Mirowski and Plehwe, *The Road from Mont Pelerin*. On the early Chicago school, see A. Bergin, "The Radical Conservatism of Frank Knight," *Modern Intellectual History* 63, no. 3 (2009): 513–38.

99. Hayek, *Road to Serfdom*, 35.

100. Ibid., 49.

101. Keynes to Hayek, 28 June 1944, Hayek Papers.

102. Hayek certainly did in his later work, *The Constitution of Liberty* (1960) and *Law, Legislation and Liberty* (1973, 1976, 1979), mainly around the legal framework within which markets could operate under conditions of fair competition.

103. R. Van Horn, "Reinventing Monopoly and the Role of Corporations: The Roots of Chicago Law and Economics," in Mirowski and Plehwe, *The Road from Mont Pelerin*, 204.

104. Hayek, *Road to Serfdom*, 37.

105. Ibid., 64.

106. Hayek to Samuelson, 18 December 1980, box 48, folder 5, Hayek Papers.

107. Ibid.

108. Samuelson was generous in his response, dated 2 January 1981:

> I have benefited so much over the years from your own writings that I shall put special attention into the effort of preparing an optimal précis of your thesis. When a prophet warns against certain "tendencies" there is a subtle problem of making clear the degree to which he believes his warnings can themselves alter the "probabilities" that what he fears should in fact ultimately occur. I shall wrestle with the problem of how to convey adequately these nuances of meaning.
>
> I am pleased to observe that the Hayekian message registers increasingly within the profession of economics. Although it was not given to Moses to enter the Promised Land, one hopes that as Friedrich Hayek moves into the 1980s he recognizes with some pleasure that his has not been the fate of Cassandra—to see and report things clearly that the world refused to put credence into.

109. Winston Churchill, election speech, 4 June 1945.

110. Hayek, *Road to Serfdom*, 91.

111. K. Tribe, "Neoliberalism in Britain, 1930–1980," in Mirowski and Plehwe, *The Road from Mont Pelerin*, chap. 1

112. I. Berlin, *Two Concepts of Liberty,* in *Four Essays on Liberty* (Oxford: Oxford University Press, 1969).

113. Hayek, *Road to Serfdom*, 101.

114. Ibid., 119–20.

115. Ibid, 123.

116. Ibid., 133.

117. Ibid., 135.

118. Ibid., 206.

119. Although this belief in the efficacy of planning engendered by the wartime experience was the grave error of the postwar settlement in Britain, according to critics—for example, future head of Margaret Thatcher's Policy Unit John Hoskyns and future chancellor of the exchequer Geoffrey Howe—the idea that having planned the economy during war, it was possible to plan during peace as well (John Hoskyns and Geoffrey Howe, interviews with the author, June and July 2007).

120. Hayek, *Road to Serfdom*, 215.

121. J. Blundell, introduction to *The Road to Serfdom,* by F. A. Hayek, Reader's Digest condensed version (London: IEA, 1999), xv.

122. "Statement of Aims," Mont Pelerin Society, 8 April 1947, quoted in Hartwell, *A History of the Mont Pelerin Society,* xvii.

123. Hartwell, *A History of the Mont Pelerin Society*, 18–19.

124. Mises to Hayek, 31 December 1946, box 38, folder 24, Hayek Papers.

125. Hayek to Leonard Read, 16 October 1947, box 20, folder 1, Hayek Papers.

126. Kim Phillips-Fein has shown how central to the resurgence of conservatism and the emergence of neoliberalism in the postwar period were the anti–New Deal businessmen in her book, *Invisible Hands: The Businessmen's Crusade against the New Deal* (New York: W. W. Norton, 2009). See also E. Fones-Wolf, *Selling Free Enterprise: The Business Assault on Labor and Liberalism* (Urbana: University of Illinois Press, 1994).

127. Hayek to Read, 16 October 1947, Hayek Papers.

128. Hayek to Read, 29 January 1948, box 20, folder 1, Hayek Papers.

129. H. C. Cornuelle to Hayek, 4 February 1948, box 20, folder 1, Hayek Papers.

130. R. Van Horn and P. Mirowski, "The Rise of the Chicago School of Economics and the Birth of Neoliberalism," chap. 4 in Van Horn and Mirowski, *The Road from Mont Pelerin*, 156. Van Horn and Mirowski argue that, through the funding of the WVF, Hayek's role in the foundation of the second Chicago school was much more crucial than has been acknowledged, more so even than Friedman's.

131. F. A. Hayek, "The Intellectuals and Socialism," *University of Chicago Law Review,* Spring 1949, 417.

132. Hayek to Popper, 13 February 1947, Popper Papers.

133. Hayek, "Intellectuals," 417.

134. Ibid., 418.

135. Ibid., 419.

136. Ibid.

137. Ibid., 420.

138. Read to Hayek, 29 October 1948, box 20, folder 1, Hayek Papers.

139. Hayek, "Intellectuals," 432–33.

140. Ibid., 429.

Chapter 3: The Rising Tide

1. A. Glyn, *Capitalism Unleashed* (Oxford: Oxford University Press, 2006); D. Harvey, *A Brief History of Neoliberalism* (Oxford: Oxford University Press, 2005); N. Klein, *The Shock Doctrine* (London: Penguin, 2008).

2. P. Mirowski, "Review of Harvey, *A Brief History of Neoliberalism,*" *Economics and Philosophy* 24 (2008): 112.

3. On the Chicago schools in general, see M. Bronfenbrenner, "On the 'Chicago School of Economics,'" *Journal of Political Economy* 70 (1962): 72–75; R. Coase, "Law and Economics at Chicago," *Journal of Law and Economics* 36 (1993): 239–54; A. W. Coats, "The Origins of the Chicago School(s)," *Journal of Political Economy* 71 (1963): 487–93; R. Emmett, *The Elgar Companion to Chicago Economics* (Cheltenham: Edward Elgar, 2010); K. Hoover, *Economics as Ideology* (Lanham, MD: Rowman and Littlefield, 2003); E. W. Kitch, ed., "The Fire of Truth: A Remembrance of Law and Economics at Chicago, 1932–1970," *Journal of Law and Economics* 26 (1983): 163–234; L. Miller, "On the 'Chicago School' of Economics," *Journal of Political Economy* 70 (1962): 64–69; D. Patinkin, *Essays on and in the Chicago Tradition* (Durham, NC: Duke University Press, 1981); M. Reder, "Chicago Economics: Permanence and Change," *Journal of Economic Literature* 20 (1982): 1–38; and W. Samuels, ed., *The Chicago School of Political Economy* (East Lansing: Michigan State University Press, 1976).

4. Angus Bergin's article on Frank Knight is an important attempt at exploring some of the nuances between the different economists of the first Chicago school: "The Radical Conservatism of Frank Knight," *Modern Intellectual History* 6, no. 3 (2009): 513–38, at 150.

5. G. Stigler, "Henry Calvert Simons," *Journal of Law and Economics* 17, no. 1 (April 1974): 5.

6. On Knight, see also J. Buchanan, "Frank H. Knight," in *Remembering the University of Chicago*, ed. E. Shils (Chicago: University of Chicago Press, 1991); F. Knight, *Selected Essays*, ed. R. Emmett, 2 vols. (Chicago: University of Chicago Press, 1999), pt. 2, chap. 6, of *The Elgar Companion to Chicago*, by R. Emmett; and R. Sally, "The Political Economy of Frank Knight: Classical Liberalism from Chicago," *Constitutional Political Economy* 8 (1997): 123–28. On Viner, see P. Samuelson, "Jacob Viner," in Shils, *Remembering the University of Chicago*.

7. On Director, see R. Coase, "Aaron Director," in *The New Palgrave Dictionary of Economics and Law,* ed. Paul Newman (New York: Macmillan, 1998), and R. Van Horn, "Aaron Director," in Emmett, *Elgar Companion to Chicago Economics,* chap. 3. On Stigler, see his autobiography, *Memoirs of an Unregulated Economist* (New York: Basic Books, 1988), and E. Nik-Khah, "George J. Stigler," in Emmett, *Elgar Companion to Chicago Economics,* 265–70. On Becker, see the Hoover Institution's retrospective collection of essays, *The Essence of Becker* (Stanford, CA: Hoover Institution, 1995).

8. On the differences between the Austrian and the Chicago schools and their alleged misrepresentation, Friedman wrote to Ed Crane, the director of the Cato Institute, on June 1, 1977:

> The fact is that insofar as there is any live movement whatsoever for reducing the scope of government, for reducing government fine-tuning and governmental intervention in the economy its major source has been the Chicago school and the group whom you so disparagingly label as monetarists. I cannot understand what

it is you propose to achieve by misrepresenting in this way what are fundamentally minor doctrinal disputes and erecting them into major differences of view.

(box 24, folder 17, Friedman Papers, Hoover Institution, Stanford University, Palo Alto, CA [hereafter "Friedman Papers"])

According to Friedman, only one major issue really separated the groups—their approach to the business cycle, though it was definitely the case that the Austrian school emphasized immutable economic law while the second Chicago school focused on positive economics, on empirical proof and the testing of data.

9. Van Horn and Mirowski, "Rise of the Chicago School of Economics," 155.

10. Ibid., 162.

11. Ibid., 149.

12. On Hayek's role, see also J. Peck, "Remaking Laissez-Faire," *Progress in Human Geography* 32, no. 1 (2008): 3–43. According to Peck, Hayek was "so often a mediator" as he pursued his organizational strategy for neoliberalism. Peck tells of the debates between the Robbins-Director faction of the Mont Pelerin Society, which wanted the society to maintain an academic bearing, and the faction around Karl Brandt of Stanford University and Albert Hunold at Geneva, which wanted to espouse a specific policy program.

13. Stigler, "Henry Simons," 1.

14. Ibid.

15. On Simons, see also C. A. Bowler, "The Papers of Henry C. Simons," *Journal of Law and Economics* 17, no. 1 (1972): 7–11; J. B. De Long, "In Defense of Henry Simons' Standing as a Classical Liberal," *Cato Journal* 9 (1990): 601–18; and A. Director, "Simons on Taxation," *University of Chicago Law Review* 14 (1946): 15–19.

16. H. Simons, "A Positive Programme for Laissez-Faire: Some Policies for a Liberal Economic Policy," chap. 2 in *Economic Policy for a Free Society* (Chicago: University of Chicago Press, 1948), 42. The essay was originally published in a public policy pamphlet edited by Harry Gideonse and published by the University of Chicago in 1934.

17. H. Simons, "Rules versus Authorities in Monetary Policy," *Journal of Political Economy* 44, no. 1 (1936): 1–30. Later still, Margaret Thatcher's chancellors of the exchequer, Geoffrey Howe and Nigel Lawson saw in the European exchange rate mechanism, for example, a source of external financial discipline that would compensate for Britain's fiscal laxness.

18. On Friedman's life, see his autobiography, written with his wife: M. Friedman and R. Friedman, *Two Lucky People: Memoirs* (Chicago: University of Chicago Press, 1999). Alan Ebenstein has also written a biography, *Milton Friedman* (London: Palgrave, 2007). On his monetary theory, see R. Woods, ed., *Milton Friedman: Critical Assessments* (London: Routledge, 1990).

19. See, e.g., M. Friedman, "The Monetary Theory and Policy of Henry Simons," *Journal of Law and Economics* 10 (October 1967): 1–13.

20. Simons, "A Positive Programme for Laissez-Faire," 42.

21. Ibid., 42.

22. Ibid., 43.

23. Ibid., 42.

24. See R. Van Horn, "Reinventing Monopoly and the Role of Corporations: The Roots of Chicago Law and Economics," in Mirowski and Plehwe, *The Road from Mont Pelerin.*

25. "Neoliberalism" was a term the Austrians had not explicitly used in their texts despite its adoption at the Colloque Walter Lippmann in 1938. But it was already in use in Germany.

26. M. Friedman, "Neo-liberalism and Its Prospects," 1951, p. 4, box 42, folder 8, Friedman Papers. A version of this piece was later published in the journal *Farmand* (February 1951, vol. 17, pp. 89–93).

27. Interestingly, Friedman in this paper identified Simons's system as neoliberal rather than laissez-faire, this despite Simons's description of his own ideas as laissez-faire. This nuance may have been because of the unpopular connotations of laissez-faire in the decades following the Great Depression. The original neoliberals, in the 1930s, saw their project as finding a middle way between laissez-faire and the New Deal—the central theme of Friedman's essay. Friedman returned to its use by the 1970s.

28. Friedman, "Neo-liberalism and Its Prospects," 4.

29. Ibid., 3.

30. Ibid., 5.

31. Alan Greenspan famously admitted, on October 23, 2008, before the House Committee on Oversight and Government Reform in response to Chairman Henry Waxman's questions that he had "found a flaw in the [free market] model that I perceived as the critical functioning structure that defines how the world works"—that "critical functioning structure" was the self-regulation of the financial markets.

32. The programs of the eight meetings (1947–57) of the Mont Pelerin Society, 1/4, Cockett Papers (copied from the Hoover Institution), London School of Economics Archives (hereafter "Cockett Papers").

33. H. Simons, "For a Free Market Liberalism," *University of Chicago Law Review* 8, no. 2 (February 1941): 213.

34. Ibid., 205.

35. The work of the Austrian school, and especially that of Mises, can also be seen partly as an attempt to counter this powerful narrative in German history through a reorientation of political economy around the individual.

36. On Adam Smith and the Scottish Enlightenment, see I. Hont, M. Ignatieff, and A. Skinner, eds., *Wealth and Virtue: The Shaping of Political Economy in the Scottish Enlightenment* (Cambridge: Cambridge University Press, 1983). On Hume, see D. Forbes, *Hume's Philosophical Politics* (Cambridge: Cambridge University Press, 1985). On both, see K. Haakonssen, *The Science of a Legislator: The Natural Jurisprudence of David Hume and Adam Smith* (Cambridge: Cambridge University Press, 1981) and his edited *The Cambridge Companion to Adam Smith* (Cambridge: Cambridge University Press, 2006).

37. N. Phillipson, *Adam Smith: An Enlightened Life* (London: Penguin, Allen Lane, 2010), 117.

38. F. A. Hayek, *The Constitution of Liberty* (Chicago: University of Chicago Press, 1960), 1.

39. Milton Friedman, unpublished paper on Adam Smith, "Highlights of Remarks for Tuck 75th Anniversary Symposium," 28 May 1976, box 55, folder 20, Friedman Papers.

40. Milton Friedman, "Adam Smith's Relevance for 1976," address to the Mont Pelerin Society, 27 August 1976, box 55, folder 21, Friedman Papers.

41. Quoted in E. Rothschild, *Economic Sentiments: Adam Smith, Condorcet, and the Enlightenment* (Cambridge, MA: Harvard University Press, 2001), 65.

42. See I. Hont and M. Ignatieff, introduction to *Wealth and Virtue*, ed. I. Hont, M. Ignatieff, and A. Skinner. See also I. Hont, *Jealousy of Trade: International Competition and the Nation-State in Historical Perspective* (Cambridge, MA: Harvard University Press, 2005).

43. The Girondins were the French liberal revolutionaries whose ascendancy preceded that of the more radical Jacobins, who presided over the Great Terror.

44. Rothschild, *Economic Sentiments*, 30.

45. Ibid., 55.

46. Ibid., "Adam Smith and Conservative Economics," chap. 2.

47. Buchanan to Hayek, undated, 1966, box 13, folder 14, Hayek Papers.

48. See Phillipson, *Adam Smith*.

49. R. Coase, Mont Pelerin Society circular, "Adam Smith's View of Man" (1976), 1, 1/4, Cockett Papers.

50. Ibid., 5.

51. Ibid., 14.

52. G. Stigler, Mont Pelerin Society circular, "The Successes and Failures of Professor Smith" (1976), 1/4, Cockett Papers.

53. A. Smith, *The Wealth of Nations*, book 4 (London: Everyman, 1991), chap. 2, 421.

54. Friedman, "Smith's Relevance for 1976," 2.

55. Ibid., 12.

56. Ibid., 4.

57. Ibid., 13.

58. Ibid., 4.

59. Ibid., 6–7.

60. Ibid., 7.

61. A. Smith, *The Wealth of Nations*, book 5, chap. 1, articles 1 and 2.

62. A. Smith, *The Theory of Moral Sentiments* (Oxford: Oxford University Press, 1976), 61. Friedman himself cannot be accused of being completely unconcerned for the disadvantaged, but, as we shall see in the next chapters, the application of neoliberal thought to policy in the Thatcher and Reagan administrations certainly did have damaging effects on "persons of poor and mean condition."

63. Hayek, *The Constitution of Liberty*, 11.

64. See especially Mises, *Human Action: A Treatise on Economics* (New Haven, CT: Yale University Press, 1949); Hayek, *The Constitution of Liberty;* and Friedman, *Capitalism and Freedom* (Chicago: University of Chicago Press, 1962).

65. Friedman, *Capitalism and Freedom*, 13.

66. Mises to Friedrich Hayek, 31 December 1946, box 38, folder 24, Hayek Papers.

67. L. Mises, introduction to *The Wealth of Nations*, by A. Smith (Washington, DC: Henry Regnery, 1952), 3.

68. Friedman, *Capitalism and Freedom*, 7.

69. Ibid., 17.

70. Ibid., 20–21.

71. Ibid., 21.

72. Ibid., 197.

73. Ibid.

74. Ibid., 199–200.

75. Ibid., 201.

76. Hayek, *The Constitution of Liberty.*

77. H. A. Johnson (personnel officer) to Friedman, 19 February 1951, box 22, folder 9, Friedman Papers.

78. Friedman, 2002 preface to *Capitalism and Freedom*, ix.

79. F. Fukuyama, *The End of History and The Last Man* (New York: Free Press, 1992).

80. Much of the literature is in German, but of what is available in English on ordoliberalism, see C. Allen, "The Underdevelopment of Keynesianism in Germany," in *The Political Power of Economic Ideas: Keynesianism across Nations,* ed. P. Hall (Princeton, NJ: Princeton University Press, 1989); A. Peacock and H. Willgerodt (with D. Johnson), eds., *Germany's Social Market Economy*, vol. 1, *Origins and Evolution*, vol. 2, *German Neoliberals and the Social Market Economy* (New York: St. Martin's Press, 1989); and A. J. Nicholls, *Freedom with Responsibility: The Social Market Economy in Germany, 1918–1963* (Oxford: Clarendon Press, 1994). See also C. Friedrich, "The Political Thought of Neo-Liberalism," *American Political Science Review* 49, no. 2 (June 1955): 509–25, and H. M. Oliver, "German Neoliberalism," *Quarterly Journal of Economics* 74, no. 1 (1960): 3–43.

81. On Eucken, see G. Meijer, "Walter Eucken's Contribution to Economics in an International Perspective," *Journal of Economic Studies* 21, no. 4 (1994): 25–37.

82. Friedrich, "The Political Thought of Neo-Liberalism," 511.

83. As mentioned in the introduction, the German neoliberals were also known as ordoliberals because of their association with the journal of the same name. "Ordo" stood for *Jahrbuch für die Ordnung von Wirtschaft und Gesellschaft*, or the Ordo Yearbook of Economic and Social Order. Hayek, Friedman, Stigler, and Buchanan all contributed to the journal as well at various points.

84. Friedrich, "The Political Thought of Neo-liberalism," 511.

85. Friedrich writes in footnote 11 of the same article:

It should be noted that writers such as Hayek and Ludwig von Mises, while obviously sharing a substantial number of the negative positions of this group—for example, the rerejection of all forms of socialism and planning—take a more traditional view, and are therefore referred to by the Neo-liberals as "palaeo-liberals"—old-timers who do not recognise the lessons of Communism and Fascism.

86. This was when the SPD disavowed Marxism and focused instead on social welfare as a means to greater equality.

87. R. M. Hartwell, *A History of the Mont Pelerin Society* (Indianapolis: Liberty Fund, 1995), 204.

88. Ibid., 19.

89. WHCF–GEN BE5, National Economy, Nixon Library, National Archives, College Park, MD.

90. "Research Report on Ludwig Erhard's Achievements," special bulletin (Great Barrington, MA: American Institute for Economic Research, August 1959), 2.

91. In *Capitalism and Freedom*, Friedman was still willing to say that antitrust laws had been useful. By December 26, 2005, in his interview with Charlie Rose, Friedman said that his previous advocacy of antitrust laws was a mistake and that they did more harm than good.

92. "Research Report on Ludwig Erhard's Achievements," 3.

93. Ibid., 2.

94. Ptak, "Neoliberalism in Germany," in Mirowski and Plehwe, *The Road from Mont Pelerin*, 104.

95. Ibid., 103.

96. See R. Van Horn, "Reinventing Monopoly and the Role of Corporations: The Roots of Chicago Law and Economics," in Mirowski and Plehwe, *The Road from Mont Pelerin*.

97. John Hoskyns, interview with the author, June 2007.

98. Geoffrey Howe, interview with the author, June 2007.

99. Nigel Lawson, interview with the author, June 2007.

100. Norman Lamont, interview with the author, July 2007.

101. See G. Becker, *The Economics of Discrimination* (Chicago: University of Chicago Press, 1957); *Human Capital: A Theoretical and Empirical Analysis, with Special Reference to Education* (Chicago: University of Chicago Press, 1964); *The Economic Approach to Human Behaviour* (Chicago: University of Chicago Press, 1976). For Peter Bauer, see *Economic Analysis and Policy in Underdeveloped Economies* (Cambridge: Cambridge University Press, 1957).

102. John Blundell, interview with the author, June 2007.

103. The paper is in the Nixon White House Central Staff Papers with a summary note to the president that states:

A central thesis of this paper is that as a rule regulation is acquired by the industry, and is designed and operated for the primary benefit of that industry.

(WHCF–EX BE5–Box 47, National Economy, Nixon Library, National Archives, College Park, MD).

104. G. Stigler, "The Theory of Economic Regulation," *Bell Journal of Economics and Management Science* 2, no. 1. (Spring 1971): 3.

105. Ibid., 4.

106. Ibid., 6.

107. Ibid.

108. Ibid., 17–18.

109. See Duncan Black, "On the Rationale of Group Decisionmaking," *Journal of Political Economy* 56 (1948): 23–36, and his book, *The Theory of Committees and Elections* (Cambridge: Cambridge University Press, 1958); Kenneth Arrow, *Social Choice and Individual Values* (New Haven, CT: Yale University Press, 1951); Anthony Downs, *An Economic Theory of Democracy* (New York: Harper, 1957); and Mancur Olsen, *The Logic of Collective Action* (Cambridge, MA: Harvard University Press, 1965).

110. See, e.g., W. Riker, *The Theory of Political Coalitions* (New Haven, CT: Yale University Press, 1962).

111. For a comparison of Buchanan and the German neoliberal Walter Eucken, see H. Leipold, "Neoliberal Ordnungstheorie and Constitutional Economics: A Comparison between Eucken and Buchanan," *Constitutional Political Economy* 1 (1990): 47–65.

112. J. Buchanan, *Public Choice: The Origins and Development of a Research Program* (Fairfax, VA: George Mason University, 2003), 5.

113. Ibid., 1.

114. Ibid., 5.

115. J. Buchanan, introduction to *The Economics of Politics*, ed. J. Buchanan (London: IEA, 1978), 17.

116. Buchanan to Arthur Seldon, April 30, 1980, box 40, folder 6, IEA Papers, Hoover Institution.

117. Buchanan, "Public Choice," 8.

118. Buchanan to Hayek, 24 November 1965, box 13, folder, 14, Hayek Papers.

119. Buchanan, "Public Choice," 8.

Chapter 4: A Transatlantic Network

1. The term "intellectual entrepreneurs" is used by John Blundell of the IEA in *Waging the War of Ideas: Why There Are No Shortcuts*, Heritage Lectures No. 254 (Washington, DC: Heritage Foundation, 1990). I have adapted his phrase.

2. Fisher to Hayek, undated, box 3, folder 7, Hayek Papers.

3. On Eisenhower, see C. J. Pach and E. Richardson, *The Presidency of Dwight D. Eisenhower* (Lawrence: University of Kansas Press, 1991); R. R. Bowie and R. H. Immerman, *Waging Peace: How Eisenhower Shaped an Enduring Cold War Strategy*

(Oxford: Oxford University Press, 1998). On the postwar British prime ministers, see P. Hennessy, *The Prime Minister* (London: Penguin, 2000), and his book on Britain in the 1950s, *Having It So Good* (London: Penguin, 2006). See also D. Sandbrook, *Never Had It So Good* (London: Little, Brown, 2005).

4. The literature on Reagan is vast, but from a favorable perspective, on his pre-presidential career, see S. F. Hayward, *The Age of Reagan*, vol. 1, *1964–1980* (New York: Prima, 2001), and vol. 2, *The Conservative Counterrevolution: 1980–89* (New York: Crown Forum, 2009). From a different perspective, see S. Wilentz, *The Age of Reagan: A History, 1974–2008* (New York: HarperCollins, 2008).

5. On Powell, see S. Heffer, *Like the Roman* (London: Weidenfeld and Nicolson, 1998).

6. In this chapter, the lowercase "conservative" is used to describe American conservatives, while "Conservative" indicates a member of the Conservative Party in Britain.

7. This was Britain's failed mission, with France, to invade the Suez Canal to prevent Egypt's General Nasser from taking control of the canal. The plan was undertaken behind the back of the United States, which refused, under Eisenhower, to back it. The result was a humiliating retreat.

8. G. H. Nash, *The Conservative Intellectual Movement in America since 1945* (Wilmington, DE: Intercollegiate Studies Institute, 1996), xv.

9. See B. Schulman, *From Cotton Belt to Sun Belt* (Oxford: Oxford University Press, 1991), and M. Lassiter, *The Silent Majority* (Princeton, NJ: Princeton University Press, 2006).

10. Nash, *The Conservative Intellectual Movement,* xvi.

11. W. F. Buckley, *God and Man at Yale* (Chicago: Henry Regnery, 1951), lix.

12. Neoconservatism is often confused with neoliberalism. Neoconservatism, however, is associated with the spreading of the creed of free markets and liberal democracy to new countries and regions. It is therefore primarily concerned with foreign policy, most famously in the arguments of proponents of the second Iraq war (2003) such as Paul Wolfowitz. Neoconservatism was the ideology of many former radical and liberals who became disillusioned with the Great Society.

13. L. Ribuffo, *The Old Christian Right: The Protestant Far Right from the Great Depression to the Cold War* (Philadelphia: Temple University Press, 1983).

14. The first Red Scare had occurred in the aftermath of World War I and the Russian Revolution in 1919–20.

15. See Lassiter, *Silent Majority*.

16. See D. Carter, *The Politics of Rage: George Wallace, the Origins of the New Conservatism and the Transformation of American Politics* (Baton Rouge: Louisiana University Press, 1995).

17. Lassiter, *Silent Majority*, 1.

18. See E. Fones-Wolf, *Selling Free Enterprise* (Urbana: University of Illinois Press, 1994), and K. Phillips-Fein, *Invisible Hands: The Businessmen's Crusade against the New Deal* (New York: W. W. Norton, 2009).

19. Though the debates surrounding the "loss of China" after 1949 indicate the way in which Republicans accused the Democrats of being poor stewards of the ship during the battles of the Cold War.

20. L. McGirr, *Suburban Warriors: The Origins of the New American Right* (Princeton, NJ: Princeton University Press, 2001), 35.

21. Ibid., 94.

22. The group's "Sharon statement of principles" was drafted by Evans with the help of Annette Kirk, Russell's wife.

23. G. Schneider, *Cadres for Conservatism: Young Americans for Freedom and the Rise of the Contemporary Right* (New York: New York University Press, 1999), 1.

24. E. J. Dionne, *Why Americans Hate Politics* (New York: Simon and Schuster, 1991), 25.

25. Note by Rab Butler, "Britain Strong and Free," 1, ACP 3/2, Conservative Party Archive, Bodleian Library, Oxford.

26. E. H. H. Green, *Ideologies of Conservatism* (Oxford: Oxford University Press, 2001), 223.

27. Ibid.

28. Ibid., 50.

29. Geoffrey Howe, interview with the author, June 2007.

30. Ibid.

31. J. Barr, *A History of the Bow Group* (London: Politicos, 2001), 51–52.

32. Geoffrey Howe, interview with the author, June 2007.

33. The Montgomery bus boycott was a peaceful direct action campaign involving civil rights activists, including Martin Luther King and Ralph Abernathy in 1955. Little Rock, Arkansas, was the center of a crisis in 1957 when nine African American students attempted to enroll at the segregated Central High School and were prevented by Governor Orval Faubus. President Eisenhower ordered the National Guard to oversee the students' successful enrollment, thereby ensuring compliance with the *Brown v. Board of Education* decision to desegregate the school system in 1954.

34. Peter Rachman was a notorious London landlord who built a property empire in West London supposedly by ruthlessly driving out protected white tenants and replacing them with new black immigrants in smaller subdivided apartments. The new tenants lacked the same legal protections as the previous longer-standing white tenants.

35. Immigration has been an issue successively exploited throughout the postwar period to the present day by hard-right groups such as the racist National Front and British National Party and the Europhobic United Kingdom Independence Party. At different times, the target was West Indians, South Asians, "asylum seekers," and Central and Eastern Europeans.

36. Hennessy, *Having It So Good,* 501.

37. In this speech, made in Birmingham on April 20, 1968, Powell suggested that immigration from the former empire had the potential to tear modern Britain apart through violence, racial disharmony, and anger.

38. Sandbrook, *Never Had it So Good*, 290.

39. British National Archives, PRO, PREM 11/5198, "Briefing Paper for Senator Goldwater."

40. NA, PRO, PREM 11/5198, note by Lord Harlech, "Goldwater—Republican Candidate."

41. M. Friedman, "Neo-liberalism and Its Prospects," 3, unpublished paper, Friedman Papers. A version of this article was published in the Norwegian neoliberal magazine *Farmand* in 1951.

42. S. Blumenthal, *The Rise of the Counter-Establishment: From Conservative Ideology to Political Power* (New York: Times Books, 1986).

43. F. A. Hayek, "The Intellectuals and Socialism," *University of Chicago Law Review* 49 (Spring 1949): 418.

44. Phillips-Fein, *Invisible Hands*, xii.

45. Ibid., 321.

46. American Enterprise Institute, *Annual Report* (Washington, DC: AEI, 2003), available at http://www.aei.org/history.

47. H. Hazlitt, "The Early History of FEE," *Freeman* 34, no. 3 (March 1984): 38–39.

48. M. Friedman and G. Stigler, *Roofs or Ceilings* (Irvington: FEE, 1946).

49. Hazlitt, "Early History of FEE," 39.

50. Ed Crane, interview with the author, October 2008.

51. Hazlitt, "Early History of FEE," 38.

52. See J. Blundell, *Waging the War of Ideas* (London: IEA, 2001), 20.

53. Ibid., 21.

54. Antony Fisher to Friedrich Hayek, 9 July 1985, box 19, folder 19, Hayek Papers.

55. At one time or another, the institute counted among its people Friedman, Hayek, Mises, Peter Bauer, Lionel Robbins, Gary Becker, George Stigler, James Buchanan, Gordon Tullock, Martin Feldstein, Reagan's future chairman of the Council of Economic Advisers, and Alan Walters, Thatcher's future chief economic adviser.

56. Ed Feulner, interview with the author, October 2008.

57. John Redwood, interview with the author, July 2007.

58. Fisher to Hayek, 23 September 1980, box 19, folder 19, Hayek Papers.

59. Leaflet, Institute for Humane Studies, "The Institute Story," date unknown, 18, box 26, folder 28, Hayek Papers.

60. Ibid., 13.

61. Ibid., 23.

62. J. Bruce-Gardyne, "Heresy Hunting in Lord North Street," *Daily Telegraph*, December 7, 1978.

63. Interviews with the author, summer 2007. This is a view confirmed by Cockett in his account of the role of British think tanks in Thatcher's economic policies, *Thinking the Unthinkable*. A different perspective is provided by Radikha Desai, who wrote one of the first scholarly accounts of neoliberal think tanks: "Second-hand Dealers in Ideas: Think-tanks and Thatcherite Hegemony," *New Left Review* 1 (January–February 1994): 27–65.

64. Margaret Thatcher, "Speech to IEA," 17 April 1987, box 19, folder 19, Hayek Papers.

65. Leon Brittan, interview with the author, July 2007.

66. Ed Feulner, interview with the author, October 2008.

67. Ibid.

68. See K. Tribe, "Neoliberalism in Britain, 1930–1980," in Van Horn and Mirowski, *The Road from Mont Pelerin*, 88.

69. Ed Feulner, interview with the author, October 2008.

70. Ibid.

71. Ronald Reagan to Eamonn Butler, 27 March 1984, box 24, folder 22, Hayek Papers.

72. At www.heritage.org/About/35thAnniversary.cfm.

73. L. Edwards, *The Power of Ideas: The Heritage Foundation at 25 Years* (Ottawa, IL: Jameson Books, 1997), 26.

74. Ibid., xiii.

75. Ed Crane, interview with the author, October 2008.

76. On Rand and her influence on the rise of the New Right in the postwar years, see J. Burns, *Goddess of the Market: Ayn Rand and the American Right* (Oxford: Oxford University Press, 2009).

77. Ed Crane, interview with the author, October 2008.

78. Ibid.

79. Ibid.

80. Box 14, folder 20, Hayek Papers.

81. Madsen Pirie and Eamonn Butler, interview with the author, September 2007.

82. Ibid.

83. See M. Pirie, *Micropolitics* (London: Wildwood House, 1988).

84. Eamonn Butler to Friedrich Hayek, 30 October 1978, box 9, folder 3, Hayek Papers.

85. He also became the president of the St. James Society, which Eamonn Butler calls "the British version of the Philadelphia and Mont Pelerin Societies."

86. D. Mason, *Revising the Ratings System* (London: Adam Smith Institute, 1985). The reviled tax was the subject of a campaign of demonstrations that culminated in riots amid 200,000 demonstrators in Trafalgar Square on March 31, 1990. The poll tax was subsequently replaced after Margaret Thatcher's fall by Environment Secretary Michael Heseltine.

87. C. Murray, *Losing Ground: American Social Policy, 1950–1980* (New York: Basic Books, 1984).

88. Bob Dole to William Hammett, 24 November 1984, box 23, folder 15, Hayek Papers.

89. David Willetts to William Hammett, 26 November 1984, box 23, folder 15, Hayek Papers.

90. Arthur Seldon to Hayek, 28 August 1975.

91. Hayek to Seldon, 7 September 1975.

92. Interview with the author, September 2007.

93. See Phillips-Fein, *Invisible Hands*.

94. Cockett, *Thinking the Unthinkable*, 80.

95. Friedman to R. Cornuelle, 23 January 1956, box 24, folder 9, Friedman Papers.

96. Box 17, folder 37, Hayek Papers.

97. Leonard Read to Hayek, 7 January 1970, box 20, folder 1, Hayek Papers.

98. George Shultz, interview with the author, February 2008.

99. Undated Memo to "Liberals of the British Isles and the Continent of Europe" on the subject of the "Interchange of Liberal Literature," box 20, folder 1, Hayek Papers.

100. Ralph Raico to Friedrich Hayek, 7 April 1977, box 14, folder 20, Hayek Papers.

101. M. Friedman, "The Limitations of Tax Limitation," *Heritage Foundation Policy Review*, Summer 1978, 11.

102. Nigel Lawson, interview with the author, July 2007.

103. On this, see Nash, *The Conservative Intellectual Movement in America*.

104. Friedman to Buckley, 3 September 1969, box 22, folder 13, Friedman Papers.

105. See Mary Brennan's *Turning Right in the Sixties* (Chapel Hill: University of North Carolina Press, 1995) and Gregory Schneider's *Cadres for Conservatism*.

106. R. Perlstein, *Before the Storm: Barry Goldwater and the Unmaking of the American Consensus* (New York: Hill and Wang, 2001).

107. Brennan, *Turning Right*, 14.

108. Ed Crane, interview with the author, October 2008.

109. Ibid.

110. Ronald Reagan, "The New Noblesse Oblige," speech to Institute of Directors, London, 6 November 1969, GO178, Gubernatorial Papers, Ronald Reagan Presidential Library, Simi Valley, CA.

111. G. Soros, "The Financial Crisis: An Interview with George Soros," *New York Review of Books*, May 15, 2008.

112. George Shultz, interview with the author, February 2008.

113. Ibid.

114. Nigel Lawson and Norman Lamont, interviews with the author, June and July 2007.

115. The Selsdon Conference was the famous shadow cabinet conference convened by Edward Heath to prepare the manifesto for the British general election of 1970. Heath's critics, especially those on the right, would later claim that Heath in government departed from the radical program agreed to at Selsdon in a series of policy U-turns. Heath loyalists hotly dispute this; they argue that a radical free market agenda was never agreed to, let alone abandoned.

116. K. Joseph, *Monetarism Is Not Enough* (London: CPS, 1976).

117. The young Thatcher had apparently read *The Road to Serfdom* in the 1940s, according to historian Richard Cockett.

118.   N. Lawson, *The View from No. 11* (London: Bantam, 1992), 1041.

119.   He added this as a postscript to *The Constitution of Liberty*, his statement of political philosophy published in 1960.

120.   Friedman to Congdon, 12 June 1979, Friedman Papers.

121.   James Buchanan to Hayek, 10 January 1963, box 13, folder 14, Hayek Papers. In the same letter, Buchanan joked to Hayek about his fame among students at the University of Virginia:

> P.S. One side story might amuse you. A team from the University of Virginia has just retired as "champions" of the College Bowl, a television quiz program that pits colleges against each other. This has been the item of notoriety here. The boys, who are all very good, have taken no economics, and they failed miserably the first few times on economic questions. However, on the last program Sunday, when they won for the fifth time and retired, one question was: What subject would you be studying if you were assigned reading from: Gustav Cassell, Alfred Marshall, and Friedrich Hayek. They passed this one with flying colors, far outdistancing the other team.

122.   Norman Lamont, chancellor under Major, and Douglas Hurd, former home and foreign secretary under Thatcher, both describe her as "heroic," while Martin Anderson, who worked in the first Reagan White house, describes the Reagan period as a "revolution." A serious historical presentation of this view is Richard Cockett's *Thinking the Unthinkable*. Its focus is on Britain, though it alludes to American developments in places, and chapters 7 and 8 are subtitled "The Heroic Age," parts 1 and 2.

Chapter Five: Keynesianism and the Emergence of Monetarism, 1945–71

1.   This chapter and the next are primarily about the political advance of a set of economic ideas. The focus is not on the detailed merits of different economic theories (the judgment of which should be left to those better qualified) but on their adoption by politicians and policymakers, whose grasp of the theory was not always clear or comprehensive. The ways in which economic ideas took hold in the political sphere through their successful promotion in a time of crisis illustrate the vagaries of the relationship between expert academic knowledge and the policy process.

2.   Nigel Lawson, interview with the author, June 2007.

3.   On Keynes, his ideas, and the spread of what became known as Keynesianism, see P. Hall, ed., *The Political Power of Economic Ideas: Keynesianism across Nations* (Princeton, NJ: Princeton University Press, 1989). On Keynesianism and its spread, see D. Winch, "Keynes, Keynesianism, and State Intervention." On Keynes's influence in the United States, see W. Salent, "The Spread of Keynesian Doctrines and Practices in the United States," chap. 2.

4. J. M. Keynes, *A Tract on Monetary Reform* (London: Macmillan, 1923, 2000), 80. This reference was to the validity of the quantity theory of money. Keynes emphasized the intervening changes in real activity while the price level adapts to changes in the quantity of money. This is the basis of Keynes's argument for a policy of price stability with a floating exchange rate. Unsurprisingly, Friedman regarded this as Keynes's best book.

5. See, e.g., chapter 1 in R. Cockett, *Thinking the Unthinkable: Think-Tanks and the Economic Counter-Revolution* (London: Fontana Press, 1995).

6. R. Skidelsky, *John Maynard Keynes*, 3 vols. (London: Macmillan, 1983, 1992, 2000), 2:xv. Keynes's first official biographer was his friend and follower, Roy Harrod. Harrod's biography was an attempt to safeguard Keynes's international, and especially American, reputation. Skidelsky's three-volume life represented more than twenty years of research. See also P. Clarke, *Keynes: The Rise, Fall and Return of Twentieth Century's Greatest Economist* (London: Bloomsbury, 2009).

7. Skidelsky, *John Maynard Keynes*, 2:xv.

8. R. Backhouse and B. Bateman, "A Cunning Purchase: The Life and Work of Maynard Keynes," in *The Cambridge Companion to Keynes*, ed. R. Backhouse and B. Bateman (Cambridge: Cambridge University Press, 2006), 15.

9. See, e.g., D. Laidler, "Keynes and the Birth of Modern Macroeconomics," in Backhouse and Batemen, *The Cambridge Companion to Keynes*, chap. 3, 51.

10. Skidelsky, *John Maynard Keynes*, 2:183.

11. Laidler, "Keynes and the Birth of Modern Macroeconomics," 51.

12. Ibid.

13. Skidelsky, *John Maynard Keynes*, 3:153

14. "Friedman: Prophet of New, New Economics?," *Washington Post*, December 31, 1967.

15. Nigel Lawson, interview with the author, June 2007.

16. R. Skidelsky, "Hayek versus Keynes: The Road to Reconciliation," in *The Cambridge Companion to Hayek*, ed. E. Feser. chap. 5 (Cambridge: Cambridge University Press, 2006), 95.

17. Ibid., 95.

18. A. W. Phillips, "The Relation between Unemployment and the Rate of Change of Money Wage Rates in the United Kingdom, 1861–1957," *Economica*, n.s., 25, no. 100 (November 1958): 283–99.

19. P. Samuelson and R. Solow, "Analytical Aspects of Anti-Inflation Policy," *American Economic Review* 50, no. 2 (May 1960): 177–94. Special issue, *Papers and Proceedings of the Seventy-second Annual Meeting of the American Economic Association*.

20. J. M. Keynes, *How to Pay for the War* (London: Macmillan, 1940).

21. Laidler, "Keynes and the Birth of Modern Macroeconomics," 54.

22. G. Peden, "Keynes and British Economic Policy," in Feser, *Cambridge Companion to Keynes*, chap. 6, 111.

23. PREM 11, PRO/NA, Roy Harrod to PM, 7 October 1957.

24. The figure estimated as healthy by Keynes was around 4 percent. Beveridge thought it should be 3 percent. The 4 percent figure was suggested in the employment white paper of 1944. This was also the aimed-for level in the United States after 1947. But after the war, the Conservative and Labour governments of the 1950s and 1960s reduced the desired level even further, arguing for below 3 percent.

25. 1824, PREM 11, NA/PRO, "The Pound Sterling," draft memoorandum by the chancellor of the exchequer.

26. Robbins said in his memoirs, *An Autobiography of an Economist* (London: Macmillan, 1976), that this intellectual disagreement was the greatest mistake of his life. The strains in the personal relationship are recounted in Hayek's letters to Popper, which are held in the Hoover Institution.

27. 1824, PREM 11, NA/PRO, paper on inflation by the prime minister.

28. "A Mere 50 Million," *Spectator*, January 10, 1958.

29. Macmillan wrote a book on political philosophy, *The Middle Way* (London: Macmillan, 1938). In this book, the future prime minister argued for a centrist approach, including a comprehensive welfare state that would include generous benefits and a move toward a basic minimum standard of living for all people.

30. Leader, *Economist*, January 11, 1958.

31. D. Sandbrook, *Never Had It So Good: Britain, 1956–63* (London: Little, Brown, 2005), 85.

32. Enoch Powell to Peter Thorneycroft, 21 February 1959, POLL 3/1/14, Powell Papers, Churchill College, Cambridge (hereafter "Powell Papers").

33. Peter Jay, interview with the author, September 2007.

34. Friedman to Buckley, 2 December 1970, box 22, folder 13, Friedman Papers.

35. Ibid.

36. Geoffrey Howe, interview with the author, June 2007.

37. Norman Lamont, interview with the author, July 2007.

38. John Hoskyns, interview with the author, June 2007.

39. Ibid.

40. Enoch Powell, speech to the Leeds Junior Chamber of Commerce, 26 September 1968, POLL 4/1/3, Powell Papers.

41. Ibid.

42. Enoch Powell, "The Fixed Exchange and *Dirigisme*," speech delivered to the Aviemore Conference, Mont Pelerin Society, 6 September 1968, POLL 4/1/3, Powell Papers.

43. Ibid.

44. Ralph Harris to Enoch Powell, 25 September 1973, POLL 1/1/49, Powell Papers.

45. Powell to Friedman, 26 August 1974, POLL 1/1/49, Powell Papers.

46. Enoch Powell, speech to the American Chamber of Commerce at the Savoy Hotel, London, 10 June 1965, POLL 4/1/1, Powell Papers.

47. Ibid.

48. S. Heffer, *Like the Roman: A Life of Enoch Powell* (London: Weidenfeld and Nicolson, 1998), 437–38.

49. Skidelsky, *John Maynard Keynes*, 3:504.

50. T. Karier, *Great Experiments in American Economic Policy* (Westport, CT: Praeger, 1997), 11.

51. Ibid., 12

52. Ibid., 13.

53. Friedman to Barry Goldwater, 13 December 1960, box 27, folder 24, Friedman Papers.

54. Ibid.

55. This was discussed in detail in chapter 2.

56. Friedman to Goldwater, 12 January 1962.

57. Nigel Lawson and Jim Boughton, interviews with the author, June 2007 (Lawson) and October 2008 (Boughton).

58. For an interesting discussion of how some economic ideas take hold while others don't see, H. Johnson, "The Keynesian Revolution and the Monetarist Counter-Revolution, *American Economic Review* 61, no. 2 (May 1971): 1–14.

59. M. Friedman and A. J. Schwartz, *A Monetary History of the United States, 1867–1960* (Chicago: University of Chicago Press, 1963).

60. M. Friedman, "The Role of Monetary Policy," address to the American Economic Association, December 29, 1967, in *The Essence of Friedman* (Stanford, CA: Hoover Institution, 1986), 388.

61. Ibid.

62. Ibid., 391.

63. Ibid., 392.

64. Ibid.

65. Ibid.

66. Ibid., 393.

67. Ibid.

68. Ibid., 396.

69. Ibid.

70. Ibid., 398.

71. Ibid., 397.

72. Ibid.

73. Norman Lamont, interview with the author, July 2007; A. Walters, *Money in Boom and Slump* (London: IEA, 1970).

74. Friedman to Harry Johnson, 15 July 1965, box 28, folder 33, Friedman Papers.

75. Johnson to Friedman, 4 August 1965.

76. Ibid.

77. Ibid.

78. Peter Bauer to Friedman, 4 October 1972, box 20, folder 27, Friedman Papers.

79. Madsen Pirie and Eamonn Butler, interview with the author, September 2007.

80. Peter Jay, interview with the author, September 2007.

81. For a good account of the contradictions and crises of American liberalism in the 1960s, see A. Matusow, *The Unraveling of America: A History of Liberalism in the 1960s* (New York: HarperCollins, 1986).

82. Karier, *Great Experiments*, 17.

83. Skidelsky, *John Maynard Keynes*, 3:504.

84. Ibid.

85. Ibid., 505–6.

Chapter Six: Economic Strategy

1. Though Friedman never accepted that monetarist policies had been properly followed in either country.

2. Some dispute this view. Kevin Hickson, in *The IMF Crisis of 1976 and British Politics* (Southampton: Tauris Academic Studies, 2005), for example, suggests that Callaghan and Healey were never converted to monetarism. Hickson argues that the Labour government relied on the classic Keynesian tools, public spending and incomes policies that were based on an idea that inflation was based on wages. However, this dismisses Callaghan's professed conversion to monetarism in his 1976 speech to the Labour Party Conference, as well as Healey's introduction of monetary targets. There is a fuller discussion of some of these issues later in the chapter.

3. *Dirigisme* was the French statist tradition of government intervention in the economy.

4. Some argue that this departure in policy marked the beginning of the end of the consensus in Britain. See, e.g., R. Skidelsky, introduction to *Thatcherism*, ed. R. Skidelsky (London: Chatto and Windus, 1988), where he argues there was a shift from "stop-go" to "go-go," the latter grounded in a belief in government "omnicompetence" (9).

5. Friedman to Peter Bauer, 12 April 1966, box 20, folder 27, Friedman Papers.

6. Bauer to Friedman, 27 April 1966, box 20, folder 27, Friedman Papers.

7. George Shultz, interview with the author, February 2008.

8. For a very good, comprehensive account of the debates over economic policy among the senior players in the Labour cabinet, as well as a thorough account of his life and politics more generally, see Ben Pimlott's biography of Wilson, *Harold Wilson* (London: HarperCollins, 1993).

9. See F. Hayek, *Prices and Production* (London: Routledge, 1935), and *The Pure Theory of Capital* (London: Routledge, 1941). On his competing currencies ideas, see F. Hayek, *Choice in Currency: A Way to Stop Inflation* and *Denationalisation of Money*, both published by the IEA in 1976. Hayek's idea was that there was no necessary or inherent need for a government monopoly on the creation and printing of currency. Instead, consumers and the market should be able provide and use any currency they

wished, which would also force a limit on the amount of money in circulation due to market forces.

10. See chapter 4, where a letter from Friedman setting out his position to Goldwater on the international monetary system is quoted. He argued that a gold standard was, though theoretically desirable, impractical.

11. Robbins to Friedman, 6 February 1952, box 32, folder 6, Friedman Papers.

12. On Nixon's presidency and its many contradictions, see R. Perlstein, *Nixonland: The Rise of a President and the Fracturing of America* (New York: Scribner, 2008). On America in the 1970s, see B. Schulman, *The Seventies: The Great Shift in American Culture, Society and Politics* (New York: Da Capo, 2002).

13. The question of whether to float the pound as an alternative to the fixed exchange rate system to combat the balance-of-payments crises that were already becoming a frequent problem was debated in Conservative Party circles in the early 1950s. Winston Churchill's government flirted with the idea of floating in 1952, when Rab Butler was chancellor. Historian Peter Hennessy has argued that this was a key moment when policy might have taken a radically different course. He suggests that the effects of the plan, known as ROBOT, would have been to alter "the country's economic and political history." According to Hennessy, "the postwar consensus would have lasted but eight years, as the new exchange rate policy would have torn up the full-employment pledge which lay at its heart together with a sheaf of other undertakings of an international character." The idea, however, was shelved and renewed agreement was reached in cabinet to stay within the Bretton Woods framework, much to the chagrin of critics such as Enoch Powell. The goal of full employment was considered too important to risk alienating the electorate. The crises of 1947 and 1949 under the preceding Labour government, which culminated in another devaluation of the pound, were not considered serious enough to warrant such a move. ROBOT subsequently disappeared from the debate. But the collapse of the Bretton Woods system in 1971 brought back the idea of floating the pound, this time out of necessity rather than choice.

14. M. Friedman, "*Money Programme* Transcript," 8, box 56, folder 20, Friedman Papers.

15. On Nixon's economic policy, see A. Matusow, *Nixon's Economy: Booms, Busts, Dollars, and Votes* (Lawrence: University Press of Kansas, 1998).

16. Memorandum to the President from Dep. Asst. to the President for Domestic Affairs Kenneth Cole, 25 November 1969, WHCF-EX BE5, Nixon Presidential Papers, National Archives, Washington, DC (hereafter "Nixon Presidential Papers").

17. Anneliese Anderson, interview with the author, February 2008.

18. See Matusow, *Nixon's Economy*.

19. Memorandum of meeting between President Nixon, George Shultz, Milton Friedman, and George Stigler, 8 June 1971, box 48, Nixon Presidential Papers.

20. White House State dinner list, 17 December 1970, WHCF [EX] CO 160, Nixon Presidential Papers.

21. Friedman to President Nixon, 13 March 1970, box 47, WHCF-EX BE5, Nixon Presidential Papers.

22. Memorandum to the President from Paul McCracken, 11 November 1969, WHCF-EX BE5, Nixon Presidential Papers.

23. Friedman to Nixon, 13 March 1970.

24. Ibid.

25. Ibid.

26. Alan Greenspan to John Ehrlichman, "Consumer Sentiment: the 1972 Election and Economic Policy," paper by Townshend-Greenspan & Co., Inc., 18 December 1970, WHCF GEN BE5, Nixon Presidential Papers.

27. Nixon (drafted by McCracken) to Friedman, 18 April 1970, box 47, WHCF-EX BE5, Nixon Presidential Papers.

28. An interesting comment on the character of the trade union movement in the United States at this time comes in a memorandum to President Nixon from his chairman of the Council of Economic Advisers, Paul McCracken, from 17 April 1969:

> Unemployment. While they expressed concern about the extent to which over-all unemployment may rise as we succeed on the inflation front, they showed only passing interest in the composition of unemployment, or in the fact that unemployment rates are highest among non-whites. The AFL-CIO may be embarrassed by the discriminatory practices of some unions, preferring not to get into the problems of non-white unemployment for fear that this would backfire on them.

> (WHCF EX BE5)

29. Policy paper, "Incomes Policy in the United Kingdom under the Labour Government," February 1970, WHCF [GEN] CO 160, Nixon Presidential Papers.

30. Peter G. Peterson to John Connally, 14 June 1971, WHCF [EX] CO 160, Nixon Presidential Papers.

31. Column by William F. Buckley, *New York Post*, August 18, 1973.

32. Friedman to Connally, 3 December 1971, box 33, folder 15, Friedman Papers.

33. G. Shultz, speech to the National Press Club, 6 January 1972, box 33, folder 15, Friedman Papers.

34. Friedman to Connally, 9 August 1971, box 24, folder 3, Friedman Papers.

35. Samuel Brittan to Friedman, 8 October 1971, box 21, folder 38, Friedman Papers. Brittan continued to make an interesting point about the representation of economists' views in the mainstream media. He suggested:

> Incidentally, it did appear to me from press reports, that there was a very large overlap both in analysis and policy recommendations in the evidence given by Samuelson, Krause and yourself to Congress; but for obvious reasons the differences were played up in reporting. May there not be a moral in this? The media have an obvious interest in emphasising disagreements among economists and then ridi-

culing them for their failure to agree. But ought not the profession to retaliate by emphasising the points of agreement?

36. Friedman to Shultz, 24 May 1973, box 33, folder 15, Friedman Papers.

37. Friedman to Brittan, 22 September 1975, Friedman Papers.

38. Arthur Burns to Nixon, 1 June 1973, box 49, Nixon Presidential Papers.

39. Friedman to Philip Crane, 30 November 1974, box 24, folder 18, Friedman Papers.

40. Douglas Hurd, interview with the author, September 2007.

41. A. Seldon, "The Heath Government in History," in *The Heath Government, 1970–1974*, ed. S. Ball and A. Seldon (London: Longman, 1996), chap. 1, 1.

42. Ibid., 14.

43. PREM 15, 42, PRO/NA, Heath, comment on letter from R. A. Allen to PM.

44. A. Cairncross, "The Heath Government and the British Economy," in Ball and Seldon, *The Heath Government*, chap. 5, 110.

45. Douglas Hurd, interview with the author, September 2007.

46. Friedman to Hayek, 7 February 1973, box 20, folder 19, Hayek Papers.

47. Letter from Friedman to Brittan, 6 January 1959, Friedman Papers.

48. Peter Jay, interview with the author, September 2007.

49. See A. Walters, *Money in Boom and Slump* (London: IEA, 1970).

50. Andrew Duguid, interview with the author, September 2007.

51. Leon Brittan, Andrew Duguid, John Hoskyns, Michael Howard, Geoffrey Howe, Douglas Hurd, Norman Lamont, and Nigel Lawson, interviews with the author, summer 2007.

52. Andrew Duguid, John Hoskyns, and Nigel Lawson, interviews with the author, summer 2007.

53. P. Jay, *The Crisis for Western Political Economy and Other Essays* (London: Deutsch, 1984), 38–39.

54. Ibid.

55. Ibid., 39.

56. For example, Brittan wrote a book in 1968 in which he laid out his frustration with the divisions that seemed to characterize modern politics:

> My main object in this essay is to argue that these qualifications [about whether one is left or right on some issues and not others] have now become so important that the left-right spectrum today obscures more than it illuminates. Political discussion, and perhaps even the conduct of politics, would accordingly benefit if it were used much less frequently. For not only is the spectrum concept misleading as a classification of political differences, but its persistence in current discussion has a positively harmful effect. It leads, as I hope to show, to the muffling of important issues, to a bias in favour of certain viewpoints against others and to the erection of unnecessary barriers between those who should be natural allies.

> S. Brittan, *Left or Right: The Bogus Dilemma* (London: Secker and Warburg, 1968), 11.

57. A. Sherman, editor's preface to *Second Thoughts on Full Employment Policy*, by S. Brittan (Chichester: Barry Rose, 1975).

58. Brittan, *Second Thoughts*, 12.

59. Ibid., 89.

60. Brittan to Friedman, 27 September 1973, Friedman Papers.

61. The trade union issue had long been a focus of some of the staunchest free market advocates. Ludwig von Mises, for example, wrote to Friedrich von Hayek in 1946 about the importance of curbing the power of the unions:

> Those who want to preserve freedom must ask for free trade, both domestic and foreign, for the gold standard, and for the reestablishment of the government's exclusive right to resort to violent coercion and suppression (this involves the abolition of the labor union privilege to "punish" strikebreakers.)

(Mises to Hayek, 31 December 1946, box 38, folder 24, Hayek Papers)

62. Norman Lamont, interview with the author, July 2007.

63. Friedman to Brittan, 17 September 1973, box 21, folder 33, Friedman Papers.

64. Brittan to Friedman, 27 September 1973.

65. Ibid. Popper's theory is discussed in chapter 1.

66. Brittan to Friedman, 27 September 1973.

67. Ibid.

68. Jay, *Crisis*, 43.

69. Friedman to Brittan, 21 August 1975.

70. Ibid.

71. The Labour Party had, of course, been founded as the political wing of the Labour movement, which continued to be the party's funder. The "social contract" was the idea that government and the unions would manage economic outcomes together through regular bilateral meetings and discussions. It was ridiculed as decision making through "beer and sandwiches" at Number 10 Downing Street (the prime minister's residence).

72. The alternative economic strategy was developed by Cambridge Keynesian economist Wynne Godley and Stuart Holland. The strategy was a response to the perceived increase in the power and market share of multinational and transnational corporations. According to Kevin Hickson: "It was necessary to increase the role of the state over the meso-economy through compulsory planning agreements, pricing policies, centrally-planned investment and further public ownership." From K. Hickson, *The IMF Crisis of 1976 and British Politics* (London: Tauris Academic Studies, 2002), 170.

Hickson suggests that the new Cambridge school, of which Godley was a leader, brought a key aspect of neoliberal philosophy into Labour Party policy through the belief in "crowding out." Godley believed that a balance-of-payments surplus needed to be restored through the introduction of import quotas and controls:

In addition, the New Cambridge Theorists argued that there was a need to restore industrial efficiency, largely through compulsory planning agreements, and the need to reduce the public sector borrowing requirement, which had a crowding-out effect on international trade and investment.

Hickson, *The IMF Crisis of 1976*, 171.

According to Paul Mosley's *The Making of Economic Policy: Theory and Evidence from Britain and the United States Since 1945* (Brighton: Harvester Wheatsheaf, 1984), this idea acted as a Trojan horse for certain neoliberal tenets. But according to Andrew Gamble, the alternative economic strategy was a prime example of a national economic strategy rather than a liberal one, see A. Gamble, *Britain in Decline: Economic Policy, Political Strategy and the British State* (London: Macmillan, 1981), 165–67.

73. J. Cronin, *New Labour's Pasts* (London: Longman, 2004), 169.

74. Prentice later became the first Labour Party defector to the Conservative Party.

75. Peter Jay, interview with the author, September 2007.

76. James Callaghan, speech to the Labour Party Conference, 28 December 1976.

77. PREM 16/799, PRO/NA, record of telephone conversation between Schmidt and Callaghan, 2 November 1976.

78. W. Simon, *A Time for Truth* (New York: Berkley Books, 1978).

79. PREM 16/800, PRO/NA, telegram from Crosland.

80. See E. Dell, *A Hard Pounding: Politics and the Economic Crisis* (Oxford: Oxford University Press, 1991).

81. PREM 16/808, PRO/NA, J. K. Galbraith, "Paper on the British Economy."

82. Ibid.

83. PREM 16/808, PRO/NA, A. J. G. Isaac, "Treasury Response to Galbraith's Paper."

84. Ibid.

85. Dell, *A Hard Pounding*, 279.

86. Ibid., 283.

87. Hickson, *The IMF Crisis of 1976*, 200.

88. Ibid., 201.

89. Peter Jay, interview with the author, September 2007.

90. D. Harvey, *A Brief History of Neoliberalism* (Oxford: Oxford University Press, 2005), 73.

91. Ibid., 73.

92. However, there is no doubt that a key neoliberal policy strategy and one that was pursued by both the Reagan and Thatcher governments after 1979 was the use of state authority to impose conditions believed to be conducive to the operation of free markets. The apparent contradiction between a supposed fear and distrust of government and a willingness to use government power to impose free markets is explained

in the work of Friedman, Hayek, and Henry Simons as the legitimate role of the state to promote the competitive order.

93. W. C. Biven, *Jimmy Carter's Economy: Policy in an Age of Limits* (Chapel Hill: University of North Carolina Press, 2002), 126.

94. George Shultz, interview with the author, February 2008.

95. Biven, *Jimmy Carter's Economy,* 193.

96. G. Howe, *Conflict of Loyalty* (London: Pan Books, 1995), 265.

97. Biven, *Jimmy Carter's Economy,* 142.

98. Ibid., 240.

99. Quoted in Biven, *Jimmy Carter's Economy,* 242.

100. Ibid., 251.

101. Friedman, "*Money Programme* Transcript," 3.

102. Ibid.

103. Quoted in Dell, *A Hard Pounding,* 231.

104. "The Right Approach to the Economy," 17 August 1977, LC (77) 160, THCR 2/6/1/161, Thatcher Archives, Churchill College, Cambridge.

105. Ibid., 2.

106. Ibid., 12.

107. Ibid., 41.

108. John Hoskyns, interview with the author, June 2007.

109. Ibid.

110. Ibid.

111. Norman Lamont, interview with the author, July 2007.

112. Leon Brittan, interview with the author, July 2007.

113. Norman Lamont, interview with the author, July 2007.

114. Ibid.

115. Nigel Lawson, interview with the author, June 2007.

116. Ibid.

117. Lawson's view of the need for external discipline later led him to support the Conservative government's entry into the European exchange rate mechanism, which he saw as an effective replacement for the Bretton Woods arrangement. This was what Lawson called "exchange rate monetarism." According to Madsen Pirie, Lawson saw the exchange rate mechanism as a "long stop against inflation." But Thatcher's main economic adviser, Alan Walters, disagreed, causing a rupture at the heart of the administration. Lawson later resigned as chancellor in 1989 over the issue.

118. "Memo to U.K. Treasury and Civil Service Committee," 10 June 1980, box 61, folder 14, Friedman Papers.

119. Ibid., 2.

120. Ibid.

121. Ibid.

122. Howard Davies, introduction to *The Chancellor's Tales: Managing the British Economy,* ed. H. Davies (Cambridge: Polity Press, 2006), 13.

123. G. Howe, *Conflict of Loyalty,* 143.

124. Cockett, *Thinking the Unthinkable,* 296.

125. On this debate see, for example, T. Congdon's book, *Keynes, Keynesians and Monetarism,* (London: Edward Elgar, 2007), and P. Minford, "Mrs Thatcher's Economic Reform Programme," in *Thatcherism,* ed. R. Skidelsky (London: Chatto and Windus, 1988).

126. Cockett, *Thinking the Unthinkable,* 263.

127. N. Lawson, "1984 Mais Lecture," available at www.margaretthatcher.org/commentary/displaydocument.asp?docid=109504.

128. Howe, *Conflict of Loyalty,* 162.

129. The Taft-Hartley Act 1947 was enacted by Congress to supervise and restrict the actions of the trade unions. It partially repealed the New Deal–era Wagner Act (1935) and was a direct response to the wave of strikes that spread across the country in 1946. Among its provisions were measures to prohibit wildcat strikes, jurisdictional strikes, solidarity or political strikes, secondary picketing, the "closed shop," and donations by unions to political parties.

130. See, e.g., J. Hacker, *The Divided Welfare State* (Cambridge: Cambridge University Press, 2002); M. B. Katz, *In the Shadow of the Poorhouse* (New York: Basic Books, 1996) and *The Price of Citizenship* (New York: Henry Holt, 2001); and J. Klein, *For All These Rights* (Princeton, NJ: Princeton University Press, 2003). See also C. Howard, *The Hidden Welfare State* (Princeton: Princeton University Press, 1997); and E. Berkowitz, *America's Welfare State: From Roosevelt to Reagan* (Baltimore: Johns Hopkins University Press, 1991).

131. The Full Employment and Balanced Growth Act of 1977 (H.R. 50, S. 50), box 46, folder 3, Hayek Papers.

132. See the correspondence of Hayek with the Committee in box 46, folder 3, Hayek Papers, and Milton Friedman's correspondence with Congressman Philip Crane in box 24, folder 18, Friedman Papers.

133. *Full Employment and Balanced Growth Act of 1977,* 1–299.

134. P. Duignan and A. Rabushka, *The United States in the 1980s* (Stanford, CA: Hoover Press, 1980).

135. Anneliese Anderson, interview with the author, February 2008.

136. E. Feulner and C. Heatherly, eds., *Mandate for Leadership: Policy Management in a Conservative Administration* (Washington, DC: Heritage Foundation, 1981).

137. Martin Anderson, interview with the author, February 2008.

138. See M. Anderson, *Revolution: the Reagan Legacy* (Stanford, CA: Hoover Press, 1990).

139. Anneliese Anderson, interview with the author, February 2008.

140. E. Rothschild, "The Real Reagan Economy," *New York Review of Books,* June 30, 1988.

141. Anneliese Anderson, interview with the author, February 2008.

142. Ibid.

143. "Improving the Nation's Air Traffic Control System," a report of the Ad Hoc Air Traffic Control Panel of the President's Science Advisory Committee, CFOA 81, Reagan Presidential Papers, Ronald Reagan Presidential Library, Simi Valley, CA.

144. Ed Feulner, interview with the author, October 2008.

145. Statement by the President, 3 August 1981, Reagan Presidential Papers.

146. George Shultz, interview with the author, February 2008.

147. Anneliese Anderson, interview with the author, February 2008.

148. Andrew Duguid, interview with the author, September 2007.

149. Douglas Hurd, interview with the author, September 2007.

150. Norman Lamont, interview with the author, July 2007.

151. Douglas Hurd, interview with the author, September 2007.

152. Norman Lamont, interview with the author, July 2007. As suggested at the end of chapter 4, for a scholarly version of this argument as it pertained to Britain, and especially the role of think-tanks, see Cockett, *Thinking the Unthinkable*.

153. Reprinted in N. Lawson, *The View from No. 11: Memoirs of a Tory Radical* (London: Bantam, 1992), 1041.

154. Norman Lamont, interview with the author, July 2007.

155. See, e.g., P. Taylor-Gooby, *Reframing Social Citizenship* (Oxford: Oxford University Press, 2009).

156. The most obvious examples would be the memoirs of Thatcher herself, *The Downing Street Years* (London: HarperCollins, 1993) and *The Path to Power* (London: HarperCollins, 1996). There are, of course, many measured and insightful memoirs, such as those of Geoffrey Howe, *Conflict of Loyalty* (London: Macmillan, 1994), and Nigel Lawson's *The View from No. 11*. On the United States, George Shultz's *Turmoil and Triumph: My Years as Secretary of State* (New York: Scribner, 1993) contains a wealth of information, and Martin Feldstein's edited volume on Reagan's economic policy, which includes contributions from people of all political colors, including Paul Volcker, *American Economic Policy in the 1980s* (Chicago: University of Chicago Press, 1993), provides a variety of perspectives on the 1980s.

Chapter 7: Neoliberalism Applied?

1. L. Vale, *Reclaiming Public Housing: A Half-century of Struggle in Three Public Neighborhoods* (Cambridge, MA: Harvard University Press, 2002), 76.

2. See, e.g., A. Brinkley, *The End of Reform* (New York: Vintage, 1995).

3. See, e.g., M. Lassiter, *The Silent Majority* (Princeton, NJ: Princeton University Press, 2006); A. Matusow, *The Unraveling of America: A History of Liberalism in the Sixties* (New York: Perennial Books, 1985); and B. Schulman and J. Zelizer, *Rightward Bound: Making America Conservative in the Seventies* (Cambridge, MA: Harvard University Press, 2008).

4. J. Deparle, *The American Dream: Three Women, Ten Kids, and a Nation's Drive to End Welfare* (New York: Viking, 2004).

5. See J. Jacobs, *The Death and Life of Great American Cities* (New York: Random House, 1961).

6. See A. Wiese, *Places of Their Own* (Chicago: University of Chicago Press, 2004).

7. N. Williams, "The 'Right-to-Buy' in England," in *Housing Economics and Public Policy*, ed. T. O'Sullivan and Kay Gibbs (Oxford: Blackwell, 2003), 235.

8. Ibid., 235.

9. On Britain and European inspirations for the New Deal, see D. Rodgers, *Atlantic Crossings* (Cambridge, MA: Harvard Belknap, 1998), chaps. 5 and 10.

10. D. Hayden, *Redesigning the American Dream* (London: W. W. Norton, 1986), 122.

11. Ibid., 122.

12. See A. Hirsch, *Making the Second Ghetto* (New York: Cambridge University Press, 1983); T. Sugrue, *The Origins of the Urban Crisis* (Princeton, NJ: Princeton University Press, 1996); R. Self, *American Babylon: Race and the Struggle for Postwar Oakland* (Princeton, NJ: Princeton University Press, 2005); and M. Lassiter, *Silent Majority: Suburban Politics in the Sunbelt South* (Princeton, NJ: Princeton University Press, 2006).

13. See, e.g., K. Kruse, *White Flight: Atlanta and the Making of Modern Conservatism* (Princeton, NJ: Princeton University Press, 2005).

14. See especially B. Schulman, *From Cottonbelt to Sunbelt* (Oxford: Oxford University Press, 1994).

15. "Redlining" was the practice of denying or increasing the cost to prohibitive levels of financial and other services to particular areas or neighborhoods. Many of these areas were, of course, racially profiled.

16. Wiese, *Places of Their Own*, 7.

17. Ibid., 108–9.

18. Hayden, *Redesigning the American Dream*, 125.

19. Ibid., 127.

20. M. O'Mara, *Cities of Knowledge: Cold War Politics, Universities, and the Roots of the Information-Age Metropolis, 1945–1970* (Philadelphia: University of Pennsylvania, 2002), vii.

21. Ibid., 3.

22. Ibid., 12.

23. On the ways in which the tax system has benefited more affluent Americans through mortgage tax relief, deductions for charitable giving, retirement saving, and higher education, see C. Howard, *The Hidden Welfare State* (Princeton, NJ: Princeton University Press, 1997).

24. P. Pierson, *Dismantling the Welfare State: Reagan, Thatcher and the Politics of Retrenchment* (Cambridge: Cambridge University Press, 1994), 75.

25. See J. Bauman, "Jimmy Carter, Patricia Roberts Harris, and Housing Policy in the Age of Limits," in *From Tenements to the Taylor Homes: In Search of an Urban Housing Policy in Twentieth Century America*, ed. J. Bauman, R. Biles, and K. Szylvian (University Park: Pennsylvania State University Press, 2000).

26. G. Galster and J. Daniell, "Housing," in *Reality and Research: U.S. Urban Policy since 1960*, ed. G. Galster, (Washington, DC: Urban Institute Press, 1996), chap. 5, 95.

27. B. Fielding, "How Useful Are Rent Supplements in Meeting Low-Income Housing Needs?" *Journal of Housing*, January 1969.

28. Galster and Daniell, "Housing," 89.

29. R. Biles, "Public Housing and the Postwar Urban Renaissance," in Bauman, Biles, and Szylvian, *From Tenements to the Taylor Homes*, 156.

30. Galster and Daniell, "Housing," 94.

31. Biles, "Public Housing," 156.

32. "Section 235 Existing Homeownership Program Suspended," *Journal of Housing*, January 1971.

33. Galster and Daniell, "Housing," 95.

34. M. K. Nenno, "A Year of Truth for the Future Course of Urban Affairs," *Journal of Housing*, February 1972.

35. "An Editorial: George Romney Resigns as HUD Secretary," *Journal of Housing*, November 1972.

36. R. Beckham, "The Housing Allowance Program: An Old Idea Will Get a New Kind of Test in 1973," *Journal of Housing*, January 1973; R. J. Struyk et al., eds., *Housing Vouchers for the Poor: Lessons from a National Experiment* (Washington, DC: Urban Institute Press, 1981), 30.

37. R. Nixon, "Nixon: The Fifth Year of His Presidency," *Congressional Quarterly*, 1974, 84-A.

38. R. Forrest and A. Murie, *Selling the Welfare State: The Privatisation of Public Housing* (London: Routledge, 1988). See also J. Burnett, *A Social History of Housing: 1815–1985* (London: Routledge, 1986); and P. Hennessy, *Never Again* (London: Vintage, 1992) and *Having It So Good* (London: Penguin, 2006).

39. In the United States, public housing estates are known as "projects." On the "problem" of British housing estates, see, e.g., Lynsey Hanley's semi-autobiographical *Estates: An Intimate History* (Cambridge: Granta Books, 2008).

40. D. Hill, *Urban Policy and Politics in Britain* (London: Macmillan, 2000), 157.

41. See chapter 10 of J. Burnett, *A Social History of Housing, 1815–1985* (London: Methuen, 1986).

42. The requirement of two bathrooms in a house with a family of five or more was reduced to one in 1951, for example. See Burnett, *Social History*, 300.

43. O. J. Hetzel, A. David Yates, and J. Trutko, *A Comparison of the Experimental Housing Allowance Program and Great Britain's Rent Allowance Program* (Washington, DC: Urban Institute, 1978), vii.

44. Enoch Powell's rise to a position of leadership of a wave of anti-immigration protest through his "Rivers of Blood" speech (delivered in Birmingham on April 20, 1968) and some of the social and economic fissures that led to such anger were discussed in chapter 3.

45. D. Feldman, "Why the English Like Turbans," in *Structures and Transformations in Modern British History*, ed. D. Feldman and J. Lawrence (Cambridge: Cambridge University Press, 2011).

46. Ibid., 291–93.

47. Forrest and Murie, *Selling the Welfare State*, 92.

48. Housing Services Advisory Group, *The Assessment of Housing Requirements* (London: Department for the Environment, 1977), 1.

49. Shelter, *And I'll Blow Your House Down—Housing Need in Britain: Present and Future* (London: Shelter, 1980), 4.

50. Burnett, *Social History of Housing*, 301.

51. Labour Party, *A New Deal for Council Housing: Interim Proposals, NEC Statement* (London: Labour Party, 1978), 1.

52. *Housing Policy: A Consultative Document*, Cmnd 6851 (London: HMSO, 1977), 1.

53. Ibid..

54. Labour Party, *A New Deal for Council Housing*, 1.

55. Forrest and Murie, *Selling the Welfare State*, 93.

56. Andrew Duguid, interview with the author, September 2007.

57. *HUD Annual Report* (Washington, DC: HUD, 1976), 8.

58. *HUD Annual Report* (Washington, DC: HUD, 1980), 5.

59. J. Bauman, "Jimmy Carter, Patricia Roberts Harris and Housing Policy in an Age of Limits," chap. 12 in Bauman, Biles, and Szylvian, *From Tenements to the Taylor Homes*, 247.

60. *The President's National Urban Policy Report* (Washington, DC: HUD, 1978), 4–5.

61. There are many studies on the processes by which blacks and other poorer people were excluded from particular American suburban and urban communities many of which were referenced earlier in the chapter, especially those by Arnold Hirsch, Kenneth Jackson, Robert Self, Tom Sugrue, and Andrew Wiese. In addition, see chapter 4 on race of Lawrence Vale's study of public housing in Boston, *From the Puritans to the Projects* (Cambridge, MA: Harvard University Press, 2000).

62. T. Hanchett, "The Other 'Subsidized Housing': Federal Aid to Suburbanization, 1940s–1960s," in Bauman, Biles, and Szylvian, *From Tenements to the Taylor Homes*.

63. A. Eden, speech to the Conservative Party Conference, October 3, 1946.

64. President Harry Truman, State of the Union address, January 5, 1949. Available at http://www.c-span.org/executive/transcript.asp?cat=current_event &code=bush_admin&year=1949.

65. M. Anderson, *The Federal Bulldozer: A Critical Analysis of Urban Renewal, 1949–62* (Cambridge, MA: MIT Press, 1965).

66. M. Friedman and G. Stigler, *Roofs or Ceilings* (Irvington: Foundation for Economic Education, 1946).

67. G. Howe, *The Future of Rent Control* (London: Bow Group, 1956).

68. Ibid., 35.

69. F. Hayek, *The Constitution of Liberty* (Chicago: University of Chicago Press, 1960), 341.

70. Ibid., 342.

71. Ibid.

72. Ibid., 345.

73. M. Friedman, *Capitalism and Freedom* (Chicago: University of Chicago Press, 1962), 178.

74. Ibid., 179.

75. Ibid.

76. Ibid., 180.

77. U.S. General Accounting Office, *Section 8 Subsidized Housing: Some Observations on Its High Rents, Costs and Inequities* (Washington, DC: US General Accounting Office, 1980), vi.

78. President's Commission on Housing, "Report" (Washington, DC: Government Printing Office, 1982), 3.

79. Stuart Butler, interview with the author, October 2008.

80. President's Commission on Housing, "Report," xxii.

81. Pierson, *Dismantling the Welfare State,* 87.

82. U.S. General Accounting Office, *Block Grants for Housing: A Study of Local Experiences and Attitudes* (Washington, DC: U.S. General Accounting Office, 1982), iv.

83. M. Katz, *The Price of Citizenship: Redefining the American Welfare State* (New York: Owl Books, 2001), 123.

84. A. Downs, *A Strategy for Designing a Fully Comprehensive Housing Policy for the Federal Government of the United States* (Cambridge, MA: MIT Housing Policy Project, 1988), 1.

85. L. Keyes and D. DiPasquale, *Housing Policy for the 1990s* (Cambridge, MA: MIT Housing Policy Project, 1988), ii.

86. For a comprehensive analysis of the history, development and outcomes of the Right to Buy policy, see C. Jones and A. Murie, *The Right to Buy: Analysis and Evaluation of a Housing Policy* (Oxford: Wiley-Blackwell, 2006).

87. Ibid., 6.

88. A. Killick, *Council House Blues* (London: Bow Group, 1976), 10.

89. Ibid., 1.

90. M. Thatcher, foreword to *Conservative Party General Election Manifesto 1979,* in *Conservative Party General Election Manifestos, 1900–1997,* ed. I. Dale (London: Routledge, 2000), 265.

91. Ibid., 277.

92. Ibid.

93. P. Malpass and A. Murie, *Housing Policy and Practice* (London: Palgrave, 1987), 99.

94. The Conservatives proposed discounts off the market rate of 33 percent after three years, rising according to length of tenancy to 50 percent after twenty years.

95. Dale, *Manifestos,* 277.

96. *Hansard Parliamentary Debates* (London: HMSO, 1980), 787.

97. Ibid., 791.

98. Ibid., 789.

99. Madsen Pirie and Eamonn Butler, interview with the author, September 2007.

100. Stuart Butler, interview with the author, October 2008.

101. Ibid.

102. Ibid.

103. Katz, *The Price of Citizenship,* 123.

104. R. Banham, P. Barker, P. Hall, and C. Price, "Non-Plan: An Experiment in Freedom," *New Society* 26 (1969): 435–43.

105. Ibid., 436.

106. P. Hall, "The British Enterprise Zones," in *Enterprise Zones: New Directions in Economic Development,* ed. R. Green (London: Sage, 1991).

107. Ibid., 181.

108. Ibid., 183.

109. The letters are available online at www.margaretthatcher.org/archives.

110. Hall, "British Enterprise Zones," 184.

111. The first eleven were in Clydebank, Belfast, Swansea, Corby, Dudley, Speke, Salford/Trafford, Wakefield, Hartlepool, Tyneside, Isle of Dogs. The second were in Allerdale, Glanford, Middlesborough, North East Lancashire, North West Kent, Rotherham, Scunthorpe, Telford, Wellingborough, Delyn, Milford Haven, Invergordon, and Tayside.

112. Hall, "British Enterprise Zones," 184.

113. Northeast = 0.36, North Central = 0.28, West = 0.59, South = 0.57. According to the report, "A value of 1.0 indicates that blacks are distributed between the central city and suburbs in the same proportion as whites; a value less than one indicates that blacks are disproportionately concentrated in the central city." Source: *The President's National Urban Policy Report, 1980* (Washington, DC: HUD, 1980), 1–16.

114. The President's Commission on Housing, *Report* (Washington, DC: Government Printing Office, 1982), xix.

115. L. Vale, *Reclaiming Public Housing: A Half-century of Struggle in Three Public Neighborhoods* (Cambridge, MA: Harvard University Press, 2002), 8.

116. Stuart Butler, interview with the author, October 2008.

117. Ibid.

118. Ibid.

119. Third Way thinking was most closely associated with the Left Communitarian ideas of Amitai Etzioni in the United States and Anthony Giddens in Britain. See, e.g., Etzioni's *The Spirit of Community: Rights, Responsibilities and the Communitarian*

Agenda, (New York: Crown Publishers, 1993) and Giddens's *Beyond Left and Right: Tthe Future of Radical Politics* (Cambridge: Polity Press, 1994).

120.   National Housing Task Force, *A Decent Place to Live: The Report of the National Housing Task Force* (Washington, DC: Government Printing Office, 1988), 4.

121.   Ibid., 2.

122.   E. Goetz, "An American Perspective," in *Stakeholder Housing: A Third Way* (London: Pluto Press, 1999), 111.

123.   *A Decade of Hope VI: Research Findings and Policy Challenges* (Washington, DC: Urban Institute, 2003), 10–11.

124.   Goetz, *American Perspective,* 112.

125.   See, e.g., Etzioni, *The Spirit of Community.*

126.   A. Van Hoffman, *House by House, Block by Block: The Rebirth of America's Urban Neighborhoods* (Oxford: Oxford University Press, 2003), 14–15.

127.   Ibid., 16.

128.   See http://www.poverty.org.uk/policies/capital receipts.shtml.

129.   Department of Environment, Transport and the Regions, *Planning for the Communities of the Future* (London: HMSO, 1998), 23.

130.   B. Jupp, *Living Together: Community Life on Mixed-tenure Housing Estates* (London: Demos, 2000), 15.

131.   *The President's Commission on Housing* (1982), xvii.

132.   Ibid., xxxv.

133.   Labour Party, *Opening Doors: Labour's Strategy for Housing* (London: 1990), 11.

134.   National Housing Task Force, *A Decent Place to Live,* 5.

Conclusion
The Legacy of Transatlantic Neoliberalism

1.   Figures taken from "% of Total Employment," in B. Supple, "British Economic Decline," in *British Economic History Since 1700,* ed. R. Floud and D. McCloskey (Cambridge: Cambridge University Press, 1994), chap. 11, 335.

2.   Supple, "British Economic Decline," 323.

3.   For example, see the tables on historical income inequality in the United States at http://www.census.gov/hhes/www/income/data/historical/inequality/index.html. For the UK, see the report of the National Equality Panel, *Anatomy of Economic Inequality in the United Kingdom: Report of the National Equality Panel* (London: London School of Economics, 2010).

4.   See P. Pierson, *Dismantling the Welfare State: Reagan, Thatcher, and the Politics of Retrenchment* (Cambridge: Cambridge University Press, 1994).

5.   Figures on the United States are from B. R. Mitchell, *International Historical Statistics: The Americas, 1750–2000* (London: Palgrave, 2003), 667. For Britain they

are from B. R. Mitchell, *International Historical Statistics: Europe, 1750–2000* (London: Palgrave, 2003), 821–23.

6. M. Friedman, "*Money Programme* Transcript," 21 April 1978, box 56, folder 20, Friedman Papers.

7. Ed Crane, interview with the author, October 2008.

8. Anneliese Anderson, interview with the author, February 2008.

9. See chapter 1, on Popper. This was how Karl Popper described the market in an interview shortly before his death.

10. "Malaise" was the description given by American commentators to Carter's televised speech to the nation delivered on July 15, 1979. In fact, he did not use the word malaise—instead, he said America was suffering from a "crisis of confidence"—but his downbeat analysis contrasted sharply with Reagan's sunny Hollywood actor persona.

11. Anneliese Anderson, interview with the author, February 2008.

12. On this point, see C. Howard, *The Hidden Welfare State* (Princeton, NJ: Princeton University Press, 1997), and J. Hacker, *The Divided Welfare State* (Cambridge: Cambridge University Press, 2002).

13. See note 3 above.

14. See J. Cassidy, *How Markets Fail* (London: Penguin, 2009).

15. See M. Lilla, "The Tea Party Jacobins," *New York Review of Books*, May 27, 2010.

Index